European Yearbook of International
Economic Law

EYIEL Monographs - Studies in European
and International Economic Law

Volume 1

EYIEL Monographs is a subseries of the European Yearbook of International Economic Law (EYIEL). It contains scholarly works in the fields of European and international economic law, in particular WTO law, international investment law, international monetary law, law of regional economic integration, external trade law of the EU and EU internal market law. The series does not include edited volumes. EYIEL Monographs are peer-reviewed by the series editors and external reviewers.

More information about this series at http://www.springer.com/series/15744

Amber Rose Maggio

Environmental Policy, Non-Product Related Process and Production Methods and the Law of the World Trade Organization

 Springer

Amber Rose Maggio
Max Planck Foundation for International
    Peace and the Rule of Law
Heidelberg, Germany

ISSN 2364-8392   ISSN 2364-8406   (electronic)
European Yearbook of International Economic Law
EYIEL Monographs - Studies in European and International Economic Law
ISBN 978-3-319-61154-9   ISBN 978-3-319-61155-6   (eBook)
DOI 10.1007/978-3-319-61155-6

Library of Congress Control Number: 2017945214

Printed on acid-free paper

This Springer imprint is published by Springer Nature
The registered company is Springer International Publishing AG
The registered company address is: Gewerbestrasse 11, 6330 Cham, Switzerland

Acknowledgements

This work was submitted as a doctoral thesis at Trier University in March 2016. While the scope of this work appears narrow, its implications are vast. It seeks to uncover the true scope of WTO obligations for States in the field of environmental regulation and, in doing so, also uncovers the lack of clarity, power accumulation and legitimacy deficit at the WTO. I hope that this book proves enlightening not only for scholars interested in the issue of NPR PPMs but also to those who seek to question the status quo of the international trade regime, and especially those that seek to reform it and create a fairer system for all.

This work would not have been possible without the vision and teaching of Akbar Rasulov. His approach to looking at WTO obligations has become my own (all errors in application are also my own), and I am very grateful for all he taught me. I would also like to thank my other PIL teachers at the University of Glasgow, Antonios Tzanakopoulos and Christian Tams. You three were an inspirational team that happily steered me towards something far more interesting than national law. Christian, many thanks to you for your continuing support—I would never have made it to Germany without it. My doctoral supervisor, Alexander Proelß, deserves my most heartfelt thanks. Alexander, thank you for supporting and encouraging me whenever I felt I was losing my way. I learned a lot from my time in Trier, and you were key to that process; I will always look back very fondly on my time working for you. Eike Blitza, I am forever indebted to you for your patience, support and friendship. There were rough times, and you helped me through. Tobias Hofmann, thank you for your sense of humour and willingness to talk about my topic when no one else would. Dorota Englender, thanks for all the crisis management chat sessions in your office—the laughter definitely helped me through! Thanks to my parents for all their encouragement—Mum and Johnnie, I could not have done it without you. A further special thanks to my Mum and Kate Manning for reading and correcting my draft—I am sure it was tedious, but your efforts were invaluable in polishing and finishing it. A special mention also goes out to everyone I met through the international PhD students programme at Trier University: great friends, a support group and a great distraction from the woes of PhD life. I am also very grateful to Christoph Herrmann, the other EYIEL editors and everyone at Springer for publishing my work; I am over the moon to see it coming together. Finally, I would like to thank my partner, Angelo Maretti. I am so grateful to you for being there through the last stage of the thesis and preparation for the oral exam. I was a nightmare, but you held my hand and helped me through.

Heidelberg, Germany   Amber Rose Maggio

Table of Cases

GATT Cases

WTO Cases

Non WTO Cases

Table of Treaties

WTO and Covered Agreements

WTO Agreement: Marrakesh Agreement Establishing the World Trade Organization, 15 April 1994, 1867 UNTS 154

General Agreement on Tariffs and Trade 1994 (annexed to the WTO Agreement)

Agreement on Technical Barriers to Trade (annexed to the WTO Agreement)

Anti-dumping Agreement (annexed to the WTO Agreement)

Agreement on Trade-Related Investment Measures (TRIMs) (annexed to the WTO Agreement)

Agreement on Sanitary and Phytosanitary Measures (annexed to the WTO Agreement)

General Agreement on Tariffs and Trade 1947, 30 October 1947, 55 UNTS 814

Tokyo Round Agreements

Agreement on Implementation of Article VI of the General Agreement on Tariffs and Trade (Antidumping Code), 12 April 1979, 1186 UNTS 814

Agreement on Implementation of Article VII of the General Agreement on Tariffs and Trade (Customs Valuation Code), 12 April 1979, 1186 UNTS 814

Agreement on Import Licensing Procedures, 12 April 1979, 1186 UNTS 814

Agreement on Interpretation and Application of Articles VI, XVI and XXIII of the General Agreement on Tariffs and Trade (Subsidies Code), 12 April 1979, 1186 UNTS 814

Agreement on Technical Barriers to Trade (Standards Code), 12 April 1979, 1186 UNTS 814

Agreement on Trade in Civil Aircraft, 12 April 1979, 1186 UNTS 814

International Dairy Agreement, 12 April 1979, 1186 UNTS 814

International Bovine Meat Agreement, 12 April 1979, 1186 UNTS 814

Differential and More Favourable Treatment and Reciprocity and Fuller Participation of Developing Countries (Enabling Clause), 12 April 1979, 1186 UNTS 814

Understanding on Notification, Consultation, Dispute Settlement and Surveillance of 28 November 1979, available at https://www.wto.org/english/docs_e/legal_e/tokyo_notif_e.pdf (last accessed on 05/03/2017)

Treaties

Agreement on the International Dolphin Conservation Program, 21 May 1998,
available at http://www.state.gov/s/l/treaty/tias/112019.htm (last accessed on
05/03/2017)

Cartagena Protocol on Biosafety to the Convention on Biological Diversity,
29 January 2000, 2226 UNTS 208

Charter of the United Nations, 26 June 1945

Convention Concerning Safety in the Use of Asbestos, 24 June 1986, 1539 UNTS
26705 (International Labour Organisation Convention 162)

Convention on Biological Diversity, 5 June 1992, 1760 UNTS 79

Convention on International Trade in Endangered Species of Wild Fauna and Flora
of 3 March 1973, UNTS 993, 14537

Convention on the Conservation of Migratory Species of 23 June 1979, 1651 UNTS
333

Statute of the International Court of Justice, 26 June 1945

Treaty on the Functioning of the European Union OJ 2012 C 326, 47

United Nations Convention on the Law of the Sea of 10 December 1982, 1833
UNTS 3

Vienna Convention on the Law of Treaties, 23 May 1969, 1155 UNTS 18323

Contents

List of Abbreviations

ASR	Articles on State Responsibility
CAA	Clean Air Act
CBD	Convention on Biological Diversity
DPCIA	Dolphin Protection Consumer Information Act
DRAMS	Dynamic Random Access Memory Semiconductors
DSB	Dispute Settlement Body
DSS	Dispute settlement system
DSU	Dispute Settlement Understanding
EC	European Communities
EEC	European Economic Community
EJIL	European Journal of International Law
EPA	US Environmental Protection Agency
ETP	Eastern Tropical Pacific
EU	European Union
GATT	General Agreement on Tariffs and Trade
GMO	Genetically modified organism
ICJ	International Court of Justice
ILC	International Law Commission
INSERM	Institut National de la Science et de la Recherche Médicale
ITLOS	International Tribunal for the Law of the Sea
ITO	International Trade Organization
JEL	Journal of Environmental Law
JIEL	Journal of International Economic Law
MFN	Most favoured nation
MPUNYBL	Max Planck Yearbook of United Nations Law
NPR PPM	Non-product related process and production method
PCIJ	Permanent Court of International Justice
RTA	Regional trade agreement
SPS	Sanitary and phytosanitary
TBT	Technical barrier to trade

TED	Turtle excluder device
TREM	Trade-restrictive environmental measure
UNCLOS	United Nations Convention on the Law of the Sea
VCLT	Vienna Convention on the Law of Treaties
WTO	World Trade Organization
YJIL	Yale Journal of International Law

Chapter 1
Introduction

This work seeks to explore the legal regime of non-product related process and production methods (NPR PPMs) in the context of trade-restrictive environmental measures (TREMs), eco-labelling requirements and sanitary measures under the World Trade Organization (WTO). The work focuses on these issues in order to give concrete examples that raise broader questions about the legitimacy of the WTO dispute settlement system (DSS) and in the attempt to explore the true position of WTO members in this complex legal regime.

Non-product related process and production methods are process and production methods that do not affect the product as such, meaning that there is no discernible difference in two products with differing NPR PPMs. A concrete example may serve to illuminate this element while also immediately demonstrating its relevance in environmental policy: thus, tuna products that have been fished using non-sustainable or environmentally damaging fishing methods are not discernible from tuna products from sustainable eco-friendly fisheries. A further example would be petroleum products produced using very energy-intensive methods, and thus highly polluting methods, being indiscernible from those from the comparatively environmentally friendly oilfields in the North Sea. This work seeks to evaluate the legal regime under the WTO for States in their attempt to regulate in this area and create potential product distinctions on the basis of NPR PPMs.

Beginning with an outline of the methodology employed to untangle the web of WTO obligations, Chap. 2 seeks to lay out an investigative framework that will be used in the rest of this work. Chapter 3 outlines the history of the General Agreement on Tariffs and Trade (GATT) in general, before more specifically focusing on the evolution of the treatment of national regulatory schemes under the GATT and WTO regimes. Chapter 4 discusses the judicial function of the WTO in detail and how it affects the issue of environmental regulatory distinctions based on NPR PPMs. The issue of 'likeness' is also explored in detail at this juncture in order to lay the foundations for its importance in the following six chapters.

© Springer International Publishing AG 2017   1
A.R. Maggio, *Environmental Policy, Non-Product Related Process and Production
Methods and the Law of the World Trade Organization*, European Yearbook of
International Economic Law 1, DOI 10.1007/978-3-319-61155-6_1

Chapters 5–10 provide the analytical backbone of the work. The six chapters can be split into three pairs: with the first of the pair providing in-depth analysis of the relevant provisions of the treaty in question and the second an overview of the relevant case law. Chapters 5 and 6 represent the central pillar of the work and concern the GATT. Chapters 7–10 concern the Agreement on Technical Barriers to Trade (TBT Agreement) and the Agreement on Sanitary and Phytosanitary Measures (SPS Agreement), which are less directly connected to the problem in question but have salient points to raise about how it is engaged with under other WTO covered agreements.

This work, despite addressing a very specific issue, raises much broader questions about the incursions of the dispute settlement system of the WTO into 'sovereign regulatory space' and the legitimacy of this system as a whole. Although the number of such critiques may have earned such attempts the designation 'tropes', it is hoped that the specific methodology chosen here brings a different approach that adds to the rich discussion surrounding the legitimacy of the WTO. Without such discussion, the impetus for reform is less evident. Thus, it is hoped that this work may in some way help to make the problems inherent in the WTO system more visible and bring them to the forefront of efforts for reform.

Chapter 2
Methodology: Sovereignty, Hohfeld and Coercion

2.1 The Issue at Hand

When a State's national regulatory measures interact with international obligations, and the execution of these measures amounts to a violation of an international obligation, the international responsibility of that State is incurred.[1] However, within the sphere of international trade law and the WTO, the incurrence and consequences of international responsibility are 'self-contained' as WTO members have 'contracted out'[2] of the general scheme of international responsibility,[3] adopting instead a specialised scheme of responsibility unique to the WTO. This specialised system of State responsibility has been described as 'the most successful scheme for implementing State responsibility yet devised'.[4] It can further be argued that responsibility under the WTO DSS is 'conceptually different' from the general regime for responsibility under international law.[5] What are the practical implications of this? It certainly means that an assessment of the responsibility of States parties to the WTO and covered agreements for the breach of obligations under these agreements requires special and differential treatment from the breach of an 'ordinary' international obligation.

---

[1]See Art. 1 Articles on State Responsibility: ILC, Responsibility of States for Internationally Wrongful Acts, GA Res. 56/83 of 12 December 2001, Annex (ASR), which states: 'Every internationally wrongful act of a State entails the international responsibility of that State.'

[2]Panel Report *Korea – Measures Affecting Government Procurement*, para 7.96.

[3]For a general treatment of the law of State responsibility see *James R. Crawford*, State Responsibility, in: Rüdiger Wolfrum (ed.) The Max Planck Encyclopaedia of Public International Law, vol. IX (Oxford, 2012), 517–533.

[4]*Ibid.*, para. 23.

[5]See *Christian Tams*, Unity and Diversity in the Law of State Responsibility, in: Andreas Zimmerman/Rainer Hofmann (eds.) Unity and Diversity in International Law (Berlin, 2006), 435, 444.

© Springer International Publishing AG 2017

A.R. Maggio, *Environmental Policy, Non-Product Related Process and Production Methods and the Law of the World Trade Organization*, European Yearbook of International Economic Law 1, DOI 10.1007/978-3-319-61155-6_2

The DSS of the WTO is an advanced judicial system in the field of international law, a system that contains compulsory jurisdiction entailing binding decisions, an appellate review process by a standing court and a separate system of consequences for breach of these international obligations.[6] Each of these factors alone could demonstrate a 'strong' international court or tribunal, and with each an element of sovereignty is ceded. That so many States, even those typically reluctant to submit to the jurisdiction of international tribunals,[7] have chosen to give the WTO DSS these powers demonstrates the importance they vest in the values and interests that this tribunal seeks to protect.

What then are these values and interests, and what is the 'grand purpose' of the WTO? Certainly, it is the judicial settlement of cases of alleged violation of obligations arising from the GATT and covered agreements. But, more than that, some authors have asserted that the WTO, and particularly its dispute settlement system, exists to protect the environment of competitive opportunity[8] established by these agreements and the concessions granted in rounds of negotiations. Protecting an environment of competitive opportunity sounds, at first, like a loose pledge to ensure that bargains struck during the various rounds are protected. It may be argued, however, that this pledge comprises more than simply protecting agreed concessions but rather goes further in that it seeks to bolster and expand a 'neoliberal' version of free market competition.[9] Environmentalists and human rights activists often level accusations that the WTO is an inherently biased system,[10] pitting free trade above all else and often to the peril of other interests, but as the dispute settlement system of a specialised regime this is surely to be expected. As an international organisation with a trade liberalisation goal and no mandate to pursue environmental protection or ensure the protection of human rights,[11] any

---

[6]Full implementation of the decision of the Panel or Appellate Body to bring the measure in question into conformity with the covered agreements is the preferred solution, with compensation and suspension of concessions being available as 'temporary measures', see Art. 22 Understanding on Rules and Procedures Governing the Settlement of Disputes (DSU).

[7]For example, the United States, which has demonstrated this reluctance, *inter alia*, with regard to the International Courts of Justice and the International Criminal Court. See Cesare P. R. Romano (ed.), The Sword and the Scales: The United States and International Courts and Tribunals (Cambridge, 2008).

[8]*David Palmeter/Petros C. Mavroidis*, Dispute Settlement in the World Trade Organization: Practice and Procedure (Cambridge, 2nd edn. 2004), 33.

[9]It is not argued here that this was the historical purpose of the GATT/WTO, nor that it is a fully institutionalised purpose of the organisation. For an in helpful discussion of the historical relationship between the GATT/WTO and neoliberalism, see *Andrew Lang*, World Trade After Neoliberalism: Re-imagining the Global Economic Order (Oxford, 2011), Ch. 4, 7 and 8.

[10]See: *Michael Jeffery*, Environmental Imperatives in a Globalised World: The Ecological Impact of Liberalising Trade, Macquarie Law Journal 7 (2007), 25, 29, stating: 'The standard of international regulation created by the GATT and the WTO is inherently biased against environmental protection and towards economic growth.'

[11]By this it will be referred to the fact that there is no textual mandate for the WTO in general, but the WTO DSS specifically, to balance their competence in the field of trade with other interests

debate in this area will necessarily involve the interlinked issues of competence and legitimacy.

The main body of this work will consist of an assessment of the ways in which WTO rules interact with national regulatory or quasi-regulatory measures (specifically trade-restrictive environmental measures—or TREMs—which make distinctions between products on the basis of NPR PPMs), how this has been dealt with by the DSS, and what implications this may have. The calls of neoliberal bias from one camp, hidden protectionism from another and environmental imperialism from a third highlight how policy priorities affect perceptions of DSS decisions and national regulatory measures. Though the question of how these perceptions interact with each other is a question of politics, the assessment of the relevant WTO obligations in this study seeks to uncover how well the differing values in this political discourse are actually protected by the current WTO regime as a matter of law and what can be done, both within the existing framework and beyond, to make the multilateral trading system its most beneficial for all parties by protecting their particular policy interests, bearing in mind the issues of competence and legitimacy.

This chapter will give an introduction to the proposed methodology[12] of the work and, with that, how it will seek to assess the power distributive consequences of WTO membership in the field of environmental policy from the perspective of 'sovereignty'.

2.2 Sovereignty

As mentioned above, this study seeks to uncover the real nature of the legal relationships created by the WTO and covered agreements and how they impact national regulatory space. In order to do this, legal analytical tools will be employed, following the work of eminent early twentieth century jurist *Wesley Newcomb Hohfeld*, to assess the relevant provisions in these treaties. An assessment of the impact of these WTO obligations necessarily raises the issue of sovereignty, how far and in what ways it is ceded to the WTO and what this means for WTO members. While the interaction of WTO obligations and environmental regulation can be assessed using a 'treaty conflict' approach, looking at obligations under

---

such as environmental protection or human rights. The fact that the obligations that stem from WTO membership are so varied and far reaching, and thus ultimately have effects in almost every imaginable situation becomes particularly problematic when it comes to their influence on human rights and the environment. The problematic nature of the scope of the power of the WTO as an organisation and how far reaching the impact of its obligations are, will, however, always bring about questions of legitimacy.

[12]The author is grateful to Dr. Akbar Rasulov, University of Glasgow, for his influence in the choice of methodology. The methodology and general approach to looking at international trade obligations applied in this work are in many ways his vision and are the result of a semester of international economic law and a masters dissertation under his supervision.

multilateral environmental agreements and how they interact with WTO obligations,[13] this work will focus primarily on national regulatory measures enacted for policy purposes. Thus, while international obligations play a minor role in this study, sovereignty is at the forefront. It is therefore necessary to first discuss both what aspects of 'sovereignty' are affected and what the consequences of this might be.

The legal nature of State sovereignty is a complex, multifaceted issue. *Oppenheim* said of sovereignty:

> There exists perhaps no conception the meaning of which is more controversial than that of sovereignty. It is an indisputable fact that this conception, from the moment when it was introduced into political science until the present day, has never had a meaning which was universally agreed upon.[14]

It is not the purpose of this work to delve into the theoretical basis of sovereignty or comment on the modern issues that arise surrounding it.[15] For the purpose of this work, only specific aspects of sovereignty will be relevant; through analysis of the implications of WTO membership on these aspects, conclusions will be drawn that may contribute to modern debate, but it is important to clarify that this work is limited in scope,[16] and any conclusions will be similarly limited.

It should be noted at this point that the elements of sovereignty addressed in this work are deemed to be more akin to political science notions of the term than strictly legal sovereignty. They may be encompassed by legal sovereignty in certain ways, but it is important to point out that States consented to becoming WTO members and can *de jure* withdraw from the regime and thus retain the relevant elements of legal sovereignty *sensu stricto*.

Krasner outlines four different ways in which the term sovereignty has been used.[17] These will provide a useful template for both analysis and exclusion:

- **international legal sovereignty**—which 'refers to the practices associated with mutual recognition, usually between territorial entities that have formal juridical recognition';

---

[13]See *Tania Voon*, Sizing Up the WTO: Trade-Environment Conflicts and the Kyoto Protocol, Journal of Transnational Law and Policy 10 (2000), 71, 77–79; *John H. Knox*, The Judicial Resolution of Conflicts Between Trade and the Environment, Harvard Environmental Law Review 28 (2004), 1, 11, and the article generally for not only a good treatment of the judicial resolution of this 'conflict', but also a good explanation as to why governments have left this sort of decision making to international tribunals.

[14]*Lassa Oppenheim*, International Law: A Treatise, vol. I (London, 3rd ed. 1920–1921), 129.

[15]For a more detailed treatment the lack of a uniform concept of sovereignty and how this affects the trade and environment debate, particularly with reference to unilateralism, extraterritorial jurisdiction and non-intervention, see *Erich Vranes*, Trade and the Environment: Fundamental Issues in International Law, WTO Law and Legal Theory (Oxford, 2009), 111–120, 179–180.

[16]Limited sectorally to WTO rules and obligations, but also limited within that field to specific agreements and types of measures.

[17]*Stephen Krasner*, Sovereignty: Organized Hypocrisy (Princeton, 1999), 3–4.

- **Westphalian sovereignty**—which 'refers to political organization based on the exclusion of external actors from authority structures within a given territory';
- **domestic sovereignty**—which 'refers to the formal organization of political authority within the state and the ability of public authorities to exercise effective control within the borders of their own polity';
- **interdependence sovereignty**—which 'refers to the ability of public authorities to regulate the flow of information, ideas, goods, people, pollutants, or capital across borders'.[18]

From even these short descriptors,[19] one can see elements of each that may be relevant to a study on national regulation (domestic sovereignty), with potential extraterritorial application (domestic sovereignty, international legal sovereignty, Westphalian sovereignty), in the field of trade (interdependence sovereignty). However, it is better in this case to attempt to exclude most aspects of 'international legal sovereignty'. The mutual recognition element in the international legal sovereignty classification could feasibly be invoked in certain cases of extraterritorial application of national legislation, but as will be seen in the cases dealt with later in this work, in the current debate this would be a stretch.

The concept of Westphalian sovereignty is more difficult to exclude. Certainly, actions of powerful States that amount to economic coercion and 'force' other States to adopt certain regulatory measures can be seen to be an encroachment on the independence-based sovereignty imagined by *Krasner* in this context, but in the limited field of internal environmental regulatory measures it may be better dealt with by one of the other models. The main focus thus will be on these two remaining conceptions of sovereignty: 'domestic sovereignty' as a State's ability to exercise effective control within its territory and 'interdependence sovereignty' as a State's ability to regulate the flow of goods[20] (and pollutants) across its borders.

Where the treaty conflict model would deal with the law of treaties and issues of international responsibility under the Vienna Convention on the Law of Treaties (VCLT)[21] and the International Law Commission's Articles on State Responsibility,[22] an assessment of the impact of WTO membership and the obligations

---

[18]*Ibid.*

[19]For further analysis of these conceptions of sovereignty see: *ibid.*

[20]While certain covered agreements also cover the flow of people (to an extent) under the GATS and the flow of information under the TRIPS Agreement, they are not the focus of this work.

[21]Art. 30 VCLT on the application of successive treaties relating to the same subject matter. And the ILC Guide to Fragmentation of IL, with respect to the idea that 'successive treaties relating to the same subject matter' could be seen to include trade and the environmental agreements, despite being within different fields of international law, as the characterisation of these as separate regimes has 'no normative value per se' and that 'The criterion of "same subject-matter" seems already fulfilled if two different rules or sets of rules are invoked in regard to the same matter'. ILC, Report of the Study Group of the International Law Commission – Fragmentation in International Law: Difficulties Arising from the Diversification and Expansion of International Law, UN Doc. A/CN.4/L.702 (2006), paras. 21–23.

[22]ILC, Responsibility of States for Internationally Wrongful Acts, GA Res. 56/83 of 12 December 2001, Annex.

stemming therefrom requires a more nuanced approach. Where one deals ostensibly not with one legal system but rather with the impact of one upon the other and then the reflection of that impact in terms of the idea of 'sovereignty' (which is a facet of the first), it is helpful to have a structured methodology of legal analysis to avoid delving into political statements. The particular methodology used here is, as mentioned above, Hohfeldian analysis: what is meant by this and its particular origins are laid out below.

2.3   Hohfeld

The way in which WTO rules impact upon sovereignty will be measured is through close analysis of the real practical impact of the relevant WTO obligations. This will be done by employing legal analysis and linguistic precision following *Wesley Newcomb Hohfeld*. Hohfeldian analysis involves breaking down jural relationships into precise categories. *Hohfeld* levelled a criticism at legal scholarship that many of the things that were termed 'rights' and 'duties' actually described different types of legal relationship and that many of his predecessors did not properly understand the distinction between rights and privileges.[23]

Hohfeld stated:

> One of the great hindrances to the clear understanding, the incisive statement, and the true solution of legal problems frequently arises from the express or tacit assumption that all legal relations can be reduced to 'rights' and 'duties,' and that these latter categories are therefore adequate for the purpose of analysing even the most complex legal interests.[24]

It would be difficult to find a lawyer or a commentator who would argue that the legal relationships and interests arising from WTO membership are simple. It is often difficult, therefore, to gain a clear understanding of the positions of WTO members. In using Hohfeldian terminology in relation to WTO 'obligations', this study seeks to demonstrate the real nature of these positions and how they affect sovereignty, in the senses laid out above.[25]

Hohfeld was an American jurist and professor of analytical jurisprudence in the early years of the twentieth century. His work was focused primarily on private law in the United States[26] and the legal relationships between private actors in that field. The characterisation of legal relationships into defined categories did not begin and

---

[23]*Joseph William Singer*, The Legal Rights Debate in Analytical Jurisprudence from Bentham to Hohfeld, Wisconsin Law Review (1982), 975, 987.

[24]*Wesley Newcomb Hohfeld*, Fundamental Legal Conceptions as Applied in Judicial Reasoning and Other Legal Essays (London, 1923), 35.

[25]See *supra*, 2.2 on sovereignty.

[26]See generally: *Hohfeld* (note 24).

end with *Hohfeld,* and there were many detractors, elaborators and supporters[27] of his proposed system. It is not argued here that this type of analysis is without defects, but it is rather employed as a useful tool in an attempt to assess the legal relationships created through WTO membership, both between members and between members and the WTO as an institution. *Singer* says of Hohfeldian analytical tools that 'their validity and importance must relate to their utility in solving some problem'.[28] It is herein proposed that the complexity of relationships under the WTO and covered agreements is our problem and that Hohfeldian analytical methods shall prove their own utility in untangling these relationships. *Hohfeld* himself did not claim that these classifications were perfect, describing fundamental legal relationships as '*sui generis,* and thus it is that attempts at formal definition are always unsatisfactory, if not altogether useless'.[29] He nevertheless set about providing his vision of a breakdown of legal relationships into individual concepts, believing that 'the most promising line of procedure'[30] lay in examining these conceptions and their relations to each other in terms of opposites and correlatives. His scheme of analysis is laid out below.

In defining the different types of relationships created by the law in the domestic private law context, a 'state' (in the sense of centralised state authority within a territory) is required, whose power can be invoked, for example, in the case of a breach of a 'duty'. In this context, the 'state' is a centralised national governmental authority with legislative and executive but particularly judicial and enforcement functions. It is well established that international law lacks this centralised governmental authority in the traditional sense, and there is no 'global state'. Therefore, in order for Hohfeldian terminology to serve as a useful tool for the analysis of international jural relationships, a specific paradigm must be adopted for this work.

In assessing whether 'freedom of contract' really constitutes a freedom at all, *Singer* states: 'Any definition of property and contract necessarily requires the state to determine the character of relations among citizens in the marketplace',[31] thus demonstrating that any functioning system of property and contract, which can easily be evidenced in international law (or at least in certain areas thereof), can be seen to constitute a 'global state' in the sense stated above, through its continued distribution of wealth and bargaining power. Therefore, in this manner, there can be said to be a 'global state' (at least in this limited context). Further, the organs of a 'state' such as this can be more easily seen in the WTO institutions, particularly as there is not only a functioning system of property and contract but also binding compulsory dispute settlement and partially centralised enforcement mechanisms.

---

[27]For a summary of the debate which raged after Hohfeld's death, see *Joseph William Singer,* The Legal Rights Debate in Analytical Jurisprudence from Bentham to Hohfeld, Wisconsin Law Review (1982), 975, 989–993.

[28]*Ibid.,* 993.

[29]*Hohfeld* (note 24), 36 – *sui generis* here denotes that classification of fundamental legal relationships is unsatisfactory due to their unique nature.

[30]*Ibid.*

[31]*Joseph William Singer,* Legal Realism Now, California Law Review 76 (1988), 465, 482.

Thus, having established a paradigmatic 'global state', what now follows is a summary of the relevant elements of Hohfeldian legal analysis for the purposes of this work. *Hohfeld* broke down the blanket terms 'right' and 'duty' and characterised them instead into eight different legal concepts.[32] These concepts can be grouped together in two ways, correlatives and opposites, in order to demonstrate types of legal relationship. When employed to analyse a real legal situation, they seek to avoid imprecise language and instead discover the real nature of the legal relationship between the relevant parties, and the real extent of their 'rights' and 'duties'.

In this work, these terms will be used to attempt to define properly the legal position and relationships not only between States parties to the WTO but also between the WTO as an institution and its members. In this second sense, the 'global state' paradigm described above is partially problematic because it itself comprises part of the 'state'. Nonetheless, it has a certain degree of legal personality as an institution in international law,[33] and therefore following *Hohfeld's* conclusion that legal relationships exist between legal persons,[34] and extending the analogy to the international plane, this point is not seriously problematic. Indeed, no one would argue that legal relationships do not exist between private citizens and the State within domestic law, though they are fundamentally different in nature to the relationships between private citizens. So although the Hohfeldian scheme is an imperfect model, it can nevertheless be used to draw interesting conclusions about that nature of the relationship between WTO member States, individually and as group, and the institution itself.

Moving onto the definitional landscape, the eight legal concepts identified by *Hohfeld* are as follows:

rights: 'claims, enforceable by state power, that others act in a certain manner in relation to the rightholder';

duties: characterised as an 'absence of permission to act in a certain manner';

privileges: 'permissions to act in a certain manner without being liable for damages to others and without others being able to summon state power to prevent those acts';

no-rights [which this work will term 'exposures'][35]: which refers to those who are in a position where they 'do not have the power to summon the aid of the state to alter or control the behaviour of others';

---

[32]*Hohfeld*, (note 24), 36.

[33]See Art VIII:1 Marrakesh Agreement Establishing the WTO (WTO Agreement), which states: 'The WTO shall have legal personality, and shall be accorded by each of its Members such legal capacity as shall be necessary for the exercise of its functions.'

[34]As opposed to between persons and objects, so ownership of property exists as a legally enforceable right to keep others from, for example, interfering with that property rather than as a legal relationship between the legal person and the object owned: see *Hohfeld* (note 24), 28–30.

[35]Following Commons, the term exposure is preferred here. Commons also utilised the term liberty rather than privilege but for reasons related to its use in the legal language in the United States which has no bearing here. See: *John R. Commons*, The Legal Foundations of Capitalism (Madison, 1923).

powers: 'state enforced abilities to change legal entitlements held by oneself or others';

immunities: characterised by 'security from having one's own entitlements changed by others';

liabilities: 'the absence of immunity from having one's own entitlements changed by others';

disabilities: the 'absence of power to alter legal entitlements'.[36]

The following work will predominantly seek to utilise the first four concepts (right, duty, privilege, no-right/exposure). It is conceded that the latter four may have some relevance in relation to the analysis of the institutional make-up of the WTO and relationships between the institution and its members, but, for reasons of length and complexity, this is outside the scope of this work.

The groupings used to demonstrate how these concepts fit into legal relationships are as follows.

Jural opposites

Right	Privilege	Power	Immunity
No-right/exposure	Duty	Disability	Liability

Jural correlatives

Right	Privilege	Power	Immunity
Duty	No-right/exposure	Liability	Disability

With regard to a certain class of acts, one would have one or the other but not both of the two opposites; for example, if State A was to have a right to do x, it would not at the same time be in a position of no-right/exposure (in relation to doing x). Correlatives express the relative positions of a legal relationship from each side; if A has a right, then B is under a corresponding duty. 'Rights are nothing but duties placed on others to act in a certain manner. Similarly, privileges are correlatives of no-rights'.[37]

However, legal relationships are often more complex than that, and various criticisms were levelled at *Hohfeld's* system—particularly related to his classifications of 'Opposites'.[38] The position of one State (State A) in relation to another (State B) in the relevant field may comprise not only a duty but within that duty a privilege in how the duty may be carried out, thus meaning that State B, who has the corresponding right to A's duty, would also be in a position of no-right/exposure.

---

[36]*Singer* (note 31), 486.

[37]*Singer* (note 23), 986.

[38]See for example: *Albert Kocourek*, Various Definitions of Jural Relation, Columbia Law Review 20 (1920), 394–412; *Commons* (note 35), 92–95.

This criticism of 'Opposites', particularly by *Kocourek*,[39] highlights a logical inconsistency in *Hohfeld's* abstract categorisation but one that, according to *Commons*, was probably due to the fact that these were intended to be used in a pragmatic sense attached to concrete cases and examples, not in the abstract.[40] *Commons* further argues that 'the logic and accuracy will be retained if we substitute the quantitative term "limits" for the indeterminate "opposites"'[41] in order that 'each set of jural relations would be interpreted as being mutually limiting, rather than logically contradictory'.[42] This substitution is particularly helpful in this study. When assessing the bargaining power and limitations on sovereignty brought about through WTO membership, breaking down legal positions as between parties is clearly helpful, but more so is an assessment of the limitations of the rights or duties, privileges or no-rights, held by a particular party.

Expanding a little further for clarity on the situation mentioned above: where State A has a duty, State B has a right—where State A has a choice in how to carry out that duty, it has a privilege. Where State A has a privilege, State B is exposed to the limit of that privilege, i.e. is in the field of no-right. These are two separate but concurrent legal positions for both States, and the scope of one part of the legal position limits the scope of the other. 'Duty and liberty vary inversely to each other, the duty increasing as the liberty diminishes, and the duty diminishing as the liberty (or privilege) increases'.[43] Therefore, State A has a duty to do x but may have a large privilege in how it may carry out x, for example a long time limit, choice of methodology, etc. The duty of State A is limited by the scope of its privilege (and this would also apply vice versa with a duty large in scope, probably crafted in very precise language, limiting the privilege of State A). State B in this situation has both of the two correlatives of State A's legal position; it has a right and is at the same time in the position of no-right, being exposed to actions occurring within the limit of State A's privilege. State B's right is of the same scope as State A's duty; where State A's duty is limited by its privilege, so too is State B's right limited by its field of exposure, which is as expansive as the privilege of State A, bearing in mind that it is the ability to call upon the 'global state' to uphold and enforce a right that makes it a right and that, in exercising a privilege, no person can call upon 'the global state' for actions occurring within that sphere. Where a duty is breached, the right holder State can apply to 'the state' to have its right enforced, but the exposure, in limiting the right, leaves this State in a position where it cannot summon the 'global state' in relation to any action happening within the sphere of privilege of the duty-holding State.

---

[39]*Kocourek* (note 38), 394–412.

[40]*Commons* (note 35), 96.

[41]*Ibid.*

[42]*Luca Fiorito*, John R. Commons, Wesley N. Hohfeld, and the Origins of Transactional Economics (2008), 6, available at: http://repec.deps.unisi.it/quaderni/536.pdf (last accessed on 05/03/2017).

[43]*Commons* (note 35), 96.

In breaking down legal positions into separate (but intrinsically inseparable) relationships, this work seeks to uncover the true nature of the relationships created by the GATT and covered agreements and the power distribution brought about by WTO membership in the field of environmental and public health regulation and, therefore, how much sovereignty (in the political science sense) has really been ceded in this area. If the chosen methodology outlined above seems a little complex in the abstract, the concrete examples used in this work will provide clarity.

The particular reason why the Hohfeldian analysis is befitting to this study is that it is essentially an assessment of one legal arena upon another: WTO membership and national regulatory space. But how can such space be measured? In international law, the concept of sovereignty means that States are only bound so far as they agree to be bound by rules of international law. WTO membership was a clear (if perhaps, from the perspective of economic bargaining power, coerced) choice of States that they can (legally, if not 100% politically realistically) withdraw from when they choose.[44] Thus, following the legal concept of sovereignty, regulatory space is restricted to agreed parameters through free choice. However, it will be argued that these 'agreed parameters' are fluid, often chosen at the whim/will of the DSS and, above all else, unclear to governments that are seeking to impose TREMs. Thus, the use of the Hohfeldian analysis in this study seeks to lay out the position of importing and exporting States vis-à-vis each other and the WTO DSS itself in relation to the WTO rules that are most important in the introduction of TREMs in the hope that it will demonstrate the parameters that exist currently, any potential room for manoeuvre, and the effects caused by and the effects on bargaining power of the obligations entailed in WTO membership.

In the simplest case of direct prohibitions on action, it is clear that Hohfeldian analysis can only say what has been said. In the more complex sphere of the WTO rules relating to NPR PPMs, Hohfeldian analysis assists in such an assessment by demonstrating what position States find themselves in under the WTO and what restrictions exist upon their regulatory freedom stemming from WTO membership (at least in the realm of TREMs and NPR PPMs). While such an undertaking cannot assist in an assessment of the effects of WTO membership on State sovereignty in the legal sense, the effects on national regulatory space and other elements that make up sovereignty in the political science sense of the term can provide a picture of the effect of one legal arena upon another.

---

[44] Art. XV WTO Agreement.

2.4 Holmes and Hale

Although the Hohfeldian analytical process laid out above will prove a useful tool for this study, there are also some other ideas raised by the 'Legal Realist' branch of juridical scholarship[45] that demonstrate themselves to be of value in assessing international trade obligations.

Oliver Wendell Holmes was a nineteenth century American judge and jurist. His 'Bad Man's Theory' of law sought to do, in many ways, what the methodology employed here seeks to do: uncover the practical implications of the law, devoid of the language of morality, in order to make the best possible predictions about it.[46] *Holmes* sought to, in his own words, 'wash it [the notion of duty] with a cynical acid and expel everything except the object of our study, the operations of the law'.[47]

Holmes argued that, in talking about rights and duties, one was doing nothing more than prophesising and that an 'evil effect' of the tying in of morality and law was that it created a situation where one considers 'the right or the duty as something existing apart from and independent of the consequences of its breach',[48] with a duty being 'nothing but a prediction that if a man does or omits certain things he will be made to suffer in this way or that way by judgment of the court; – and so of a legal right'.[49] He thus sought to strip away abstract thinking about the nature of rights and duties and looked at them instead only through the lens of consequence.

Further, with regard to his 'Bad Man's Theory', *Holmes* argued:

> If you want to know the law and nothing else, you must look at it as a bad man, who cares only for the material consequences which such knowledge enables him to predict, not as a good one, who finds his reasons for conduct, whether inside the law or outside of it, in the vaguer sanctions of conscience.[50]

And

> the notion of legal duty, to which already I have referred. We fill the word with all the content which we draw from morals. But what does that mean to a bad man? Mainly, and in the first place, a prophecy that if he does certain things he will be subjected to disagreeable consequences by way of imprisonment or compulsory payment of money. But from his point of view what is the difference between being fined and being taxed a certain sum for doing a certain thing?[51]

The application of this sort of approach to some areas of international law may raise an eyebrow or two—for instance, looking at *jus cogens* norm violation in

---

[45] As with Hohfeld, outlined above, legal realist scholarship predominantly sought to reimagine classical legal scholarship related to United States private law. For a concise summary of the history, contentions and conclusions of the legal realist scholars, see *Singer* (note 31).

[46] *Oliver Wendell Holmes*, The Path of Law, Harvard Law Review 10 (1897), 457.

[47] *Ibid.*, 462.

[48] *Ibid.*, 458.

[49] *Ibid.*

[50] *Ibid.*, 459.

[51] *Ibid.*, 461.

terms of cost/benefit analysis—but in terms of economic law, it is a useful way in which to abandon notions of 'right and wrong' in the concepts of right and duty. This is employed not only to try to uncover how parties are really using the law, but also when they are choosing to breach their obligations, the reasons why they are choosing to do so. Where penalties are treated in the same way as taxes on behaviour from both a theoretical and a practical (by States) point of view, the rhetoric of rights and duties becomes more than simply a prescriptive code and can rather be seen as a series of points of reference from which States can choose to depart, if they can afford the consequences due to their economic bargaining power. In positions of differing bargaining power, these rules will affect different parties differently—a bad man weighs the consequences of his actions in terms of what he can afford, and this can differ greatly.

Bargaining power was also a theme central to the work of *Robert Hale*, writing in the mid-twentieth century. Following the legal realist tradition of re-examining classical legal scholarship, *Hale* sought to similarly wash the law with a cynical acid in order to discover its operations.[52] This is precisely what this work sets out to do: breaking down of complex legal relationships using the Hohfeldian analytical tradition; assessing the law from the bad man's point of view, after *Holmes*; and seeking to assess coercion, compulsion and bargaining power, following *Hale*.

Hale sought to demonstrate that legal systems create burdens, both through **coercive measures**, such as penalties or taxes,[53] and by 'the state' enforcing the private rights of others[54] (which amounts to enforcing private coercion).[55] *Hale* viewed coercion as a concept that had, like *Holmes*' rights and duties, been imbued with connotations of morality. Stripping away those connotations, he claimed of his work on coercion that 'to call an act coercive is not by any means to condemn it'.[56] He saw it rather as a useful term by which the real machinations of marketplace interaction could be described.

Hale viewed the role of 'the state' in private transactions as not only abstaining from interference with property rights but also as actively 'forcing' the non-owner to desist from interfering with property without the consent of the owner.[57] In order to gain this consent, and avoid the consequences of the law, the non-owner 'may be willing to obey the will of the owner, provided that the obedience is not in itself more unpleasant than the consequences to be avoided'.[58] This echoes back to

---

[52]Following the language of *Holmes* (note 46), see *Robert Lee Hale*, Force and the State: A Comparison of 'Political' and 'Economic' Compulsion, Columbia Law Review 35 (1935), 149, 153.

[53]See above, *Holmes* (note 46), 641 and *Hale* (note 52), 153.

[54]*Robert Lee Hale*, Coercion and Distribution in a Supposedly Non-Coercive State, Pol. Sci. Q. 38 (1924), 470–478.

[55]See generally: *ibid.*

[56]*Ibid.*, 471.

[57]*Ibid.*

[58]*Ibid.*, 472.

Holmes' 'Bad Man', who makes material choices about obeying the law on the basis of its consequences. What *Hale* sought to show here is that even though a 'non-owner' chooses to obey the law in a particular instance, based on a preference for the consequences of one bad option over another, this cannot be distinguished in any meaningful way from him being coerced into this path of action, based on his relative bargaining position vis-à-vis the 'property owner'.

Hale argued further that it is the law of property that coerces people into working for others, and making deals that may be unfavourable to them, and on the other side it is what motivates employers and those with greater bargaining power into paying more, or offering a more favourable terms, as they seek to avoid the possibility of unpleasant circumstances (related to the retention, enjoyment and growth of their own property) by the withholding of payment/labour or services in ways protected by the law.

Applying this analogy in a broader way to States under international law requires again the caveat that it is not argued here that coercion and compulsion are the prime movers in all areas of international law, but that they are certainly a helpful lens through which to assess international trade law and economic relationships. While the law of property and contract is somewhat adjusted on the international plane, it is clearly possible to apply *Hale's* approach to the sort of legal relationships, which are the concern of this study. The contract analogy broadens out into States with unequal bargaining power agreeing to become members of the WTO and their acceptance of tariff bindings and other potentially negative consequences that arise from membership—such as the limitations placed on their ability to regulate certain matters internally, which will be the focus of this work—being based on coercion. Thus, where a State with substantially less economic bargaining power makes an agreement with a stronger economic power, in our case by becoming party to the WTO, this decision should be viewed not simply as a 'meeting of the minds' based on *consensus ad idem* and sovereign equality. Rather, the coercion that *Hale* demonstrated in the domestic marketplace is equally evidenced here.

2.5 Coercion

Economic coercion in general in international law has been 'traditionally difficult to define'[59] but can broadly be seen to include the threat or use of 'measures of an economic – contrasted with diplomatic or military – character taken to induce a State to change some policy or even its governmental structure'.[60] Evidently, this is of a slightly different nature to the analogy made above in relation to coercion with

---

[59]*Barry E. Carter*, Economic Coercion, in: Rüdiger Wolfrum (ed.) The Max Planck Encyclopaedia of Public International Law, vol. III (Oxford, 2012), 291, 292 (para. 1).

[60]*Andreas F. Lowenfeld*, International Economic Law (Oxford, 2002), 698.

regard to international agreements, in this case exemplified by becoming party to the WTO.

With regard to the conclusion of treaties and the legality of coercion, the VCLT contains two provisions on coercion, which dictate:

Article 51: Coercion of a representative of a State
The expression of a State's consent to be bound by a treaty which has been procured by the coercion of its representative through acts or threats directed against him shall be without any legal effect.

Article 52: Coercion of a State by the threat or use of force
A treaty is void if its conclusion has been procured by the threat or use of force in violation of the principles of international law embodied in the Charter of the United Nations

Article 51 VCLT is clearly not of relevance to the sort of coercion imagined in this study. Article 52 VCLT is likewise not easy to analogise without employing a broad-reaching interpretation of the threat or use of force to include economic measures.[61] Furthermore, it is unlikely in the extreme that any State would argue that the WTO and covered agreements are void on the basis of coercion, making this matter purely academic.

Looking more generally at force and economic coercion in international law: while some developing countries have argued that the Art. 2 (4) United Nations Charter prohibition on the use of force encompasses economic force,[62] the fact that a proposal to extend this provision to include the use of economic coercion was rejected in the negotiations[63] of the Charter seriously undermines this claim.[64] Indeed, in 1993, the United Nations Secretary-General noted:

There is no clear consensus in international law as to when coercive measures are improper, despite relevant treaties, declarations, and resolutions adopted in international organizations which try to develop norms limiting the use of such measures.[65]

And he further stated that 'the intent criterion [in establishing whether a measure amounts to economic coercion] does not include measures imposed with the intent of changing the economic policies of the receiving State'.[66] It would be difficult to argue, therefore, that economic coercion would be covered by the term 'threat or

---

[61]Indeed proposals to include 'economic and political pressure' in the wording of Art. 52 were rejected, though an annex to the Final Act did include the Declaration on the Prohibition of Military, Political or Economic Coercion in the Conclusion of Treaties. See *Olivier Corten*, Article 52 Convention of 1969, in Olivier Corten/Pierre Klein (eds.), The Vienna Conventions on the Law of Treaties: A Commentary, vol. II (2011) 1201, 1205–1211.

[62]*Carter* (note 59), para. 6.

[63]See *Albrecht Randelzhofer/Oliver Dörr*, Article 2(4), in Bruno Simma *et al.* (eds.) The Charter of the United Nations: A Commentary, vol. I (Oxford, 3rd edn. 2012), 200, 209.

[64]*Carter* (note 59), para. 6.

[65]GA, Economic Measures as a Means of Political and Economic Coercion against Developing Countries: Note by the Secretary General, UN Doc. A/48/535 (1993), Agenda Item 91 (a) at 2(a).

[66]*Ibid*, 2(b).

use of force' in the VCLT,[67] and it is clearly not recognised as such in any way that could amount to a norm of customary international law. Further, the specific reference by the Secretary-General that the intent criterion, which was also described as 'the most important criteria'[68] in establishing economic coercion, would not encompass measures designed to change the *economic* policies of another State would appear to rule out the sort of coercion that was the basis of conclusion of the WTO and covered agreements. Although the terms of these treaties are not measures in the way the Secretary-General was describing, it is possible to loosely analogise them with the continued imposition of high tariff barriers as the negative consequences that act as the leverage to coerce States with lesser economic bargaining power to become party to the WTO. These 'negative consequences' have the 'intention of changing the policies of the receiving State', and specifically economic policies, and therefore do not meet this most important intent criteria laid out by the Secretary-General.

However, national regulatory measures designed to protect the environment or public health that have extraterritorial effects could feasibly be designed with the intent that their consequences change the policies of the receiving State in the fields of the environment and health. They would therefore be measures with extraterritorial effect, the consequences of which would coerce States into changing non-economic policies, and meet the Secretary-General's definition of economic coercion.

2.6   Summary

The analytical structure that this work will follow has been outlined above. It includes not only methodological analysis of the relevant legal positions but also special areas of interest for the analysis of law and policy in the fields of national environmental and health regulation, and international obligations. The overarching point of reference will always be sovereignty, how the relevant provisions affect the sovereignty of WTO members, and how far and in what ways members are differentially affected due to differing economic bargaining power.

This analytical structure can be summarised as follows:

- Hohfeldian analysis: breaking down legal relationships to better understand their implications;
- following *Holmes*: looking at the law through the eyes of the 'Bad Man', washing it with cynical acid and attempting to assess the function of the law in terms of its consequences;

---

[67]Art. 52 VCLT.

[68]GA, Economic Measures as a Means of Political and Economic Coercion against Developing Countries: Note by the Secretary-General, UN Doc. A/48/535 (1993), Agenda Item 91 (a) at 2(b).

- following *Hale*: assessing how bargaining power is allocated and coercion applied through WTO membership, uncovering the real machinations of the marketplace in international trade law while bearing in mind that any connotations of morality attached to the language of coercion serve only to obfuscate these machinations.

Chapter 3
Historical Development of the WTO DSS and National Environmental and Public Health Regulation

3.1 Overview

The following chapter will now go on to give an introduction to the content of the relevant provisions of the WTO and covered agreements in the area of environmental and health regulation, particularly in reference to non-tariff barriers to trade and more specifically labelling requirements and border measures (including import bans) on the basis of NPR PPMs.

Before this, however, it is necessary to include an institutional overview of the WTO and particularly its DSS in order to understand the issue raised in context. To do so, the structure and function of the WTO as an organisation will be summarised, and then the Dispute Settlement Understanding (DSU) and DSS system will be described and analysed in order to lay out how this advanced dispute settlement system was designed to operate. In order to fully understand the institution, the history of the GATT will also be summarised, chiefly in order to show how the particular history of the international trading regime has influenced the current position of the WTO. The importance of the institutional structure and functioning of the DSS cannot be understated; the DSS has been described as 'in all probability, the most effective area of adjudication in the entire area of public international law'.[1] In order to understand the allocation of bargaining power by the organisation between parties, and between parties and the organisation itself, it is necessary to fully understand how the organisation and its DSS function.

---

[1]*David Palmeter/Petros C. Mavroidis*, Dispute Settlement in the World Trade Organization: Practice and Procedure (Cambridge, 2nd edn. 2004), 234.

© Springer International Publishing AG 2017
A.R. Maggio, *Environmental Policy, Non-Product Related Process and Production Methods and the Law of the World Trade Organization*, European Yearbook of International Economic Law 1, DOI 10.1007/978-3-319-61155-6_3

3.2   The GATT, WTO, DSU and DSS

An in-depth history of the GATT and Uruguay Round negotiations that led to the formation of the WTO is beyond the scope of this work. It will suffice to give a brief overview of the history of the two regimes, particularly highlighting points of interest in relation to the environment, development and institutional outlook. Furthermore, the differences between the dispute settlement system of the GATT and the WTO DSS will be analysed in more detail as the understanding of its operation enables a deeper appreciation of how and why its measures may be able to restrict national regulatory space.

The GATT 1947, negotiated at the same time as the Havana Charter for an International Trade Organisation (ITO) (which never came into effect), was never intended to be a permanent 'organisation' but rather a stopgap to facilitate international trade while the negotiations and ratifications of the Havana Charter took place.[2] The 23 original GATT 'Contracting Parties'[3] comprised 13 developed and 10 developing countries,[4] and by the end of the Torquay Round (1950) the total stood at 14, with developed countries numbering 20.[5] Although in the next decade little happened to change this balance of developed/developing countries, decolonisation in the 1960s in particular 'produced a sharp change in the numerical balance', with 52 of the 77 GATT contracting parties in 1970 being developing countries.[6] The Uruguay Round, which began in September 1986 and involved seven and a half years of 'arduous negotiations',[7] was the first round of negotiations where developing countries really played an active role.[8] The Round involved 123 negotiating parties and eventually produced the Marrakesh Agreement Establishing the World Trade Organization (with final act, annexes and protocol). The GATT 1947 was incorporated into the new WTO regime, and, alongside the inclusion of other multi- and plurilateral agreements (such as the SPS and TBT Agreements, which will be discussed below), the whole GATT DSS underwent a drastic change through the introduction of the DSU.

---

[2]For a comprehensive history on the relationship between the Havanna Charter, the ITO and the GATT, as well as analysis as to the reasons for its failure, see *Robert E. Hudec*, The GATT Legal System and World Trade Diplomacy (London, 2nd edn. 1990), 23–61.

[3]The fact that the GATT was never intended to be an organisation can also be evidenced in the choice of language here, as 'Contracting Parties' was used rather than 'Members'.

[4]The original developing country members were Brazil. Burma, China, Ceylon, Chile, Cuba, India, Pakistan, Syria and Lebanon. See: *Robert E. Hudec*, Developing Countries in the GATT Legal System (Cambridge, 1987), 23.

[5]*Ibid.* The developed countries at this point and included all major developed countries except Japan and Switzerland.

[6]*Ibid.*, 24–25.

[7]*William R. Cline*, Evaluating the Uruguay Round, The World Economy 18 (1995), 1.

[8]ODI, The GATT Uruguay Round, Overseas Development Institute Briefing Paper (1987), 4.

Although after the failure of the overly ambitious ITO to materialise[9] the GATT spent 'the better part of its first ten years of existence waiting and hoping for the creation of a permanent organizational structure'[10], this never occurred. Indeed, until the birth of the WTO in 1995, the GATT regime was characterised by 'institutional flexibility'.[11] In 1947, there was no GATT Secretariat, but a small interim commission was set up for the ITO (ICITO) in order to pave the way for its establishment. When this did not come to pass, it became the *de facto* GATT Secretariat.[12] In 1960, the contracting parties created a formal council, which then became the 'principal permanent institution for the GATT 1947'.[13]

Due to its origin and history, the GATT DSS was understandably also endowed with the same 'institutional flexibility' as the 'organisation' itself. Many States found this beneficial, and it can be described as one of the strengths of the GATT DSS,[14] particularly by WTO critics, in contradistinction to the more rigid system in operation under the WTO. The GATT DSS was a regime that evolved through practice[15] and functioned based on diplomacy and cooperation. The GATT was described as 'a flexible instrument, modified sometimes in its structure and *modus operandi* so as to adapt to the economic and political conditions in which world trade develop[ed]',[16] and this not only allowed for but also encouraged a flexible approach to dispute settlement.[17] Ambiguity and flexibility were utilised in the GATT regime on the basis of pragmatism, which was balanced with a legal approach.[18] The importance of this balance, and pragmatism generally in the regime, can be seen as based on the subject matter the GATT intended to govern.

---

[9]The ITO was effectively 'killed' by the failure of US Congress to approve it. In fact, in 1950, the US Department of State declared it to be dead. See *Palmeter/Mavroidis* (note 1), 2.

[10]*Hudec* (note 2), 67.

[11]*Ibid.*

[12]*John H. Jackson*, The Evolution of the World Trading System: The Legal and Institutional Context, in: Daniel Bethlehem *et al.* (eds.), The Oxford Handbook of International Trade Law (2009), 30, 35; see further *Wolfgang Benedek*, General Agreement on Tariffs and Trade (1947 and 1994), in: Rüdiger Wolfrum (ed.) The Max Planck Encyclopaedia of Public International Law, vol. IV (Oxford, 2012), 312, 315 (paras. 14–15).

[13]*Jackson* (note 12), 36.

[14]See *Miles Kahler*, International Institutions and the Political Economy of Integration (Washington DC, 1995), 27, who describes this flexibility as being 'Particularly important, because the General Agreement was very difficult to amend, a principal explanation for the gradual proliferation of side agreements'.

[15]*Hudec* (note 2), 75–108.

[16]*Oliver Long*, Law and its Limitations in the GATT Multilateral Trading System (Heidelberg, 1985), 5.

[17]*Andrew Lang*, World Trade After Neoliberalism: Re-imagining the Global Economic Order (Oxford, 2011), 202–205 (emphasis added). *Lang* pays particular attention here to the fact that the text of the GATT 'represented only a very partial and even misleading window onto the normative universe of the GATT's legal system' and that greater heed should be paid to the 'large body of informal norms which sprang up in and around the formal texts' which 'structured the interpretation and application of the law'.

[18]*Long* (note 16), 61.

As a purpose-oriented trade 'regime', this balance helped ensure that crucial issues could be dealt with both effectively and realistically.[19] Furthermore, '[a]mbiguity was important as a way of ensuring sufficient flexibility in the law to permit it to express whatever informal community consensus existed at any particular point in time'.[20] Thus, any description of the GATT and the GATT DSS requires not only analysis of the legal text on which the regime was based but also the prevailing conditions at the relevant moment. This is, of course, a truism in many areas of law, but the particular importance given to trade diplomacy by the contracting parties and the pendulum of opinion on economic models in the time of the GATT makes this point key in this context. '[T]hroughout the history of the GATT, contracting parties [. . .] responded constructively and positively to international economic and political conditions, without having undue regard to legal technicalities.'[21]

The GATT 'institutional system' was purposely far more limited than that of the proposed ITO, and the whole agreement was framed from the outset as a 'trade agreement' in order that its quick ratification could be facilitated.[22] This meant that the contracting parties initially sought to 'avoid making the GATT a formal international organization',[23] and although it did later gain a more formal structure, it has been described as 'provisional for almost half a century'.[24] The history of the GATT as an organisation, and particularly its DSS, should not be viewed as a natural, linear progression from flexibility to formality that culminated in the Uruguay Round (and thus the 'rigid' system of the WTO). Rather, the changing political and historical context of the period conditioned expectations of dispute settlement in the trade context, and this in turn changed the expected and actual function of the GATT and its DSS.[25] Decolonisation and the growth of developing country membership, economic conditions in post-war Europe and the birth and growth of the EEC, the post-war economic supremacy of the United States (and its comparative 'decline') and the way in which the DSS itself functioned are all factors that contribute to the fact that it is possible to describe the GATT institution and DSS differently depending on the particular period of time in question. Some periods were characterised by a stance of 'antilegalism' by the US and the EEC,[26]

---

[19]*Ibid.*, 62.

[20]*Lang* (note 17), 204.

[21]*Long* (note 16), 62.

[22]Particularly by the United States, whose requirement for congressional ratification was in fact the major blow to the ITO. This is in contrast to the substantive obligations of the GATT which were 'a faithful copy of the ITO's Commercial Policy Chapter as it then stood'. See *Hudec* (note 2), 50.

[23]*Ibid.*, 51.

[24]WTO, Understanding the WTO (5th edn. 2011), 15. Art. XXIX: GATT 1947 provides, in fact, that 'Part II of this Agreement shall be suspended on the day on which the Havana Charter comes into force'.

[25]For a thorough history of the legal system of the GATT, see *Hudec* (note 2); *Robert E. Hudec, Enforcing International Trade Law: The Evolution of the Modern GATT Legal System* (London, 1993).

[26]*Hudec* (note 2), 34. Particularly the period in the 1960s where very few cases were brought, and none at all in the last six years of the decade, *ibid*, 31.

or particular friction between the two economic superpowers leading to more litigation.[27] The 1970s saw an emergence of a period of stagnation, and the 1973/5-9 Tokyo Round both brought some reform to the DSS and strengthened some of its features.[28] The greatest divergence of opinion in this period between the US and the EEC was over whether contracting parties would have the automatic right to convene a Panel in the event of a complaint (US) or if potential defendants could continue to block the possible formation of a Panel (EEC). The reforms emanating from the Round gave each side a victory of sorts but 'did not, however, resolve the tensions between the [...] positions'.[29] The DSS in the early 1980s experienced a growth in reputation due to its increased volume of activity and satisfactory results[30] following the implementation of the Tokyo Round Agreements.[31]

By this period, the organisation had succeeded, through the various rounds, in lowering tariffs. The agreements negotiated at the Tokyo Round were the first to cover areas that represented trading obstacles that occurred behind the borders, so-called non-tariff barriers to trade. The greater reach of these agreements, alongside 'a series of economic recessions in the 1970s and early 1980s, [which] drove governments to devise other forms of protection for sectors facing increased foreign competition',[32] meant that the GATT and its DSS were both in a better position and under greater pressure to provide stability to the international trading system. A more operational DSS meant, however, a more visible DSS: greater visibility and a wider purview also meant that the weaknesses (or 'birth defects' as some have categorised them)[33] in the ad hoc, diplomatic DSS of the GATT became more apparent. Thus, by the beginning of the Uruguay Round negotiations in 1986, a clear case could be made for the need for a much strengthened DSS in any new organisation that would be produced as a result of the Round.

The two key issues here are the policy change of the GATT in terms of what sort of measures were regulated internationally, first after the Tokyo Round with non-tariff barriers to trade and then to a far greater extent following the institution of the WTO, and the huge change in the institutional make-up of the 'organisation',

---

[27]Ibid., generally and particularly 39–40, 54.

[28]Though also created some problems that were not solved until the introduction of the WTO DSU.

[29]Hudec (note 2), 57.

[30]Ibid., 129.

[31]The Tokyo Round was the first major round that tackled non-tariff barriers to trade and included the Agreement on Implementation of Article VI of the General Agreement on Tariffs and Trade (Antidumping Code), the Agreement on Implementation of Article VII of the General Agreement on Tariffs and Trade (Customs Valuation Code), Agreement on Import Licensing Procedures, Agreement on Interpretation and Application of Articles VI, XVI, and XXIII of the General Agreement on Tariffs and Trade (Subsidies Code), Agreement on Technical Barriers to Trade (Standards Code), Agreement on Trade in Civil Aircraft, International Dairy Agreement, International Bovine Meat Agreement and the Differential and More Favourable Treatment and Reciprocity and Fuller Participation of Developing Countries (Enabling Clause).

[32]Understanding the WTO (note 24), 17.

[33]See Jackson (note 12), 32–35.

particularly the DSS, after the Uruguay Round. The evolution of the importance of the GATT DSS has been outlined above, and the following will go into more detail about the GATT to WTO institutional changes, both in general but also more specifically in regard to how dispute resolution changed and why this is of importance in this study.

3.3 GATT DSS to WTO DSS

The reason for the importance of the GATT, its DSS and the decisions of its DSS in any study of international trade law are provided in Art. XVI:1 of the WTO Agreement. The article states:

> Except as otherwise provided under this Agreement or the Multilateral Trade Agreements, the WTO shall be guided by the decisions, procedures and customary practices followed by the CONTRACTING PARTIES to GATT 1947 and the bodies established in the framework of the GATT 1947.

As outlined above, the GATT was envisaged as a trade agreement and transformed itself 'in a pragmatic and incremental manner' into a *de facto* international organisation.[34] The GATT 1947 provided little in the way of institutional structure. Article XXV GATT 1947 required meetings 'from time to time',[35] with the first to be convened by the UN Secretary-General in 1948,[36] at which all parties would have one vote and decisions were to be 'taken by a majority of votes cast'.[37] Obligations arising under the GATT could be waived by a decision of the contracting parties with a two-thirds majority vote.[38] However, as the actual working of the *de facto* organisation evolved, some fairly elaborate, makeshift, powerful procedures[39] came into existence to enable the organisation to function,[40] and some of these procedures did not follow even the loose organisational structure laid out in Art. XXV. The provision made for voting rights and majorities in the GATT was not followed, and decisions were taken not by majority voting but by consensus. The consequences of this consensus-based decision-making that characterised the GATT years of particular importance here are that Panel reports were also adopted, or not, on the basis of consensus, meaning that the losing party could block the adoption of a report—a manifestation of the diplomatic rather than legal nature of the GATT DSS.

Panels were (and continue to be, though in a slightly different manifestation under the WTO) the cornerstone of the GATT DSS. There was no express provision

---

[34] *Peter Van den Bossche*, The Law and Policy of the World Trade Organization (Cambridge, 2nd edn. 2008), 80.

[35] Art. XXV:1 GATT 1947.

[36] Art. XXV:2 GATT 1947.

[37] Art. XXV:3 GATT 1947; Art. XXV:4 GATT 1947.

[38] Art. XXV:5 GATT 1947.

[39] *Jackson* (note 12), 31.

[40] *Van den Boscche* (note 34), 80.

for their establishment as Art. XXIII GATT 1947 only provided for the referral of disputes over nullification or impairment of benefits accruing under the Agreement to the contracting parties, who would 'promptly investigate any matter so referred to them and shall make appropriate recommendations [. . .] or give a ruling on the matter, as appropriate'.[41] Around this vague provision, the system of *ad hoc* Panel dispute settlement eventually emerged, arranged in a manner modelled on, but with important differences to, conventional arbitration tribunals.[42]

Although at the outset disputes under the GATT were generally dealt with using diplomatic means, in the first half of the 1950s '[i]t was decided that rather than use a "working party" composed of nations [. . .], a dispute would be referred to a "panel" of experts'.[43] Panels were made up of three or five experts who were chosen from a list put together by the GATT Chairman.[44] These experts acted 'in their own capacities and not as representatives of any government'.[45] The change from working parties to Panels served to 'legalize' the dispute settlement process in the GATT,[46] and, despite the systems' 'birth defects', the 'GATT had managed to establish an instrument that could focus the few mildly coercive pressures it had been granted, sharply and effectively'.[47] The GATT DSS was further strengthened by the Understanding on Notification, Consultation, Dispute Settlement and Surveillance of 28 November 1979[48] produced during the Tokyo Round, which included the Annex: Agreed Description of the Customary Practice of the GATT in the Field of Dispute Settlement.[49] This Annex contained a much more detailed institutional/procedural framework for the GATT DSS, particularly as regards Panel procedure.[50]

However, as outlined above, the process of consensus decision-making meant that the reports issued by Panels were adopted only with the consent of the 'losing' party to any dispute, who was able to block the consensus,[51] meaning that, in effect, every member had a veto power. This 'handicap' of the GATT DSS was indeed

---

[41] Art. XXIII:2 GATT 1947.

[42] Particularly as the adoption of their reports remained *Georges Abi-Saab*, The Appellate Body and Treaty Interpretation, in: Malgosia Fitzmaurice/Olufemi Elias/Panos Merkouris (eds.), Treaty Interpretation and the Vienna Convention on the Law of Treaties: 30 Years On (Leiden, 2010), 97, 102.

[43] *Jackson* (note 12), 46. For the functioning of the working party system, see further *Hudec* (note 2), 78–80. The panel system began evolving in 1952 upon the suggestion of Mr. Johan Melander of Norway, and was used *ad hoc* for the next 3 years. By 1955 it was decided that the panel system was a success, and its use was cemented in practice.

[44] *Hudec* (note 2), 85.

[45] *Jackson* (note 12), 46.

[46] *Hudec* (note 2), 88.

[47] *Ibid.*, 92.

[48] *Palmeter/Mavroidis* (note 1), 8.

[49] BISD 29S/13, 15.

[50] Paras. 3–6.

[51] Although this became diplomatically problematic by the 1980, it was still part of the GATT DSS. See *Jackson* (note 12), 48–49.

utilised by the losing parties to disputes (though Panel decisions came to be accepted by the losing parties in approximately 90% of cases).[52] Panels, furthermore, could only be constituted on the basis of the consent of the parties—a far cry from the compulsory, binding DSS of the WTO. A further problem with the GATT DSS arose due to procedural issues as there was no guidance as to how the separate dispute settlement procedures that were introduced in the Tokyo Round Agreements[53] should be assessed by the Panels or how they should fit into the GATT system overall.[54]

The finely constructed architecture of the WTO can be held in stark contrast to the *ad hoc* GATT. Between 1986 and 1994, negotiators finally accomplished what was not possible with the ITO: a vision of an international organisation, responsible for trade and centred on (and designed to maximise) stability in international trading relationships. The WTO is not comparable to the EU or the UN in terms of institutional complexity; however, unlike these organisations, it did not grow incrementally but was produced fully formed as an organisation in 1995. The organisational structure of the WTO is set out in Arts. IV and VI of the WTO Agreement. It is comprised of the Ministerial Conference (which meets every 2 years)[55]; the General Council (which meets 'as appropriate')[56]; the General Council sitting as the Dispute Settlement Body (DSB)[57]; the General Council sitting as the Trade Policy Review Body[58]; smaller councils reporting to the General Council for Trade in Goods, Trade in Services and Trade-Related Aspects of Intellectual Property Rights (TRIPS), each with their own committees,[59] as well as committees on issues such as Trade and Environment and Trade and Development[60]; and smaller working groups.[61] The WTO also has its own Secretariat, provided for in Art. VI of the WTO Agreement.

Under the General Council sitting as the DSB sit the dispute settlement Panels and the Appellate Body. The DSB is responsible for constituting a Panel on the request of a complaining party, and following any such request a Panel 'shall be established [...] unless [...] the DSB decides by consensus not to establish a panel'.[62] Once a Panel Report has been issued, it is considered by the DSB,[63] and

---

[52]*Hudec*, Enforcing International Trade Law (note 25), 278.

[53]See note 31.

[54]*Jackson* (note 12), 49.

[55]Art IV:1 WTO Agreement.

[56]Art. IV:2 WTO Agreement.

[57]Art IV:3 WTO Agreement.

[58]Art VI:4 WTO Agreement.

[59]Art. IV:5 WTO Agreement.

[60]Art. IV:6 WTO Agreement.

[61]See *Van den Bossche* (note 34), 118, for a helpful table demonstrating how the organisational structure is set out, and *ibid.*, 117–138 for in-depth analysis as to the institutional structure of the WTO.

[62]Art. 6 DSU.

[63]Art 16.1 DSU.

then it 'shall be adopted' by the DSB, unless one of the parties to the dispute appeals to the Appellate Body.[64] Reports of the Appellate Body 'shall be adopted by the DSB and unconditionally accepted by the parties to the dispute unless the DSB decides by consensus not to adopt the report'.[65] The language used here is clearly strong, indicating the intended strength of the dispute settlement process under the WTO. What is really important, however, is the 'reverse consensus' procedure used for the adoption of DSS reports.[66] Reverse consensus provides the WTO with the *de facto* automatic adoption of Panel and Appellate Body reports, as the General Council sitting as the DSB includes representatives from every member,[67] including the 'winning' party to any given dispute. Reverse consensus dictates that every member would have to agree **not** to adopt a report, which is exceedingly unlikely, though not technically impossible.[68] This particular institutional make-up demonstrates the desire to maintain some of the tenets of the diplomacy-based GATT system while ensuring that compulsory, binding dispute settlement underpins the new regime. A sharp contrast can be seen in the 'balance between legal approach and pragmatism'[69] of the GATT and the rule-constrained hierarchal WTO DSS. Although parties technically do have the possibility to prevent reports of the DSS from becoming binding, a fact that made the system easier to achieve consensus on during the Uruguay Round negotiations, the reality of the situation means that in the last 18 years this possibility has never been utilised—so that it is possible to say that the reports issued by the DSS are *de facto* automatically binding upon the parties.

The WTO DSS has also remedied the 'legally fragmented previous "GATT à la carte" system' and provided an 'integrated dispute settlement system'[70] by

---

[64] Art. 16.4 DSU.

[65] Art. 18 DSU.

[66] Art. IX:1 WTO Agreement iterates that the practice of decision-making by consensus followed under the GATT 1947 'shall continue'. Reverse consensus was first introduced to the GATT system in 1989 through the adoption of the 'Montreal Rules' and then made permanent through their adoption into the WTO regime, see: *Palmeter/Mavroidis* (note 1), 10–11.

[67] Art. IV:2 WTO Agreement.

[68] The possibility can be imagined where a Panel or Appellate Body decision is a clear and flagrant misinterpretation of a rule under one of the agreements, or more likely a report which vastly encroaches upon the autonomy of WTO members by reading standards of review of obligations into the agreements which do not exist and were not agreed upon in the negotiations. But again, the likelihood of a party to a dispute having their claims upheld but nevertheless agreeing that the report should not be adopted is remote. The power of the DSB to withhold consent to the adoption of a report has been described as 'more illusory than real', see *Palmeter/Mavroidis* (note 1), 15. In fact, 'It is generally expected that virtually every WTO dispute settlement final report will be adopted: WTO, The Future of the WTO: Addressing Institutional Challenges in the New Millennium (2004), 50 (2004 Sutherland Report).

[69] *Long* (note 16), 61.

[70] *Ernst-Ulrich Petersmann*, International Trade Law and the GATT/WTO Dispute Settlement System 1948–1996: An Introduction, in: Ernst-Ulrich Petersmann (ed.), Studies in Transnational Economic Law: International Trade Law and the GATT/WTO Dispute Settlement System (Neuwied, 1997), 54–55.

providing in Art. 1 (2) DSU that 'To the extent that there is a difference between the rules and procedures of this Understanding and the special or additional rules and procedures set forth in Appendix 2, the special or additional rules and procedures in Appendix 2 shall prevail'. As Appendix 2 lists the special or additional rules and procedures contained in the covered agreements, the DSU prevents any possible confusion or any possibility of 'rule shopping'[71] and ensures coherency in the DSS.

As indicated above, the WTO 'shall be guided by the decisions' of the GATT contracting parties (Art. XVI:1 WTO Agreement), and as reports of Panels under the GATT were adopted by the contracting parties before becoming binding, then such guidance can certainly be seen to emanate from GATT Panel reports. Indeed, the body of GATT case law has been described as forming part of the *acquis* of the GATT DSS.[72] Thus, despite the fact that there is no doctrine of precedent in the WTO DSS, the decisions of the GATT Panels, along with all decisions made by the WTO DSS, are of central importance in analysing the interpretation and application of the rights and obligations of WTO members. 'Even in the most controversial disputes, the WTO membership and Panels have generally accepted the interpretations and findings of the Appellate Body as part of WTO law', though 'sometimes, Appellate Body reports have needed to mature before Members accepted them as part of WTO *acquis*'.[73] The role and importance of both GATT and WTO Panel or Appellate Body reports will be returned to later in the section on the judicial function of the WTO and treaty interpretation.[74]

3.4 National Environmental and Health Regulatory Autonomy and the GATT

To many, it is not apparent at first glance why the WTO has such far-reaching implications in the field of either international or national regulation in relation to environmental and health matters. The reason, however, becomes clear when looking at the historical development of the GATT. Although initially designed to be a way to bring down tariffs and to prevent more crippling tariff wars like those

---

[71]*Ibid.*, 55.

[72]*Petersmann* (note 70), 56. '*Acquis*' is a term used in EU law in reference to the content, principles and political objectives of the treaties, the legislation adopted in application of the treaties, the case law of the Court of Justice, declarations of the Union etc. See EU, Summaries of EU Legislation: Glossary, available at http://europa.eu/legislation_summaries/glossary/community_acquis_en.htm. The Appellate Body has also made reference to the GATT case law in the context of the 'acquis' of the GATT, see Appellate Body Report *Japan –Taxes on Alcoholic Beverages*, para. 14, stating: 'Adopted panel reports are an important part of the GATT *acquis*'.

[73]*Isabelle Van Damme*, Treaty Interpretation by the WTO Appellate Body (Oxford, 2009), 6; see further *James K. R. Watson*, The WTO and the Environment: Development of Competence Beyond Trade (Oxford, 2013), 84–88.

[74]See *infra*, Chap. 4.

that characterised the interwar years,[75] the later GATT rounds of negotiations began to address domestic measures that constituted non-tariff barriers to trade,[76] as these 'became more prominent as trade barriers' as tariffs were progressively cut.[77] Non-tariff barriers to trade encompass a wide variety of measures[78] and can be described as 'any measure (public or private) that causes internationally traded goods or services, or resources devoted to the production of these goods and services, to be allocated in such a way as to reduce real world income'.[79]

The annual WTO World Trade Reports[80] include a section on non-tariff measures, and the report from 2012 is dedicated to this issue.[81] This report contains a table of classifications of types of non-tariff measures that can constitute a barrier to trade, and it may be helpful to see these classifications in order to better imagine the types of governmental measure that could involve both environmental and health concerns and also fit into one of these categories:

(A) **sanitary and phytosanitary measures**;
(B) **technical barriers to trade**;
(C) pre-shipment inspection and other formalities;
(D) price control measures;
(E) licences, quotas, prohibitions and other quantity control measures;
(F) **charges, taxes and other para-tariff measures**;
(G) finance measures;
(H) anti-competitive measures;
(I) **trade-related investment measures**;
(J) distribution restrictions;
(K) restrictions on post-sales services;
(L) **subsidies (excluding export subsidies)**;
(M) **government procurement restrictions**;
(N) **intellectual property**;
(O) rules of origin;
(P) export-related measures.[82]

---

[75]*Lang* (note 17), 191–192; *Jörg Philipp Terhechte*, Non-Tariff Barriers to Trade, in: Rüdiger Wolfrum (ed.) The Max Planck Encyclopaedia of Public International Law, vol. VII (Oxford, 2012), 750, 752–753 (paras. 14–18).

[76]See *Lang* (note 17), 218–220, for a discussion of the reasons for the substantive shift and how it was brought about.

[77]*Palmeter/Mavroidis* (note 1), 5.

[78]*C. Coughlin/G. E. Wood*, An Introduction to Non-Tariff Barriers to Trade, 71 Federal Reserve Bank of St Louis (1989), 31, 33.

[79]*Terhechte* (note 75), para. 1, quoting *Robert Baldwin*, Nontariff Distortions of International Trade (Washington DC, 1970), 5.

[80]2003–2012 Reports available at: http://www.wto.org/english/res_e/reser_e/wtr_e.htm.

[81]WTO, World Trade Report 2012: Trade and Public Policies: A Closer Look at Non-Tariff Measures in the 21st Century (2012).

[82]*Ibid.*, 101.

The measures that have been highlighted have an obvious and direct link to environmental or health measures, while the others could also come into play in any number of ways in the complex regulatory measures enacted by governments.

The question is then raised: how and when do these non-tariff measures constitute a barrier to trade? Certainly, it is clear that in order to do so they must be crafted in such a way as to violate one of the substantive provisions of the GATT or covered agreements. Depending on the way in which the national regulatory measure operates, it may conflict with Art. XI 'General Elimination of Quantitative Restrictions', which is a most important provision in this regard as it constitutes a general prohibition that 'forms one of the cornerstones of the GATT system'.[83] Article XI states, in its operative part:

> 1. No prohibitions or restrictions other than duties, taxes or other charges, whether made effective through quotas, import or export licences or other measures, shall be instituted or maintained by any contracting party on the importation of any product of the territory of any other contracting party or on the exportation or sale for export of any product destined for the territory of any other contracting party.

As mentioned previously, an all-out ban, or an import ban, may be one of the ways in which governments chose to regulate goods on their internal markets that have been produced in a way that they deem to be detrimental to the environment or may cause them concern in relation to public health (both inside and outside their territorial jurisdiction). These are, however, not the only types of measures that constitute quantitative restrictions. The 1996 Decision on Notification Procedures for Quantitative Restrictions from the Council for Trade in Goods[84] lays out a list of such measures, which can encompass the following:

– prohibitions;
– prohibitions except under defined conditions;
– global quotas;
– global quotas allocated by country;
– bilateral quotas (i.e., anything less than a global quota);
– automatic licensing;
– non-automatic licensing;
– quantitative restrictions made effective through state-trading operations;
– mixing regulations;
– minimum price, triggering a quantitative restriction;
– 'voluntary' export restraints.[85]

---

[83]Panel Report *Turkey – Restrictions on Imports of Textile and Clothing Products*, para 9.63.
[84]G/L/59 of 10 January 1996.
[85]*Ibid.*, Annex.

Excluding perhaps voluntary export restraints,[86] it is easy to see how each of these could be implemented by governments seeking to prevent/limit market access for foreign products whose process and production methods cause concern in the health or environmental fields.

The key here is the phrase 'market access'. If the measure—and Art. XI is notable for the fact that it refers to 'other measures' and not simply laws or regulations—is a border measure, then it comes within the remit of Art. XI. If, however, the measure constitutes an internal measure, then it will come to be assessed under Art. III on 'National Treatment on Internal Taxation and Regulation'. The relevant parts of Art. III lay out:

> 1. The contracting parties recognize that **internal taxes and other internal charges, and laws, regulations and requirements affecting the internal sale**, offering for sale, purchase, transportation, distribution or use of products, and internal quantitative regulations requiring the mixture, processing or use of products in specified amounts or proportions, **should not be applied to imported or domestic products so as to afford protection to domestic production.**
>
> 2. The products of the territory of any contracting party **imported into the territory of any other contracting party shall not be subject, directly or indirectly, to internal taxes or other internal charges of any kind in excess of those applied, directly or indirectly, to like domestic products.** Moreover, no contracting party shall otherwise apply internal taxes or other internal charges to imported or domestic products in a manner contrary to the principles set forth in paragraph 1.
>
> 4. The products of the territory of any contracting party imported into the territory of any other contracting party **shall be accorded treatment no less favourable than that accorded to like products of national origin in respect of all laws, regulations and requirements affecting their internal sale, offering for sale, purchase, transportation, distribution or use. [...].**[87]

While Art. XI seeks to restrict and prohibit measures that affect the follow of goods on to the markets of member states, Art. III serves to ensure these products seeking to enter the market are not discriminated against vis-à-vis domestic products. In order to apply the appropriate legal regime, this distinction must be made. However, it is no easy task to distinguish border measures from behind-the-border measures, as many of these 'behind-the-border' measures are applied at the time of importation.[88]

Annex I to the GATT provides notes and supplementary provisions, and in this respect *Ad* Art. III provides:

> Any internal tax or other internal charge, or any law, regulation or requirement of the kind referred to in paragraph 1 which **applies to an imported product and to the like domestic product** and is collected or enforced in the case of the imported product at the time or point of importation, is nevertheless to be regarded as an internal tax or other internal charge, or a

---

[86]Though it is more than conceivable that, when operated on a bilateral basis, it would be possible to also employ them in preventing market access for foreign products whose process and production methods cause concern in the health or environmental fields.

[87]Art. III GATT 1947 (emphasis added).

[88]*Van den Bossche* (note 34), 7.

law, regulation or requirement of the kind referred to in paragraph 1, and is accordingly subject to the provisions of Article III.[89]

The Art. I:1 'General Most-Favoured-Nation Treatment' (MFN) obligation is the other main obligation of relevance under that GATT. It is complementary to the Art. III non-discrimination obligation in that it seeks to prevent any discrimination as between trading partners, so that imports from one country are not granted more favourable treatment than those of another. Article I is a lengthy provision, which reads in its operative part:

> With respect to customs duties and charges of any kind imposed on or in connection with importation or exportation [. . .] and with respect to the method of levying such duties and charges, and with respect to all rules and formalities in connection with importation and exportation [. . .] any advantage, favour, privilege, or immunity granted by any contracting party to any product originating in or destined for any other country shall be afforded immediately and unconditionally to the like product originating in or destined for the territories of all other contracting parties.[90]

While it is difficult to imagine the MFN obligation being violated by national regulations that genuinely seek to protect environmental or health concerns—due to the fact that any country's specific regulation would *prima facie* appear to first discriminate against certain parties rather than try to attempt to raise environmental/ health standards[91]—this is too superficial a view.

The type of advantage imagined in Art. I:1 can be construed broadly, similar to the term 'like products'.[92] This, coupled with the fact that such advantage must be granted 'immediately and unconditionally' so as not to breach the MFN obligation, means that there are myriad of possible environmental or health-based regulatory mechanisms that could apply at or behind the border that have the possibility to discriminate between goods based on their origin and thus violate Art. I:1.

From this we can then, for the most part, reasonably distinguish between measures falling under Art. XI as being measures applied to imported products only, measures falling under Art I:1 that grant advantages and result in discrimination between trading partners and measures falling under Art. III as being those that apply to both domestic and imported products—even if they are applied to imported products at the point of importation. What becomes key when assessing measures such as those falling under Arts. I:1 and III of the GATT is the idea of 'like products', a phrase that appears in Arts. I:1, III:2, III:4 and *Ad* Art. III. What can really be considered to be like products, and what factors the WTO DSS takes into consideration when determining the 'likeness' of a product, is key to this study. In assessing whether the process and production methods of a product affect the

---

[89]*Ad* Art. III GATT 1947.

[90]Art I:1 GATT.

[91]Explicitly, regulations that discriminate between products due to their origin rather than their PPMs or environmental/health impact would be very unlikely to meet the Art. XX general exceptions laid out below.

[92]See *infra*, Sect. 4.5.

likeness of that product to one with environmentally damaging process and production methods—though the end product remains the same, NPR PPMs—this work will attempt to summarise and engage with the historical and ongoing debate in this area, assess the law as it stands and question whether the current interpretation model is satisfactory for parties on either side of the debate. In terms of the impact of WTO membership on State sovereignty, the importance of the breadth of the phrase 'like products' cannot be understated. In actual terms, 'the broader the concept [of like products], the broader the jurisdiction of international trade law becomes (narrowing the scope of national regulatory autonomy)'.[93]

While still looking specifically at the legal regime under the GATT, the key focus is not only on the scope of the prohibitions provided for in Arts. III and XI but also on how the GATT Art. XX 'General Exceptions' operates. If a measure put in place restricts imports, adversely affects imports vis-à-vis domestic products or discriminates between trading partners and therefore violates the obligations laid out in Arts. I:1 III or XI, it may nevertheless be justified by one of the exceptions laid out in Art. XX.

The relevant parts of Art. XX dictate:

> Subject to the requirement that such measures are not applied in a manner which would constitute a means of arbitrary or unjustifiable discrimination between countries where the same conditions prevail, or a disguised restriction on international trade, nothing in this Agreement shall be construed to prevent the adoption or enforcement by any contracting party of measures:
> [...]
> (b) necessary to protect human, animal or plant life or health; [...]
> (g) relating to the conservation of exhaustible natural resources if such measures are made effective in conjunction with restrictions on domestic production or consumption;
> [...].

These so-called 'environmental exceptions' have been tested in the WTO DSS,[94] and what sort of regulatory regimes appear to be permitted under them will be assessed not only through analysis of the text of the provisions but further from the interpretations of the GATT and WTO Panels and decisions of the Appellate Body. The importance of the 'chapeau' of Art. XX has also been made clear by various Panels and the Appellate Body, and any analysis of the functioning of Art. XX is not complete without assessing how the chapeau is interpreted and how this affects the invocation of one of the environmental exceptions contained in Art. XX (b) and (g).

---

[93]Won-Mog Choi, Like Products in International Trade Law: Towards a Consistent GATT/WTO Jurisprudence (Oxford, 2003), ix (preface).

[94]See, for example, GATT Panel Report United States – Restrictions on the Import of Tuna (Tuna/ Dolphin I), DS21/R 1991, para. 2.7 (unadopted); GATT Panel Report United States – Restrictions on the Import of Tuna, DS29/R 1994, paras. 2.1–2.15 (unadopted); Panel Report, United States – Standards for Reformulated and Conventional Gasoline; Appellate Body Report United States – Standards for Reformulated and Conventional Gasoline; Panel Report United States – Import Prohibition of Certain Shrimp and Shrimp; Appellate Body Report United States – Import Prohibition of Certain Shrimp and Shrimp Product; and infra, Chap. 6.

3.5   Environmental and Public Health Regulation: SPS and TBT Agreements

The TBT and SPS Agreements are central to any study of environmental or health regulation under the WTO. While the TBT Agreement applies to 'technical regulations and standards, including packaging and labeling requirements, and procedures for assessment of conformity with technical regulations and standards',[95] the SPS Agreement applies to 'all sanitary and phytosanitary measures which may, directly or indirectly, affect international trade'.[96] 'Sanitary and phytosanitary measures' are loosely defined by the WTO as 'food safety and animal and plant health measures'[97] but more precisely include the following:

Any measure applied:
(a) to protect animal or plant life or health within the territory of a Member from risks arising from the entry, establishment, or spread of pests, diseases, disease-carrying organisms or disease-causing organisms;
(b) to protect human or animal life or health within the territory of the Member from risks arising from additives, contaminants, toxins or disease-causing organisms in foods, beverages or foodstuffs;
(c) to protect human life or health within the territory of the Member from risks arising from diseases carried by animals, plants or products thereof, or from the entry, establishment or spread of pests; or
(d) to prevent or limit other damage within the territory of the Member from the entry, establishment or spread of pests.[98]

Thus, while the TBT applies to a broad range of circumstances, the SPS is more limited. The application of the SPS Agreement in the context of the measures imagined in this work is therefore also more limited than the TBT. This is the case particularly as any NPR PPM labelling scheme or import ban would foreseeably be crafted in such a way as to apply to only a part of a range of products that some parties believe should all be treated together as 'like products'. Many of the SPS measures, however, aim to regulate risks that are not related to production methods or would influence the end product in such a manner that it would no longer be considered 'like' the products to which the regulation does not apply. The main exceptions are SPS measures concerning genetically modified organisms (GMOs), which will be discussed in the context of the SPS Agreement.[99]

The application of one or other of these agreements (or both) depends on the type of governmental measure in question. However, due to the potential for overlap, the

---

[95]See Preamble 5, TBT Agreement. Annex 1 TBT Agreement provides more specific definitions for the terms 'Technical regulation', 'Standard' and 'Conformity assessment procedures'.

[96]Art. 1 SPS Agreement.

[97]See http://www.wto.org/english/tratop_e/sps_e/sps_e.htm.

[98]Art. 1 Annex A SPS Agreement.

[99]See *infra*, Chap. 9.

scope of the TBT Agreement has been limited in favour of the SPS Agreement,[100] so that when the SPS applies to a certain measure that would ordinarily also be covered by the TBT, only the SPS Agreement applies 'even if they take the form of technical regulations, standards or conformity assessment procedures'.[101] It was recognised by the Panel in the *EC – Biotech* case, however, that 'to the extent the requirement at issue is applied for a purpose not covered by Annex A(1) of the *SPS Agreement*, it can be viewed as embodying a non-SPS measure'[102] and thus 'falls to be assessed under the *TBT Agreement*, to the extent it embodies a non-SPS measure'.[103] Hence, it is not only the type of measure that is of concern in differentiating a TBT from an SPS measure but also its purpose. Furthermore, single measures can have more than one purpose[104] and must be assessed under the relevant agreement to the extent that the measure embodies either an SPS or a non-SPS measure. In assessing which part of a particular measure is covered by which covered agreement, Panels 'are not obliged to base their decision solely on the arguments of the parties'.[105]

The relationships between the TBT and the GATT, and the SPS and the GATT are, however, of a different nature. The general rule in cases of conflict is laid out in the General Interpretative Note to Annex 1A of the WTO Agreement, which states that in the event of a conflict between the GATT and a provision of one of the other agreements listed in Annex 1A to the WTO Agreement, 'the provision of the other agreement shall prevail to the extent of the conflict'. However, this rule only applies in situations of conflict of rules or obligations (establishing a sort of hierarchy of speciality). In cases where there is no conflict, measures falling within the scope of one of the covered agreements will also be assessed under the GATT, so that, for example, a measure deemed TBT compliant would still be assessed under the provisions of the GATT. In the *EC – Bananas III* case, the Appellate Body laid out that the measure in question ought to have been assessed first under the relevant covered agreement (in this case the Agreement on Import Licencing Procedures) before being assessed under the GATT as 'this agreement deals specifically, and in detail'[106] with the relevant issues. Furthermore, '[i]f the Panel had done so, then

---

[100]Art. 1.5 SPS Agreement states 'The provisions of the agreement do not apply to sanitary or phytosanitary measures as defined in Annex A of the Agreement on the Application of Sanitary and Phytosanitary Measures'. The TBT Agreement is also limited in favour of the Agreement on Government Procurement (Art. 1.4 TBT Agreement).

[101]*Van den Bossche* (note 34), 815.

[102]Panel Report *European Communities – Approval and Marketing of Biotech Products*, para. 7.167.

[103]*Ibid.*

[104]*Van den Bossche* (note 34), 816.

[105]*Palmeter/Mavroidis* (note 1), 23. See also Panel Report *European Communities – Measures Affecting Asbestos and Asbestos -Containing Products*, para. 8.32.

[106]Appellate Body Report *European Communities – Regime for the Importation, Sale and Distribution of Bananas*, para. 204.

there would have been no need for it to address the alleged inconsistency with Article X:3(a) of the GATT 1994'.[107]

The Panel in *EC – Asbestos* then went on to elaborate on this point specifically in relation to the TBT Agreement, demonstrating the procedural hierarchy. In this case there was no conflict; however, the hierarchy served to demonstrate how the Panel ought to proceed in an assessment of violation of the GATT and covered agreements, and violation under a covered agreement would remove the need for any subsequent assessment under the GATT. The Panel stated:

> In order to decide upon the order in which our consideration should proceed, in the way suggested by the Appellate Body, the hypothesis should be that, if the Decree is a 'technical regulation' within the meaning of the TBT Agreement, then the latter would deal with the measure in the most specific and most detailed manner. Consequently, in our view it must first be determined whether the Decree is a technical regulation within the meaning of the TBT Agreement. If this is the case, we shall start considering this case by examining the ways in which the Decree violates the TBT Agreement. If we find that the Decree is not a 'technical regulation', we shall then immediately start to consider it in the context of the GATT 1994.[108]

Unlike in its relationship with the TBT Agreement, the SPS Agreement does not have a relationship of mutual exclusivity with the GATT, and as with the TBT and GATT, 'to the extent that it is discriminatory, or constitutes a quantitative restriction, [a measure is] also caught, in principle, by the rules of the GATT'.[109] However, unlike the TBT Agreement, Art. 2.4 SPS Agreement contains a presumption of consistency with the GATT, so that if a measure is found to be consistent with the SPS, then the rebuttable presumption is created that it is also consistent with the GATT. Article 2.4 reads SPS 'measures which conform to the relevant provisions of this Agreement shall be presumed to be in accordance with the obligations of the Members under the provisions GATT 1994 [...] in particular the provisions of Art. XX (b)'. No explicit guidance has been issued by the DSS in relation to the procedural hierarchy in assessing measures under the SPS Agreement and the GATT as in the above quoted *EC – Asbestos* Panel Report. However, it would be 'logical',[110] following the presumption of consistency, to follow the same procedure, and this was also so reasoned and carried out by the Panel in the *EC – Hormones* dispute.[111]

---

[107]*Ibid.*

[108]Panel Report *European Communities –Measures Affecting Asbestos and Asbestos-Containing Products*, para. 8.17. See further: Panel Report *European Communities – Trade Description of Sardines*, paras. 7.14–7.19 generally, and specifically at para. 7.15 stating 'Appellate Body suggests that where two agreements apply simultaneously, a panel should normally consider the more specific agreement before the more general agreement'.

[109]*Van den Bossche* (note 34), 841.

[110]*Ibid.*

[111]Panel Report *European Communities – Measures Concerning Meat and Meat Products (Hormones) (Canada)*, para. 8.45; Panel Report *European Communities – Measures Concerning Meat and Meat Products (Hormones) (US)*, para. 8.42.

3.6 Summary

This chapter has sought to lay out the history of the GATT/WTO and the significant changes in the institutional structure that are of importance in any modern study of the interaction of the WTO DSS and State sovereignty (in the political science sense) in the realm of environmental protection. An overview of the central legal framework has also been laid out in order to enable an appreciation of the regime as a whole in the way it interacts with national environmental regulatory structures. A detailed analysis of the interpretation, application and implications of these provisions will appear in Chaps. 5–10, after a more in-depth assessment of treaty interpretation (as carried out by the GATT Panels, and WTO Panels and the Appellate Body), the judicial role and function of the WTO DSS and the term 'like products'.

Chapter 4
The Judicial Function of the WTO

4.1 Overview

In simple terms, the WTO's sophisticated dispute settlement mechanism makes it a distinctive organization.[1]

This quotation from *Pascal Lamy*, former Director-General of the WTO,[2] clearly recognises the importance of the WTO DSS in the particular and distinctive position of the WTO. Indeed, as quoted above, the WTO DSS is 'in all probability, the most effective area of adjudication in the entire area of public international law'.[3] Thus, the WTO DSS operates in such a manner that is almost unique in effectiveness in the realm of public international law. This section aims to elaborate on some of the previous points raised as to why this is and incorporate other facets of the DSS that have not yet been mentioned that also contribute to the effectiveness of the system. It is on the basis of such an effective DSS that the criticisms raised in this study must be viewed, as it puts them in marked relief to similar criticisms (for example, those of overreach and illegitimacy) raised under other international regimes. It is the very effectiveness of the WTO DSS that leads to such a power concentration in the institution, and, unlike other international tribunals, the compulsory dispute settlement means that States cannot simply choose another forum if they lose trust in the WTO DSS. The WTO DSS is at the heart of all criticisms

---

[1]*Pascal Lamy*, The Place and Role of the WTO in the International Legal Order: Address before the European Society of International Law (May 2006), available at: http://www.wto.org/english/news_e/sppl_e/sppl26_e.htm (last accessed on 05/03/2017).

[2]Pascal Lamy was Director-General of the WTO from 2005–2013. See: http://www.wto.org/english/thewto_e/dg_e/pl_e.htm (last accessed on 05/03/2017).

[3]*David Palmeter/Petros C. Mavroidis*, Dispute Settlement in the World Trade Organization: Practice and Procedure (Cambridge, 2nd edn. 2004), 234.

© Springer International Publishing AG 2017

A.R. Maggio, *Environmental Policy, Non-Product Related Process and Production Methods and the Law of the World Trade Organization*, European Yearbook of International Economic Law 1, DOI 10.1007/978-3-319-61155-6_4

levied in this study as its actions and position combine to exacerbate the threat to sovereignty created by WTO membership.

Though other methods of consensual dispute settlement, such as mediation, conciliation and good offices, are mentioned in the DSU[4] and are used in practice by parties,[5] it is the judicial arm of the WTO that is of particular interest in this study as it involves the 'adjudication with real consequences'[6] that affects parties in ways that traditional consensual dispute settlement methods do not. The DSU itself recognises the importance of the DSS within the WTO system, with Art. 3.2 DSU stating: 'The dispute settlement system of the WTO is a central element in providing security and predictability to the multilateral trading system.'

The WTO DSS has exclusive and compulsory, but not general, jurisdiction.[7] Any disputes that occur in relation to obligations arising under the WTO and covered agreements must be litigated before the WTO DSS and not another international court.[8] Article 23 (1) DSU states:

> When Members seek redress of a violation of obligations or other nullification or impairment of benefits under the covered agreements, they shall have recourse to, and abide by, the rules and procedures of this Understanding.

This obligation sets up two different legal relationships: first, between disputing parties themselves and, second, between parties and the WTO (DSS) as an institution. Although it is not immediately apparent from the text of the provision, it creates a right for disputing parties. A disputing party has a right, vis-à-vis the other party to the dispute, that the dispute will not be taken to any other forum (assuming there exists another competent forum to hear the dispute) as, following *Singer*, '[r]ights are nothing but duties placed on others to act in a certain manner'.[9]

Thus, the duty to take recourse to the WTO DSS limits the freedom of States to find the forum of their choice to resolve a dispute under the WTO and covered agreements, but it also strengthens the position of other States in that they have

---

[4] Art. 5 DSU.

[5] Furthermore, 'The DSU expresses a clear preference for solutions mutually acceptable to the parties reached through negotiations, rather than solutions resulting from adjudication'. See *Peter Van den Bossche*, The Law and Policy of the World Trade Organization (Cambridge, 2nd edn. 2008), 173 and 171–178 generally.

[6] Appellate Body Report *Canada – Continued Suspension of Obligations in the EC – Hormones Dispute*, para. 352.

[7] It should be noted, however, that there is no provision comparable to Art. 36 of the Statute of the International Court of Justice which lays out the jurisdiction of the DSS in DSU or any other of the covered agreements. See *Palmeter/Mavroidis* (note 3), 17. The jurisdiction of the DSS, though not laid out explicitly, can be found in Arts. 1, 2, 3.1, 6, 7, 17.6 and 17.13 DSU: *ibid.*

[8] *Ernst-Ulrich Petersmann*, International Trade Law and the GATT/WTO Dispute Settlement System 1948–1996: An Introduction, in: Ernst-Ulrich Petersmann (ed.), Studies in Transnational Economic Law: International Trade Law and the GATT/WTO Dispute Settlement System (Neuwied, 1997), 55.

[9] *Joseph William Singer*, The Legal Rights Debate in Analytical Jurisprudence from Bentham to Hohfeld, Wisconsin Law Review (1982), 975, 986.

security in their position of knowing where a dispute will be heard if they have obligations owed to them violated or if they themselves violate their obligations. This position of security that accompanies the right of all States to have their disputes heard by the WTO DSS is coupled by a corresponding loss of freedom of choice of forum for disputes. This compromise can certainly be seen as a factor that strengthens the multilateral trading system by centralising adjudicative decision-making authority, preventing forum shopping (which may undermine the WTO DSS and WTO itself) and importantly preventing (for the most part) any disparity in legal reasoning or contradicting applications of the law.

Though these benefits seem at first hand to offer a clear justification for why States chose to give up this particular freedom at Uruguay, the fact that such a duty rarely exists in international law generally should emphasise the importance of this concession.[10] Importantly from the perspective of environmentalists, if a dispute involves both environmental and trade matters, then the obligation contained in Art. 23 (1) DSU prevents them from utilising any forum that is more suited to passing judgment on matters relating to environmental protection, as far as the dispute relates to redress for 'violation of obligations or other nullification or impairment of benefits under the covered agreements'.

The other legal relationship created by this provision relates to the WTO DSS and States, with States being in a position of no-right (or are exposed) in relation to the choice of forum for disputes under the WTO and covered agreements. The WTO DSS is in a position of privilege as the sanctioned forum in the 'WTO legal order'. This particular legal relationship cannot be characterised in terms of right and duty as it is not possible to talk about the ability to invoke the 'state', nor can it meaningfully be asserted that the duty on States to utilise the WTO DSS as the forum for their disputes is a duty owed to the DSS—as highlighted above, it is a duty owed to other States and specifically the other State in a particular dispute. The privilege/exposure relationship between the State and the institution creates a clear distribution of power in favour of the institution. As was outlined in Chap. 2, it is also the case that the legal relationships created under the WTO and covered agreements distribute power not only among the States parties to the WTO but also between States and the WTO itself. The greater the amount of power ceded to the WTO, the greater the loss of 'sovereignty'—in the political science sense of the term. In this way, we can see that the judicial functions of the WTO also serve to alter the bargaining power of the members.

This alteration in bargaining power is a natural consequence of the creation of a new judicial body (if the WTO DSS can be so described). It is nothing new or explosive to say that the DSS has power because States gave it power. What is

---

[10]Exclusive jurisdiction is possessed by many human rights bodies, but is often coupled with an obligation to first exhaust any possible national remedies. The International Tribunal for the Law of the Sea is a specialist tribunal, but without exclusive jurisdiction and parties to the United Nations Convention on the Law of the Sea (of 10 December 1982, 1833 UNTS 3), are only subject to compulsory jurisdiction in certain instances and not specifically at the ITLOS (See Part. XV UNCLOS). The ICJ has general jurisdiction but not compulsory.

important here is to map out how and in what ways States gave power to the DSS as any appraisal of the real position of States can only be undertaken on the basis of a plain statement of how and in what ways power was ceded and is distributed.

Coming back to the judicial function of the WTO DSS, it is necessary to now sketch out a few further defining elements, alongside exclusive jurisdiction, of the 'most effective' adjudicative body in public international law.[11] As will already be clear from the foregoing, the birth of the WTO changed the old GATT Panel system dramatically, *inter alia* by including an Appellate Body in the adjudicative process. This means that instead of the decisions of the Panels being the final judgment, reports can be appealed to a 'quasi-court of appeal'. 'The introduction of a level of appeal, it was thought, would counterbalance the reverse consensus rule',[12] making the package deal of the new DSS more palatable to States.[13] Panel reports shall be adopted by the DSB 'unless a party to the dispute formally notifies the DSB of its decision to appeal or the DSB decides by consensus not to adopt the report'.[14] This means that either party—the 'winning' or 'losing' party—can choose to appeal the report of the Panel.

The Appellate Body is, in terms of the judicial function of the WTO, more like a 'traditional' court than the Panel system. The Appellate Body is a standing body composed of seven persons, of which three serve on each case.[15] The Appellate Body members are to be distinguished experts in international trade law[16] and are appointed for a term of 4 years.[17] Though there is provision in the DSU that the members of the Appellate Body be 'broadly representative of the WTO member-ship',[18] this may be more difficult to achieve in real terms as Appellate Body members cannot have any affiliation with their home governments when serving, and it may be difficult for developing countries particularly to part with such highly trained trade specialist lawyers for a potential 8-year term.[19] This poses problems in terms of legitimacy and representativeness and could be argued to apportion more bargaining power in real terms to developed countries, which have a comparative wealth of such specialists. Of the 24 Appellate Body members since the birth of the WTO, however, 12 have come from developing countries.[20] This leads to the

---

[11]*Palmeter/Mavroidis* (note 3), 234.

[12]*Isabelle Van Damme*, Treaty Interpretation by the WTO Appellate Body (Oxford, 2009), 5.

[13]In the 2004 Sutherland Report, the creation of the right to appeal was described as '[t]he balancing element in the DSU': WTO, The Future of the WTO: Addressing Institutional Challenges in the New Millennium (2004), 50 (para. 219).

[14]Art. 16.4 DSU.

[15]Art. 17.1 DSU.

[16]Art 17.3 DSU.

[17]With the possibility of one re-appointment: Art. 17.2 DSU.

[18]Art. 17.3 DSU.

[19]Art. 17.3 DSU.

[20]See: http://www.wto.org/english/tratop_e/dispu_e/ab_members_descrp_e.htm (last accessed on 05/03/2017).

conclusion that, to date, in practice, this provision has worked effectively towards developing country participation at the highest adjudicative level of the DSS.

4.2 Binding Decisions

Decisions of the WTO DSS are binding upon parties after the adoption of the Panel or Appellate Body Report by the DSB. Though they are couched in the language of recommendations, the implementation and compliance mechanisms provided for in the DSU, as well as the possibility of sanctioned retaliatory measures by the winning party to the dispute, ensure the binding status of the reports issued by the DSS. As in every area of international law, compliance with adopted reports of the DSS can be problematic as there is no centralised global enforcement body. What is more, as will be laid out later in this section, the differing bargaining power of the parties to the WTO means that the consequences of paying compensation or facing a suspension of concession for non-compliance weigh differently and therefore incentivise compliance differently.

As outlined above, due to the reverse consensus rule contained in Arts. 16.4 and 17.14 DSU, the recommendations contained in the reports of the Panels and Appellate Body are adopted *de facto* automatically by the DSB. This reverse consensus rule is the cornerstone of the effectiveness of the DSS as it prevents the veto power of any one party and also has the effect of neutralising the bargaining power of influential States in this part of the process.[21]

In laying out the primary purpose of the DSS, Art. 3.7 of the DSU states:

> In the absence of a mutually agreed solution, the first objective of the dispute settlement system is usually to **secure the withdrawal of the measures concerned** if these are found to be inconsistent with any of the provisions of any of the covered agreements.[22]

It is thus explicitly within the remit of the rulings of the DSS to attempt to ensure that national regulatory measures are amended when they are found to be in contravention of a WTO rule, unless a mutually agreed solution can be found. The legitimacy of DSB recommendations in carrying out such a function cannot be called into question in a legal sense as it is clear from the text of this provision that this was the intended consequence entering into the DSU Agreement, with this being stated as its primary objective in securing compliance.

Article 21.1 DSU states: 'Prompt compliance with recommendations or rulings of the DSB is essential in order to ensure the effective resolution of disputes to the benefit of all Members.' It is clear that non-compliance would weaken both

---

[21]States have, furthermore, 'refrain[ed] from making their own binding unilateral judgments on whether other parties have acted inconsistently', further neutralising influence in a similar manner, as well as substantially strengthening the system: see 2004 Sutherland Report (note 13), 50 (para. 220).

[22]Emphasis added.

confidence in the WTO and the integrity of the organisation itself. Thus, in order to ensure this 'essential' compliance, the DSU lays out an elaborate procedure for the 'Surveillance of Implementation of Recommendations and Rulings'. Article 21 DSU obliges States to inform the DSB of its intentions in respect of implementation of decisions, which, if not carried out immediately due to impracticality, should be carried out within a reasonable period of time.[23] In order to effectively ensure compliance and resolve problems of disagreement as to whether compliance has actually occurred, Art. 21.5 obligates the parties to resort to dispute settlement procedures, 'including wherever possible the original panel'. The availability of these review processes, alongside the possibility for compensatory/'retaliatory' measures, discussed below, 'strengthens the authority' of the decisions emanating from the DSS.[24]

In cases where a party does not implement the recommendation or ruling of the DSS within a reasonable period of time, it is possible for the other party to claim compensation or suspend concessions vis-à-vis the non-implementing party. This right, provided for in Art. 22 DSU, is limited to 'temporary measures', as is made explicit in the first sentence of the article. These temporary measures are not 'preferred to full implementation of a recommendation to bring a measure into conformity with the covered agreements'.[25] Compensation is voluntary, meaning no financial penalty will be imposed upon a State without its consent.[26]

The debate as to whether recommendations of the DSB are binding, in the sense that they create a legal obligation to comply, has been described as 'exhaustively covered'[27] and is summed up by *Jackson*, who states that 'there is overwhelming support for the view that the result of an adopted dispute settlement report [...] create[s] an international law obligation to comply with that report'.[28] But what

---

[23] Art. 3 DSU. What constitutes a reasonable period of time clearly varies on a case-by-case basis, but Art. 3 (a)-(c) DSU lay out some guidance. Members can propose a time period which will constitute a reasonable period of time if approved by the DSB, the parties to the dispute can mutually agree a period of time, or a period of time will be determined through binding arbitration. Furthermore, it was laid out in the arbitration award in the *EC – Hormones* dispute that a 'reasonable period of time for implementation' should be considered as 'the shortest period possible within the legal system of the Member to implement the recommendations of and rulings of the DSB', see Award of the Arbitrator, *EC – Hormones (Article 21.3(c))*, para. 26. This is now considered to be the 'core rule in establishing a reasonable period of time', *Van den Bossche* (note 5), 221.

[24] *Caroline E. Foster*, Science and the Precautionary Principle in International Courts and Tribunals (Cambridge, 2011), 282.

[25] Art. 22.1 DSU.

[26] Art. 22.1 DSU states: 'Compensation is voluntary and, if granted, shall be consistent with the covered agreements.'

[27] *John Errrico*, The WTO in the EU: Unwinding the Knot, Cornell International Law Journal 44 (2011), 179, 195.

[28] *John H. Jackson*, International law Status of WTO Dispute Settlement Reports: Obligation to Comply or Option to 'Buy Out'?, AJIL 98 (2004), 109, 123.

does this 'international law obligation' really entail?[29] As outlined above, the State found to be in breach of an obligation must implement the recommendations of the DSS/DSB within a reasonable period of time, or face possible retaliatory measures. The implementation of the recommendation of the DSB is the 'one final remedy'[30] envisaged in the WTO system, with the other two possibilities being 'temporary remedies which can be applied awaiting the withdrawal (or amendment) of the WTO inconsistent measure'.[31] In so far as 'temporary remedies' go, however, one can clearly point to the continued suspension of obligations in the *EC – Hormones* dispute in assessing how what was envisaged can work in practice.[32] The ability of strong diverse economies to subsume such retaliatory measures clearly affects the distribution of bargaining power created not only by the DSU but also by the WTO and covered agreements altogether.

The rules laid out in Arts. 21 and 22 of the DSU constitute a *lex specialis* to general international law in the field of international responsibility. The ILC Articles on the Responsibility of States for Internationally Wrongful Acts[33] are generally considered to (largely) represent customary international law in this area and provide a framework for understanding the consequences of a breach of an international obligation, particularly in terms of the invocation of the international responsibility of the State in breach of such an obligation.

In *Korea – Procurement*, the Panel laid out that

> international law applies to the extent that the WTO treaty agreements do not 'contract out' from it. To put it another way, to the extent there is no conflict or inconsistency, or an expression in a covered WTO agreement that implies differently, we are of the view that the customary rules of international law apply to the WTO treaties and to the process of treaty formation under the WTO.[34]

This is clearly an important statement about the position of customary law in the WTO regime. What is interesting in the present study, however, is what it says about the areas of customary international law that WTO membership 'contracts out' of.

---

[29]There is no scope in this work for any address or analysis of the question of whether it is really possible to compare WTO obligations with other obligations under public international law. It suffices here to say that Jackson's summation of the status of WTO obligations, alongside the real consequences produced for their breach gives sufficient evidence to the position that both the academic and State position regard them as binding, if not 100% analogous with other internationally binding obligations.

[30]*Van den Bossche* (note 5), 218.

[31]*Ibid.*, 219.

[32]The request for consultations in the *EC – Hormones* dispute between the United States and the European Communities was received on 26th of January 1996, the Panel Report was issued on 18th August 1997, the Appellate Body report on the 16th January 1998 and a mutually acceptable solution for implementation was notified on 25th September 2009. See: http://www.wto.org/english/tratop_e/dispu_e/cases_e/ds26_e.htm (last accessed on 05/03/2017).

[33]ILC, Responsibility of States for Internationally Wrongful Acts, GA Res. 56/83 of 12 December 2001, Annex (ASR).

[34]Panel Report *Korea-Measures – Affecting Government Procurement*, para. 7.96.

Articles 21 and 22 DSU, and the DSU generally, contain a system of dispute settlement entailing specific remedies and enforcement procedures that are clearly not those contained in the ILC's Articles or in customary law. Where international law generally provides for reparation, restitution, compensation, satisfaction and possible countermeasures in the event of the breach of an international obligation,[35] it is clear from the foregoing that the WTO rules governing breach of an obligation under the WTO or covered agreements produce vastly different consequences, consequences that have indeed 'contracted out' of the general international law system of State responsibility. Most importantly, this WTO-specific system of responsibility has limited the ability of States to respond unilaterally to a perceived breach of an international obligation owed to them. This limitation includes a limitation in interpretation of obligations, finding of violation and choice of consequences. This limitation is clearly linked to the desire to remove trade disputes from the realm of political leverage, as it has the reciprocal function of contracting WTO obligations out of the general international law regime of countermeasures[36] and can be seen to tie in to the purpose of the GATT to end tariff wars.

The limitation seeks to somewhat neutralise inequalities in bargaining power by ensuring consistency in the decision-making process and application of the law, and preventing economically powerful States from using trade countermeasures as a form of coercion. While limiting the freedom of action of States by placing them under a duty to use the WTO DSS and not that of general international law, the WTO DSS also provides all other States with rights vis-à-vis each other that they will not use the customary system of State responsibility. Such limitations that provide security can be seen to benefit all States, though they clearly at the same time apportion a large amount of decision-making power to the DSS that was once part of their 'sovereignty'.

4.3 Standard of Review

> WTO rules are not so rigid or so inflexible as not to leave room for reasoned judgements in confronting the endless and ever-changing ebb and flow of real facts in real cases in the real world.[37]

---

[35]Arts. 34–37, 42 ASR.

[36]Except in limited consequences. Article XXI (c) GATT 1947 provides an exception in terms of economic sanctions used as countermeasures, provided that they are taken 'to prevent any contracting party from taking any action in pursuance of its obligations under the United Nations Charter for the maintenance of international peace and security'. This has the consequence that States will not be held in breach of their obligations under the WTO and covered agreements if they implement trade restrictive measures in pursuance of fulfilling a UN Security Council Resolution obligation. This particular exception clearly does not allow for any degree of unilateralism in terms of the application of trade related economic countermeasures, and is therefore also in line with other purposes of removing unilateralism from the trading system, see *infra*, 6.5.6.

[37]Appellate Body Report *Japan – Taxes on Alcoholic Beverages*, pg. 31.

So said the Appellate Body in the *Japan – Alcohol* report, but what exactly are the parameters of WTO rules? Disputes arise where national regulatory measures appear to fall foul of WTO rules, but how far and in what ways does the DSS take these regulatory measures into account in difficult cases concerning sensitive policy areas, such as the environment or public health? A term borrowed from national administrative law employed in this context asks—what is the standard of review employed by the DSS? How much deference, also a term with origins in administrative law, is, or should be, shown to governmental decision-makers by an international trade tribunal? As the Panel in *US – Cotton* noted, however, there is an inherent danger in the employment of terms from national legal systems in the WTO context as they 'inevitably carry with them many connotations from these national legal systems'.[38] Nevertheless, important parallels can be drawn between the fields of national and global governance, and divergences potentially better analysed by means of comparison.[39]

OESCH deftly sums up the concept of standard of review within the WTO as being 'to what depth and with what intensity the national policy determination should be reviewed'[40] and as a baseline for defining 'whether and to what extent, Panels should respect a WTO member's measure although they would prefer a different factual conclusion or legal interpretation'.[41]

It is important to note here that although this section may make reference to the DSS generally, it should be the case that only Panels engage in review of governmental decisions and decision-making as the Appellate Body hears appeals 'on the basis of errors of law',[42] meaning that their reports are 'limited to issues of law covered in the panel report and legal interpretations developed by the panel'[43] and do not extend to reviewing national policy determinations, which are dealt with more appropriately by the Panels at first instance. As will be seen later, however, the Body does not always stick to this as its 'completing the legal analysis' and reviewing issues that were ignored by the Panel at first instance come dangerously close to doing precisely that.

The DSU itself contains no explicit standard of review for Panels to implement. The reason for this failure was not oversight but rather the inability of negotiators to agree during the Uruguay Round. While some argued for a rigorous and intrusive

---

[38]Panel Report *United States – Transitional Safeguard Measure on Combed Cotton Yard from Pakistan*, pg. 97 (para. 7.35, footnote 93).

[39]This position is not shared by all. *Matthias Oesch*, Standards of Review in WTO Dispute Resolution (Oxford, 2003), 7–8, talks of the irrelevance of domestic standard of review concepts in the analysis of the standard of review in the WTO. This work will not assess the application of these various standards in the domestic context, though the benefit of comparison with fixed standards of review is not ruled out.

[40]*Oesch* (note 39), 13.

[41]*Ibid.*, 14.

[42]*Ross Becroft*, The Standard of Review in WTO Dispute Settlement: Critique and Development (Cheltenham, 2012), 1.

[43]Art. 17.6 DSU.

standard,[44] others sought greater deference to governmental decision-making procedures.[45] The issue was judged to be of such importance that it was almost a dealbreaker during the negotiations[46] and ultimately was too contentious to reach consensus on.[47] In the end, therefore, there is no explicit treaty provision upon which Panels can base their review standard.

The Appellate Body has held, however, that although there is no explicit standard of review in the DSU (or GATT and covered agreements except in Art. 17.6 (i) of the Anti-Dumping Agreement), this failure

> resolves itself into the issue of whether or not the Panel, in making the above and other findings referred to and appealed by the European Communities, had made an 'Objective assessment of the matter before it, including an *objective assessment of the facts*[. . .]'[48]

The Appellate Body is here quoting Art. 11 DSU and, perhaps not wholly convincingly, 'develop[ing] the jurisprudence of its legal content'.[49] In a Panel's objective assessment of the facts of a given case, is it entitled to replace a governmental decision with its own, so long as it is based on such an objective assessment? The precise degree of deference to be shown, if any, is not abundantly clear from the Appellate Body's reasoning or from the text of Art. 11 DSU.

The Appellate Body's role in the standard of review process, though unable to review national decisions or decision-making procedures itself, is, following the reasoning in *EC – Hormones*, through assessing whether Panels have 'failed to make an "objective assessment" of the matters before them, as required by Art. 11'.[50] Moreover, the Appellate Body has stated:

> An allegation that a panel has failed to conduct the 'objective assessment of the matter before it' required by Article 11 of the DSU is a very serious allegation. Such an allegation goes to the very core of the integrity of the WTO dispute settlement process itself.[51]

This demonstrates both the importance of Panels and the Appellate Body striking the right balance in this regard and the importance of its own ability to review whether a Panel has fulfilled its obligation under Art. 11 DSU. If simply the allegation of such a failure 'goes to the very core of the integrity' of the DSS, then the Appellate Body's role in ensuring an actual failure to conduct such an assessment has not taken place is clearly of central importance to the integrity of the

---

[44]E.g. The European Communities, except perhaps in Anti-dumping matters, see *Oesch* (note 39), 76.

[45]E.g. The United States, see *ibid.*, 73.

[46]*John H. Jackson*, WTO and the New Sovereignty, ASIL Proceedings 88 (1994), 139.

[47]*Oesch* (note 39), 7.

[48]Appellate Body Report *European Communities – Measures Concerning Meat and Meat Products (Hormones)*, pg. 43 (para. 119).

[49]*Palmeter/Mavroidis* (note 3), 152.

[50]*Ibid.*

[51]Appellate Body Report *European Communities – Measures Affecting the Importation of Certain Poultry Products*, pg. 46 (para. 133).

system.[52] The Appellate Body then went on to state that such an allegation is 'a claim that the panel [...] denied the party submitting the evidence fundamental fairness, or what in many jurisdictions is known as due process of law or natural justice'.[53]

It is clear then that the application of the appropriate standard of review is appreciated by the DSS as being central to any proper administration of justice but also that there is no precise treaty basis for its determination contained in the DSU or elsewhere. The remainder of this section will seek to address the following questions: how can the question of the appropriate standard of review be approached, how has this issue been dealt with to date, and what are the implications of this in terms of national environmental or health regulatory mechanisms within the DSS and the WTO system generally?

Oesch conceptualises standard of review as a spectrum, with '*de novo* review'[54] at one end and 'total deference'[55] at the other. *De novo* review would be constituted by a Panel reviewing all elements of a national governmental decision/decision-making process and replacing it with its own interpretation. Total deference would, on the other hand, identify a governmental exercise in decision-making and then defer to it as it would view governments as better placed to make such decisions. Though *Oesch* argues that it is unlikely that it would be appropriate for a specific degree of deference to be applied by Panels, as 'the proper standards of review may differ depending on the particular circumstances of a case',[56] it is argued here that this provides a lack of certainty about the actual nature of the obligations provided for in the WTO and covered agreements (except the Anti-Dumping Agreement, which will not be addressed in this work), decreasing legal certainty and hindering good governance. From *Oesch's* spectrum, there are many possible standards available for a future amendment of the DSU,[57] and it is not the task of this work to identify what the most appropriate would be. Rather, the following will attempt to outline the past and current standards applied and then provide further analysis as to why the current state of affairs may be deemed detrimental to WTO members, though probably less so to the institution itself.

It is important to point out at this stage that this study only seeks to assess the standard of review of the DSS in relation to questions of fact. Clearly, the standard

---

[52]Jackson identifies two separate standards of review operating within the WTO system. The first applies to the standard applied by panels in their review of members' decisions/decision making processes and the second applies to the Appellate Body in its review of Panel decisions. *John H. Jackson*, Sovereignty, The WTO and Changing Fundamentals of International Law (Cambridge, 2006), 169. In this section the main focus is clearly on the first standard, though as can be seen here in its interpretation of the application of Art. 11 DSU the Appellate Body does have some, albeit indirect, interaction with the first standard.

[53]*Ibid.*

[54]*Oesch* (note 39), 15.

[55]*Ibid.*

[56]*Ibid.*

[57]Though this is politically unlikely, if not unfeasible.

of review of questions of law is also a major issue, particularly in areas where the legal provisions in the WTO and covered agreements are imprecise and offer the possibility of more than one interpretation. It is put forward here that for a functioning system of dispute settlement in an area as contentious as international trade, it can easily be seen as appropriate for organs of the DSS to carry out *de novo* review of legal questions raised in disputes between parties. The decisions of the Panels are also reviewed by the Appellate Body in this respect, and the applicable standard is, following *EC – Hormones*, also objective assessment.[58] In areas where the law lacks formal realisability,[59] it is of course arguable that deference could be shown towards States' interpretation of obligations in cases of sensitive policy overlap. The potential impact upon the integrity of the multilateral trading system and particularly its DSS means that this sort of argument could lead to a fundamental change in the nature of the legal relationships produced through WTO membership (as it would appear to allow for differing but equally valid interpretations of the law) and thus a fundamental change in the legal system itself. Such radicalism is not proposed here.

Moving on, there will now be an assessment of the application of the standard of review of factual situations, looking first to the GATT 1947. As is laid out above, the dispute settlement provisions of the original GATT treaty were very limited and contained no reference at all to anything like a standard of review—it is more than doubtful if it would have been conceivable in 1947 that the GATT would develop a DSS, never mind one that was not simply aimed at tariff-related trade matters but also reached so far as the potential review of national regulation.[60] As the GATT DSS developed in reality, however, so did the standard of review. Panels were increasingly in the position, with the juridification of the GATT[61] and extension of its ambit to domestic regulatory measures as non-tariff barriers to trade, 'to elaborate on the appropriate standards of review applicable in specific cases'.[62]

Following the introduction of the Tokyo Codes, Panels had not only a greater ability to review domestic legislation but also greater guidance as to how this ought to be carried out.[63] The 1979 Understanding on Dispute Settlement[64] laid out, in Art. 16, that 'a panel should make an objective assessment of the matter before it,

---

[58]*Becroft* (note 42), 51.

[59]Formal realisability is condition by which treaty obligations, or any legal duties, can provide a clear and concise standard by which states can assess whether, when facing litigation, they have fulfilled their duty or not. Unclear, imprecise obligations which do not provide surety lack formal realisability.

[60]Indeed, the first decision which touched on standard of review in the GATT showed a highly deferential approach. See: GATT Panel Report *United States – Fur Felt Hats*, pg. 30; *Becroft* (note 42), 40.

[61]*Oesch* (note 39), 60.

[62]*Ibid.*

[63]See *Becroft* (note 42), 40–42.

[64]The blueprint for what would become the DSU.

including an objective assessment of the facts of the case [...]'. This guidance, as with the jurisprudence of the Appellate Body in *EC – Hormones*, is not entirely enlightening. An 'objective' assessment of the facts can arguably produce more than one different assessment, depending on the policy area that is prioritised. Without suggesting that the WTO DSS should take into consideration other policy areas, it becomes clear that complex regulatory mechanisms and objective assessment may produce alternate outcomes, depending on who is carrying out such an assessment and for what purpose. The GATT 1947 had to, and now the WTO DSS must, without any further guidance, decide whether, and if so when and in what ways, they can prefer their own interpretation to that of members. This is not carried out in every case in an entirely *ad hoc* manner but rather relies on previous jurisprudence to determine the applicable standard in a given case. To this jurisprudence, this study now turns.

The DSS has 'struggled with [the] broader question of standard of review',[65] but the jurisprudence has been argued to reveal a gradual 'movement towards a *de novo* standard, and the adaptation of the standard to the specific provisions of different WTO agreements, thus potentially creating more than one standard'.[66] In *EC – Hormones*, the Appellate Body further attempted to define the standard of review by stating that 'the applicable standard is neither *de novo* review as such, nor "total deference," but rather "an objective assessment of the facts"'.[67] Following the *EC – Hormones* Report, the Appellate Body, in making an assessment of the conformity of the Panel decision with Art. 11, ruled in *Australia – Salmon* that it did not '"deliberately disregard", "refuse to consider", "wilfully distort", or "misrepresent"'[68] the evidence in the case, nor did it carry out an '"egregious error that calls into question the good faith" of the Panel'[69] and therefore did not 'abuse its discretion in a manner which even comes close to attaining the level of gravity required for a claim under Article 11 of the DSU to prevail'.[70]

This reasoning of the Appellate Body demonstrates the limitations of Art. 11 and of the Body itself in relation to the standard of review within a system with such broad overlap with areas of domestic regulation. There is clearly a vast difference between a precisely defined standard of review, comprising how far and in what ways Panels can review national decisions and decision-making procedures and replace them with their preferred interpretation, and the test applied by the Appellate Body in *Australia – Salmon* measuring whether the Panel deliberately disregarded, refused to consider, wilfully distorted or misrepresented the evidence

---

[65] *Jackson* 2006 (note 52), 171.

[66] *Becroft* (note 42), 52.

[67] Appellate Body Report *European Communities – Measures Concerning Meat and Meat Products (Hormones)*, pg. 43 (para. 117).

[68] Appellate Body Report *Australia – Measures Affecting Importation of Salmon*, pg. 78 (para. 266).

[69] *Ibid.*

[70] *Ibid.*

presented to it. It can also be argued that bad faith and the misapplication of a standard of review are conceptually different and that 'it may be possible to apply the correct standard of review without failing to exercise good faith, or vice versa',[71] a point that clearly undermines the reasoning of the Appellate Body in this case.

The Appellate Body in *Australia – Salmon* did not find a violation of Art. 11. However, in *US – Wheat Gluten*,[72] it was found that the Panel had 'failed to properly carry out this standard of review'.[73] In this case, the European Communities appealed on the basis of the Panel's appreciation of the evidence presented to it. The EC argued that the 'Panel failed in this case to make an "objective" factual and legal assessment of all relevant evidence, because it failed to provide an adequate and reasonable explanation for its findings'.[74] The Appellate Body agreed in part with this reasoning, first stating that they

> cannot base a finding of inconsistency under Article 11 simply on the conclusion that we might have reached a different factual finding from the one the panel reached. Rather, we must be satisfied that the panel has exceeded the bounds of its discretion, as the trier of facts, in its appreciation of the evidence[75]

The particular breach of Art. 11 DSU occurred in relation to the Panel's reliance on supplementary evidence rather than the original report submitted to it by the US.[76] The Appellate Body found 'the Panel's conclusion is at odds with its treatment and description of the evidence supporting that conclusion'.[77] A similar conclusion was reached by the Appellate Body in its review of the Panel decision in *US – DRAMS* and *US – Continued Zeroing*.[78]

In the *US – Continued Suspension* case,[79] the Appellate Body ruled that the Panel had not accorded the appropriate amount of deference to the evidence presented, stating:

> The Panel seems to have conducted a survey of the advice presented by the scientific experts and based its decisions on what the majority of experts, or the opinion that was most thoroughly reasoned or specific to the question at issue, agreed with the conclusion drawn

---

[71]*Becroft* (note 42), 52.

[72]Appellate Body Report *United States – Definitive Safeguard Measures on Imports of Wheat Gluten from the European Communities*.

[73]*Ibid.*, pg. 45 (para. 148).

[74]*Ibid.*, pg. 9 (para. 24).

[75]*Ibid.*, pg. 46 (para. 151).

[76]For a thorough treatment of the categorical difference in terms of errors of law and errors of fact made by Panels, see: *Oesch* (note 39), Ch. 6–11.

[77]*Ibid.*, pg. 50 (para. 161).

[78]Appellate Body Report *United States – Countervailing Duty Investigation on DRAMS*; Appellate Body Report *United States – Continued Existence and Application of Zeroing Methodology*.

[79]Appellate Body Report *United States – Continued Suspension of Obligations in the EC – Hormones Dispute*.

in the European Communities' risk assessment. This approach is not consistent with the applicable standard of review under the *SPS Agreement*.[80]

The Appellate Body ruled that the Panel rather ought to have

first looked at the European Communities' risk assessment. It should then have determined whether the scientific basis relied upon in that risk assessment came from a respected and qualified source. The Panel should have sought assistance from the scientific experts in confirming that it had properly identified the scientific basis underlying the European Communities' risk assessment or to determine whether that scientific basis originated in a respected and qualified source. The Panel should also have sought the experts' assistance in determining whether the reasoning articulated by the European Communities on the basis of the scientific evidence is objective and coherent, so that the conclusions reached in the risk assessment sufficiently warrant the SPS measure.[81]

While it is clear from a comparison of the two that, in the first instance, the Panel conducted something more akin to *de novo* review than what the Appellate Body deemed appropriate, it is not immediately apparent from the description of the appropriate action by the Panel what 'applicable standard of review under the *SPS Agreement*'[82] actually is. Indeed, based on the 'objective assessment of the matter before it' test laid out in the original *EC – Hormones* judgment, it is even arguable that the Panel in this instance, by taking into account the majority position that was 'most thoroughly reasoned or specific to the question at issue' in its assessment of the risk assessment, did in fact carry out an objective assessment of the matter before it. Clearly, the Appellate Body did not think so as it saw, in this instance, that deference was required while *de novo* review of the risk posed and the risk assessment conducted was not appropriate. But where is the legal textual basis for this? And what is the specific legal basis for their elaboration of what the Panel in fact ought to have carried out so as not to violate Art. 11 DSU? The approach taken in this case by the Appellate Body was reaffirmed by the Panel in *Australia – Apples*,[83] which stated: 'The Panel finds no reason to articulate a standard of review that departs from such guidance',[84] despite arguments put forward by Australia that 'the standard of review must maintain the balance between trade liberalization goals and domestic regulatory rights'.[85] The standard of review elaborated in *US – Continued Suspension* is recognised by neither the DSS nor States as employing 'total deference'. Nevertheless, it can be seen to constitute a move along the spectrum towards deference to governmental decisions and decision-making processes.

However, as stated above, some commentators clearly see a general move towards *de novo* review in the DSS.[86] How can these apparently conflicting positions be brought together? The important point is that the general move towards

---

[80]*Ibid.*, para. 598.

[81]*Ibid.*

[82]*Ibid.*

[83]Panel Report *Australia – Measures Affecting the Importation of Apples from New Zealand.*

[84]*Ibid.*, para 7.222.

[85]*Becroft* (note 42), 55–56; *Australia – Apples*, first written submission, 180–183.

[86]*Becroft* (note 42), 52.

de novo review is not claimed to be consistent, and particularly not in relation to the standard of review applied in the case of Art. 5.1 of the SPS Agreement, which is argued to be moving towards more deference.[87] Indeed, *Becroft* states that 'this more deferential approach may be confined to disputes under the SPS Agreement'.[88] However, *Oesch* notes that, in general, '[c]orresponding to the panels' active and intrusive approach to fact-finding, the standard of review of the "raw" evidence has been quite close to *de novo* review'[89] in cases involving economic data, scientific evidence or 'traditional GATT cases'[90] but not generally. Appraisal of scientific evidence is a key element in the Art. 5.2 SPS risk assessment obligation,[91] illustrating further that not only is the jurisprudence inconsistent but so is the related academic commentary, or, alternatively, a deferential review is shown to the general risk assessment requirement but not where assessing the scientific evidence of the risk assessment. Either position, both lacking any legal textual basis, can be seen to reflect an inconsistent application of standard of review and a lack of formal realisability in terms of WTO obligations in the realm of their impact on, or interference with, national regulatory measures.

Further complicating the debate surrounding the standard of review, *Palmeter* and *Mavroidis* have argued that 'there is broad and growing case law making it clear that panels are not going to conduct *de novo* review'.[92] The case law cited in support of the second point of view includes *EC – Hormones*, *US – Lamb Safeguards*[93] and *US – Cotton Yarn*.[94] Furthermore, *Palmeter* and *Mavroidis* question the ability of Panels to fulfil the 'objective assessment' required by Art. 11 DSU 'without considering [the facts] afresh'.[95] They point to a 'substantial evidence' test familiar to lawyers from the US, whereby Panels do not replace governmental decisions with their own interpretations of factual circumstances but rather weigh the support for the position adopted and make their assessment based on whether the governmental decision is supported by at least substantial evidence.[96] Where there is support for the position that 'the facts provide a basis for the decision of the authorities', then the Panels will likely find the measure to be WTO consistent, but where it appears that all of the support is for the opposing position, then they are more likely to find that the facts do not provide a basis for the national decision.

---

[87]*Ibid.*, 56.

[88]*Ibid.*

[89]*Matthias Oesch*, Standards of Review in WTO Dispute Resolution, JIEL 6 (2003), 635, 650.

[90]*Ibid.*, 651 (emphasis added).

[91]Art. 5.2 SPS states: 'In the assessment of risks. Members shall take into account available scientific evidence, relevant process and production methods [...]'.

[92]*Palmeter/Mavroidis* (note 3), 154.

[93]Appellate Body Report *United States – Safeguard Measures on Imports of Fresh, Chilled or Frozen Lamb Meat from New Zealand and Australia*.

[94]Appellate Body Report *United States – Transitional Safeguard Measure on Combed Cotton Yarn from Pakistan*.

[95]*Palmeter/Mavroidis* (note 3), 154.

[96]*Ibid.*, 155.

This is something quite removed from *Oesch's* spectrum of review. This assertion by *Palmeter* and *Mavroidis* is not sufficiently substantiated in order for their analysis to be proven or rebuffed, but it does provide a further insight into the quagmire of standard of review employed currently in the WTO DSS.

The purpose of this section is not to provide a general or specific standard of review that ought to be included in a future revision of the DSU.[97] Rather, it seeks to show the deficiencies in the current 'standard of review' in operation in the DSS, as it fails to provide legal certainty or any degree of formal realisability, bringing the legitimacy of the DSS and the WTO itself into question. Without formal realisability, States cannot know in advance the exact scope of their legal obligations, and this puts them firmly in the position of no-right in comparison to the DSS, which has a large privilege in this regard. As WTO members, States therefore cannot know in advance the precise degree to which their domestic regulatory measures will be reviewed by the DSS, putting them in a particularly weak position when they choose to regulate matters internally that relate in any way to products with a foreign origin. Furthermore, the DSS decides for itself the particular standard to apply, and then the review process, which could limit the privilege of the DSS, is also carried out internally and therefore increases and concretises this privilege, without any greater legitimacy.

As all WTO members are exposed to the lack of specific standard of review in any of the WTO Agreements (except in the Anti-Dumping Agreement) in the same manner, the power distributive consequences are an appropriation of power by the DSS, and its corresponding loss by all parties. As outlined above, however, the fact that it is possible for States with more (economic) bargaining power to bear the consequences of retaliatory measures under the DSU means that they are in a position of privilege *de facto* in relation to when and in what ways they carry out their obligations under the DSS (or rather bring their measures into conformity following the review of the Panel that finds them in breach). Thus, this other layer, in terms of distribution of bargaining power, means that they retain more than a nominal advantage vis-à-vis States with significantly less bargaining power and vis-à-vis the DSS.

The following section will now go on to address another partially problematic feature of the judicial function of the WTO: treaty interpretation.

---

[97]For a full treatment of the benefits of the introduction of a general standard of review and how this may be modified, using a precise legal test in Agreement-specific cases where a general standard may not be appropriate, see *Becroft* (note 42), 100–154.

4.4 Treaty Interpretation and the GATT/WTO

4.4.1 Position of DSS/the Appellate Body in Treaty Interpretation

> It should not be surprising that panels and the Appellate Body make law or complete the applicable law, when they consider it necessary.[98]

In order for any international treaty to function in a meaningful way, interpretation and application are necessary. Indeed, '[t]reaties are incomplete. Nothing is decided comprehensively in advance. Treaties reflect a negotiated political compromise and will leave issues unanswered, unprovided for, or unclear.'[99] Thus, as mentioned above, in order for the WTO DSS to fulfil its function of providing a benchmark of stability and security, it is inherent in the powers of the DSS to be able to interpret the WTO and covered agreements in a meaningful way, and part of that must be to create workable solutions to factual problems as and when they arise. When negotiated, the texts of the agreements could not and did not foresee every eventuality that would arise in the application of the WTO legal regime, nor are international treaties generally negotiated in order to make sure every possible factual outcome is prescribed and provided with a firm legal solution. However, as will be seen in the close analysis of the provisions of the GATT and TBT and SPS Agreements, the lack of precision and formal realisability, and thus the interpretative competence granted (and power transferred) to the DSS, raise huge questions about the legitimacy of the regime.

Nevertheless, it is an inevitability in the process of interpretation and application of legal norms contained in treaties that international judicial bodies develop and create law, and '[t]oday, it is no longer convincing to only think of international courts in their role of settling disputes',[100] with their role as lawmakers being described as 'beyond dispute'.[101] Furthermore, in the field of the WTO, 'as a matter of fact adjudicatory practice has developed some of trade law's cardinal norms'.[102]

However, it is clear, based on the principles of State sovereignty, and, more broadly, the rule of law, that it is not only problematic but also illegitimate for judicial bodies to have real norm-creating power. The precise position of the 'rule of law' within the international system is beyond the scope of this work, and the author recognises the many inherent problems in transplanting this formal doctrine of national legal systems into the international sphere. However, it is clear that

[98]*Van Damme* (note 12), 110.

[99]*Ibid.*

[100]*Armin von Bogdandy/Ingo Venzke*, Beyond Dispute: International Judicial Institutions as Lawmakers, in: Armin Von Bogdandy/Ingo Venzke (eds.), International Judicial Lawmaking (Heidelberg, 2012), 3.

[101]*Ibid.*, 4.

[102]*Ingo Venzke*, Making General Exceptions: The Spell of Precedents in Developing Article XX GATT into Standards for Domestic Regulatory Policy, in: Bogdandy/Venzke (note 279), 179, 180.

some of the elements of the rule of law can be evidenced in international law, and it is argued here that it certainly applies in international judicial decision-making, in so far as it would be contrary to the rule of law for international judicial bodies to apply the law in an arbitrary manner, or create wholly new norms and obligations, thereby preventing any security in the position of States in their understanding of their legal rights and obligations at any given time. In this way, it is related to the idea of formal realisability, discussed above.[103]

Where, then, can the line be drawn in terms of necessity and legitimacy? How far can the WTO DSS, or any other international judicial body, go beyond what could be considered 'ordinary interpretation' into what is often described as 'judicial legislation'? The simple answer appears to be that there is no answer, and this huge debate is, again, beyond the scope of this work. What will be done instead, below with the most important example of the definition of 'like products' in the WTO and covered agreements, and later in the specific contexts of the relevant provisions, is an attempt to assess how far into judicial legislation the DSS can be demonstrated to have reached, what this means in terms of power distribution and benefit, and whether this can be claimed to be something that threatens the legitimacy of the WTO system as a whole.

The particular problem of judicial legislation produces not only criticisms of illegitimacy directed at the WTO, but it is also manifestly contrary to Art. 19.3 DSU. Article 19.3 states: 'in their findings and recommendations, the panel and Appellate Body cannot add to or diminish the rights and obligations provided in the covered agreements'. Where the Panels engage in such behaviour, the Appellate Body has the power to overrule such decisions, but where the Body itself does so, or does not find a breach of Art. 19.2 DSU by the Panel, then the quasi-automatic adoption of DSS recommendations by the DSB means that there is very little to restrain the Appellate Body or prevent judicial legislation. The fine line between interpretation necessitated by factual circumstances of vague provisions and that which goes beyond is hard to draw (particularly in the case of the WTO due to such imprecise obligations), and the will of WTO members should be taken into account in doing so. A more secure grounding for WTO members could be achieved through reform of the DSU and more precise boundaries being drawn. In the meantime, the Art. IX:2 WTO Agreement 'authoritative interpretation' mechanism may be the tool to overcome this, and is discussed below.[104]

First of all, however, this section will lay out some of the most important issues in treaty interpretation under the WTO generally, from the 'incorporation' of customary law by Art. 3.2 DSU and the role of the VCLT and customary rules of interpretation in the DSS generally to the potential 'need' for a broader approach in the WTO.

---

[103]See *supra*, note 59. For more on the position of the rule of law in international law, see: *Simon Chesterman*, The Rule of Law, in: Rüdiger Wolfrum (ed.) The Max Planck Encyclopaedia of Public International Law, vol. VIII (Oxford, 2012), 1014–1022.

[104]See *infra*, 4.4.7.

4.4.2 Article 3.2 DSU

> Concerns about the role of panels and the Appellate Body include claims of judicial legislation and overreaching.[105]

Based on the forgoing, this is not surprising. Where the DSU provides no precise formulation for a particular power granted to the Panels or Appellate Body, they are left in a position of privilege to decide for themselves (to an extent) where the limits of their discretion are. Of course, the (however remote) possibility of the DSB unanimously overruling a recommendation of the DSU means that they are prevented from acting in a way that is manifestly contrary to the role envisaged for them in the DSU. However, overreaching[106] (in terms of standard of review) and judicial legislation (in the interpretation of the WTO and covered agreements) attract much criticism not only because they are 'inappropriate' functions for a dispute settlement body to carry out but also because within the WTO system the DSS is almost untouchable in these areas (in contrast to other international fora characterised by consensual dispute settlement).

Panels and the Appellate Body tend to cling closely (and vocally) to the idea that their interpretation of WTO law is 'in accordance with customary rules of interpretation of public international law' (Art. 3.2 DSU), and they often make reference to rules of the VCLT as embodying customary law in this area.[107] Article 3.2 DSU is key here in its direct incorporation of customary rules of interpretation into the DSU. However, the precise role of customary law in WTO dispute settlement in general is far less certain. Furthermore, while Art. 3.2 DSU may incorporate customary rules of interpretation into the DSU, the provision does not exactly place the DSS under the firm obligation to apply the rules exclusively or in their entirety. The provision states that the 'Members recognize' that the DSS serves 'to clarify the existing provisions of the agreements in accordance with customary rules of interpretation of public international law'. How far the legal consequences of this slightly imprecise provision affect the freedom of the DSS in its choice of methods of treaty interpretation is unclear. The provision reads more like a preambular paragraph, in that it appears to set out the 'object and purpose of the treaty',[108] rather than containing any firm legal content.[109] However, many scholars

---

[105]*Van Damme* (note 12), 7.

[106]See comments of former Appellate Body Member James Bacchus, who denies that the Body has overreached, but agrees that perhaps the criticism of overreaching could be levelled at the system as a whole, *James Bacchus*, WTO Appellate Body Roundtable, ASIL Proceedings (2005), 175, 178, stating: 'it could be argued that the system is overreaching'.

[107]See, for example, Appellate Body Report *United States – Standards for Reformulated and Conventional Gasoline*, pg. 16–17; Appellate Body Report *Japan – Taxes on Alcoholic Beverages II*, pg. 104.

[108]*Makane Moïse Mbengue*, Preamble, in: Rüdiger Wolfrum (ed.) The Max Planck Encyclopaedia of Public International Law, vol. VIII (Oxford, 2012), 397 (para. 4).

[109]Furthermore, if you compare this provision (Art. 3.2 DSU) with what is contained in the WTO Agreement (binding the whole organization including the DSS) then it raises further doubt that it

are of the view that Art. 3.2 DSU does in fact 'require' the DSS to utilise customary rules of interpretation.[110]

Furthermore, following the International Court of Justice (ICJ) in the 1980 *Interpretation of the Agreement of 25 March 1951 Between the WHO and Egypt* Advisory Opinion, '[i]nternational organizations are subjects of international law and, as such, are bound by any obligations incumbent upon them under rules of general international law'[111]—at least in so far as they have not 'contracted out' of them, following the doctrine of *lex specialis*. This means that the DSS is bound, as an organ of an international organisation and thus a subject of international law, by general international law to apply the rules of customary international law that are incumbent upon it. The rules of customary law relating to treaty interpretation are such rules, and thus the content of Art. 3.2 DSU is, from the perspective of general international law at least, irrelevant to the obligations of the DSS. A breach of this general obligation, however, would be external to the WTO system and is separate from the focus of this chapter. How the DSS itself evaluates its relationship with customary law and implements the customary rules on treaty interpretation is addressed in the following sections.

Briefly going back to the point made about *lex specialis*: *lex specialis*, as it applies to the relationship between customary law and treaties, dictates that 'in a concrete case treaty rules usually prevail over customary rules because of their specialty, as very often treaty rules introduce limitations and exceptions to areas of freedom set out in customary rules'.[112] Whether this would be the case in relation to the rules of treaty interpretation is questionable, though the particular nature of economic relationships and obligations may mean that this power is inherent in the DSS as a sort of 'implied power', as it is required for them to be able to carry out

---

was so intended to create an obligation on the DSS then without doing so expressly – Art. XVI:1 WTO Agreement reads: 'Except as otherwise provided under this Agreement or the Multilateral Trade Agreements, the WTO shall be guided by the decisions, procedures and customary practices followed by the CONTRACTING PARTIES to GATT 1947 and the bodies established in the framework of the GATT 1947.'

[110]See, for example, *Alexander M. Feldman*, Evolving Treaty Obligations: A Proposal for Analyzing Subsequent Practice Derived from WTO Dispute Settlement, NYU Journal of International Law and Politics 41 (2008–2009), 655, 677.

[111]ICJ, *Interpretation of the Agreement of 25 March 1951 between the WHO and Egypt*, Advisory Opinion of 20 November 1980, ICJ Reports (1980), 73, 89–90 (para. 37).

[112]*Tullio Treves*, Customary International Law, in: Rüdiger Wolfrum (ed.) The Max Planck Encyclopaedia of Public International Law, vol. II (Oxford, 2012), 937, 955 (para. 87). See further Iran-US Claims Tribunal, *Amoco v. Islamic Republic of Iran*, 27 ILM 1316 (1998), para. 112, stating: 'As a *lex specialis* in the relations between the two countries, the Treaty supersedes the *lex generalis*, namely customary international law. This does not mean, however, that the latter is irrelevant. On the contrary, the rules of customary law may be useful in order to fill in possible *lacunae* of the Treaty, to ascertain the meaning of undefined terms in its text or, more generally, to aid interpretation and application of its provisions.'

their other functions laid out in the DSU.[113] An implied power has been described as 'a term [. . .] being read into the organization's statute not in order to modify it or add to the members' burdens, but in order to give effect to what they agreed by becoming parties to the constitutional treaty'.[114] Thus, in this case, it could be argued that the parties to the WTO intended that the DSS have the ability not only to utilise customary rules of treaty interpretation but also to limit the rules and/or extend them as they see fit in order to best interpret the obligations of such a particular nature as are contained in the WTO and covered agreements. If the question is 'can the DSS function effectively without such powers?' and the answer, if we follow the remarks contained in the 2004 Sutherland Report,[115] is probably no, then it would appear that a relatively strong case could be made for the idea that this is indeed an 'implied power' of the DSS.[116] However, these are again questions of general international law and have limited relevance within the WTO system itself.

4.4.3   Interaction with the Vienna Convention on the Law of Treaties

The way in which the DSS applies the customary Vienna Convention rules has been described thus:

> [T]he Appellate Body has tried to justify its interpretations on the basis of the VCLT without treating the VCLT as a rigid, binding structure of rules, though exceptions exist and have sometimes been excessive. This understanding of the Articles 31 to 33 VCLT as principles, not rules, is not yet sufficiently appreciated by WTO law and its audience.[117]

Furthermore, the fact that the understanding in international law generally that the customary rules relating to treaty interpretation do not begin and end with Arts. 31–33 VCLT and the fact that these customary rules are 'broader than the principles codified in the VCLT ha[ve] not been sufficiently appreciated by some

---

[113]*Krzysztof Skubiszewski*, Implied Powers of International Organizations, in: Yoram Dinstein (ed), International Law at a Time of Perplexity: Essays in Honour of Shabtai Rosenne (Leiden, 1989) 855 *et seq*. See also *Niels M*. Blokker, International Organizations or Institutions, Implied Powers, in: Rüdiger Wolfrum (ed.) The Max Planck Encyclopaedia of Public International Law, vol. VI (Oxford, 2012), 18–26.

[114]*Skubizewski* (note 113), 860.

[115]Formal realisability is condition by which treaty obligations, or any legal duties, can provide a clear and concise standard by which states can assess whether, when facing litigation, they have fulfilled their duty or not. Unclear, imprecise obligations which do not provide surety lack formal realisability.

[116]*Van Damme* (note 12), 189–191, also explores the idea of inherent powers of the WTO DSS, but in a slightly different context.

[117]*Ibid.*, 56.

members'.[118] In this context, *Van Damme* draws particular attention to a statement of the Appellate Body in *EC – Computer Equipment*, which reads: 'the only rules which may be applied in interpreting the meaning of a concession are the general rules of treaty interpretation set out in the Vienna Convention',[119] though she also points to the fact that the DSS has applied principles that are not contained in Arts. 31 and 32 VCLT.[120]

Article 31 VCLT lays out an obligation that treaties shall be interpreted in good faith, in accordance with the ordinary meaning of the terms used, in their context and in light of their object and purpose.[121] The article then goes on to elaborate on the meaning of context in this provision, making reference to 'any agreement' relating to the treaty that was 'made between all the parties in connexion with the conclusion of the treaty'[122] or 'any instrument made by one of the parties in connexion with the conclusion of a treaty and accepted by the other parties as an instrument related to the treaty'.[123] This elaboration of context is 'relatively narrow'[124] and may be seen as overly restrictive in the trade context, and where customary law would allow for a broader approach then it is likely that the DSS would follow it.

Furthermore, Art. 31 (3) (a)–(c) allows for other factors to be taken into account, as well as the context, such as 'any subsequent agreement between the parties regarding the interpretation of the treaty or the application of its provisions',[125] 'any subsequent practice'[126] and 'any relevant rules of international law applicable in relations between the parties'.[127] Moreover, Art. 31 (4) VCLT provides that 'a special meaning shall be given to a term if it is established that the parties so intended'. How exactly this could be established is unclear, though reference to the *travaux preparatoires* may prove useful. Similarly, the Art. IX:2 WTO Agreement mechanism for the Ministerial Conference and the General Council to adopt authoritative interpretation would appear to fall into this category.[128]

---

[118]*Ibid.*, 57.

[119]Appellate Body Report *European Communities – Customs Classification of Certain Computer Equipment*, para. 84.

[120]See *Van Damme* (note 12), 57.

[121]Art. 31 (1) VCLT.

[122]Art. 31 (2) (a) VCLT.

[123]Art. 31 (2) (b) VCLT.

[124]*Michael Lennard*, Navigating by the Stars: Interpreting the WTO Agreements, JIEL 5 (2002), 17, 24.

[125]Art. 31 (3) (a) VCLT; see *infra*, 4.4.7 for detail on the Art IX:2 WTO Agreement procedure on authoritative interpretation and how this unutilised tool may constitute an opportunity for such 'agreements' to be concluded in relation to the WTO.

[126]Art. 31 (3) (b) VCLT.

[127]Art. 31 (3) (c) VCLT.

[128]Though it has also been argued that these interpretations would be legally binding on the DSS. Article IX:2 WTO Agreement is discussed in greater detail below, or see *Claus-Dieter Ehlermann/ Lothar Ehring*, The Authoritative Interpretation Under Article IX:2 of the Agreement Establishing

Article 32 VCLT provides that recourse may be had to supplementary means of interpretation, including preparatory works, to confirm a meaning deduced under Art. 31 VCLT or where an interpretation under Art. 31 leaves the meaning ambiguous, obscure or leads to an absurd or unreasonable result:

> The Appellate Body does not readily turn to supplementary means of interpretation, other language versions, subsequent practice, or special meanings on its own initiative. These principles of interpretation differ from the principles of contextual and effective interpretation, which the Appellate Body applies almost as a matter of course.[129]

Van Damme explains that the reason why this is so is partly due to the residual character of Art. 32 and further that '[t]he application of other non-codified principles of treaty interpretation also offers an explanation and may rule out that Article 31 results in a manifestly absurd or unreasonable result'.[130] Moreover, the reluctance may be based on the particular difficulties of relying on the *travaux preparatoires* relating to a set of treaties that were 'negotiated by a heterogeneous group with particular and diverse interests',[131] and in such cases it may be more helpful to rely on legal fictions to 'mov[e] from theoretical impasses to practical solutions'.[132]

The Appellate Body has, however, repeatedly emphasised that 'the elements of Articles 31 and 32 are not hierarchically structured'[133] and that they are 'connected and mutually reinforcing components of a *holistic exercise*'.[134] Despite this, even former Appellate Body members are willing to admit that the 'textualism of the Appellate Body'[135] is represented by a 'strong adherence' to grammatical analysis, based partly on 'economic rationales'.[136]

---

the World Trade Organization: Current Law, Practice and Possible Improvements, JIEL 8 (2005), 803 *et seq.*

[129]*Van Damme* (note 12), 305.

[130]*Ibid.*, 310.

[131]*Ibid.*, 313.

[132]*Ibid.* Furthermore, Van Damme makes particular reference to the fact that it is very difficult in the case of the WTO and covered agreements to find 'accessible, trustworthy, and representative preparatory work having probative value', *ibid.*, 316; see also *Bacchus*, WTO Roundtable (note 106), 179, stating: '[W]e all know there is no negotiating history. There certainly is nothing that rises to the level of what would be considered preparatory work under Article 32 of the Vienna Convention'.

[133]*Malgosia Fitzmaurice/Panos Merkouris*, Canons of Treaty Interpretation, in Malgosia Fitzmaurice/Olufemi Elian/Panos Merkouris (eds.), Treaty Interpretation and the Vienna Convention on the Law of Treaties: 30 Years On (Leiden, 2010), 153, 183.

[134]Appellate Body Report *United States – Continued Existence and Application of Zeroing Methodology*, para. 268. See also: Appellate Body Report *Canada – Certain Measures Concerning Periodicals*, 478–9; Appellate Body Report *United States – Import Prohibition of Certain Shrimp and Shrimp Products*, para. 152; and *Van Damme* (note 12), 310–327.

[135]*Mitsuo Matsushita*, WTO Roundtable (note 106), 180.

[136]*Ibid.*

In this field, the Appellate Body has created its own jurisprudence—a singular jurisprudence that may strongly contribute to a growing isolation of the WTO regime in international law. Though greater reliance on supplementary means of interpretation would not 'remedy' this 'problem', more explicit guidance for the DSS in any future revision of the DSU could help to ensure that some degree of coherence is achieved. Or, on the other hand, the DSS may continue in the same vein but without such cries of illegitimacy, lack of transparency and 'overreaching'—clearly a potential benefit for the system as a whole.

4.4.4 Article 31 (3)(c) VCLT

Taking a step 'back' in the analysis of the Vienna Convention, in the context of WTO treaty interpretation special mention must be made of the relationship of the DSS to Art. 31 (3)(c) VCLT. This particular rule arguably views international law as one coherent system and allows for agreements made in subsections of international law to have potential relevance in the interpretation of a treaty in other sections. It has been described as a potential 'means to mitigate the effects of the much-described fragmentation of international law'[137]: even from a legal pluralist vision of the international legal order, it can be seen to have a potentially useful function in its 'integrative effects'.[138]

The Panel in *EC – Biotech* made the decision not to take into account the Convention on Biological Diversity (CBD)[139] and the Biosafety Protocol,[140] based on its interpretation of the wording of Art. 31 (3)(c). The Panel made explicit reference to the wording of the provision and deduced therefrom that 'those rules of international law which are "applicable in the relations between the parties" that are to be taken into account in interpreting a treaty'[141] were not to include any rules stemming from treaties that not all WTO members are parties to.[142] The Panel chose not to differentiate from the wording of Art. 31 (2)(a) VCLT, which makes reference to 'all the parties', and Art. 31 (3)(c), which only refers to 'the parties'. In the view of the Panel, the reference to 'all the parties' in Art. 31 (2)(a) is necessitated by its relationship to Art. 31 (2)(b), and no such parallel can be drawn with

---

[137]*Oliver Dörr*, Article 31, in: Oliver Dörr/Kirsten Schmalenbach (eds.), The Vienna Convention on the Law of Treaties: A Commentary (Heidelberg, 2012), 521, 560.

[138]*Tomer Broude*, Principles of Normative Integration and the Allocation of International Authority: The WTO, The Vienna Convention on the Law of Treaties, and the Rio Declaration, Loyola International Law Review 6 (2008), 173–207.

[139]Convention on Biological Diversity, 5 June 1992, 1760 UNTS 79.

[140]Cartagena Protocol on Biosafety to the Convention on Biological Diversity, 29 January 2000, 2226 UNTS 208.

[141]Panel Report *European Communities – Approval and Marketing of Biotech Products*, para. 7.68.

[142]*Ibid.*

Art. 31 (3)(a).[143] The Panel then expanded on the notion that although the obligation to 'take into account' such rules of international law exists, 'no particular
outcome is prescribed'.[144]

In multilateral treaties that create multilateral obligations, or obligations *erga
omnes*, such as multilateral human rights treaties, it is clear that such an interpretation of Art. 31 (3)(c) may be justified. However, the WTO and covered agreements, although being multilateral, produce a series of bilateral relationships
between the parties, and it is at least feasible to imagine a different interpretative
stance on this issue.

The approach of the Panel has been described thus: 'the Panel found that a treaty
interpreter could rely on such a treaty only if found useful but that under no
circumstance was he obliged to do so',[145] and further:

> While the Panel's interpretation of the reference in Article 31 (3) (c) of the Vienna
> Convention to 'rules applicable in the relations between the parties' may not be manifestly
> wrong, it does not contribute to building channels of dialogue in an increasingly fragmented
> international legal system. The Panel's apparent attempt to avoid conflicts between relevant
> rules of international law led it to conclude that the Vienna Convention did not establish a
> legal obligation for interpreting bodies to take into account treaties that were not ratified by
> all parties to the treaty being interpreted. However, this conclusion stands at odds with the
> responsibility of an interpreting body to take into account those treaties, especially when
> they address issues of global concern where the interests of the international community are
> involved.[146]

While the invocation of the particular responsibility of an interpreting body in
issues of major global concern appears to be more political and/or aspirational, the
critique of the failure to build a dialogue within the international legal system ties
into the idea mentioned above of the potential 'integrative effects' of Art. 31 (3)(a).
There is no overarching obligation on dispute settlement bodies to create greater
integration in the system, but the repeated failure to do so may produce yet more
criticism of illegitimacy. However, at the same time, it must be recognised that
were the DSS to take into account international treaties not binding on all parties, or
not binding on all parties to the particular dispute, then such a method may fall foul
of the *pacta tertiis* rule, a fundamental principle in international law.[147] Thus, the
line to be tread by the DSS in this regard is not so easy or clear-cut. The possibility
of revisions and reform to the DSU at Doha (or any future Round) could enable the
DSS to navigate its relationship with customary rules of treaty interpretation with
greater ease and legitimacy, and most perhaps importantly on a firm legal basis.

The reason why Art. 31 (3)(a) is of relevance in this study becomes clear when
the judgment of the Appellate Body in the *US – Shrimp/Turtle* is recalled. In this

---

[143]*Ibid.*, footnote 242.

[144]*Ibid.*, para. 7.69.

[145]Center for International Environmental Law, EC-Biotech: Overview and Analysis of the
Panel's Interim Report (2006), 49.

[146]*Ibid.*, 49–50.

[147]*Malgosia Fitzmaurice*, Third Parties and the Law of Treaties, MPYBUNL 6 (2002), 37, 38.

case, discussed below,[148] the Appellate Body made explicit reference to a treaty concluded by the United States in the context of the lawfulness of domestic legislation.[149]

4.4.5 In Dubio Mitius?

It has been argued by *Dörr*, drawing on the differing approaches of the Appellate Body in *EC – Hormones* and *China – Publications and Audiovisual Products*,[150] that, in respect of treaty interpretation, the WTO DSS began with a policy of *in dubio mitius* but later shifted to a less deferential approach.[151] The doctrine of *in dubio mitius*, or principle of restrictive interpretation, means that when there is any doubt as to the meaning of a treaty provision, it should be interpreted by the court or tribunal in a manner that 'entails the lesser obligation for sovereign states'.[152] The *EC – Hormones* Appellate Body Report elaborates it as a principle for use:

> if the meaning of a term is ambiguous, that meaning is to be preferred which is less onerous to the party assuming an obligation, or which interferes less with the territorial or personal supremacy of a party, or involves less general restrictions upon the parties.[153]

Is this then an example of the DSS using customary means of interpretation not contained in the VCLT to take a broader approach? *Van Damme* is quick to point out that the DSS makes reference to this principle in only one judgment[154] and states that 'it is doubtful whether it qualifies as a general principle of law or is part of customary law'.[155] She furthermore argues that were it to be applied, it ought to be applied, following the reasoning of the PCIJ,[156] as a last resort and not as it was applied by the Appellate Body in the *EC – Hormones* case.[157] *In dubio mitius* should, therefore, not be seen as the starting point from which the DSS has deviated

---

[148]See Ch. 6.6.

[149]See also EC – Biotech and the attempted invocation of *inter alia* The Biosafety Protocol: Panel Report *European Communities – Approval and Marketing of Biotech Products*, para. 7.78.

[150]Appellate Body Report *China – Measures Affecting Trading Rights and Distribution Services for Certain Publications and Audiovisual Entertainment Products*.

[151]*Dörr* (note 137), 538–539.

[152]*Ibid.*, 538.

[153]Appellate Body Report *European Communities – Measures Concerning Meat and Meat Products (Hormones)*, para. 165 (footnote 154, quoting R. Jennings/A. Watts (eds.) Oppenheim's International Law, 9th ed. Vol. I (1992), 1278).

[154]*Van Damme* (note 12), 63.

[155]*Ibid.*, 62.

[156]In cases such as: PCIJ, *Competence of the International Labour Organization in Regard to International Regulation of the Conditions of Labour of Persons Employed in Agriculture*, PCIJ (1922) Ser. B, No. 2; PCIJ, *The S.S. Wimbledon*, PCIJ (1923) Ser. A, No. 1, 35. See further *Van Damme* (note 12), 60–64.

[157]*Van Damme* (note 12), 60–65.

but rather a one-off, misapplication of a method of treaty interpretation that has not been considered to be part of the canons of treaty interpretation for quite some time. The rule has been described as 'lacking a good modern authority'[158] and, as early as 1961, was described by LORD MCNAIR as 'from an age in which treaties were interpreted not by legal tribunals, and not even much by lawyers but by statesmen and diplomats'.[159]

This one example of the use of the principle by the Appellate Body should not then be seen as the repeated application of this doctrine within the DSS (or as a starting point from which it moved away) but does help to emphasise the position of the Appellate Body and how it approaches treaty interpretation. The Appellate Body is not reined in by firm enough language in the DSU and therefore can, in the exercise of this almost unlimited privilege, freely produce such anomalies. The question as to whether an *in dubio mitius* approach might be a possible solution to the interpretative and legitimacy problems highlighted in this work is an interesting one but unlikely to win the support of WTO members.

It should be pointed out that it is not possible to compare the DSS with other international tribunals as, due to the principle of consent, such erroneous interpretation would inevitably lead to States avoiding the use of such fora. As the WTO DSS provides compulsory, binding dispute settlement (and the disadvantages of non-membership are too substantial, meaning that leaving is not a political reality), the DSS is placed in a position of almost unlimited privilege in this regard. Were the WTO members to begin to use the Art. IX:2 authoritative interpretation mechanism (discussed below), it could help to limit the DSS in such cases and provide a more legitimate basis for further jurisprudence.

4.4.6 Broader Approach and Necessity

The 'relatively narrow'[160] Vienna Convention approach, as discussed above, may be too narrow in the trade context. However, the appropriateness of treaty interpretation in its broader (than the VCLT) customary sense was also brought into question by the 2004 Sutherland Report for the WTO. The report stated:

> 234. There is, nevertheless, some controversy about the degree to which general international law should be utilized in the jurisprudence and determinations of the WTO dispute settlement system. Clearly, it seems to be the case that international law will have relevance, but that there are risks about pushing that relevance too far. [. . .]

> 235. The customary international law rules of interpretation are, themselves, sometimes questionable when applied in the context of very detailed and intricate economic

---

[158]*Lennard* (note 124), 63.

[159]*Arnold D. McNair*, The Law Treaties (1961), 765, quoted in *Lennard* (note 124), 63.

[160]*Lennard* (note 124), 25.

obligations of the WTO. There are many different techniques that can be used for interpreting a treaty, and the Appellate Body has utilized many of the rules that are necessary.[161]

What is key here is the concept of necessity, implying that customary rules of interpretation are available to the DSS to be used when they feel them to be necessary, but where they are unnecessary, other methods of interpretation are not only conceivable but actually utilised. The VCLT rules themselves are 'not exclusive',[162] and they 'do not prevent the interpreter from applying other principles compatible with the general rule laid down in Art. 31'.[163] 'Necessity' is perhaps ever so slightly less plausible in cases where the DSS limits its application of customary rules, but the argument could still be made in such instances.

Furthermore, it is important to point out at this stage that it is not only within the WTO DSS that the question is raised as to whether treaty interpretation is and/or should be considered in the specific subsection/system of the international legal order it is applied. The idea of 'special principles of treaty interpretation' has also been explored in reference to, for example, human rights law[164] and international criminal law.[165] Indeed, one can 'note the emergence of different hermeneutics across the landscape of judicial treaty interpretation'.[166] Whether this phenomenon is constituted, bolstered or in fact a result of judicial lawmaking is debatable, and it is probably true that in each 'area' of international law, before each different tribunal and possibly in every case, the relationship functions differently. Indeed, the ILC's Report on Fragmentation in International Law[167] states:

System integration governs all treaty interpretation, the other relevant aspects of which are set out in the other paragraphs of articles 31–32 VCLT. These paragraphs describe a process of legal reasoning, in which particular elements will have greater or less relevance depending upon the nature of the treaty provisions in the context of interpretation. In many cases, the issue of interpretation will be capable of resolution with the framework of the treaty itself.[168]

This recognition of the fact that the nature of the treaty provisions and the context in which they exist influence the relevance of factors in legal reasoning

---

[161]WTO, The Future of the WTO: Addressing Institutional Challenges in the New Millennium (2004), 53–54.

[162]*Dörr* (note 137), 538.

[163]*Ibid.*

[164]*Van Damme* (note 12), 58 (footnote 124); *George Lestas*, Strasbourg's Interpretive Ethic: Lessons for the International Lawyer, EJIL 21 (2010), 509–541.

[165]*Leena Grover*, A Call to Arms: Fundamental Dilemmas Confronting the Interpretation of Crimes in the Rome Statute of the International Criminal Court, EJIL 21 (2010), 543–583.

[166]*Joseph H. H. Weiler*, The Interpretation of Treaties – A Re-examination: Preface, EJIL 21 (2010), 507.

[167]ILC, Report of the Study Group of the International Law Commission – Fragmentation in International Law: Difficulties Arising from the Diversification and Expansion of International Law, UN Doc. A/CN.4/L.702 (2006).

[168]*Ibid.*, para. 18.

demonstrates that although at some level the critique at the WTO that its application of customary rules of interpretation falls short of what is required, it is clear that divergence is a necessary product of context. Whether such divergence should be seen 'as an incorrect application of the Vienna Convention rules or proof that these rules are outdated or should not fully apply to a particular tribunal',[169] or rather simply demonstrating the fact 'that tribunals have a varying degree of interpretation space within which they must select between different interpretative techniques',[170] is contested. It is argued here that within the field of 'interpretation space' no formal criticisms can be raised in terms of 'regime divergence' in interpretation, and if the divergence goes further afield still, then it is the responsibility of the WTO members to use (or at least attempt to use) the authoritative interpretation mechanism contained in Art. IX:2 of the WTO Agreement, discussed below.

4.4.7   Article IX:2 WTO Agreement

The debate as to whether treaty interpretation is an art or a science has a long history.[171] The idea that we may be attempting to treat interpretation as a science, and thus apply legal tenets to it on an erroneous basis, provides criticism of the way in which works such as this handle treaty interpretation. But again—this broad theoretical question can only change the approach by degrees, and what is relevant here is whether the 'failure' of the DSS to utilise customary means of interpretation has any legal significance.

The Appellate Body can clearly 'overrule' Panel decisions if their chosen method of interpretation goes so far as to breach the Art. 3.2 DSU 'obligation' to interpret the agreements 'in accordance with customary rules of interpretation of public international law'. In fact, the Appellate Body often chooses to do so in a methodical manner, giving a wealth of practice within the WTO as to the application of the VCLT rules on treaty interpretation.[172] The systematic approach of the

---

[169]*Joost Pauwelyn/Manfred Elsig*, The Politics of Treaty Interpretation: Variations and Explanations across International Tribunals, in: Jeffrey L. Dunoff/Mark A. Pollack (eds.), Interdisciplinary Perspectives on International Law and International Relations (Cambridge, 2012), 445.

[170]*Ibid.*, 446.

[171]See further *Panos Merkouris*, Interpretation is an Art, is a Science, is an Art, in: Malgosia Fitzmaurice/Olufemi Elian/Panos Merkouris (eds.), Treaty Interpretation and the Vienna Convention on the Law of Treaties: 30 Years On (Leiden, 2010), 1–14, who finally concludes: 'Interpretation is a science, that is artful, an art that is scientific; a science that has characteristics that transform it into art, which art in turn partakes of such scientific elements that make it a science, and so on and so forth'.

[172]See, for example, Appellate Body Report *China – Measures Affecting Trading Rights and Distribution Services for Certain Publications and Audiovisual Entertainment Products*, paras. 338–413.

Appellate Body in the review of the application of the rules of the Vienna Convention by Panels ensures that the 'rule' contained in Art. 3.2 DSU is upheld.

However, what is the case when the application of the Vienna Convention rule/customary law on treaty interpretation is being carried out by the Appellate Body and not Panels? The approach of the Appellate Body to treaty interpretation has been described as one that 'privileges the textual and contextual [...] and grudgingly and sparingly analyzes the teleological'.[173] Is this a 'breach' of Art. 3.2 DSU? What are the possible repercussions of such an application of customary law (i.e. misapplication)? It is also possible to draw on the examples given in the foregoing section of potential areas of overreaching and judicial legislation, as well as the concrete examples provided later in this work. As outlined above, within the WTO the only possibility to 'overrule' an Appellate Body report is by the non-adoption of the report by the DSB, and as they are adopted with 'quasi-automaticity'[174] this would only be possible in very exceptional circumstances.

What then remains to tame a (largely hypothetical) overly active Appellate Body whose decisions have now gone so far as to surely be described as *ultra vires*? Or even in non-hypothetical cases where States may be unhappy with the interpretation or reasoning applied by the DSS generally? In fact, there is an—until now completely unused—option for WTO members: the issuance of an authoritative interpretation under Art. IX:2 WTO Agreement.

Article IX:2 states:

> The Ministerial Conference and the General Council shall have the exclusive authority to adopt interpretations of this Agreement and of the Multilateral Trade Agreements. In the case of an interpretation of a Multilateral Trade Agreement in Annex 1, they shall exercise their authority on the basis of a recommendation by the Council overseeing the functioning of that Agreement. The decision to adopt an interpretation shall be taken by a three-fourths majority of the Members. This paragraph shall not be used in a manner that would undermine the amendment provisions in Article X.

This procedure is 'mentioned'[175] in Art. 3.9 DSU, which is a without-prejudice clause ensuring that nothing in the DSU prejudices the rights of the members to 'seek authoritative interpretation of provisions of a covered agreement through decision-making under the WTO Agreement'. Although this provision has never been used, *Ehlermann* and *Ehring* argue persuasively that if it were to be implemented, it would be possible to consider these interpretations as producing legal effects and binding the DSS.[176] Such a mechanism provides a potential form of check and balance: while the reverse consensus rule is insurmountable, a three-fourths majority in the DSB is conceivable and could therefore assist in ensuring that the DSS does not extend too far into judicial legislation, as the WTO members

---

[173]*Douglas A. Irwin/Joseph Weiler*, Measures Affecting the Cross-Border Supply of Gambling and Betting Services (DS 285), World Trade Review 7 (2008), 71, 90.

[174]*Ehlermann/Ehring* (note 128), 812.

[175]*Ibid.*, 804.

[176]*Ibid.*, 807–812.

would then be able to issue an authoritative interpretation 'overruling' the decision of the DSS.

This is, of course, notwithstanding the voting problems that have plagued the WTO.[177] As Art. IX:1 WTO Agreement lays out: 'The WTO shall continue the practice of decision-making by consensus followed under the GATT 1947. Except as otherwise provided, where a decision cannot be arrived at by consensus, the matter shall be decided by voting. [...].' The practice of the WTO, however, indicates that whenever a decision is to be made, then it will be made by consensus. Voting in the 'consensus-dominated practice of the WTO'[178] has become a 'nearly total taboo',[179] but this could be remedied through practice, and thus the authoritative interpretation function of the Ministerial Conference and the General Council under Art. IX:2 WTO Agreement remains a practical and potentially viable opportunity for States to rein in any judicial legislation or *ultra vires* methods of treaty interpretation (leading to unforeseeable results) by the DSS and particularly the Appellate Body.

This section has focused on how treaty interpretation in the DSS functions, how it interacts with the VCLT and customary law, and some of the perceived problems of the regime. Overreaching and judicial legislation may be problems inherent in any dispute settlement regime, but the particular features of the WTO DSS (certainly in comparison to other international dispute settlement fora) present particular problems. The lack of precise standard or review and fairly loose obligation to apply customary rules of interpretation not only invite but create problems of a lack of legal certainty, and this problem should be remedied in order to preserve the autonomy of States in areas where they did not elect to cede their 'sovereignty'. As a more concrete example, and also because it has particular relevance to this study, the issue of 'like products' will be addressed next.

4.4.8   Problems in Interpretation: Like Products

National regulatory space, and especially the reach of the WTO into national regulatory space, is a particular focus of this work. Why then is the interpretation of the term 'like products' of particular relevance?

> [T]he specific coverage of these [WTO] obligations hinges upon the definition and resulting scope of 'like products'. A broad interpretation of the like products relationship would broaden the coverage of the basic WTO obligations, whereas narrow would reduce it.[180]

---

[177]*Ibid.*, 818.

[178]*Ibid.*, 806.

[179]*Ibid.*, 818.

[180]*Won-Mog Choi*, Like Products in International Trade Law: Towards a Consistent GATT/WTO Jurisprudence (Oxford, 2003), ix.

The reason for this is that the term 'like products' is used, *inter alia*, in the MFN and national treatment obligations outlined above. Where a WTO member is prevented from discriminating against 'like products' originating abroad, or from discriminating between 'like products' originating from different trading partners, then the scope of 'like products' determines the scope of these obligations. There is no definition of 'like products' given in the GATT or other covered agreements, but the phrase has produced a significant amount of jurisprudence in the DSS. In *Japan – Alcoholic Beverages*, the Appellate Body ruled that there was no single definition of likeness to be applied unanimously throughout the texts but rather referred to an 'accordion of likeness', stating that for different provisions:

> The concept of 'likeness' is a relative one that evokes the image of an accordion. The accordion of 'likeness' stretches and squeezes in different places as different provisions of the *WTO Agreement* are applied. The width of the accordion in any one of those places must be determined by the particular provision in which the term 'like' is encountered as well as by the context and the circumstances that prevail in any given case to which that provision may apply.[181]

Hudec describes two possible interpretations of the phrase within the WTO— either that it can be observed that the phrase appears in more than one GATT provision and that its meaning is likely to 'vary from one GATT provision to another'[182] or, going further, that

> [T]here may be identifiable and describable differences in the policy contexts of the various GATT Articles in which the term 'like product' is used, and that these policy differences may yield identifiable differences in the meaning, or at least in the range of meaning, accorded to that term from one Article to another.[183]

The statement of the Appellate Body in the *Japan – Alcohol* case that the 'the context and the circumstances that prevail in any given case' are relevant to the interpretation of 'like products' certainly appears to indicate that the meaning of the term can vary on a case-by-case basis—clearly posing problems of legal certainty and formal realisability. Further analysis of the jurisprudence of the DSS will later assess to what extent these problems actually exist under the WTO.

In the GATT, the term 'like products' appears in Arts. I:1; II:2(a); III:2; III:4; VI:1(a), (b)(i); VI:4; IX:1; X:2(c)(i),(ii); XIII:1; XVI:4; XIX:1(a), (b), with the terms 'like merchandise' and 'like commodities' also featuring several times in the agreement. The phrase also appears multiple instances in the covered agreements.[184] A full comparison of the possible policy reasons for differences in interpretation of each or any of these provisions and analysis of the jurisprudence relating to the actual interpretation of each of these articles by the DSS is beyond

---

[181] Appellate Body Report *Japan – Taxes on Alcoholic Beverages*, pg. 21.

[182] *Robert E. Hudec*, 'Like Product': The Differences in Meaning in GATT Articles I and III, in: Thomas Cottier/Petros Mavroidis (eds.), Regulatory Barriers and the Principle of Non-Discrimination in World Trade Law (Ann Arbor, 2000), 101.

[183] *Ibid.*, 101–102.

[184] Including Arts. 2.1, 5.1.1, 5.2.1, 5.2.5 of the TBT Agreement.

the scope of this work. The importance of the interpretation(s) of this phrase in some of the provisions becomes clear, however, when one takes into account the potential 'likeness' of environmental NPR PPMs.

Are two products that share the same physical characteristics but different (in terms of their impact on the environment) process and production methods 'like' in WTO law? If so, how far and in what ways is it possible for governments to enact legislation that makes product distinctions on the basis of these PPMs and relates to trade (including tariffs, import bans, other border measures, behind-the-border measures/non-tariff barriers to trade, labelling schemes, etc.)? The main provisions to be focused on here are as follows: Arts. I:1, where trading partners have products potentially deemed to be 'like' but with vastly different environmental impacts—can the non-environmentally friendly products be treated differently? Art. III:2, can taxes or other charges be applied to 'non-environmentally friendly' products of foreign origin that share the same physical characteristics as 'environmentally friendly' domestic products, in excess of what is applied to the domestic 'like products'? Art. III:4, can less favourable treatment 'in respect of all laws, regulations and requirements affecting their internal sale, offering for sale, purchase, transportation, distribution or use' be accorded to 'like products' of a foreign origin whose only difference to domestic products lies in the PPMs? And, finally, in relation to the GATT, what impact does 'likeness' that does not take into account PPMs—or what impact to NPR PPMs—have on the application of Art. XX general exceptions?

Furthermore, within the context of the TBT Agreement, what is the position of 'like products', how does this concept function in relation to technical barriers to trade and what is the relationship between 'like products' interpretations under the TBT and GATT?

The next section will seek to address some of the main substantive differences identified in the meanings of like products in these provisions (except Art. XX), whether the differing interpretations of the phrase are justified/justifiable, and what implications this has on the WTO DSS and on WTO members, from a power distributive point of view. The following chapter will go on to assess the provisions of the GATT and look more closely at how 'like products' functions in each instance.

Hudec points comfortably to the 'policy goals' behind differences in the interpretation of 'like product',[185] but how far this is justifiable in terms of the VCLT or broader customary means of interpretation (discussed above) is contestable. Are these policy goals providing part of the 'context' of the treaty, in terms of its interpretation—and what is the basis of this? It is clear from the arguments in relation to the structure of Art. III:2 (discussed below) that a different interpretation is plausible in this instance, but can this be extended more broadly to the concept 'accordion of likeness' put forward by the Appellate Body? The meaning of 'like

---

[185]*Hudec* (note 182), 108.

products' in Arts. I:1, III:2, III:4 and in the TBT Agreement, particularly with reference to NPR PPMs, will be discussed below.

During the drafting process, the wording 'identical or similar products' was used in conjunction with the national treatment obligation.[186] Though the term 'like products' is not defined anywhere in the WTO and covered agreements, the concepts of 'identical' and 'similar' are. Identical products are defined in Art. 15 of the Customs Evaluation Agreement as being

> Identical goods which are the same in all respects including physical characteristics, quality and reputation. Minor differences in appearance would not preclude goods otherwise conforming to the definition as being regarded as identical.

Similar goods are defined by Art. 15 as

> Similar goods means goods which, although not alike in all respects, have like characteristics and like component materials which enable them to perform the same functions and to be commercially interchangeable. The quality of the goods, their reputation and the existence of a trademark are among the factors to be considered in determining whether goods are similar.

The definition also 'seems to be shared by the Antidumping Agreement as well as the SCM [Subsidies and Countervailing Measures] Agreement'.[187] How these 'firm' (or certainly firmer) textual definitions of terms compare with the jurisprudence of the DSS in relation to 'like products' will be evidenced in the next section, dealing specifically with likeness in WTO jurisprudence.

4.5 Likeness in WTO Jurisprudence: Determined on a Case-by-Case Basis?

4.5.1 Likeness and MFN

Likeness, as outlined above, varies in meaning depending (at the very least) on the provision in question. Article I:1 states:

> any advantage, favour, privilege or immunity granted by any contracting party to any product originating in or destined for any other country shall be accorded immediately and unconditionally to the like product originating in or destined for the territories of all other contracting parties.

The main elucidation of the meaning of 'like product' under Art. I:1 comes from a GATT Panel Report. In *Spain – Unroasted Coffee*, the Panel assessed the characteristics of the products, their end uses and the tariff regimes of other

---

[186]*Choi* (note 180), 107; UN ECOSOC, Draft Report of the Technical Subcommittee of Committee II, UN Doc. E/PC/T/C.II/54 (1946), 4–5.

[187]*Choi* (note 180), 13.

members[188] while stating that 'organoleptic differences resulting from geographical factors, cultivation methods, the processing of the beans, and the genetic factor'[189] were 'not sufficient reason to allow for a different tariff treatment'.[190] As this case is one of the only GATT cases that fully treated and expanded on the idea of like products, it has been cited by many of the following cases in the GATT and also the WTO DSS, whether they concerned the definition of the phrase in Art. I or other GATT articles.[191]

This is not, however, the end of the story. In more recent reports being issued from the DSS, the importance of consumers' tastes and habits as a factor in likeness has been included in the interpretation of likeness. This does not mean that NPR PPMs can now affect whether a product is 'like', but if they are environmentally damaging then it could lead to a huge sway in consumers' tastes and habits and may even affect the competitiveness of such products. At the very least, it can be said that such an outright explicit rejection of such NPR PPMs as in *Spain – Unroasted Coffee* may arguably be treated differently today due to the inclusion of this factor as part of an assessment of likeness.[192]

The uncertainty of the parameters of 'like products' under Art. I:1 raises problems of formal realisability as it is not possible for States to understand the extent of their obligations and legislate accordingly. This raises issues of legitimacy and increases the likelihood of judicial lawmaking and overreach from the WTO, which further exacerbates the problem of legitimacy.

4.5.2   Art. III:2 Jurisprudence in Relation to Like Products

Article III:2 reads:

> The products of the territory of any contracting party imported into the territory of any other contracting party shall not be subject, directly or indirectly, to internal taxes or other internal charges of any kind in excess of those applied, directly or indirectly, to like domestic products. Moreover, no contracting party shall otherwise apply internal taxes or other internal charges to imported or domestic products in a manner contrary to the principles set forth in paragraph 1.*

The particular controversy of the interpretation of 'like products' under Art. III:2 was put to rest in 1996 when the Appellate Body 'overruled' two previous GATT Panel interpretations of the term in this article. The Panels in *United States – Measures Affecting Alcoholic and Malt Beverages*[193] and *United States – Taxes*

---

[188]*Van den Bossche* (note 5), 330.

[189]GATT Panel Report *Spain – Tariff Treatment of Unroasted Coffee*, para. 4.6.

[190]*Ibid.*

[191]*Hudec* (note 182), 116.

[192]*Van den Bossche* (note 5), 331.

[193]GATT Panel Report *United States — Measures Affecting Alcoholic and Malt Beverages*. See *Van den Bossche* (note 5), 354–355.

on Automobiles[194] had both relied on interpretations of the phrase 'like products' that did not actually assess the likeness of the products at all, or at least not in the way any textual approach to treaty interpretation would comfortably allow. The Panels instead looked at the 'aims' and the 'effects' of the production distinction. They assessed 'whether the product distinction in question had the "aim" of protecting domestic industry, and the question whether that product distinction had the "effect" of protecting the domestic industry'.[195] The WTO DSS, however, in *Japan – Alcohol* not only laid out the accordion of likeness analogy but also made the pronouncement that the so-called aims and effects test was an inappropriate interpretation of Art. III:2. The Appellate Body agreed with the Panel in this case that 'like products' ought to be interpreted narrowly in relation to Art. III:2.

The Body stated:

> Because the second sentence of Article III:2 provides for a separate and distinctive consideration of the protective aspect of a measure in examining its application to a broader category of products that are not 'like products' as contemplated by the first sentence, we agree with the Panel that the first sentence of Article III:2 must be construed narrowly so as not to condemn measures that its strict terms are not meant to condemn.[196]

Furthermore, with regard to the aim and effects test, the Panel noted 'that the proposed aim-and-effect test is not consistent with the wording of Article III:2, first sentence' and 'that the basis of the aim-and-effect test is found in the words "so as to afford protection" contained in Article III:1' but that Art. III:2 'contains no reference to those words'.[197] The Panel thus rejected the 'aims and effects' test in the context of Art. III:2. The Appellate Body affirmed the reasoning of the Panel in this regard.[198]

This rejection of 'aim and effects' of product distinction aimed to eliminate the assessment of product distinctions based on regulatory intent[199] as such intent may be impossible to determine and because such an interpretation of Art. III:2 could affect the Art. XX GATT general exceptions. The Panel noted:

> the list of exceptions contained in Article XX of GATT 1994 could become redundant or useless because the aim-and-effect test does not contain a definitive list of grounds justifying departure from the obligations that are otherwise incorporated in Article III. The purpose of Article XX is to provide a list of exceptions, subject to the conditions that they 'are not applied in a manner which would constitute a means of arbitrary or unjustifiable discrimination between countries where the same conditions prevail, or a disguised restriction of international trade', that could justify deviations from the obligations imposed under GATT. Consequently, in principle, a WTO Member could, for

---

[194]GATT Panel Report *United States – Taxes on Automobiles*, para. 5.10.

[195]*Hudec* (note 182), 103.

[196]Appellate Body Report *Japan –Taxes on Alcoholic Beverages*, pg. 19–20.

[197]Panel Report *Japan –Taxes on Alcoholic Beverages*, para 6.16.

[198]Appellate Body Report *Japan –Taxes on Alcoholic Beverages*, pg. 23.

[199]*Van den Bossche* (note 5), 352.

example, invoke protection of health in the context of invoking the aim-and-effect test. The Panel noted that if this were the case, then the standard of proof established in Article XX would effectively be circumvented. WTO Members would not have to prove that a health measure is 'necessary' to achieve its health objective.[200]

Instead, under Art. III:2, the term, alongside being construed narrowly, should be

examined on a case-by-case basis. This would allow a fair assessment in each case of the different elements that constitute 'similar' product. Some criteria were suggested for determining, on a case-by-case basis, whether a product is 'similar': the products end-uses in a given market; consumers' tastes and habits, which change from country to country, the products' properties, nature and quality.[201]

The Appellate Body in *Japan – Alcohol* found that this approach, quoted from the 1970 Report on *Border Tax Adjustments*, was 'helpful in identifying on a case-by-case basis the range of like products that falls within the limits of Article III:2, first sentence, of the GATT 1994'.[202] Other factors that have been assessed include tariff classification.[203]

Much has been made of the particular structure of Art. III:2 in the interpretation of 'like products', and this is because the second sentence includes an obligation not to 'apply internal taxes or other internal charges to imported products in a manner contrary to the principles set forth in paragraph 1', those being that, *inter alia*, taxes, charges, laws, regulations and requirements 'should not be applied to imported or domestic products so as to afford protection to domestic production'.[204] In *Japan – Alcohol*, the Appellate Body described Art III:1 thus:

Article III:1 articulates a general principle that internal measures should not be applied so as to afford protection to domestic production. This general principle informs the rest of Article III. The purpose of Article III:1 is to establish this general principle as a guide to understanding and interpreting the specific obligations contained in Article III:2 and in the other paragraphs of Article III, while respecting, and not diminishing in any way, the meaning of the words used in the texts of the other paragraphs.[205]

An *Ad Note* to Art. III:2 reads:

A tax conforming to the requirements of the first sentence of paragraph 2 would be considered to be inconsistent with the provisions of the second sentence only in cases where competition was involved between, on the one hand, the taxed product and, on the other hand, a directly competitive or substitutable product which was not similarly taxed.

---

[200]Panel Report *Japan – Taxes on Alcoholic Beverages*, para 6.17. For further analysis of Art. XX exceptions, see Ch. 6.5.

[201]Report of the Working Party on *Border Tax Adjustments* (1970), para. 18; Appellate Body Report *Japan –Taxes on Alcoholic Beverages*, pg. 23.

[202]Appellate Body Report *Japan –Taxes on Alcoholic Beverages*, pg. 23.

[203]See, for example, GATT Working Party Report *Australia – Ammonium Sulphate*, para. 8; GATT Panel Report *EEC – Measures on Animal Feed Proteins*, para. 4.22.

[204]Art. III:1 GATT.

[205]Appellate Body Report *Japan –Taxes on Alcoholic Beverages*, pg. 18.

So while Art. III:2 first sentence is informed by Art. III:1, the first sentence does not specifically invoke it. The *Ad Note* assists in the interpretation of the relationship between the two sentences by providing an example of a situation where a specific type of conduct would breach the obligation contained in the second sentence but not the first. The generally accepted interpretation of Art. III:2 first sentence is that it is 'concerned with the treatment of "like" products, whereas the second sentence is concerned with the treatment of "directly competitive or substitutable" products'[206]—a 'broader category' than like products.[207]

As can be seen from the foregoing, the interpretation of 'like products' under Art. III:2 is of a complex nature and has not been interpreted consistently by the DSS. Although the structure of the provision and its relationship with the *Ad Note* may feasibly have been intended by the parties to produce a different meaning for the phrase 'like products' in this provision, the approach of the DSS has not brought greater clarity, and the scope of the phrase in this provision is still lamentably vague. While a more precise definition from the DSS may result in judicial lawmaking (which is currently carried out without overarching justification), it would at least provide legal certainty that would benefit the regime as a whole.

4.5.3 Article III:4 National Treatment Obligation and Like Products

As mentioned above, the structural difference between Art. III:2 and Art. III:4 has led to the accordion of likeness being squeezed differently in each case. Article III:4, first sentence, reads:

> The products of the territory of any contracting party imported into the territory of any other contracting party shall be accorded treatment no less favourable than that accorded to like products of national origin in respect of all laws, regulations and requirements affecting their internal sale, offering for sale, purchase, transportation, distribution or use.

There is no equivalent second sentence in Art. III:4 like the one that appears in Art. III.2.[208] As the inclusion and interpretation of the second sentence of Art. III:2 materially affects the interpretation of like products in the first sentence, the lack of such a sentence in Art. III:4, following the canons of treaty interpretation, must produce a material difference in the interpretation of the phrase in Art. III:4. While it is 'currently unclear exactly how the scope of "like products" differs between the two provisions',[209] some guidance has been provided in jurisprudence of the DSS.

---

[206]*Hudec* (note 182), 106.

[207]*Ibid.*

[208]The second sentence of Art. III:4 relates specifically to transport charges, and is not of relevance in the assessment of like products.

[209]*Nathalie Bernasconi-Osterwalder/Daniel Magraw/Maria Julia Olivia/Morcos Orellana/Elizabeth Tuerk*, Environment and Trade: A Guide to WTO Jurisprudence (London, 2006), 10.

In *EC – Asbestos*, the issue of 'like products' was directly addressed by the Appellate Body. The Body stated:

> In previous Reports, we have held that the scope of 'like' products in this sentence is to be construed 'narrowly'. This reading of 'like' in Article III:2 might be taken to suggest a similarly narrow reading of 'like' in Article III:4, since both provisions form part of the same Article. However, both of these paragraphs of Article III constitute specific expressions of the overarching, 'general principle', set forth in Article III:1 of the GATT 1994. As we have previously said, the 'general principle' set forth in Article III:1 'informs' the rest of Article III and acts 'as a guide to understanding and interpreting the specific obligations contained' in the other paragraphs of Article III, including paragraph 4. Thus, in our view, Article III:1 has particular contextual significance in interpreting Article III:4, as it sets forth the 'general principle' pursued by that provision. Accordingly, in interpreting the term 'like products' in Article III:4, we must turn, first, to the 'general principle' in Article III:1, rather than to the term 'like products' in Article III:2.[210]

In this case, the Appellate Body found that, due to this difference, a difference in interpretation was required between the two articles. The Body 'explained the parameters within which' like products under Art. III:4 'must fall' in order that the article maintained its 'desired consistency'.[211] 'Like products' under Art. III:4 must then 'be broader than Art. III.2's "like products", but not as broad as the combined scope of Art. III:2's two products categories'.[212] However, it is unclear 'where in that continuum' 'like products' actually lie under Art. III:4, and the Body itself stated that 'it is difficult, if not impossible, in the abstract, to indicate precisely where on this spectrum the word "like" in Article III:4 of the GATT 1994 falls'.[213]

While from a structural perspective this disparity in interpretation may have some basis, the approach of the DSS thus far has been too imprecise to give any greater clarity to WTO members about the scope of their obligations. This is a fairly serious assertion, on the basis that the coverage of the WTO obligations 'hinges upon the definition and resulting scope of "like products". A broad interpretation of the like products relationship would broaden the coverage of the basic WTO obligations, whereas narrow would reduce it.'[214] If the interpretation of 'like products' is largely indeterminate, changes dramatically over time and is essentially at the will of the DSS, then so is the scope of the basic WTO obligations (MFN and national treatment).

Furthermore, it has been noted that the economic emphasis of the Appellate Body in its assessment in *EC – Asbestos* has raised concerns '[w]hether such an economic emphasis can adequately take into account environmental or health

---

[210] Appellate Body Report *European Communities – Measures Affecting Asbestos and Asbestos-Containing Products*, para. 93.

[211] *Bernasconi-Osterwalder et al.* (note 209), 12.

[212] *Ibid.*

[213] Appellate Body Report *European Communities – Measures Affecting Asbestos and Asbestos-Containing Products*, para. 99.

[214] *Choi* (note 180), ix.

concerns arising from trade in certain products'.[215] Such a position can be evidenced in the emphasis of the Appellate Body that 'a determination of "likeness" under Art. III.4 is, fundamentally, a determination about the nature and the extent of the competitive relationship between and among products'. The relationship between economic objectives and like products will be dealt with below in relation to the thesis put forward by *Choi*, but first a paradigm of interpretation put forward by *Hudec* to attempt to explain 'like products' in the GATT will be explored.

4.5.4 A Paradigm?

Hudec assessed that in order to reconcile the 'apparent conflict between the wording of Paragraphs 2 and 4 of Article 3',[216] we need to assume that either 'the term "like product" simply has a different meaning in Paragraph 4'[217] or that the term 'like products' is broader than assumed. *Hudec* favoured the second explanation for its ability to explain the disparity in structure, arguing that, following this interpretation, the phrase like products 'includes a lot of what we would normally call "not-like-but-directly-competitive" products, and that the second sentence of Paragraph 2 is meant to cover only quite dissimilar goods'.[218] Although he admitted that this approach would lead to a very narrow interpretation of 'directly competitive' in Art III:2, he still believed that 'it was the most logical way to make paragraphs 2 and 4 at least roughly consistent despite their quite different structures'.[219]

The interpretation of 'like products' in Art. I:1 for *Hudec* can feasibly be applied differently to different measures as

> Although the words of Article I:1 appear to apply the same MFN principle to each of these different subject areas, defined in terms of what appears to be the same 'like product' concept, the fact that the provision covers so many different measures raises the possibility that the content of the MFN rule may not be the same for each area.[220]

In Arts. I and III, it can be argued that the MFN and national treatment obligations have similar policy goals and are similar from an economic perspective

---

[215]*Bernasconi-Osterwalder et al.* (note 209), 14.

[216]*Hudec* (note 182), 107.

[217]*Ibid.*

[218]*Ibid.*, 107–108.

[219]*Ibid.*, 108. Hudec also concedes here that this would mean that there was disparity in the application of the national treatment obligation, with broader protection for foreign products against tax discrimination than other types of regulatory discrimination. He outlines that this could be justified, however, by arguing: '(a) Differences in tax rates are inherently arbitrary, and thus should be harder to justify than regulatory distinctions. (b) It is easier to trace the competitive effects on tax differences (money charges) on dissimilar but competitively related products than it is to trace the effects of regulatory distinctions on such products.'

[220]*Ibid.*, 109.

as both prohibit a sort of protectionist, market-distorting behavior.[221] *Hudec* found that the justification for any difference in interpretation between 'like products' in Art. I:1 and Art. III could be based, however, on the fact that while in the application of Art. I:1 'like products' concerns tariffs, in the application of Art. III it does not. Article I, by allowing tariffs, inherently and implicitly also allows tariff protection. *Hudec* saw that it was thus necessary for governments to have the ability to draw lines between products: 'in order to confine protection to those imports which do in fact threaten domestic producers, and also to confine tariff liberalization to those products for which the removal of protection will be found acceptable to domestic interests'.[222] A further issue that must be addressed by Art. I is that of reciprocity in tariff negotiation and the problem of 'free riders' (those benefitting from the concessions given by others without contributing themselves). *Hudec* argued that this is not explicitly done in Art. I, although

> governments have agreed, tacitly, that they may discriminate against free riders by making fine product distinctions in their tariffs – product distinctions that are calculated to limit the benefit of tariff reductions to the countries that have not granted equivalent concessions in return.[223]

These two fundamental differences can be invoked to support the distinct interpretation of Art. I and Art. III, as they are not in any way relevant to the interpretation of 'like products' in Art. III.

Hudec's subsequent analysis of the case law of the WTO DSS did not, however, support his thesis on either count. Although coming to the problem of 'like products' from the policy perspective served to produce, at least partially, a convincing paradigm for differentiating the interpretation of like products in Art. III:2 and Art. III:4, and Art. III and Art I.1 of the GATT, the case law did not provide adequate support for treating this method of differentiation as constituting an actual description of the meaning and function of 'like products' in these articles. In fact, he concluded that due to the likelihood that subsequent decisions will tend to a 'narrower rather than broader interpretation',[224] 'it may be a long time before the policy distinctions argued for [. . .] are accepted by WTO decisions'.[225]

The conclusions of *Hudec* were drawn based on the case law available at the time of publication (2000) and reaching back to the early GATT days. Since the paper was published, there has not been a huge amount of expansion or divergence in the case law of the DSS, and none explicitly in support of *Hudec's* paradigm. The

---

[221]*Ibid.*, 108–9.

[222]*Ibid.*, 109.

[223]*Ibid.*, 109. In support of his argument Hudec cites the distinctions made in: GATT Panel Report *Spain – Tariff Treatment of Unroasted Coffee*; GATT Panel Report *Germany – Treatment by Germany of Imports of Sardines*. It should be noted, however, that this tacit agreement is not considered by Hudec to be far reaching and can only be utilised in limited circumstances. See *ibid.*, 109–112.

[224]*Ibid.*, 120.

[225]*Ibid.*, 121.

EC – Asbestos Appellate Body Report, discussed above, did attempt to produce a semblance of clarity in describing the relationship between Art. III:2 and Art III:4, but stopped short of providing any actual clarity. The long-awaited *EC – Biotech* Panel report chose not to address the issue of likeness at all but rather made its recommendations based on the conformity of the measures in question with the SPS Agreement (which has no 'like products' related MFN or national treatment obligations).

What can be seen, however, is a broadening of the concept of 'like products' in such a manner that the DSS can be said to have 'marched deep into the territory of traditional regulatory autonomy'.[226] This argumentation is based on the introduction of potential or future competition as a feature of 'likeness' that will be considered by the DSS in its assessment.[227] This particular feature was introduced by the Panel in *Korea – Alcoholic Beverages* and upheld by the Appellate Body. In its appeal, Korea argued that the Panel had erred in its interpretation of 'directly competitive or substitutable product' by relying on 'potential competition'.[228] This development has been described by *Choi* as creating such a divergence in the coverage of likeness under the WTO that 'the WTO tribunal seems to be equipped with an accordion in each hand – one being the traditional "accordion of provision-by-provision" and the other the brand-new "accordion of potentiality"'.[229]

4.5.5   An Economic Basis for Interpretation?

In *Choi's* seminal work on like products ('Like Products' in International Trade Law: Towards a Consistent GATT/WTO Jurisprudence) the aim of 'Mastering the Accordion' is specifically set out.[230] In order to do so, *Choi* proposes an economic basis for the interpretation of 'like products' in which economic theory is applied in international economic law. This is achieved through economic analysis of market forces in order to assess whether products are truly like. The approach is partially supported by the WTO DSS case law as, beginning in the *Japan – Alcoholic Beverages* case, the Appellate Body began a new approach to the determination of like products that included 'directly competitive or substitutable products' and 'explicitly puts emphasis on the marketplace'.[231] *Choi* seeks to expand on this development to see the Appellate Body and then the DSS gravitate more strongly towards economic analysis. *Choi* defines economic analysis as 'an analysis that is based on efficiency and a welfare maximising way of thinking and that employs

---

[226]*Choi* (note 180), 154.

[227]*Ibid.*

[228]Appellate Body Report *Korea – Taxes on Alcoholic Beverages*, pg. 32 (para. 111).

[229]*Choi* (note 180), 30.

[230]*Ibid.*, 1.

[231]*Choi* (note 180), xxi.

econometric tools to the utmost extent possible and concepts developed in the science of economics'.[232]

While this approach is laudable in several ways, above all for the proposed consistency it would introduce (according to *Choi*), there are also several problems with the idea, the foremost being the lack of textual basis for such an interpretation. Although the broad idea could certainly be read into the provisions on 'like products', in exploring the idea further *Choi* appears at times to enter into the realm of unbridled speculation that cannot be reconciled with the texts of the agreement, and going beyond what the DSS has until now contemplated. The fact that this approach was also not what was imagined by negotiators,[233] and thus may be argued to potentially affect the balance struck at Uruguay, is also a significant factor in the (lack of) legitimacy of any such approach.

4.5.6   Like Products and the TBT

As mentioned above, 'like products' is also a phrase that is included in the TBT Agreement. What is important to note here is that the interpretation deviates from that in respect of the GATT (as the accordion will be squeezed differently depending on the context) and thus raises further issues of consistency, legal certainty and formal realisability.

The 'likeness' of the products under Art. 2.1 TBT was particularly at issue in *US – Clove Cigarettes*.[234] The Panel in this case took a 'purpose based' approach,[235] which the Appellate Body rejected in favour of a competition-based approach. The Body stated that a determination of likeness under Art. 2.1 is 'a determination about the nature and extent of a competitive relationship between and among the products at issue'.[236] This move appears to, in some ways, parallel the jurisprudence of the DSS under the GATT in relation to a move towards the competitiveness of the products at issue. Further jurisprudence from the DSS is required in order to assess better the parameters of 'like products' under the TBT Agreement.

---

[232]*Ibid.*, 171–172.

[233]See, e.g., *ibid.*, 94–95.

[234]Panel Report *United States – Measures Affecting the Production and Sale of Clove Cigarettes*; Appellate Body Report *United States – Measures Affecting the Production and Sale of Clove Cigarettes*.

[235]Panel Report *United States – Measures Affecting the Production and Sale of Clove Cigarettes*, para. 7.119; *Peter Van den Bossche/Werner Zdouc*, The Law and Policy of the World Trade Organization (Cambridge, 3rd ed. 2013), 866.

[236]Appellate Body Report *United States – Measures Affecting the Production and Sale of Clove Cigarettes*, para. 120.

4.5.7 Likeness in WTO Jurisprudence: NPR PPMs

The question of the interpretation of 'like products' is fundamental in any assessment of the regulatory freedom of States in the area of environmental protection as many processes and production methods are damaging to the environment but do not affect the end product. The following chapters will explore the provisions of the GATT and TBT and the relevant case law in context with respect to this issue. The crux of the problem can be seen very clearly from the following two quotations. The first comes from an unadopted GATT Panel Report and the second from a recent textbook on the law and policy of the WTO:

> Article III:4 calls for a comparison of the treatment of imported tuna *as a product* with that of domestic tuna *as a product*. Regulations governing the taking of dolphins incidental to the taking of tuna could not possibly affect tuna as a product. Article III:4 therefore obliges the United States to accord treatment to Mexican tuna no less favourable than that accorded to United States tuna, whether or not the incidental taking of dolphins by Mexican vessels corresponded to that of United States vessels.[237]

> [t]he concept of 'likeness' has evolved since the 1991 *US – Tuna (Mexico)* case. The question of whether NPR PPMs may be of relevance in the determination of 'likeness' now requires a more nuanced answer than that given by the Panel in *US – Tuna (Mexico)*. It should be noted that NPR PPMs may have an impact on consumer preferences and tastes, and thus on the nature and the extent of the competitive relationship between products.[238]

Together these quotations demonstrate the problem as it was, the possible change and development in the law, and how important the interpretation of 'like products' is to address the issues in this study.

This section has given a brief overview of the problems of interpretation of the phrase 'like products' and demonstrates how pervasive they are in the system. There is no consistency in interpretation, no firm adherence to the text of the agreements or negotiating history and a clear lack of legal certainty and formal realisability in this area. Furthermore, the jurisprudence of the DSS in this regard may be seen as amounting to judicial lawmaking, which furthers problems of legitimacy for the system as a whole. The deficiencies in this area lead to an increased likelihood of litigation, creating a larger burden on developing countries, which may suffer from a lack of expertise both in the legal teams that would represent them in Geneva and also in crafting legislation. The problem with a lack of legal certainty and formal realisability in the context of drafting legislation is clear; national law cannot be invoked to excuse the breach of an international obligation, and the difficulty in crafting legislation so as not to fall foul of international obligations creates a particular burden in this context. States do not (and cannot) know the extent of their obligations and are thus discouraged from

---

[237]GATT Panel Report *United States – Restrictions on Imports of Tuna Restrictions on the Import of Tuna (Tuna/Dolphin I)*, para. 5.15.

[238]*Van den Bossche* (note 5), 381.

legislating or must calculate the potential consequences of litigation before legislating—disadvantageous for all States but a particular burden for developing States.

4.6   Summary

This chapter has sought to highlight some of the most problematic areas within the judicial functioning of the WTO DSS. The judicialisation of the DSS since its inception in 1994 means that whatever the intention of the drafters and negotiating parties is, when it is assessed today, it is as a fully functioning judicial dispute settlement organ. The problems raised in this chapter must be addressed in order for this powerful judicial body to continue to function with legitimacy. The answer to these problems would ideally come in the form of renegotiation and amendment to the DSU, but bearing in mind the failed Doha Round this may be unrealistic. In this context, the authoritative interpretation function under Art. XI:2 would be a possible avenue to be pursued by WTO members in order to ensure that the interpretation of some of the most controversial provisions of the WTO and covered agreements reflects the will of the members.

Chapter 5
Trade-Restrictive Environmental Measures and the GATT

5.1 Overview

In the preceding chapters, the particular history and structure of the WTO has been discussed, alongside a more in-depth assessment of the role and function of the DSS and some of its particularly problematic areas. This chapter will now go on to examine the provisions of the GATT that are relevant in the context of national regulatory mechanisms and, also with reference to case law the following chapter of this chapter, attempt to assess the regulatory freedom of WTO members and their relative bargaining power.

5.2 Article I:1—Most Favoured Nation

5.2.1 Content of the Norm

The Art. I:1 most favoured nation clause reads:

> With respect to customs duties and charges of any kind imposed on or in connection with importation or exportation or imposed on the international transfer of payments for imports or exports, and with respect to the method of levying such duties and charges, and with respect to all rules and formalities in connection with importation and exportation, and with respect to all matters referred to in paragraphs 2 and 4 of Article III,* any advantage, favour, privilege or immunity granted by any contracting party to any product originating in or destined for any other country shall be accorded immediately and unconditionally to the like product originating in or destined for the territories of all other contracting parties.

The MFN obligation contained in Art. I:1 seeks to eliminate discrimination between trading partners. It may not be immediately apparent why a measure that is, on its face, origin neutral and non-discriminatory (such as a charge imposed on the import of a certain product, extraneous to the tariff binding, or a higher tariff for

© Springer International Publishing AG 2017
A.R. Maggio, *Environmental Policy, Non-Product Related Process and Production Methods and the Law of the World Trade Organization*, European Yearbook of International Economic Law 1, DOI 10.1007/978-3-319-61155-6_5

a particular product that is also origin neutral) may nevertheless be deemed to violate Art. I:1. Creating such charges or implementing other trade-restrictive measures that are also levied within the State in question and apply to all trading partners equally appears to be an attempt to even the playing field, rather than discrimination or protectionism. However, what is important in this context is the interpretation of 'like products'. When the products are treated as 'like', even if the NPR PPMs are, on the one hand, environmentally friendly and, on the other, 'highly polluting', then when charges applied only apply to a product produced in a particular State or group of States but not to others, the argument could be made that such a charge was discriminatory and a breach of the MFN obligation. This could occur, for example, in a situation where a particular product is produced in developing countries using NPR PPMs that are harmful to the environment but with environmentally friendly NPR PPMs in developed countries.

In *EC – Bananas III*, the Appellate Body stated:

> The essence of the non-discrimination obligations is that like products should be treated equally, irrespective of their origins. As no participant disputes that all bananas are like products, the non-discrimination provisions apply to *all* imports of bananas, irrespective of whether and how a Member categorizes or subdivides these imports for administrative or other reasons.[1]

Though in the case of bananas such reasoning appears solid, the policy considerations involved in the differential treatment of products with differing NPR PPMs are not so obviously covered by it. In fact, as will be demonstrated in the following chapters, it is not so clear that such agreement now exists (and even in the case of bananas, it is a hugely controversial question whether those that have been genetically modified can be considered 'like' those that have not). Some of the major issues surrounding 'like products' were highlighted in the previous chapter in the context of the role of the WTO DSS in treaty interpretation.[2]

The obligation contained in Art. I:1, though described as 'the cornerstone of the GATT',[3] and continuing to be 'both central and essential to assuring the success of a global rules-based system for trade in goods',[4] was described by the 2004 Sutherland Report thus:

> MFN is no longer the rule; it is almost the exception. Certainly, much trade between the major economies is still conducted on an MFN basis. However, what has been termed the 'spaghetti bowl' of customs unions, common markets, regional and bilateral free trade areas, preferences and an endless assortment of miscellaneous trade deals has almost reached the point where MFN treatment is exceptional treatment.[5]

---

[1] Appellate Body Report *European Communities – Regime for the Importation, Sale and Distribution of Bananas*, pg. 81 (para. 190).

[2] See Ch. 4.11.

[3] Appellate Body Report *European Communities – Conditions for the Granting of Tariff Preferences to Developing Countries*, pg. 41 (para. 101).

[4] Appellate Body Report *United States – Section 211 Omnibus Appropriations Act of 1998*, pg. 85 (para. 297).

[5] WTO, The Future of the WTO: Addressing Institutional Challenges in the New Millennium (2004), para. 60.

The existence of such customs agreements or free trade areas must be borne in mind in any assessment of the impact of the MFN obligation. The acceptance of preferential trade agreements (through Art. XXIV) of any sort under the WTO further enhances the bargaining power of strong diverse economies as they have the ability to enter into more agreements and on better terms than developing countries. As such, they are able to choose with a higher degree of freedom against whom they wish to 'discriminate'[6] by not entering into such preferential agreements with them. Although the language of Art. I:1 speaks of 'any advantage, favour, privilege or immunity' being 'accorded immediately and unconditionally to the like product originating in or destined for the territories of all other contracting parties', the acceptance of preferential trade agreements under the WTO means that this obligation only applies to such advantages that are granted outside of these preferential arrangements.

According to the WTO website, 'As of 31 January 2014, some 583 notifications of RTAs [Regional Trade Agreements] (counting goods, services and accessions separately) had been received by the GATT/WTO. Of these, 377 were in force.'[7] Thirty-one preferential trade arrangements are also listed on the website.[8] All WTO members are parties to at least one regional trade agreements.[9] It should also be noted that the Art. I:1 obligation 'concerns not only advantages granted to other WTO Members, but also advantages granted to other countries (including non-WTO Members)'.[10]

Coming back to the provision itself, the Art. I:1 most favoured nation clause lays out a three-tier test of consistency:

- whether the measure at issue confers a trade 'advantage' of the kind covered by Art. I:1;
- whether the products concerned are 'like products'; and

---

[6]Although it must be underlined that this 'discrimination' is still taking place within the framework of the WTO and covered Agreements, so that while it is discrimination *de facto* – in terms of giving preferences to some and not to others – it is not incompatible with the GATT non-discrimination provisions.

[7]http://www.wto.org/english/tratop_e/region_e/region_e.htm (last accessed on 05/03/2017).

[8]http://ptadb.wto.org/ptaList.aspx (last accessed on 05/03/2017).

[9]See WTO, Regionalism: Friends or Rivals?, available at: http://www.wto.org/english/thewto_e/whatis_e/tif_e/bey1_e.htm (last accessed on 05/03/2017). Mongolia was for a considerable time the only member not party to a regional trade agreement, but has now concluded one with Japan: https://docs.wto.org/dol2fe/Pages/FE_Search/FE_S_S006.aspx?Query=%28%20@Symbol=%20wt/reg*%20and%20n%29%20and%20%28%20@Title=%20mongolia%20%29&Language=ENGLISH&Context=FomerScriptedSearch&languageUIChanged=true# (last accessed on 05/03/2017).

[10]*Peter Van den Bossche*, The Law and Policy of the World Trade Organization (Cambridge, 2nd edn. 2008), 328.

- whether the advantage at issue is granted 'immediately and unconditionally' to all like products originating in or destined for the territory of another contracting party.[11]

To fulfil the first point, the advantage must be with respect to 'customs duties and charges of any kind imposed on or in connection with importation or exportation or imposed on the international transfer of payments for imports or exports, and with respect to the method of levying such duties and charges, and with respect to all rules and formalities in connection with importation and exportation, and with respect to all matters referred to in paragraphs 2 and 4 of Article III'. Articles III:2 and III:4 cover 'internal taxes or other internal charges of any kind in excess of those applied, directly or indirectly, to like domestic products' and 'laws, regulations and requirements affecting their internal sale, offering for sale, purchase, transportation, distribution or use'. According to the Panel in *EC – Commercial Vessels*, the application of the MFN obligation to the matters referred to in Arts. III:2 and III:4 'refers to the subject matter of those provisions in terms of their substantive legal content'.[12] The exception to Art. III:4 for domestic subsidies contained in Art. III:8 (a) also exists in relation to what is covered substantively in Art. I:1.[13]

The areas in which these advantages can be granted are expressly stipulated, but what then is meant by advantages? It is recognised that in the interpretation of Art. I:1, Panels and the Appellate Body have cast 'a very wide net'.[14] It covers not only advantages *sensu stricto* but also the application of trade disadvantages to some WTO members and not to others (or other non-WTO member trading partners). The types of measures that have been construed as advantages must relate to the measures listed above, and a complete list is not possible. Some examples include whether a tariff is bound or not,[15] the application of consular taxes[16] and 'tax and customs duty benefits'.[17]

Whatever the advantage is, the applicability of Art. I:1 in relation to this study is relevant where these advantages have been conferred on the basis of differences in products that do not affect the end product. The particular interpretation of the term 'like products', the second point in the three-tier test of consistency, is thus of

---

[11] Slightly adapted from *Van den Bossche, ibid.*, 325.

[12] Panel Report *European Communities – Measures Affecting Trade in Commercial Vessels*, para. 7.75.

[13] *Ibid.*; see also *Van den Bossche* (note 10), 328.

[14] *Ibid.*, 326.

[15] GATT Panel Report *Spain – Tariff Treatment of Unroasted Coffee*, para. 4.3.

[16] GATT, Ruling by the Chairman: The Phrase 'Charges of Any Kind' in Article 1:1 in Relation to Consular Taxes, BISDII/12 (1948).

[17] Panel Report *Indonesia – Certain Measures Affecting the Automobile Industry*, para. 14.147. See further *Van den Bossche* (note 10), 326–327. The more controversial debate on the applicability of Art. I:1 to advantages in the fields of safeguards, anti-dumping duties and countervailing duties are not relevant to this study, but see further *ibid.*, 327.

crucial importance here. Although in the previous chapter it was mentioned that, due to the fact that 'consumers' tastes and habits' are now to be included in any assessment of 'likeness' under Art. I:1, and this could mean that the interpretation of like products under Art. I:1 would not wholly rule out a differential treatment on the basis of NPR PPMs, it continues to be the 'prevailing view' that they are not relevant and that 'products produced in an environmentally unfriendly manner cannot be treated differently from products produced in an environmentally friendly manner on the sole basis of the difference in PPMs'.[18]

For example, in *EC – Fur Seals*, the products concerned[19] were all considered 'like', despite a major difference in their hunting operations.[20] In this case, Canada and Norway sought to challenge the consistency of an EU Regulation[21] that conditioned market access on whether the hunting of the seals had been 'traditionally conducted by Inuit and other indigenous communities and contribute[d] to their subsistence', ruling out commercial hunting: clearly trade-restrictive measures based on a sort of NPR PPM. In the case, Norway and Canada challenged, *inter alia*, the conformity of the regulation with Art. I:1 on the basis that seal products from Greenland would qualify for the exception but that products originating in their territories would not. The Panel and then the Appellate Body agreed.

The Appellate Body stated that

> while virtually all Greenlandic seal products are likely to qualify under the IC exception for access to the EU market, the vast majority of seal products from Canada and Norway do not meet the IC requirements for access to the EU market. Thus, the Panel found that, 'in terms of its design, structure, and expected operation', the measure at issue detrimentally affects the conditions of competition for Canadian and Norwegian seal products as compared to seal products originating in Greenland. Based on these findings, the Panel considered, correctly in our view, that the measure at issue is inconsistent with Article I:1 because it does not, 'immediately and unconditionally', extend the same market access advantage to Canadian and Norwegian seal products that it accords to seal products originating from Greenland.[22]

---

[18]*Van den Bossche* (note 10), 331.

[19]The case concerned products: 'either processed or unprocessed, deriving or obtained from seals, including meat, oil, blubber, organs, raw fur skins and tanned fur skins, as well as articles (such as clothing and accessories, and omega-3 capsules') made from fur skins and oil', see Panel Report *European Communities – Measures Prohibiting the Importation and Marketing Of Seal Products*, para. 2.2; Art. 2 (2) Regulation (EC) No 1007/2009 of the European Parliament And Of The Council of 16 September 2009 dictates that '"seal product" means all products, either processed or unprocessed, deriving or obtained from seals, including meat, oil, blubber, organs, raw fur skins and fur skins, tanned or dressed, including fur skins assembled in plates, crosses and similar forms, and articles made from fur skins'.

[20]Appellate Report *European Communities – Measures Prohibiting the Importation and Marketing Of Seal Products*, paras. 7.592–7.600.

[21]Regulation (EC) No 1007/2009 of the European Parliament And Of The Council of 16 September 2009.

[22]Appellate Body Report *European Communities – Measures Prohibiting the Importation and Marketing Of Seal Products*, para. 5.95.

This clearly demonstrates that even if the measures are origin neutral on their face (though perhaps not in design), they will be considered to breach Art. I:1 if they result *de facto* in discrimination.

In this case, the products here were considered to be like:

> based on *inter alia* the following criteria: (a) the properties, nature, and quality of the products; (b) the end-uses of the products; (c) consumers' tastes and habits; and (d) the tariff classification of the products.[23]

The European Union did 'not contest that all seal products are "like products", irrespective of the distinction drawn in the measure between non-conforming and conforming products'.[24] The particular reasons why the EU did not attempt to distinguish the products concerned on the basis of 'likeness' may be manifold. In particular, a partial ban may not have been judged to reflect 'consumers' tastes and habits' in the same way that the Art. XX (a) moral exception (as was successfully invoked in this case)[25] appears to justify the ban but not the exceptions to it. In this case, the Appellate Body found that the invocation of public morals for the ban was provisionally justified under Art. XX (a) but that the exception for traditionally hunted seal products meant that the EU ban did not meet the requirements of the chapeau of Art. XX.[26] This demonstrates that even where the likeness of products is not brought into question, treating products differently on the basis of NPR PPMs may lead regulations to fall foul of other provisions of the GATT.

The interpretation of 'like products' under Art. I:1 for the moment appears to be restricted to the characteristics of the products, their end uses, the tariff regimes of other members[27] and consumers' tastes and habits,[28] while 'organoleptic differences resulting from geographical factors, cultivation methods, the processing [. . .], and [. . .] genetic factor[s]'[29] likely would not be 'sufficient reason to allow for a different tariff treatment'[30] or other discrimination under Art. I:1. Though the inclusion of 'consumer tastes and habits' could be viewed as a stepping stone towards the inclusion of NPR PPMs in an assessment of the likeness of products, it must be strongly stated that this is currently a very controversial proposition, and

---

[23]Panel Report *European Communities – Measures Prohibiting the Importation and Marketing Of Seal Products*, para. 7.136.

[24]*Ibid.*, para. 7.138.

[25]Appellate Body Report *European Communities – Measures Prohibiting the Importation and Marketing Of Seal Products*, pg. 193.

[26]The Chapeau of Art. XX GATT requires 'Subject to the requirement that such measures are not applied in a manner which would constitute a means of arbitrary or unjustifiable discrimination between countries where the same conditions prevail, or a disguised restriction on international trade, nothing in this Agreement [. . ..]'. See *infra*, 5.5.4.

[27]*Van den Bossche* (note 10), 330.

[28]*Ibid.*, 331.

[29]GATT Panel Report *Spain – Tariff Treatment of Unroasted Coffee*, para. 4.6.

[30]*Ibid.*

it would be a monumental development in the interpretation by the DSS of 'like products' under the GATT, were this to come about.

The final element in the three-tier test for consistency comprises whether the advantage at issue is granted 'immediately and unconditionally' to all like products originating in or destined for the territory of another contracting party. The conditionality element appears on its face to mean that once an advantage is conferred to one member or trading partner, it must be granted to all WTO members without (any) additional conditions being imposed. However, a review of the jurisprudence of the DSS demonstrates that this term and its interpretation lack clarity and consistency.

In *Indonesia – Autos*, the Panel stated that 'any such advantage (here tax and customs duty benefits) cannot be made conditional on any criteria that is not related to the imported product itself'.[31] Whether the term 'related to the product' encompasses NPR PPMs is doubtful, and following the general logic and interpretative methodology of the DSS, it is the better argument that it does not. However, in *Canada – Autos*, the Panel put forward an altogether different interpretation of the unconditionality requirement. In this case, they found that 'the term "unconditionally" does not mean that all conditions are prohibited. The imposition of conditions that do not discriminate between products on the basis of their origin is not inconsistent with Article I:1.'[32] This interpretation is certainly tailored to the purpose of Art. I:1 as a non-discrimination clause and would tend to rule out origin-neutral environmentally motivated advantages. The situation is, however, further complicated by the fact that the Panel in *EC – Tariff Preferences* saw 'no reason not to give that term its ordinary meaning under Article I:1, that is "not limited by or subject to any conditions"'.[33] Thus, it is shown in the jurisprudence of the DSS that there exists no uniform interpretative approach to this element and thus to this provision. As demonstrated above, such a lack of clarity means a lack of formal realisability, placing the WTO DSS in a position of privilege and giving it more power.

5.2.2 Analysis

What then can be taken from this brief description of Art. I:1? Hohfeldian analysis of the provision demonstrates that it creates a duty on States when conferring any

---

[31]Panel Report *Indonesia – Certain Measures Affecting the Automobile Industry*, para. 14.143.

[32]*Van den Bossche* (note 10), 333: see Panel Report *Canada – Certain Measures Affecting the Automotive Industry*, para. 10.29.

[33]Panel Report *European Communities – Conditions for the Granting of Tariff Preferences to Developing Countries*, para. 7.59. This report was not appealed by the European Communities, see: Appellate Body Report *European Communities – Conditions for the Granting of Tariff Preferences to Developing Countries*, para. 124 (footnote 259); *Van den Bossche* (note 10), 333–334.

sort of advantage on a trading partner in relation to a specific product in relation to the items listed in Art. I:1 and Arts. III:2 and III:4 to confer them also immediately and unconditionally to all other WTO members. This falls under the Hohfeldian characterisation of duty as it constitutes the absence of permission to confer advantages to one trading partner without immediately and unconditionally extending it to all other WTO members. This duty can also be expressed as an enforceable right for the other parties. The right of the other parties is then limited by the privilege held by the duty holder, to the extent of the privilege contained within the duty.[34] What does this mean in terms of Art. I:1? Here it can be clearly shown that the privilege of the duty-holding State in carrying out its duty is very limited as the obligation applied to 'any sort of advantage', 'immediately and unconditionally' (and not, for example, to a certain category of advantages, within a time frame, depending on certain conditions). This demonstrates that the duty placed on States by Art. I:1 is of a robust character as it is not limited to any great extent by freedoms of action on the part of the duty holder. If a State grants any advantage, it must then be granted immediately and unconditionally to all other WTO member trading partners.

Even the interpretation of Art. I:1, however, is not as simple as it seems. The differing interpretations of the meaning of 'unconditionally' demonstrate some of the privilege that may or may not be accorded to the duty bearer. If 'unconditionally' means, following the Panel in *Indonesia – Autos*, that an advantage 'cannot be made conditional on any criteria that is not related to the imported product itself'[35] or, following the Panel in *Canada – Autos*, that unconditionally 'does not mean that all conditions are prohibited'[36] or rather, following the Panel in *EC – Tariff Preferences*, that it means quite simply 'not limited by or subject to any conditions',[37] then the Hohfeldian analysis becomes more difficult as different results are yielded from the two opposing positions, while the middle way appears to provide uncertainty. The interpretation laid out in *EC – Tariff Preferences* is in line with the above Hohfeldian analysis, in that this interpretation would only allow for a very limited privilege in the carrying out of the duty and thus a strong right on the part of exporting States. On the other hand, the position of the Panel in *Indonesia – Autos* (while not necessarily providing for any flexibility with regard to NPR PPMs) does give the importing State more freedom of manoeuvre in that conditionality is permitted, at least in reference to criteria related to the product itself. This permissible conditionality is a privilege that limits the duty of the importing State, and thus the right of the exporting State is also reduced (as the sphere of no-right is increased, and no-right and right are mutually limiting principles).[38] If, on the

---

[34]See *supra*, 2.3.

[35]Panel Report *Indonesia – Certain Measures Affecting the Automobile Industry*, para. 14.143.

[36]Panel Report *Canada – Certain Measures Affecting the Automotive Industry*, para. 10.29.

[37]Panel Report *European Communities – Conditions for the Granting of Tariff Preferences to Developing Countries*, para. 7.59.

[38]See *supra*, 2.3.

other hand, the vague pronunciation in *Canada – Autos* is assessed, then it cannot be properly determined what the precise boundaries of the duty of the importing State are. The assertion that 'unconditionally' 'does not mean that all conditions are prohibited' does not provide any further guidance as to what conditions are and are not prohibited, and although this position can be reconciled with *Indonesia – Autos*, it cannot with *EC – Tariff Preferences*.

The interpretation of Art. I:1 is indeterminate, and thus the precise rights and duties brought about are correspondingly so. In terms of distributive impact analysis, this places more power in the hands of the DSS vis-à-vis States as further litigation is required before formal realisability can be assured. Although it is legally possible for the WTO members to issue an authoritative interpretation under Art. IX:2 GATT (or unanimously reject a Panel or Appellate Body Report),[39] and thus the power is only shifted *prima facie* to the WTO DSS, until this provision is used for the first time it is better to view it as being *de facto* in the hands of the Panels and Appellate Body. While legal certainty and formal realisability may increase the duties and diminish the regulatory freedom of States as among themselves, this is countered by the corresponding growth in the rights of other members (and a growth also in the rights of the duty holder too, as all members have the same duties). Imprecise legal provisions and inconsistent interpretation, however, represent an overall loss of rights and freedoms and an increase in the power of the DSS.

This loss is likely best not described in purely legal terms:

> It is self-evident that in an exercise of their sovereignty, and in pursuit of their own respective national interests, the Members of the WTO have made a bargain. In exchange for the benefits they expect to derive as Members of the WTO, they have agreed to exercise their sovereignty according to the commitment they have made in the *WTO Agreement*.[40]

The argument put forward here by the Appellate Body is valid, and goes to the very heart of the criticisms made in this study. It is of course true that States exercised their sovereignty in becoming WTO members, and this consent to limitation can be withdrawn and is not *de jure* permanent.[41] Making reference to the definitions of sovereignty provided in Chap. 2, it should be clear that although these different types of sovereignty are constitutive parts of sovereignty in the legal sense in international law, they are being used here in the political science sense for this very reason: consent.

However, this is too simplistic. Global governance is a hugely complex area where law and politics intertwine at every turn. It is too rudimentary to say that States consented to the WTO and therefore we must accept the functionality and

---

[39] See *supra*, 4.4.7.

[40] Appellate Body Report *Japan – Taxes on Alcoholic Beverages II*, pg. 15.

[41] Art. XV:1 of the Marrakesh Agreement Establishing the World Trade Organization provides: 'Any Member may withdraw from this Agreement. Such withdrawal shall apply both to this Agreement and the Multilateral Trade Agreements and shall take effect upon the expiration of six months from the date on which written notice of withdrawal is received by the Director-General of the WTO.'

power distribution of the system as it presently stands. Understanding how, where and to what extent power is distributed by WTO membership is part of the process of legitimisation of global governance. Critique should breed better governance and through better governance better law. Imprecise law, though it may have been consented to by the members, can only be a tool for good governance in as far as it is sometimes necessary in order to achieve agreement. In hotly contested issues such as human rights or the crime of aggression, enacting such vague laws is a legitimate and helpful tool in bringing about progress. In the field of trade obligations, designed to create a web of bilateral legal relationships, these benefits do not (for the most part) exist.

The two key elements of *Krasner's* conception of sovereignty that are invoked in this context are 'domestic sovereignty' and 'interdependence sovereignty'. Domestic sovereignty 'refers to the formal organization of political authority within the state and the ability of public authorities to exercise effective control within the borders of their own polity'.[42] What, then, is really meant by effective control? If a State is a member of an international organisation, through which it has consented to compulsory binding dispute settlement under a range of vague provisions—meaning it cannot know in advance whether its measures will be in conformity with its obligations or not—then national regulatory space is limited in an uncertain and unpredictable way. The result of this can be either a regulatory 'chilling effect',[43] in which States attempt to limit their regulatory mechanisms in particular areas in order to avoid infringement of their obligations, or the risk of continuous litigation—neither of which can be completely resolved with the notion of 'effective control', in a limited sense. These arguments will be returned to following further analysis of the GATT and the TBT and SPS Agreements.

Before moving on to an assessment of the other substantive non-discrimination clause in the GATT (Art. III), brief mention should be made again of the relationship between Art. I:1 and preferential trade areas. Under Art. XXIV:5, it is stipulated that nothing in the GATT shall prevent 'as between the territories of contracting parties, the formation of a customs union or a free trade area', so long as 'duties and other regulations of commerce' 'shall not on the whole be higher or more restrictive than the general incidence' prior to the introduction of the customs union (Art. XXIV:5(a)) or free trade area (Art. XXIV:5(b)). Article XXIV constitutes an exception to, *inter alia*, Art. I:1 of the GATT. As outlined above, the possibility for strong diverse economies to enter into more beneficial agreements under Art. XXIV means that they benefit more from this exception to Art. I:1. All contracting parties may make use of this exception, but in terms of distributive impact analysis, it benefits developed countries more than developing countries. They have greater ability to enter into the agreements that benefit them the most and

---

[42]*Stephen Krasner*, Sovereignty: Organized Hypocrisy (Princeton, 1999), 3–4.

[43]See, for example, *Alberto Alemanno*, Public Perception of Food Safety Risks Under WTO Law: A Normative Perspective, in: Geert Van Calster/Denise Prevost (eds.), Research Handbook on Environment, Health and the WTO (Cheltenham, 2013), 270, 272 (footnote 9).

greater capacity to bargain for concessions from partners that will benefit them more. Moreover, when two strong post-industrial economies enter into a free trade agreement, such as the proposed Transatlantic Trade and Investment Partnership (TTIP) between the United States and the European Union,[44] then the fact that they do not then have to roll out advantages conferred under the MFN clause of the GATT can be seen to be to the disadvantage of all other members.

Of course, it could be argued that WTO membership does not necessarily need to benefit all parties equally. What speaks against this assumption is the second paragraph of the preamble to the Marrakesh Agreement Establishing the World Trade Organization, which recognises the members'

> relations in the field of trade and economic endeavor should be conducted with a view to raising standards of living, ensuring full employment and a large and steadily growing volume of real income and effective demand, and expanding the production in goods and services, while allowing for the optimal use of the world's resources in accordance with the objective of sustainable development, seeking both to protect the environment and to enhance the means for doing so in a manner consistent with their respective needs and concerns at differing levels of economic development,

and in the third paragraph

> there is need for positive efforts designed to ensure that developing countries, and espe-cially the least developed among them, secure a share in the growth in international trade commensurate with the needs of their economic development.[45]

Although the preamble to a treaty does not generally consist of binding obliga-tions but rather 'defines, in general terms, the purposes and considerations that led the parties to conclude the treaty',[46] there is no reason not to highlight the incon-sistency of the provisions of the GATT with the purposes of the treaty. Where non-discrimination clauses (such as Art. I:1 MFN) can be seen to further the objectives laid out in the preamble, exceptions that favour developed countries and allow them to circumvent the MFN clause by privileging some trading partners over others clearly do not. Furthermore, as Art. III:2 of the Marrakesh Agreement obligates the WTO as an institution to 'facilitate the implementation, administration and operation, and further the objectives, of this Agreement [. . .]', this inconsis-tency ought to be, at the very least, addressed by the organisation in some way.

The exception in Art. XXIV of the GATT constitutes a privilege that limits the duty imposed by Art. I:1 (as duties and privileges are mutually limiting principles). As the right of the other State is merely another way of expressing the other side of the legal relationship, it is also limited by the exception in Art. XXIV. As this exception is available to all members *de jure*, but *de facto* benefits some more than others, through the prism of distributive impact analysis it clearly places more power in the hands of developed countries. From the Bad Man's point of view, the

---

[44]See: http://ec.europa.eu/trade/policy/in-focus/ttip/ (last accessed on 05/03/2017).

[45]Marrakesh Agreement Establishing the World Trade Organisation.

[46]*Makane Moïse Mbengue*, Preamble, in: Rüdiger Wolfrum (ed.) The Max Planck Encyclopaedia of Public International Law, vol. VIII (Oxford, 2012), 397 (para. 1).

exception constitutes the ability to discriminate against some trading partners, at the price of allowing freer trade with others. It provides another set of consequences for the Bad Man to assess, not simply conformity or non-conformity with the 'tax' of possible retaliatory suspension of concessions or compensation. This is particularly problematic from the perspective of developing countries as their ability to pay such a 'tax' is limited, and thus they are more likely to choose the least costly option of adherence with the obligations, while this coercive pressure[47] does not apply to developed countries in the same way. Thus, for the wealthy, developed 'Bad Man State', Art. I:1 does not restrict the possible policy choices in the same way as for developing countries.

5.3 Article III National Treatment

5.3.1 Content of the Norm

Article III of the GATT, as has already been laid out, contains the second (set) of the major non-discrimination obligation(s) in the GATT. The Art. III:2 and Art. III:4 obligations analysed in the following sections complement the Art. I:1 MFN non-discrimination clause by ensuring that not only do WTO members not discriminate between trading partners, but also that they do not discriminate against them vis-à-vis domestic production. Article III is the central provision in the elimination of protectionism. It protects expectations not of any particular trade volume but rather of the equal competitive relationship between imported and domestic products.[48]

The GATT Panel, in *Italy – Agricultural Machinery*, provided that

> the intention of the drafters of the Agreement was clearly to treat imported products in the same way as the like domestic products once they had been cleared through customs. Otherwise indirect protection could be given.[49]

Article III covers only internal measures as border measures are dealt with by Arts. II and XI. Preventing protectionism through non-tariff barriers to trade, i.e. internal measures, constitutes the 'broad purpose' of Art. III.[50]

Article III:2 seeks to eliminate protectionism by providing that

> The products of the territory of any contracting party imported into the territory of any other contracting party shall not be subject, directly or indirectly, to internal taxes or other internal charges of any kind in excess of those applied, directly or indirectly, to like

---

[47] See Ch. 2.4–2.5.

[48] Appellate Body Report *Japan – Taxes on Alcoholic Beverages II*, pg. 16.

[49] GATT Panel Report *Italy – Agricultural Machinery*, para. 11.

[50] Appellate Body Report *Japan – Taxes on Alcoholic Beverages II*, pg. 16, where it also makes clear that based on this broad purpose of avoiding protectionism means that the obligation covers both measures that are subject to tariff bindings and those that are not.

domestic products. Moreover, no contracting party shall otherwise apply internal taxes or other internal charges to imported or domestic products in a manner contrary to the principles set forth in paragraph 1.*

And Art. III:4 provides:

The products of the territory of any contracting party imported into the territory of any other contracting party shall be accorded treatment no less favourable than that accorded to like products of national origin in respect of all laws, regulations and requirements affecting their internal sale, offering for sale, purchase, transportation, distribution or use.

In the previous chapter, analysis was made of the relationship between these two paragraphs in Art. III. Although that will not be explored in more detail here, explicit reference is made here to that analysis in order to carry out the appropriate Hohfeldian and distributive impact analyses. Recalling that the textual differences in Arts. III:2 and III:4 have resulted in (with some guidelines) a 'case-by-case' approach[51] to the categorisation of 'like products', it is immediately apparent that this article lacks formal realisability. Although in law many areas are categorised by this sort of judicial leeway, and indeed if the rules are too rigorously applied without regard to the particularities of the case at hand it can be argued that can create unjust burdens, it is argued here that in the field of trade—and particularly with regard to the obligations themselves—such imprecision creates unjustifiable burdens on importing States.

As with Art. I:1, the lack of precision in the provision creates a duty of indeterminate scope, making it difficult for States to assess the scope of their own obligations. This removes power from States and centres it instead in the WTO DSS, again limiting 'sovereignty'—in the political science sense of the term.

The obligation in Art. III:2 contains a two-tier test, laid out by the Appellate Body in *Canada – Periodicals* to be constituted by

- whether imported and domestic products are like products;
- whether the imported products are taxed in excess of the domestic products.

'If the answers to both questions are affirmative, there is a violation of Article III:2 first sentence.'[52] Although this appears at first to be a relatively clear-cut obligation, the analysis of the term 'like products' in the preceding chapter demonstrates that this is not the case. What products are then considered to be like under Art. III:2—could a WTO member create a tax on the sale of imported items based on their environmentally damaging NPR PPMs that was in conformity with Art. III:2? What about a tax that would not apply to domestic products as their PPMs are less/not damaging to the environment?

As laid out previously, the 'aim and effects' test originally relied on by GATT Panels[53] was deemed an inappropriate interpretation of Art. III:2 by the Appellate

---

[51]See Appellate Body Report *European Communities – Measures Affecting Asbestos and Asbestos-Containing Products*, para. 40.

[52]Appellate Body Report *Canada – Certain Measures Concerning Periodicals*, pg. 22.

[53]GATT Panel Report *United States — Measures Affecting Alcoholic and Malt Beverages*; GATT Panel Report *United States – Taxes on Automobiles*, para. 5.10; Ch. 4.

Body in *Japan – Alcohol*.[54] Rather, the products' end uses in a given market, consumers' tastes and habits, the products' properties, nature and quality[55], and tariff classification[56] of the products in question will be assessed. Though these factors provide some guidance, the likeness of products will be decided on a 'case-by-case' basis.

While Art. III:2 deals with national treatment for taxation, Art. III:4 lays out a non-discrimination obligation relating to behind-the-border regulatory measures. Although Art. III:4 specifies no less favourable treatment for like products of foreign origin 'in respect of all laws, regulations and requirements affecting their internal sale, offering for sale, purchase, transportation, distribution or use', many of the regulatory measures fall under the TBT Agreement, which will be analysed separately below. As laid out in Chap. 3, the general rule in cases of conflict is laid out in the General Interpretative Note to Annex 1A of the WTO Agreement, which states that in the event of a conflict between the GATT and a provision of one of the other agreements listed in Annex 1A to the WTO Agreement, 'the provision of the other agreement shall prevail to the extent of the conflict'. Following the procedural hierarchy referred to by the Panel in *EC – Asbestos*, first regulatory measures will be assessed to see if they fall within the category 'technical regulation'; if so, they will be assessed under the TBT Agreement and, if not, then under the GATT.[57]

Article III: 4 also lays out a two-tier test:

- whether the imported products are like products;
- whether the imported products receive treatment less favourable than like products of national origin in respect of all laws, regulations and requirements.

What can be seen with a comparison to the test for Art. III: 2 is that the major difference between the two paragraphs is in the type of measure covered by them (i.e., taxes versus other regulations).[58] However, as highlighted in Chap. 4, there is a difference in the interpretation of 'like products' in these two paragraphs based on the structural difference of the provision.[59] While it is 'currently unclear exactly how the scope of "like products" differs between the two provisions',[60] as outlined

---

[54]See Panel Report *Japan –Taxes on Alcoholic Beverages*, para 6.16; Appellate Body Report *Japan –Taxes on Alcoholic Beverages*, pg. 23.

[55]Report of the Working Party on *Border Tax Adjustments* (1970), para. 18; Appellate Body Report *Japan –Taxes on Alcoholic Beverages*, pg. 23.

[56]See, for example, GATT Working Party Report *Australia – Ammonium Sulphate*, para. 8; GATT Panel Report *EEC – Measures on Animal Feed Proteins*, para. 4.22.

[57]Panel Report *European Communities – Measures Affecting Asbestos and Asbestos-Containing Products*, para. 8.17.

[58]Though it should be noted that in certain circumstances Art. III:4 may also be deemed to apply to taxes, see: Panel Report *Mexico – Tax Measures on Soft Drinks and Other Beverages*, para. 2.113; *Van den Bossche* (note 10), 372.

[59]See *supra*, Chap. 4.

[60]*Nathalie Bernasconi-Osterwalder/Daniel Magraw/Maria Julia Olivia/Morcos Orellana/Elizabeth Tuerk*, Environment and Trade: A Guide to WTO Jurisprudence (London, 2006), 10.

above, the main difference appears to be a broader interpretation in Art. III:2 on the basis of the structural difference. Note is made once again of the *Ad Note* to Art. III:2, which reads:

> A tax conforming to the requirements of the first sentence of paragraph 2 would be considered to be inconsistent with the provisions of the second sentence only in cases where competition was involved between, on the one hand, the taxed product and, on the other hand, a directly competitive or substitutable product which was not similarly taxed.

However, 'laws, regulations and requirements affecting [...] internal sale, offering for sale, purchase, transportation, distribution or use' that conform to the requirement in Art. III:4 are not subject to such a secondary test. The overarching purpose and relevance of the difference between the two provisions in the WTO system remains, despite some further elucidation in case law,[61] unclear.

A further notable factor about Art. III:4 is that although it covers mostly governmental regulatory measures, it also covers requirements that can emanate from private action, so long as there is sufficient nexus with a governmental measure.[62] Thus, depending on whether there has been sufficient governmental involvement or support with a private measure that amounts to a *de facto* requirement, then Art. III:4 can be invoked by the exporting State. In the context of NPR PPMs, this is not likely to occur in relation to labelling requirements[63] as they are covered by the TBT Agreement. However, other examples could be imagined in this area, such as self-regulating, government-endorsed industry requirements ('compliance with which is necessary in order to obtain an advantage'[64]), which exclude the sourcing of unsustainable raw materials, such as timber. Depending on the precise nature of the measure in question, it may also be covered by the TBT Agreement, but it remains important to highlight the possibility of non-governmental requirements being caught under Art. III:4.

5.3.2   Analysis

Beginning with Art. III:2, the obligation contained therein can be seen as a Hohfeldian duty as it contains an 'absence of permission' to directly or indirectly impose charges on imports that are in excess of those applied directly or indirectly to like domestic products. Thus, importing States have a 'right'—enforceable by the WTO DSS—that their 'like products' receive the same treatment as domestic products in the application of 'internal taxes or other charges'. The obligation is

---

[61] See *supra*, Chap. 4.

[62] Panel Report *Canada – Certain Measures Affecting the Automotive Industry*, paras. 10.106–10.107; *Van den Bossche* (note 10), 373.

[63] See *infra*, Chap. 7.

[64] See: Agreement on Trade-Related Investment Measures (TRIMs), Annex, para. 1; *Van den Bossche* (note 10), 373.

indirectly formulated: 'shall not be subject to', describing the position of the right holder, rather than a positive formation, such as 'shall not subject'. Nevertheless, the provision creates a claim that others act in a certain manner in relation to the right holder and thus constitutes a Hohfeldian right. As outlined in Chap. 2, '[r]ights are nothing but duties placed on others to act in a certain manner'.[65]

The scope of this duty on importing States lies in its application to 'internal taxes or other internal charges of any kind' that are applied 'in excess' of those applied to like domestic products. 'Internal taxes or other internal charges of any kind' is clearly very broad as all charges not deemed to be taxes will also be caught within the obligation of the importing State (such taxes and charges are to be distinguished from import taxes and charges as '[w]hat is important [. . .] is that the *obligation* to pay a charge must accrue due to an internal event, such as the distribution, sale use or transportation of the imported product'[66]). Furthermore, the phrase 'directly or indirectly' serves to broaden the scope of the duty further by ensuring that 'indirect' taxes or charges that accrue due to an internal event are also covered by the national treatment obligation and cannot be in excess of those applied to like domestic products.

These elements demonstrate that the scope of the duty, and thus that of the right, is very broad. On the other hand, the phrase 'like products', as discussed in the previous chapter, is inherently indeterminate, and although there are certain elements that will be taken into account by the DSS when assessing likeness under Art III:2, it is 'the context and the circumstances that prevail in any given case' that really affect its interpretation.[67] Thus, this crucial element in the determination of the scope of the duty lacks formal realisability, thus preventing WTO members from being able to anticipate the scope of their obligations and legislate accordingly. This clearly moves power from WTO members to the DSS, which disadvantages both importing and exporting States. In relation to NPR PPMs, based on the criteria discussed above, it is very unlikely that they will affect the 'likeness' of a product in a negative manner. Thus, if such products are identical except on the basis of their PPMs, then the duty under Art. III:2 can be seen to be broad, and the privilege of the importing State in how it carries out its obligation is very limited. The right of the exporting State is thus also broad and the field of exposure/no-right very narrow. The major power distribution in relation to this provision, however, is not from importing to exporting States but rather to the WTO DSS, as the provision's scope is inherently indeterminate and thus must be assessed on a case-by-case basis.

---

[65] *Joseph William Singer*, The Legal Rights Debate in Analytical Jurisprudence from Bentham to Hohfeld, Wisconsin Law Review (1982), 975, 986.

[66] Appellate Body Report *China – Measures Affecting Imports of Automobile Parts*, para. 162. Import taxes are customs duties and are covered by tariff bindings and not the national treatment obligation.

[67] Appellate Body Report *Japan – Taxes on Alcoholic Beverages*, pg. 21.

The further qualifier in Art. III:2 second sentence ('Moreover, no contracting party shall otherwise apply internal taxes or other internal charges to imported domestic products in a manner contrary to the principles set forth in paragraph 1.*') introduces a further obligation to ensure that, *inter alia*, internal taxes and other charges are not applied as a means 'to afford protection to domestic production'. As laid out in Ad Art. III:2, taxes that conform with the obligation contained in the first sentence of Art. III:2 are considered inconsistent with the second sentence 'only in cases where competition was involved between, on the one hand, the taxed product and, on the other hand, a directly competitive or substitutable product which was not similarly taxed'. Thus, taxes that have been found to be in conformity with Art. III:2 first sentence may fall foul of the rule in the second sentence. As outlined above, the inclusion of the second sentence (alongside its Ad Article) serves to limit the interpretation of 'like products' in Art. III:2 first sentence as those that are 'directly competitive or substitutable' are caught by the obligation contained in the second sentence—a 'broader category' than 'like products'.[68]

This affects the Hohfeldian analysis thus: although its inclusion makes the interpretation of 'like products' in the first sentence more determinate (on the basis of exclusion), the secondary obligation serves to create a wider sphere of duty, in which not only 'like products' in their narrow sense but also 'directly competitive and substitutable products' (wider even than the widest possible reading of 'like products') are subject to a national treatment obligation. This separate but intimately related duty is both more widely, in terms of the products caught by it, and more restrictively formulated.

The restriction comes by way of the proviso that such internal taxes and charges 'should not be applied to imported or domestic products so as to afford protection to domestic production'. This wording may inform the first sentence of Art. III:2, but it is incorporated explicitly into the second sentence. This limits the application of the national treatment obligation (re internal taxes and charges) in relation to 'directly competitive and substitutable products' to those taxes and charges that are applied so as to afford protection to domestic products. Thus, the duty is limited and so is the right. Importing States therefore have the privilege to apply taxes and other internal charges to such products (so long as they are not 'like' in the narrow sense of the first sentence), and the exporting State is exposed to such behaviour. However, as the characterisation of products as 'like' or 'directly competitive or substitutable' can only be adjudged on a case-by-case basis, such a distinction serves to once more transfer power to the DSS from States, whose ability to appropriately legislate such fine technical distinctions is compromised by the lack of formal realisability in this provision. Moreover, such minor distinctions are more likely to cause disparate effects for developing countries that may lack expertise or

---

[68]*Robert E. Hudec*, 'Like Product': The Differences in Meaning in GATT Articles I and III, in: Thomas Cottier/Petros Mavroidis (eds.), Regulatory Barriers and the Principle of Non-Discrimination in World Trade Law (Ann Arbor, 2000), 106.

fear litigation before the WTO—perhaps leading to regulatory freeze or reluctance to implement national environmental schemes that may involve TREMs.

Moving on to Art. III:4, a related obligation of national treatment is contained in respect of laws, regulations and requirements affecting internal sale, offering for sale, purchase, transportation, distribution or use. In Art III:4, the obligation comprises the duty to accord 'treatment no less favourable' to imported products vis-à-vis 'like products of national origin'. As in Art III:2, a Hohfeldian right is contained in this provision as it creates a claim that others act in a certain manner in relation to the right holder. Thus, it also creates a duty on importing States. The scope of the duty extends to a relatively broad number of actions, encompassing as it does 'laws, regulations and requirements' that affect 'internal sale, offering for sale, purchase, transportation, distribution or use'. Indeed, it is difficult to imagine a more comprehensive enumeration in relation to the treatment of imported goods (with the exception of taxes and other charges, included in Art. III:2, and more specific technical or sanitary measures, which are dealt with under the TBT and SPS Agreements respectively). On the other hand, the mechanism of the duty ('to accord treatment no less favourable') leaves importing States with a large privilege in their choice of regulatory action. It is not possible for them to offer imported 'like products' less favourable treatment than domestic products without being in contravention of the Art III:4 obligation, but they can choose different regulatory mechanisms for dealing with such imported products. This regulatory freedom can of course be very helpful for States in addressing policy concerns while at the same time ensuring that protectionism is not interfering with the free flow of goods. This freedom limits the duty and is thus a privilege of the importing State. It leaves exporting States in the position of no-right/exposure as they have no right to demand, e.g., identical treatment, but only treatment 'no less favourable'.

However, in this study, the focus is TREMs based on NPR PPMs, and thus the 'likeness' of the imported products is the key issue. As demonstrated above, NPR PPMs are not (yet) recognised by the WTO DSS as a factor that affects the 'likeness' of products under Art. III:4, although elements connected to NPR PPMs such as consumer tastes and habits may be taken into account. Thus, although the privilege contained in the duty of Art III:4 enables importing States to treat imported products differently, this must not amount to treatment less favourable. Different regulatory schemes may thus be permissible, but not trade-restrictive measures that favour domestic products that do not have NPR PPMs that are detrimental to the environment. As above, the precise interpretation of 'likeness' is indeterminate and may change, but as it stands today TREMs (as they are restrictive) based on NPR PPMs will fall foul of the obligation in Art. III:2 and Art. III:4.

5.4 Article XI General Elimination of Quantitative Restrictions

Moving on from MFN and national treatment, Art. XI:1 contains the other main weapon in the free trade arsenal of the GATT: the obligation to eliminate quantitative restrictions. Article XI:1 states:

> No prohibitions or restrictions other than duties, taxes, or other charges, whether made effective through quotas, import or export licenses or other measures, shall be instituted or maintained by any contracting party on the importation of any product of the territory of any other contracting party or on the exportation or sale for export of any product destined for the territory of any other contracting party.

Article XI:1 thus not only creates an obligation not to create or maintain quotas or import/export licences but also refers to prohibitions in general, meaning this article also creates an obligation to eliminate import bans. All TREMs that constitute an import ban will be in contravention of this provision, as demonstrated by the decision of the DSS in the *US – Shrimp/Turtle* judgment, in which an import ban on shrimp caught without the use of turtle excluder devices was found to have violated Art. XI of the GATT.[69] This case will be addressed in the next chapter.[70]

As Art. XI:1 refers to 'measures' generally, it has been interpreted to include all measures and not only those enacted by the legislature. Indeed, the GATT Panel in *Japan – Semi-Conductors* stated:

> This wording indicated clearly that any measure instituted or maintained by a contracting party which restricted the exportation or sale for export of products was covered by this provision, irrespective of the legal status of the measure.[71]

De facto restrictions that amount to quantitative restrictions are also covered.[72]

Article XI is complemented by Art. XIII:1, which creates an MFN-like[73] obligation on importing States that enact measures under Art. XI to ensure that they are not applied in a discriminatory manner.

Article XIII:1 states:

> No prohibition or restriction shall be applied by any contracting party on the importation of any product of the territory of another contracting party or on the exportation of any product destined for the territory of any other contracting party, unless the importation of the like product of all third countries or the exportation for the like product to all third countries is similarly prohibited or restricted.[74]

---

[69]Panel Report *United States – Import Prohibition of Certain Shrimp and Shrimp Products*, paras. 7.17, 8.1; Appellate Body Report *United States – Import Prohibition of Certain Shrimp and Shrimp Products*.

[70]See Ch. 6.6.

[71]GATT Panel Report *Japan – Trade in Semi-Conductors*, para. 106.

[72]Panel Report *Argentina – Measures Affecting the Export of Bovine Hides and the Import of Finished Leather*, para. 11.17, where the panel expressed 'no doubt' that such measures are also covered by Art XI.

[73]*Van den Bossche* (note 10), 455.

[74]Emphasis added.

Article XIII thus brings 'like products' into any assessment of measures instituted under Art. XI. The precise relationship of Art. XIII with the general exceptions contained in Art. XX is not clear at first sight. In the *US – Shrimp/Turtle* judgment, the Panel first established that there was a violation of Art. XI and thus did not examine the further claims that the US measure violated both Art. I:1 and Art. XIII:1.[75] From the language of the provision, it would appear that the Panel ought to have assessed the measure's conformity with Art. XIII:1 after finding a breach of Art. XI:1, but reference to other case law on Art. XIII:1 demonstrates that the provision is aimed at ensuring MFN-like non-discrimination for the prohibitions and restrictions permitted by Art. XI.[76] For example, in the GATT case *EEC – Apples I (Chile)*, a violation of Art. XIII:1 was found due to an import restriction that was deemed not to be like the voluntary export restraints agreed upon with the other parties (Argentina, Australia, New Zealand and South Africa).[77]

Whether Art. XI amounts to a general 'right of market access' has been much debated, and following *Hohfeld* we can see that the legal relationship created by Art. XI:1 is one of right and duty. The provision creates an actionable right for exporting States that no prohibitions or restrictions (other than duties, taxes or other charges) be imposed or maintained. This can in turn be described as a duty on importing States not to impose or maintain (and thus to eliminate) such prohibitions or measures. The express limitation of the duty not to include 'duties, taxes, or other charges, whether made effective through quotas, import or export licenses or other measures,' alongside the express exceptions contained in Art XI:2, may demonstrate that this right is not one of general, broad scope. Furthermore, the existence of the general exceptions in Art. XX go on to limit the scope of the duty further. How far and in what ways this affects the general 'right of market access' will be dealt with in the following subsection covering Art. XX.

The express exceptions contained in Art XI:2 refer to (a) prohibitions or restrictions temporarily applied to relieve critical shortages of foodstuffs; (b) prohibitions or restrictions necessary for the application of standards or regulations for the classification, grading or marketing of commodities in international trade; and (c) **restrictions** on any agricultural or fisheries product necessary to enforce measures that (1) restrict qualities of like or substitutable domestic products, (2) remove a temporary surplus of like or substitutable domestic product or

---

[75]See *Marlo Pfister Cadeddu*, Turtles in the Soup? An Analysis of the GATT Challenge to the United States Endangered Species Act Section 609 Shrimp Harvesting Nation Certification Program for the Conservation of Sea Turtles, Geo. Int'l Envtl. L. Rev 11. (1998–1999), 179, 193; Citing the Appellate Body in *US – Wool Shirts*, the Panel stated: 'A panel need only address those claims which must be addressed in order to resolve the matter in issue in the dispute.', see Panel Report *United States – Import Prohibition of Certain Shrimp and Shrimp Products*, para. 7.22; Appellate Body Report *United States – Measure Affecting Imports of Woven Wool Shirts and Blouses from India*, pg. 19.

[76]For example, the exceptions to Art XI:1 contained in Art. XI:2 (a)-(c).

[77]See *Van den Bossche* (note 10), 455; GATT Panel Report *EEC – Restrictions on Imports of Apples from Chile*, para. 4.11.

(3) restrict quantities permitted to be produced for animal products directly dependent on the imported quantity (where domestic production of such is negligible). While Art. XI:2 (a) and (b) includes exceptions to both prohibitions and restrictions, Art. XI:2 (c) uses more restrictive language and only includes restrictions and not prohibitions. Indeed, this textual difference was highlighted by the GATT Panel in *United States – Prohibition of Imports of Tuna and Tuna Products from Canada*, which 'felt that the provisions of Article XI:2(c) could not justify the application of an import prohibition'.[78]

These exceptions clearly demonstrate concrete restrictions on the 'right of market access' and limitations on the duty contained in Art. XI:1 on importing States. These exceptions thus constitute privileges, as they limit the duty. Although Art. XI:2 (a) and (b) is couched in relatively broad language, it refers to very specific instances and thus does not limit the duty contained in Art XI:1 to a significant extent. The exception/privilege contained in Art. XI:2 (c)(i) may have had relevance in relation to TREMs based on NPR PPMs where they amount to an import ban (for example, a ban on cod imports from unsustainable fisheries), but two elements remove this from the sphere of possibility. First of all, only restrictions and not prohibitions are permissible under Art. XI:2 (c), thus a ban on imports from fisheries that are damaging to the environment would not be possible, and secondly, even if the DSS were to ignore this textual difference, the provision states: 'restrict qualities of like or substitutable domestic products'. Even if the products were not deemed to be like based on NPR PPMs, they would certainly be 'substitutable' in most domestic markets and would therefore not meet the requirements of the exception in Art. XI:2 (c)(i) either.

Thus, although it can be seen that there are some important limitations to the duty contained in Art. XI, it should still be regarded as a wide-ranging one that removes significant power from the importing State. As noted in Chap. 2, *Krasner's* 'interdependence sovereignty' conception of sovereignty 'refers to the ability of public authorities to regulate the flow of information, ideas, goods, people, pollutants, or capital across borders'.[79] It is clear that Art. XI:1, if assessed without reference to Art. XX, completely removes the ability of WTO members to regulate the flow of goods across their borders (as inherent in such an ability must be the ability to prevent the flow of goods if desired), except in the very limited circumstances prescribed in Art. XI:2 (a)–(c). Thus, it must be seen that with reference to this facet of sovereignty, States have ceded much under Art. XI:1, and it is a very broad duty. With regard to NPR PPMs, it appears that any TREMs based on NPR PPMs that amount to an import ban would be ruled out—and as noted above not caught by the exceptions contained within Art. XI.

---

[78]GATT Panel Report *United States – Prohibition of Imports of Tuna and Tuna Products from Canada*.

[79]See Ch. 2.2.

5.5 Article XX General Exceptions

From the foregoing, it can be seen that Arts. I:1, III:2, III:4 and XI:1 GATT exclude the possibility, at first instance, that TREMs based on NPR PPMs can be deemed compatible with the obligations under the substantive obligations of the GATT. The interpretation of 'like products' discussed above and the wide-ranging obligation contained in Art. XI mean that if a country imposes a trade-restrictive measure not amounting to a ban but based on NPR PPMs, it will fall foul of the Art. I:1 or Art. III obligations as the distinction made between products with environmentally friendly TREMs will not be recognised by the WTO DSS, and if they amount to a ban, they will be contrary to Art. XI:1. The GATT, however, contains its own general exception clause in Art. XX, and how these exceptions interact with TREMs based on NPR PPMs will be explored in this section.

Next to the controversial issue as to whether 'like products' applies to products treated differently by TREMs based on NPR PPMs comes the controversial issue as to how the general exceptions apply to them if such products are treated as 'like'. As we have already seen from the foregoing, and will be explored in greater detail in Part II on case law, it is generally not in conformity with the WTO obligations to treat products differently based solely on their process or production methods, even if the overarching goal might be environmental protection. Therefore, how the exceptions to the main substantive obligations of the GATT are applied is of central importance in the analysis of how much regulatory freedom States have to create TREMs. If the products are not 'like', then there has been no violation of Art. I:1, Art. III:2 or Art. III:4. If the products are 'like', then the TREM must fit under one of the subheadings of Art. XX and meet the requirements of the chapeau in order to be permissible under the WTO. Following the reasoning of the GATT Panel in *US – Section 307*, Panels must first find a violation of one of the substantive provisions of the GATT and then go on to see if it can be justified under Art. XX.[80]

Although the word 'environment' never appeared in the GATT 1947, many of its provisions are of direct relevance to the environment.[81] Article XX contains ten subheadings, of which three are of particular relevance in relation to environmental concerns.

Article XX, including the 'environmental exceptions', reads:

> Subject to the requirement that such measures are not applied in a manner which would constitute a means of arbitrary or unjustifiable discrimination between countries where the same conditions prevail, or a disguised restriction on international trade, nothing in this Agreement shall be construed to prevent the adoption or enforcement by any contracting party of measures:
>
> (a) necessary to protect public morals;

---

[80]GATT Panel Report *United States – Section 337 of the Tariff Act of 1930*, para. 5.9, where the Panel stated 'If any inconsistencies with Art. III:4 were found, the Panel would then examine whether they could be justified under Art. XX (d).'

[81]*P. K. Rao*, The World Trade Organization and the Environment (Basingstoke, 2000), 97.

(b) necessary to protect human, animal or plant life or health;

[...]

(g) relating to the conservation of exhaustible natural resources if such measures are made effective in conjunction with restrictions on domestic production or consumption; [...].

The chapeau of Art. XX is made up of the obligation contained in the introductory clause of the provision. This clause is widely referred to in literature and by the WTO DSS itself as the 'chapeau'. Article XX (b) and (g) is the traditional 'environmental exceptions' of the GATT, while the relevance of Art. XX (a) may rise in prominence in environmental issues.

The two-tier test contained within Art. XX can be summarised as requiring

- that one of the exceptions in (a)–(j) are met by the measure in question; and
- that the requirements of the chapeau are also met.[82]

This two-tier test reflects the order in which the measure will be analysed to see if it qualifies as an exception under Art. XX. Although the chapeau of Art. XX comes before the individual subheadings, when a measure is assessed, the chapeau is the final part of the test. The reason for this was elaborated on by the Appellate Body in *US – Shrimp/Turtle*:

> The sequence of steps [...] reflects, not inadvertence or random choice, but rather the fundamental structure and logic of Article XX.[83]

> The task of interpreting the chapeau so as to prevent the abuse or misuse of the specific exemptions provided for in Article XX is rendered very difficult, if indeed it remains possible at all, where the interpreter [...] has not first identified and examined the specific exception threatened with abuse.[84]

The language employed here by the Appellate Body may be seen as a telling demonstration of their attitude towards the invocation of the environmental exceptions under Art. XX. This theme will be discussed in greater detail below, but here it suffices to point out that even in the attempt to organise the analytical structure of interpretation for Art. XX, the Appellate Body refers to the exceptions as being 'threatened with abuse'. That is not to say, however, that incentives do not exist for governments to create TREMs for the purposes of disguised protectionism,[85] but

---

[82] Adapted from *Van den Bossche* (note 10), 620.

[83] Appellate Body Report *United States – Import Prohibition of Certain Shrimp and Shrimp Products*, para. 119.

[84] *Ibid.*, para. 120.

[85] See *Nita Ghei*, Evaluating the WTO's Two Step Test for Environmental Measures Under Article XX, Colo. J. Int'l Envtl. L. & Pol'y 18 (2007), 117–150, for detail on the incentives governments have to create TREMs as a form of disguised protectionism. Here the author makes the argument that the two step test, as it has been applied by the WTO DSS, has been thus far successful in distinguishing between TREMs that are disguised protectionism and those that are enacted for policy reasons only.

such immediately hostile language may be argued as indicating the approach of the DSS to the use of environmental exceptions in general.

A TREM seeking to fall under one of the exceptions of Art. XX must then first meet the requirements of one of the sub-paragraphs. In assessing the sub-paragraphs, it is the measure itself that will be assessed, and in the later chapeau stage, the application of the measure will be assessed.[86]

5.5.1 Article XX (a)

Article XX (a) is an interesting example of what might come to be a site of contestation over environmental matters in the future as it may come to be seen in some States that the import and sale of products with environmentally damaging PPMs becomes a moral issue. Although the Appellate Body has repeatedly noted that 'It is undisputed that WTO Members have the right to determine the level of protection [. . .]'[87] under Art. XX, it remains true that while the other environmental exceptions contain elements that can (at least to some extent) be assessed objectively (the protection of human, animal or plant life or health and the conservation of exhaustible natural resources), the protection of public morals is subjective and variable as between countries in ways that the other exceptions are not. Although different levels of protection may be chosen under Art. XX (b) or (g), entirely different moral values may be invoked under Art. XX (a), and it is not possible for other States to object. As demonstrated in the *EC – Fur Seals* case, a partial prohibition can be seen as necessary to protect public morals but will struggle to meet the requirements of the chapeau.[88] Whether environmental protection can go on in the future to be deemed to be 'necessary to protect public morals' remains to be seen. However, the *EC – Fur Seals* case may provide some indication that cases that involve wildlife conservation (a part of environmental protection) may be best suited to explore this possibility.[89]

5.5.2 Art. XX (b)

Article XX (b) allows exceptions to main substantive provisions of the GATT for measures that are 'necessary to protect human, animal or plant life or health'. As

---

[86]See Panel Report *Brazil – Measures Affecting Imports of Retreaded Tyres*, para. 7.107.

[87]See Appellate Body Report *European Communities – Measures Affecting Asbestos and Asbestos-Containing Products*, para 168.

[88]See: *supra*, 5.2; Appellate Body Report *European Communities – Measures Prohibiting the Importation and Marketing Of Seal Products*, pg. 193.

[89]See above 5.2 for detail of this case in the context of 'like products' and MFN.

mentioned above, although the level of protection will be left for States to decide, the measure will be assessed to ensure it is 'designed to protect life and health of humans, animals, or plants' and that it is necessary to do so.[90]

This constitutes a two-part test:

- the measure must be designed to protect the life or health of humans, animals or plants;
- the measure must be necessary to achieve such protection.[91]

The design of the measure to protect 'human, animal or plant life or health' has been described as 'relatively easy to apply and has not given rise to major interpretative problems',[92] citing evidence such as the *Thailand – Cigarettes* case,[93] in which it was

> accepted that smoking constituted a serious risk to human health and that consequently measures designed to reduce the consumption of cigarettes fell within the scope of Article XX (b).[94]

This, of course, can only be seen in a positive light. But what can it tell us about environmental TREMs based on NPR PPMs? If an analogy were to be drawn with the *Thailand – Cigarettes* case, then it would be necessary that the State enacting the TREM was doing so in order to protect the health of persons within the borders of the other contracting party. With smoking, such an analogy cannot so easily be drawn (banning the import of cigarettes certainly will not stop people in other countries from smoking them, whereas environmentally damaging PPMs harm the environment in another member's territory—at first instance at least). Perhaps, then, it is the production of something that is 'highly polluting' in its PPMs? High levels of pollution not only cause damage in the area in which the pollutants are released but can also cause transboundary harm (through, e.g., smog and acid rain) and contribute to global problems such as climate change. Thus, it is possible for a State to aim to protect the health and environment of its own population through TREMs based on PPMs. It is, however, questionable whether such measures would reasonably de deemed to be (1) necessary to protect human, animal or plant life or health or, (2) even if meeting that test, able to meet the requirements of the chapeau (discussed below).

The interpretation of 'necessary' (as opposed to 'relating to' in (g), for example) has been particularly controversial in the history of the GATT. In assessing whether a measure falls under Art. XX (a), (b) or (d), Panels must determine whether the measure in question is 'necessary' to fulfil one of the legitimate objectives contained in these sub-paragraphs.[95] The reason for this controversy is that the

---

[90]*Van den Bossche* (note 10), 622.

[91]Emphasis added.

[92]*Van den Bossche* (note 10), 622.

[93]GATT Panel Report *Thailand – Restrictions on Importation and Internal Taxes on Cigarettes*.

[94]*Ibid.*, para. 73.

[95]*Bernasconi-Osterwalder et al.* (note 60), 149.

interpretation of the word 'necessary' led some GATT Panels to conclude that measures would not fulfil this requirement unless there was no GATT-consistent or less inconsistent measure available to the contracting party implementing the measure.[96] The Panel in *Thailand – Cigarettes*, following the reasoning in *United States – Section 337*,[97] saw no good reason to differentiate between the use of the word 'necessary' in Art. XX (b) and Art. XX (d).[98] Article XX (d) provides an exception for laws and regulations that are 'necessary to secure compliance' with other laws or regulations that are not inconsistent with the GATT.[99]

The major criticism levelled at this interpretation by the Panel is that, by insisting upon the 'least-trade-restrictive' approach, it was 'failing to give adequate consideration to societal values other than trade'.[100] While consistent interpretation may be desirable in terms of the need for legal certainty and formal realisability,[101] it is important to differentiate the critique of 'like products' and the 'accordion of likeness'. The justifications relied on by the DSS are patchy and largely without firm textual basis, the process removes powers from States and gives it the DSS and it is not clear that the interpretation of the DSS could have been foreseen by the negotiating parties. On the other hand, the argument that the interpretation of necessity in the context of Art. XX (b) to the GATT should not be influenced by the importance of the societal value protected as an exception to other GATT obligations does not raise the same criticisms. In fact, it appears to be within the very purpose of Art. XX (b) that it removes this particular area of policy from the confines of the GATT system (except, of course, when such measures are applied in such a manner as to result in arbitrary or unjustifiable discrimination).

Furthermore, while it was suggested previously that the quagmire of interpretation that surrounds 'like products' is problematic and results in a concentration of power in the WTO DSS, if a difference was recognised here on the basis of the purpose of the particular sub-paragraph, then the result would be the opposite: the power would remain in the hands of the State attempting to 'protect human, animal or plant life or health', a result that would appear to be concurrent with the purposes of Art. XX (b). Article XX (d) should rightly be considered to be a procedural

---

[96]See *Van den Bossche* (note 10), 624; GATT Panel Report *Thailand – Restrictions on Importation and Internal Taxes on Cigarettes*, para. 81.

[97]GATT Panel Report *United States – Section 337 of the Tariff Act of 1930*, para. 3.56 *et seq.*

[98]GATT Panel Report *Thailand – Restrictions on Importation and Internal Taxes on Cigarettes*, para. 74.

[99]The provision goes on to specify that it includes those laws and regulations 'relating to customs enforcement, the enforcement of monopolies operated under paragraph 4 of Article II and Article XVII, the protection of patents, trade marks and copyrights, and the prevention of deceptive practices'.

[100]*Bernasconi-Osterwalder et al.* (note 60), 149.

[101]Formal realisability is condition by which treaty obligations, or any legal duties, can provide a clear and concise standard by which states can assess whether, when facing litigation, they have fulfilled their duty or not. Unclear, imprecise obligations which do not provide surety lack formal realisability.

exception included to ensure that certain measures that contravene substantive provisions of the GATT, but that are necessary to secure compliance with other laws or regulations that are not GATT inconsistent, should also be granted an exception. Such measures can clearly be distinguished from measures enacted under Art. XX (b) that themselves enact policy that aims to protect human, animal or plant life or health.

The approach taken by the GATT Panels with respect to Art. XX (d) was confirmed by the Appellate Body in *Korea – Beef*, though slightly tempered.[102] In this report, the Appellate Body included additional factors in the necessity test and importantly stated:

> We believe that, as used in the context of Article XX (d), the reach of the word 'necessary' is not limited to that which is 'indispensable' or 'of absolute necessity' or 'inevitable'. Measures which are indispensable or of absolute necessity or inevitable to secure compliance certainly fulfil the requirements of Article XX (d). But other measures, too, may fall within the ambit of this exception.[103]

Other factors to be included were 'relative importance of the common interests or values that the law or regulation to be enforced is intended to protect',[104] 'the extent to which the measure contributes to the realization of the end pursued, [and] the securing of compliance with the law or regulation at issue'.[105] Although this partially broadened the interpretation of necessity under Art. XX (d), it remains difficult to justify its wider application under Art. XX (b).

5.5.3 Article XX (g)

The other major environmental exception contained in the GATT is Art. XX (g), which lays out that an exception to the substantive provisions of the GATT is available for measures 'relating to the conservation of exhaustible natural resources if such measures are made effective in conjunction with restrictions on domestic production or consumption'.

Article XX (g) contains a two-part test:

- measures must relate to the conservation of exhaustible natural resources;
- any such measures must also be made effective in conjunction with restrictions on domestic production or consumption.[106]

---

[102] Appellate Body Report *Korea – Measures Affecting Imports of Fresh, Chilled and Frozen Beef.*
[103] *Ibid.*, para. 161.
[104] *Ibid.*, para. 162.
[105] *Ibid.*, para. 163.
[106] *Van den Bossche* (note 10), 634, casts Art. XX (g) as containing a three-part test, emphasis first on 'relating to' and then on the 'conservation of exhaustible natural resources'. There is logic to this this distinction, and this work will seek to make the definitional distinction clear while remaining with a two-part test.

The second criterion included in the test is a safeguard to ensure that if measures are taken by States to conserve natural resources in a way that affects trade, they must also ensure that such resources are being protected domestically. The necessity of this part of the test is perhaps questionable as any such measures taken that were not matched by similar restrictions on domestic consumption would inevitably not reach the requirement of the chapeau that the application of such measures should not amount to 'arbitrary or unjustifiable discrimination'.[107]

The first criterion raises two interesting issues. The first is that measures enacted under Art. XX (g), in contrast to measures under, *inter alia*, Art. XX (b), which must be necessary for the fulfilment of the desired policy goal, must only be related to the conservation of natural resources. Though it is not immediately apparent from the text of the provision what the precise difference is between 'necessary'[108] and 'related to', it is certain that necessity constitutes a higher bar to be reached than the mere 'related to'. It could be argued, in fact, that any measure that was in any way (and even only very remotely) connected to the conservation of exhaustible natural resources would fulfil this requirement.

The interpretation of 'relating to' has undergone quite significant revision in the jurisprudence of the GATT/WTO DSS. In the *Canada – Herring and Salmon* GATT Panel Report, the Panel recognised that, in contradistinction to 'necessary', 'Article XX (g) does not only cover measures that are necessary or essential for the conservation of exhaustible natural resources but a wider range of measures'.[109] The Panel, however, went on to limit the interpretation of 'relating to' to measures that are 'primarily aimed at the conservation of an exhaustible natural resource'[110] on the basis that

> the purpose of Article XX (g) in the General Agreement was not to widen the scope for measures serving trade policy purposes but merely to ensure that the commitments under the General Agreement do not hinder the pursuit of policies aimed at the conservation of exhaustible natural resources.[111]

Although the 'primarily aimed at' appears to be a limitation of the simpler and broader language of 'relating to', the justification of the Panel here appears to be reasonable and consummate with attempting to uphold the interpretation of the phrase with the purpose of Art. XX in general.

The interpretation of the GATT Panel was upheld by the Appellate Body in *US – Gasoline*, but with the proviso that '"primarily aimed at" is not itself treaty language and was not designed as a simple litmus test for inclusion of exclusion from Article XX (g)'.[112] The Appellate Body pointed to the 'substantial

---

[107] See *infra*.

[108] See *supra*, 5.5.2 on the problematic definition of 'necessary' in this article.

[109] GATT Panel Report *Canada – Measures Affecting Exports of Unprocessed Herring and Salmon*, para. 4.6.

[110] *Ibid.*

[111] *Ibid.*

[112] Appellate Body Report *United States – Standards for Reformulated and Conventional Gasoline*; pg. 17.

relationship' that 'existed between the baseline establishment rules and the policy objective of preventing further deterioration of the level of air pollution'.[113] This elucidation supported the direction taken by the Panel in *Canada – Herring and Salmon* while at the same time discouraging focus on the language in the GATT Panel's Report in favour of an assessment of the relationship of the measure to the policy aim. Although this can also be seen to step away from the language of 'relating to', it is similarly backed up by the aim of Art. XX in general. An assessment of the relationship in this manner was further elaborated on by the Appellate Body in *US – Shrimp/Turtle*, in which a 'close and real relationship between the measure and policy objective'[114] was deemed necessary in order to fulfil the 'relating to' criterion.[115]

The second issue raised by the second part of the Art. XX (g) test is what can be considered to be 'exhaustible natural resources'. Certainly, at the time of the negotiation of the original GATT, the intention of the parties may have been to create an exception for a rather narrower exception for the 'conservation of "mineral" or "non-living" natural resources'.[116] This particular issue came to the fore in the *US – Shrimp/Turtle* case, where the complainants contended 'that a "reasonable interpretation" of the term "exhaustible" is that the term refers to "finite resources such as minerals, rather than biological or renewable resources"'.[117] However, rather than adopt this restrictive interpretation, the Appellate Body decided on an evolutionary approach to treaty interpretation in the light of what has been learned from 'modern biological sciences'.[118] The Body stated:

> The words of Art. XX (g), 'exhaustible natural resources', were actually crafted more than 50 years ago. They must be read by a treaty interpreter in the light of contemporary concerns of the community of nations about the protection and conservation of the environment.[119]

Furthermore, the Appellate Body went on to elaborate on the reason as to why such an evolutionary interpretative technique should be undertaken by the DSS:

> While Article XX was not modified in the Uruguay Round, the preamble attached to the WTO Agreement shows that the signatories to the Agreement were, in 1994, fully aware of the importance and the legitimacy of environmental protection as a goal of national and international policy. The preamble of the WTO Agreement – which informs not only the

---

[113]*Van den Bossche* (note 10), 636.

[114]*Ibid.*, 637.

[115]Report of the Appellate Body *United States – Import Prohibition of Certain Shrimp and Shrimp Products*, para. 141.

[116]*Van den Bossche* (note 10), 634, referring to the complainants in the *US – Shrimp/Turtle* case, see *infra*, 6.5.

[117]Report of the Appellate Body *United States – Import Prohibition of Certain Shrimp and Shrimp Products*, para. 127.

[118]*Ibid.*, para. 128.

[119]*Ibid.*, para. 129.

GATT 1994, but also the covered agreements – explicitly acknowledges the goal of sustainable development.[120]

This recognition of the effect of the preamble in informing the interpretation of the WTO and covered agreements and the recognition that it was 'too late in the day'[121] to plump for such a restricted interpretation, particularly as two GATT Panel reports had recognised fish as an 'exhaustible natural resource',[122] can be seen as one of the prime examples of the inherent flexibility of the vague nature of the GATT being interpreted by the DSS in such a way as to allow for policy space and environmental protection by States. Although this is certainly positive from the perspective of environmentalists, it would be preferable in terms of legal certainty to have more firm provisions. This example, however, being largely uncontroversial and uncontested throughout the history of the GATT/WTO, is likely to constitute firm jurisprudence that is more likely to be built upon and expanded to include more environmental issues rather than tightened.

Indeed, the example of Art. XX (g) and fisheries could be seen by some, particularly if the WTO remains in Doha-stasis, as a beacon of hope for the inclusion of a more broad sway of environmental measures under the Art. XX exceptions. For example, a truly evolutionary interpretation could see the environment more generally as being an exhaustible natural resource. The environment itself may be difficult to define, but the examples of air[123] and water free from pollution, ozone level depletion and climate change could all be potential fields of Art. XX (g) contestation in the future, if the relationship between trade and the environment remains solely in the realm of the current (unrevised) WTO and covered agreements.

5.5.4   The Chapeau

As outlined above, after the specific exceptions contained in Art. XX (a)–(g) have been assessed, and the measure in question is deemed to have met the requirements, the DSS will then move on to assess the conformity of the measure in question with the chapeau of Art. XX.

---

[120]*Ibid.*

[121]*Ibid.*, para. 131.

[122]*Ibid.*; GATT Panel Report *United States – Prohibition of Imports of Tuna and Tuna Products from Canada*, where it was argued that there was 'little question that tuna stocks were potentially subject to over-exploitation and exhaustion', para. 3.8, and it was accepted by both parties and the Panel that Tuna are 'an exhaustible natural resource in need of conservation management', para. 4.9; GATT Panel Report *Canada – Measures Affecting Exports of Unprocessed Herring and Salmon*, where it also was agreed by both parties that 'salmon and herring were exhaustible natural resources', para. 3.29.

[123]Already successfully invoked as an exhaustible natural resource in *US – Gasoline*, see Appellate Body Report *United States – Standards for Reformulated and Conventional Gasoline*, pg. 18.

The chapeau of Art. XX reads:

> Subject to the requirement that such measures are not applied in a manner which would constitute a means of arbitrary or unjustifiable discrimination between countries where the same conditions prevail, or a disguised restriction on international trade, nothing in this Agreement shall be construed to prevent the adoption or enforcement by any contracting party of measures.

The chapeau is designed to ensure that when exceptions to the substantive obligations of the GATT are invoked, they are not used as a mere pretext by the invoking State in order to discriminate (arbitrarily or unjustifiably) against a trading partner or to disguise protectionist restrictions on trade while, at the same time, ensuring that any measures that come under the Art. XX general exceptions 'should not be so applied as to frustrate or defeat the legal obligations of the holder of the right under the substantive rules of the [GATT]'.[124]

The application of the chapeau is controversial in practice, as if too strictly applied it removes the potency of the exceptions, while too liberal an interpretation would allow the frustration or defeat of the obligations of the right holder. The precise way in which this fine line can be adjudged is not clear but will be indicated where measures are 'applied reasonably, with due regard to the legal duties of the party claiming the exception and the legal rights of the other parties concerned'[125]; they must 'maintain a balance' while ensuring that 'the right to invoke one of those exceptions is not to be rendered illusory'.[126] The fact that the right holder's position must be taken into account at all is questionable in the application of a rule and exception constellation, though the focus of the chapeau on the application of the measure,[127] rather than its contents,[128] may serve to mitigate any prejudicial effects of such an approach on the State invoking the exception.

The 'second tier' analysis of the chapeau contains three elements:

- arbitrary discrimination between countries where the same conditions prevail;
- unjustifiable discrimination between countries where the same conditions prevail;
- a disguised restriction on international trade.[129]

Furthermore, the first two of these elements contain a three-part test:

- the application of the measure must result in discrimination;
- the discrimination must be arbitrary or unjustifiable;

---

[124]*Ibid.*, pg. 21 (gasoline).

[125]*Ibid.*

[126]Appellate Body Report *United States – Import Prohibition of Certain Shrimp and Shrimp Products*, para. 156.

[127]Appellate Body Report *United States – Standards for Reformulated and Conventional Gasoline*, pg. 20.

[128]*Ibid.*

[129]See Appellate Body Report *United States – Import Prohibition of Certain Shrimp and Shrimp Products*, para. 150.

- the discrimination must occur between countries where the same conditions prevail.[130]

In reference to the discrimination involved under the chapeau, interpretative problems could arise—as there is necessarily discrimination in the application of the measure in question if it has been found to breach Art. I or III of the GATT. This would appear to (at least theoretically) negate the very purpose of general exceptions. In order to avoid such problems, the Appellate Body made clear in *US – Gasoline* that '[t]he provisions of the chapeau cannot logically refer to the same standard(s) by which the violation of a substantive rule has been determined to have occurred'.[131]

The Body further stated:

> The chapeau is further animated by the principle that while the exceptions of Article XX may be invoked as a matter of legal right, they should not be so applied as to frustrate or defeat the legal obligations of the holder of the right under the substantive rules of the [GATT]. If those exceptions are not to be abused or misused, in other words, the measures falling within the particular exceptions must be applied reasonably, with due regard both to the legal duties of the party claiming the exception and the legal rights of the other parties concerned.[132]

This approach was confirmed by the Body in *US – Shrimp/Turtle* decision.[133]

The discrimination cannot thus refer to the normal type of prohibited discrimination in Arts. I and III of the GATT[134]: it must be arbitrary or unjustifiable. The fact that the exceptions contained in Art. XX can be 'invoked as a legal right', but ought not to be applied so as to defeat the substantive obligations of the GATT, is a potential limitation of the practical application of general environmental exceptions, particularly when the Appellate Body makes statements such as the following: 'In our view, the language of the chapeau makes clear that each of the exceptions [. . .] is a limited and conditional exception.'[135] However, as highlighted above, the focus of the chapeau on the application of the measure, rather than its specific contents, means that this criticism may fail to meet the mark.

'Arbitrary or unjustifiable discrimination between two countries where the same conditions prevail' encompasses discrimination between trading partners[136] but also against a trading partner vis-à-vis domestic production,[137] mirroring both Art. I and Art. III GATT.

---

[130]*Ibid.*

[131]Appellate Body Report *US – Standards for Reformulated and Conventional Gasoline*, pg. 23.

[132]*Ibid.*, pg. 22.

[133]See Appellate Body Report *United States – Import Prohibition of Certain Shrimp and Shrimp Products*, para. 151. See further: *Bernasconi-Osterwalder et al.* (note 60), 119–122.

[134]Appellate Body Report *US – Standards for Reformulated and Conventional Gasoline*, pg. 21.

[135]Appellate Body Report *US – Import Prohibition of Certain Shrimp and Shrimp Products*, para. 158.

[136]Appellate Body Report *US – Standards for Reformulated and Conventional Gasoline*, pg. 21.

[137]*Ibid.*

Further, following the Appellate Body in *US – Shrimp/Turtle*:

> It may be quite acceptable for a government, in adopting and implementing a domestic policy, to adopt a single standard to all its citizens throughout the country. However, it is not acceptable, in international trade relations, for one WTO Member to use an economic embargo to *require* other Members to adopt essentially the same comprehensive regulatory program, to achieve a certain policy goal, as that in force within that Member's territory, *without* taking into considerations different conditions which may occur in the territories of those other Members.

> We believe that discrimination results not only when countries in which the same conditions prevail are differently treated, but also when the application of the measure at issue does not allow for any inquiry into the appropriateness of the regulatory program for the conditions prevailing in those exporting countries.[138]

Thus, against the specific wording of the chapeau, the DSS will take into account discrimination that occurs that fails to take into account different conditions. This quotation demonstrates, above all, that in the case where a policy decision is made in an importing State that has the effect of requiring exporting States to adopt the same regulatory program, then this will not be justified *unless* the differing conditions existing in the exporting State are taken into account.

What would this then mean for TREMs based on NPR PPMs? The result depends on the relative bargaining power of the importing and exporting States, on their level of economic development and feasibly also on their own environmental policies. Import bans on the basis of NPR PPMs necessarily '*require* other Members to adopt essentially the same comprehensive regulatory program to achieve a certain policy goal', or they will face exclusion from that market. This means that if an importing State creates a TREM restricting imports on the basis of NPR PPMs and thus discriminates against or between trading partners (probably both), then it must inquire as to the appropriateness of the measure on the basis of the conditions prevailing in the exporting country/ies (alongside ensuring that such a measure does not constitute arbitrary or unjustifiable discrimination against/between countries where the same conditions prevail). The example of GMOs, which will be examined in detail in a later chapter, may pose particular problems here as food products containing GMOs are produced in both developed and developing countries,[139] meaning that the particular policy reasons for the exporting countries' reliance on such crops may result from different bases. Whether this could mean that a ban on GMO containing products from developed countries (in so far as it is not covered by the SPS Agreement) would be justified but

---

[138] Appellate Body Report *United States – Import Prohibition of Certain Shrimp and Shrimp Products*, paras. 164–165.

[139] The largest field areas for GMO crops were recorded in 2013 as being: USA (70.1 Million hectare), Brazil (40.3), Argentina (24.4), India (11.0), Canada (10.8) and China (4.2). See http://www.gmo-compass.org/eng/agri_biotechnology/gmo_planting/257.global_gm_planting_2013.html (last accessed on 05/03/2017).

not justified if from developing countries seems inherently unlikely but appears plausible on the basis of the reasoning laid down in *US – Shrimp/Turtle*.

5.5.5 Analysis

Article XX (a), (b) and (g) constitutes exceptions to the substantive rules laid out in Arts. I, III and XI of the GATT. While the duties on the importing State (and thus the rights of the exporting States) are laid out in the substantive provisions,[140] the question arises as to the precise nature of the legal relations created by Art. XX. Although the Appellate Body described the nature of Art. XX by stating that 'Article XX may be invoked as a matter of legal right',[141] following *Hohfeld* what we actually see in Art. XX is a privilege. It is a sphere of action that limits the duties imposed on the importing State by Arts. I, III and XI. It is itself then limited by the duties that are incumbent upon the importing State wishing to make use of the particular exception contained in one of the sub-paragraphs. Thus, while the rights and duties laid out in Arts. I, III and XI contain specific privileges and exposures— the general ones contained in the exceptions serve to reduce the scope of these duties further.

Article XX (a) provides importing States with a privilege of potentially very wide-ranging (but as yet not fully tested in the realm of NPR PPMs) scope that may prove the decisive 'environmental exception' in the future, if States become more creative with their invocation of the exceptions due to Doha deadlock or increased domestic pressure for TREMs. The privilege contained in Art. XX (a) is limited by the conditions for its exercise (duties): (1) that the measure protects public morals and (2) that it is necessary to do so. As outlined above, the sphere of Art. XX (a) is potentially very broad as feasibly any issue can be invoked on the basis of protection of public morality—and, following the Panel in *US – Gambling*, 'each WTO member has considerable discretion to determine what practices would violate the moral code of the community'.[142] This discretion (due to the culture-specific and thus subjective nature of public morality), despite the inclusion of 'necessary' in Art. XX (a) (see above section on Art. XX (b) for analysis of this term), constitutes a far-reaching privilege that serves to severely restrict the duties contained in the substantive provisions of the GATT. As outlined above, this possibility has already been partially tested in the *EC – Fur Seals* case and may be the best option for introducing a total ban on products with environmentally

---

[140]See also Appellate Body Report *United States – Standards for Reformulated and Conventional Gasoline*, pg. 22.

[141]*Ibid.*

[142]*Robert Howse/Joanna Langille*, Permitting Pluralism: The Seals Products Dispute and Why the WTO Should Accept Trade Restrictions Justified by Noninstrumental Moral Values, YJIL 37 (2011), 367, 413; Panel Report, *United States — Measures Affecting the Cross-Border Supply of Gambling and Betting Services*, para. 6.461.

damaging NPR PPMs in the future, providing that the WTO member involved can establish that the protection of the environment within its polity is a moral issue.

The privilege contained in Art. XX (b), on the other hand, is not so wide ranging. It is further limited by the duties that the measure must be designed to protect the life or health of humans, animals or plants and that the measure must be necessary to achieve such protection. As discussed above, a further privilege is included in the first of these duties as States can determine their own level of protection. The 'necessity' requirement, which is a further duty limiting the privilege of Art. XX (b), was demonstrated in the foregoing as having been subject to problematic interpretation (i.e., the analogous interpretation of necessary in this article with the procedural Art. XX (d)). As highlighted above, the interpretation of this concept in this manner blurs exceptions enacted for policy and procedural purposes and thus removes the intended policy-protective element of Art. XX (b), further limiting the scope of this privilege and thus increasing the scope of the duties contained in both the substantive provisions and those within the exceptions themselves.

Article XX (g) is similarly a privilege, limiting the scope of the duties contained in Arts. I, III and XI of the GATT. It is itself limited by the conditions imposed upon its exercise, i.e. that the measures imposed must relate to the conservation of exhaustible natural resources and that any such measures must also be made effective in conjunction with restrictions on domestic production or consumption. As discussed above, the scope of 'relating to' is broader than that of 'necessary' under Art. XX (b). Nevertheless, the relatively narrow interpretation employed by the DSS has limited the possibilities of Art. XX (g) and narrowed the scope of the privilege—again widening the duties of the importing State. The second element that ensures that such measures must be made effective in conjunction with restrictions on domestic consumption is perhaps superfluous, due to the chapeau, but also lacks relevance in the context of TREMs, which this work assumes are not intentionally protectionist in nature and thus ought to be accompanied by such domestic restrictions.

These privileges (Art. XX (a), (b) and (g)) have individual limitations in the form of the duties contained therein (explained above). However, the chapeau is also of relevance here as it introduces a general limitation on all exceptions—and thus constitutes a duty on the State attempting to justify its measure under one of the exceptions. The requirements of the chapeau that States attempting to make use of one of the exceptions cannot discriminate in an arbitrary or unjustifiable manner and the discrimination must occur between countries where the same conditions prevail (or fail to take into account where different conditions prevail) limit the privileges of the importing State in its application of measures under Art. XX. This limitation in the scope of the privilege has the consequence of broadening and strengthening the duties contained in the substantive provisions of the GATT.

While the reasons for the inclusion of the chapeau are clear, with regard to Art. XI and the 'right of market access' under the GATT, this further limitation, alongside the limitations included in the sub-paragraphs themselves, can be seen to strengthen the robust character of the obligation to eliminate quantitative restrictions under the GATT. Thus, the 'right' contained in Art. XI is a Hohfeldian right (see above), and after analysis of the spheres of exposure (the privileges of the importing States), it can be demonstrated that Art. XI does indeed contain a broad right of market access. When assessed against *Krasner's* Interdependence Sovereignty (which 'refers to the ability of public authorities to regulate the flow of information, ideas, goods, people, pollutants, or capital across borders'), such a right for other WTO members is demonstrated to be a sizable ceding of this element of sovereignty. While it is of course beneficial for a State when exporting, this loss of the ability to control the flow of goods is a legitimate concern for States, particularly in instances where they are dissatisfied with the interpretation and application of Art. XX in its ability to allow for them to legislate on policy issues. This is of course particularly problematic in the case of TREMs based on NPR PPMs.

Moving back to Art. XX itself, as can be seen from the foregoing, the conditions imposed on States hoping to use the Art. XX exceptions are fairly extensive and fraught with interpretational uncertainty or based upon the more than questionable jurisprudence of the DSS (particularly with regard to the interpretation of 'necessary' in Art. XX (b) and (d)). Here, it is thus demonstrated that when attempting to define the precise parameters arising from GATT obligations (both the substantive duties and the Art. XX privilege/exceptions), States are faced with judicial law-making, overreach, a lack of formal realisability and thus uncertainty. What is clear from a power distributive perspective is that the combination of Arts. I, III and XI with Art. XX places yet more power in the hands of the DSS. Thus, when attempting to establish the effect of the WTO on national regulatory space in the area of environmental regulation, it is clear that, at least in the application of TREMs, this is significantly encroached upon.

Due to the lack of formal realisability, the precise parameters are even more difficult to assess (as all attempts to see effects on space are necessarily difficult), but by tracing the position of States in their legal relations and seeing where power is distributed by these relations, it is clear that from *Krasner's* four sovereignty markers, three are affected. Westphalian sovereignty, which 'refers to political organization based on the exclusion of external actors from authority structures within a given territory', can clearly be seen to be affected through the concentration of power in the hands of the DSS in relation to TREMs; domestic sovereignty, which 'refers to the formal organization of political authority within the state and the ability of public authorities to exercise effective control within the borders of their own polity', can be seen to be affected in terms of the constraints upon national regulatory space, which are evidenced in the above analysis; and interdependence sovereignty, which 'refers to the ability of public authorities to regulate the flow on information, ideas, goods, people, pollutants, or capital across borders', is clearly affected in cases in which States are not allowed to apply TREMs to NPR PPMs as, in this case, States are no longer able to regulate what crosses their borders while at the same time not acting in contravention of their obligations under the WTO. Where three of the four manifestations of sovereignty are affected by this arm of the WTO, it must be stated that WTO membership, at least in this field, has a substantial negative effect on sovereignty.

Article XX (a), (b) and (g) constitutes the environmental exceptions to the substantive obligations contained in the GATT (as outlined, Arts. I, III, XI are of particular relevance in this study). As mentioned above, the importance of the exceptions in relation to NPR PPMs hinges particularly on the question of whether they can be included (at all, or more importantly as the decisive criterion) in an assessment of the 'likeness' of products. If not, and a violation is found based on a TREM, then the efficacy of the environmental exceptions to protect policy choices vis-à-vis trade commitments comes into play.

From the foregoing analysis, it can be seen that interpretation of the exceptions is not always favourable to policy decisions and that the system of rule and exception encroaches upon national regulatory space and thus upon sovereignty, in the political science sense of the term. Though it is clear from the preceding that NPR PPMs will (at present) not render products 'unlike' and even if they are seen to fall under one of the environmental exceptions may face significant problems overcoming the additional duties in the chapeau, Part II of this chapter will map out a selection of the GATT/environmental cases from the beginning of the GATT to the present day in order to assess the application of the measures analysed above by the DSS in depth.

5.6 Developing Countries and the GATT

As is clear from the foregoing, many of the issues raised in relation to environmental policy, NPR PPMs and the WTO involve developing countries. Developing countries are offered special treatment under the GATT in Part VI—entitled 'Trade and Development'. This section offers a series of principles and objectives to assist in their development, alongside commitments for developed countries to aid in this assistance. The provisions consist of loose obligations for developed countries: 'shall to the fullest extent possible – that is, except when compelling reasons [. . .] make it impossible to', 'accord high priority', 'make every effort', 'have special regard', as well as a joint action framework to assist in development.

The way in which these issues are addressed does not directly deal with the problems raised in this study, but it should be noted that such obligations on developed States could be given more emphasis in future negotiations in order that some of the more harmful effects of the WTO system may be mitigated for developing countries. In this way, it might be possible to move some of the non-tariff barrier to trade policy issues away from the development agenda, by refocusing the debate on what developed countries can proactively do to assist development while at the same time continuing to be able to follow their own desired development and health policies.

Furthermore, the 1979 Decision on Differential and More Favourable Treatment, Reciprocity and Fuller Participation of Developing Countries, or the 'Enabling Clause', provides developing countries with an additional mechanism under the GATT to give them preferential and more favourable treatment. The enabling clause allows developed countries, under the Generalised System of Preferences, to offer 'non-reciprocal preferential treatment (such as zero or low duties on imports) to products originating in developing countries'. However, 'preference-giving countries unilaterally determine which countries and which products are included in their schemes'.[143] Despite the good intention of the Enabling Clause, it clearly hands more power to developed countries, which can further choose who they discriminate against. While removing such a power may harm some developing countries, it is fairer to attempt to structurally readjust the system in favour of developing countries—or at least less to their detriment.

---

[143]https://www.wto.org/english/tratop_e/devel_e/dev_special_differential_provisions_e.htm (last accessed on 05/03/2017).

Chapter 6
Environmental Cases Under the GATT

6.1 Overview

> Until the late 1980s, even as the environmental movement was growing in all the industrial countries, it was only sporadically suggested that the concerns of environmentalists and conservationists were in conflict with the objectives with the GATT and related movements to reduce trade barriers. It was occasionally suggested that trade contributes to economic growth, that increased economic activity leads to increased pollution, and therefore that trade is bad and so are rules discouraging or forbidding restrictions on trade. But on the whole these suggestions did not win favour.[1]

As mentioned previously,[2] a strict doctrine of precedent does not exist within the WTO (as elsewhere in international law), but there is significant value[3] given to the reports by both the DSS, in any future reports covering the same issue, and by States, which may choose to rely on such reports when enacting policy. Therefore, any assessment of the issue of NPR PPMs and environmental policy under the WTO necessitates an evaluation of the relevant case law to date. Although the extensive coverage here may seem lengthy, it is necessary in order to give a proper impression of how these issues are dealt with, not only by the Panels and Appellate Body but also by WTO Members themselves. In this way, this part helps deepen understanding of the problems raised through their application, and not merely in the abstract, under the WTO and covered agreements.

The environmental cases/relevant cases under the GATT 47 that will be addressed here are as follows:

---

[1]*Andreas F. Lowenfeld*, International Economic Law (Oxford, 2002), 314.

[2]See *supra*, Chap. 3 and *James K. R. Watson*, The WTO and the Environment: Development of Competence Beyond Trade (Oxford, 2013), 84–88.

[3]*Watson* (note 2), 84.

© Springer International Publishing AG 2017
A.R. Maggio, *Environmental Policy, Non-Product Related Process and Production Methods and the Law of the World Trade Organization*, European Yearbook of International Economic Law 1, DOI 10.1007/978-3-319-61155-6_6

- *United States – Restrictions on the Import of Tuna (Tuna/Dolphin I),*
- *United States – Restrictions on the Import of Tuna (Tuna/Dolphin II),*
- *United States – Standards for Reformulated and Conventional Gasoline,*
- *United States – Import Prohibition of Certain Shrimp and Shrimp Products,*
- *European Communities – Measures Affecting Asbestos and Asbestos-Containing Products.*

Although the other environmental cases dealt with later under the TBT and SPS Agreements also involved GATT infringements, these cases are better assessed under the more specific agreements involved.

6.2 Tuna/Dolphin I

6.2.1 Facts and Arguments of the Parties

The *Tuna/Dolphin* GATT decisions are probably the most controversial trade/environment cases to date. Following the above quotation,[4] the prevailing approach to possible trade/environment clashes was, for a long time, a rough estimation that although there was perhaps a potential for problems between the two regimes, it warranted no great cause for concern. However, this changed irrevocably with the GATT Panel decisions in the *Tuna/Dolphin* cases.

The first *Tuna/Dolphin* case was brought by Mexico following the imposition of an embargo on yellowfin tuna caught using purse-seine nets in the Eastern Tropical Pacific (ETP) affecting Mexico, Venezuela, Vanuatu, Panama and Ecuador.[5] Due to the particular circumstances that exist there, the 'intentional encirclement of dolphins with purse-seine nets [was] used as a tuna fishing technique only in the Eastern Tropical Pacific Ocean'.[6] According to Section 101 (a) (2) of the US Marine Mammal Protection Act of 1972,[7] the US Secretary of the Treasury was obligated[8] to ban the importation of 'commercial fish or products from fish which have been caught with commercial fishing technology which results in the incidental kill or incidental serious injury of ocean mammals in excess of United States standards'. On this basis, on 28 August 1990, the US Government imposed an embargo on 'imports of commercial yellowfin tuna and yellowfin tuna products harvested with purse-seine nets in the ETP'.[9] In the following months, this embargo

---

[4]*Lowenfeld* (note 1), 314.

[5]GATT Panel Report *United States – Restrictions on the Import of Tuna (Tuna/Dolphin I)*, DS21/R 1991, para. 2.7 (unadopted).

[6]*Ibid.*, para. 2.2.

[7]Marine Mammal Protection Act of 1972, 16 U.S.C. 1361–1407.

[8]GATT Panel Report *United States – Restrictions on the Import of Tuna (Tuna/Dolphin I)*, DS21/R 1991, para. 2.5 (unadopted).

[9]*Ibid.*, para. 2.7.

was adjusted, partially lifted and reintroduced,[10] and the further stipulation was included that tuna that was imported into the US had to be accompanied by a NOAA Form 370-1 'Yellowfin Tuna Certificate of Origin' providing that the tuna had not been harvested with purse-seine nets in the ETP by vessels from Mexico, Venezuela or Vanuatu[11] and demonstrating the origin of the tuna products.[12] Also of relevance in this case was the Dolphin Protection Consumer Information Act, enacted on 28 November 1990. This Act specified a 'labelling standard for any tuna product exported from or offered for sale'[13] in the US and made it an offence to distribute tuna products that may have 'falsely suggest[ed] that the tuna contained therein was fished in a manner not harmful to dolphins',[14] if they were, *inter alia*, 'harvest[ed] in the Eastern Tropical Pacific Ocean by a vessel using purse-seine nets which does not meet certain specified conditions for being considered dolphin safe'.[15]

Mexico requested that the Panel find that, *inter alia*, the US embargo was inconsistent with Art. XI of the GATT[16] and that the 'conditions of comparison between yellowfin tuna regulation in the United States and in another country' were inconsistent with Art. III GATT.[17] Mexico further sought that the Panel finds the Dolphin Protection Consumer Information Act to be inconsistent with the US's obligations under Arts. I and XI of the GATT.[18]

The United States argued that the Marine Mammal Protection Act embargo was justified under Art. III:4 GATT, and even if it was not, then it would fall under Arts. XX (b) and XX (g) general exceptions.[19] The US argued that, in this case, Art. XI did not apply as the regulations in question were 'laws, regulations and requirements affecting the internal sale, offering for sale, purchase, transportation, distribution or use of yellowfin tuna harvested in the ETP with purse-seine nets'.[20] With regard to the Dolphin Protection Consumer Information Act, the US argued that Arts. I and III applied as the measures in question focused on where the tuna was caught and not the country of origin of the export. The US further argued that the measure was not inconsistent with these articles.[21]

---

[10]*Ibid.*, para. 2.7–2.8.

[11]*Ibid.*, para. 2.8.

[12]*Ibid.* Also at issue in this case were exports into the US from 'intermediary nations': *ibid.*, para. 2.10.

[13]GATT Panel Report *United States – Restrictions on the Import of Tuna (Tuna/Dolphin I)*, DS21/R 1991, para. 2.12 (unadopted).

[14]*Ibid.*

[15]*Ibid.* Under the WTO, labelling is now an issue covered by the TBT Agreement and will be dealt with below in Chaps. 7–8.

[16]GATT Panel Report *United States – Restrictions on the Import of Tuna (Tuna/Dolphin I)*, DS21/R 1991, para. 3.1 (a) (unadopted).

[17]*Ibid.*, para. 3.1 (b).

[18]*Ibid.*, para. 3.3.

[19]*Ibid.*, para. 3.6.

[20]*Ibid.*, para. 3.11.

[21]*Ibid.*, para. 3.8.

In relation to Art. XX, Mexico argued:

> [N]othing in Article XX entitled any contracting party to impose measures in the imple-
> mentation of which the jurisdiction of one contracting party would be subordinated to the
> legislation of another contracting party. It could be deduced from the letter and spirit of
> Article XX that it was confined to measures contracting parties could adopt or apply within
> or from their own territory. To accept that one contracting party might impose trade
> restrictions to conserve the resources of another contracting party would have the conse-
> quence of introducing the concept of extraterritoriality into the GATT, which would be
> extremely dangerous for all contracting parties.[22]

6.2.2   Panel Report

The Panel's findings noted that under the Marine Mammals Protection Act, the
United States conditioned market access on the provision of satisfaction by countries wishing to export yellowfin tuna products caught in the ETP that the overall
regulatory regime regarding the taking of mammals is comparable to the United
States, specifically that it must be proved that 'the average rate of incidental taking
of marine mammals by its tuna fleet operating in the ETP is not in excess of 1.25
times the average incidental taking rate of United States vessels operating in the
ETP during the same period'.[23]

The Panel laid out four points of contention that it would first assess for GATT
consistency and then, if they were found to be inconsistent, in light of the Art. XX
general exceptions.[24] These four points covered (1) the import ban under the
Marine Mammals Protection Act, (2) the import ban from 'intermediary nations',[25]
(3) the potential extension of the ban to all fish products from Mexico and (4) the
provisions of the Dolphin Protection Consumer Information Act, in particular the
labelling requirements.[26]

In the Panel's analysis of the first point, it focused on the nature of the tuna
products in question (although avoiding the language of 'like products', as later
developed under the WTO). With regard to the import embargo under the Marine
Mammals Protection Act, the Panel stated that it did not 'prescribe fishing techniques that could have an **effect on tuna as a product**'.[27] The Panel did not view
the embargo as a measure that fell under Art. III:4[28] but further stated that 'Article
III:4 calls for a comparison of the treatment of imported tuna as a product with that

---

[22]*Ibid.*, para. 3.33.

[23]*Ibid.*, para. 5.2.

[24]*Ibid.*, para. 5.7.

[25]See *supra*.

[26]GATT Panel Report *United States – Restrictions on the Import of Tuna (Tuna/Dolphin I)*, DS21/
R 1991, para. 5.7 (unadopted).

[27]*Ibid.*, para. 5.10 (emphasis added).

[28]See *ibid.*, paras. 5.11–5.15.

of domestic tuna as a product. Regulations governing the taking of dolphins incidental to the taking of tuna could not possibly affect tuna as a product.'[29] The Panel ruled that were Art. III:4 to apply in this case, then the United States must offer treatment no less favourable to tuna products from Mexico on the basis that the products could not be distinguished, 'whether or not the incidental taking of dolphins by Mexican vessels corresponds to that of United States vessels'.[30] With regard to a violation of Art. XI:1, the Panel found a clear violation.[31]

The attempted invocation of Art. XX general exceptions by the US led the Panel to describe Art. XX as a 'limited and conditional exception from obligations under other provisions of the General Agreement, and not a positive rule establishing obligations in itself',[32] whose burden of proof rests on the contracting party invoking the exception.[33]

With regard to Art. XX (b), the Panel sought to answer the key question as to 'whether Article XX(b) covers measures necessary to protect human, animal or plant life or health outside the jurisdiction of the contracting party taking the measure'[34] and in doing so turned to the drafting history of the GATT[35] as the answer was not apparent from the wording of the provision.[36] The Panel found that such extraterritorial effects were not envisaged during the drafting of the Havana Charter and, furthermore, that such an interpretation would indeed be harmful to the multilateral trading system itself. The Panel stated:

> The Panel considered that if the broad interpretation of Article XX(b) suggested by the United States were accepted, each contracting party could unilaterally determine the life or health protection policies from which other contracting parties could not deviate without jeopardizing their rights under the General Agreement. The General Agreement would then no longer constitute a multilateral framework for trade among all contracting parties but would provide legal security only in respect of trade between a limited number of contracting parties with identical internal regulations.[37]

The Panel went on to assess that even if the GATT were intended to permit extra-jurisdictional protection of life and health, the US measure would not meet the requirement of necessity set out in that provision as the Panel held that the US must first exhaust all GATT-consistent measures available to it in the pursuance of its dolphin protection standards.[38] The Panel suggested that this would also include the

---

[29]*Ibid.*, para. 5.15.

[30]*Ibid.*

[31]*Ibid.*, paras. 5.17–5.19.

[32]*Ibid.*, para. 5.22.

[33]*Ibid.*

[34]*Ibid.*, para. 5.25.

[35]See the history of the GATT/Havana Charter in Sect. 3.2.

[36]GATT Panel Report *United States – Restrictions on the Import of Tuna (Tuna/Dolphin I)*, DS21/R 1991, (unadopted), 5.25–5.26.

[37]*Ibid.*, para. 5.27.

[38]*Ibid.*, para. 5.28.

'negotiation of international cooperative agreements'.[39] The Panel found, thus, that Art. XX (b) could not be relied upon to justify the measures in question.

The US attempt to rely on the exception contained in Art. XX (g) was similarly excluded on the basis of the extra-jurisdictional protection, with the further explanation from the Panel that even if Art. XX (g) allowed such extraterritoriality, the US measure was not capable of fulfilling the requirement of being 'related to' the conservation of natural resources. This was the case as it was not 'primarily aimed at' dolphin conservation, based on the argument that as the maximum dolphin taking rate for Mexico at any given time was dependant on the rate recorded by US vessels, such a 'limitation on trade based on such unpredictable conditions could not be regarded as being primarily aimed at the conservation of dolphins'.[40] This argument does not appear to be particularly sound and was not further expanded on by the Panel.

As regards the second point covering the import ban from 'intermediary nations', the Panel similarly found that Art. III did not apply and that the ban violated Art. XI:1. The ban was also not found to be covered by the exceptions in Art. XX (b) or (d).[41] The third point was not deemed to be a violation as, although such a measure was envisaged in legislation,[42] the legislation 'did not require trade measures to be taken'.[43] The final point, labelling requirements, was deemed to fall not under Art. XI:1 of the GATT but rather under Art. I:1. In this respect, the Panel also found no violation as the measure was 'applied to all countries whose vessels fished in this geographical area and thus did not distinguish between products originating in Mexico and products originating in other countries'.[44]

In its concluding remarks, the Panel stated:

> The Panel wished to underline that its task was limited to the examination of this matter 'in the light of the relevant GATT provisions', and therefore did not call for a finding on the appropriateness of the United States' and Mexico's conservation policies as such.[45]

The Panel went on to point out that, in its view, the GATT imposed 'few constraints on a contracting party's implementation of domestic environmental policies'[46] as the rights to tax imports and domestic production were provided,[47] but '[a]s a corollary to these rights, a contracting party may not restrict imports of a product merely because it originates in a country with environmental policies

[39]Ibid.

[40]Ibid., para. 5.33.

[41]Ibid., para. 5.35–5.40.

[42]Section 8 of the Fishermen's Protective Act (Pelly Amendment) P.L. 92-219 (85 Stat. 786).

[43]GATT Panel Report United States – Restrictions on the Import of Tuna (Tuna/Dolphin I), DS21/R 1991, para. 5.21 (unadopted).

[44]Ibid., para. 5.43.

[45]Ibid., para 6.1.

[46]Ibid., para. 6.2.

[47]Ibid.

different from its own'.[48] With regard to the general exceptions, the Panel stated that it was necessary for these exceptions to have limits, and were Art. XX to 'permit import restrictions in response to differences in environmental policies',[49] then it would be preferable for the contracting parties to amend the GATT or waive the obligations altogether rather than have this substantiated through the interpretation of Art. XX.[50]

6.2.3   Analysis

From this GATT case, several issues are raised that are relevant to this study. The issue at hand concerns the regulation of NPR PPMs, and the Panel clearly pronounced that the legislation at hand did not create a standard based on anything that could have an effect on tuna as a product—thus proscribing the possibility of such products being treated as 'like'. With regard to the invocation of Art. XX, the Panel made it clear that no positive rules were included in the exceptions but rather limited and 'exceptional' exceptions to the main substantive rules of the GATT. Despite being convinced of the position that measures that apply extraterritorially, such as those involved in this case, are not covered by the Art XX exceptions, the Panel nonetheless addressed reasons why, even if this were not the case, these measures would fail to meet the requirements of Art. XX (b) and (g). With regard to the Art. XX (b) exception, the GATT Panel proclaimed that even if extraterritorial rules were permissible under Art XX, that would not apply in this case as the United States did not exhaust all other GATT-consistent measures. Article XX (g) would not have been able to be successfully invoked, as the measure in question could not meet the 'primarily aimed at' requirement.

6.3   Tuna/Dolphin II

6.3.1   Facts and Arguments of the Parties

The second of the two GATT *Tuna/Dolphin* Panels gave its report in 1994, just before the WTO came into operation. A largely identical factual background to *Tuna/Dolphin I* applied in this case.[51] In *Tuna/Dolphin II*, the EEC and the Netherlands requested that the Panel find the US' preliminary and intermediary import

---

[48]*Ibid.*

[49]*Ibid.*, para. 6.3.

[50]*Ibid.*

[51]Although there were some developments in the interim period, see GATT Panel Report *United States – Restrictions on the Import of Tuna*, DS29/R 1994, paras. 2.1–2.15 (unadopted).

embargoes on tuna products caught using purse-seine nets to be inconsistent with their obligations under the GATT (Arts. III and XI:1). The United States sought to argue that the measures were consistent with their substantive obligations under the GATT, and if not, then they meet the requirements of the exceptions under Art XX,[52] stating 'that there was no requirement in Article XX (g) for the resources to be within the territorial jurisdiction of the country taking the measure'.[53] The EEC and the Netherlands were of the opposite view, claiming that 'the resource to be conserved had to be within the territorial jurisdiction of the country taking the measure' and that 'the United States measures were not related to the conservation of an exhaustible natural resource under Article XX (g)'.[54]

6.3.2   Panel Report

The Panel found that Art. III did not apply in this case[55] but that 'the embargoes imposed by the United States were "prohibitions or restrictions" in the terms of Article XI'.[56] In this instance, the Panel was not persuaded of the view that Art. XX (g) was limited to nature conservation within the territory of the United States,[57] but neither was it persuaded that 'measures taken so as to force other countries to change their policies, and that were effective only if such changes occurred, could not be primarily aimed either at the conservation of an exhaustible natural resource'.[58] The embargoes thus failed to meet the requirements of Art. XX (g). With regard to the invocation of Art. XX (b) to 'protect the life or health of dolphins',[59] the Panel similarly found that it was within the range of measures that would be covered by Art. XX (b)[60] but that the US measures could not be said to be 'necessary', and thus the requirements for Art. XX (b) were also not met.[61]

In its concluding remarks, the Panel described the crux of the case as whether 'in the pursuit of its environmental objectives, the United States could impose trade embargoes to secure changes in the policies which other contracting parties pursued within their own jurisdiction'.[62] In this vein, the Panel felt that the correct approach to this case was to evaluate whether, through the exceptions under Art. XX, the

---

[52]*Ibid.*, paras. 5.1–5.11.
[53]*Ibid.*, para. 5.11.
[54]*Ibid.*
[55]*Ibid.*, para. 5.9.
[56]*Ibid.*, para. 5.10.
[57]*Ibid.*, para. 5.20.
[58]*Ibid.*, para. 5.27.
[59]*Ibid.*, para. 5.28.
[60]*Ibid.*, para. 5.33.
[61]*Ibid.*, para. 5.39.
[62]*Ibid.*, para. 5.42.

contracting parties had agreed to allow import embargoes on the basis of, *inter alia*, the protection of human, animal or plant life or health or the conservation of exhaustible resources.[63] The Panel found, 'after reviewing this issue in the light of the recognized methods of interpretation [...] that none of them lent any support to the view that such an agreement was reflected in Article XX'.[64]

6.3.3   Analysis

In this case, the Panel departed widely from the interpretation of Art. XX by the Panel in *Tuna/Dolphin I* in finding that measures falling under Art. XX were not limited to the territory of the contracting party. However, the Panel concluded that the measure in question could not fall under Art. XX because its extraterritorial purpose to change the policies of exporting States could not be 'necessary', or 'primarily aimed at', within the meaning of Art. XX (b) and (g). The Panel clung to the purpose of Art. XX in coming to this conclusion and did not make any room for the evolutionary interpretation of GATT obligations that may be deemed appropriate, considering the evolution and development of environmental priorities of States.

6.3.4   Tuna/Dolphin I and II

As mentioned above, the *Tuna/Dolphin* GATT Panel Reports are probably the most infamous cases under the GATT and led to intense scrutiny of the GATT in relation to environmental protection. This is not particularly surprising as they were very high-profile cases that involved a subject matter that easily captured the attention of environmentalists and the wider public. What is more surprising, however, is that the infamy surrounding these cases often neglects to properly take into account the fact that they were unadopted by the DSB after being issued by the Panel and thus do not properly form part of the '*aquis*' of the DSS. That being said, even unadopted reports can have some persuasive value, as demonstrated by the Appellate Body in *Japan – Alcohol*, confirming the position of the Panel that 'a panel could nevertheless find useful guidance in the reasoning of an unadopted panel report that it considered to be relevant', despite the fact that such reports 'have no legal status in the GATT or WTO system since they have not been endorsed through decisions by the CONTRACTING PARTIES to GATT or WTO Members'.[65]

---

[63]*Ibid.*

[64]*Ibid.*

[65]Appellate Body Report *Japan –Taxes on Alcoholic Beverages*, pg 14–15.

The two major decisions made by the Panels in these cases were as follows: (1) environmental laws cannot extend beyond national boundaries, so that 'no nation can enact a law protecting the global commons or the species inhabiting them if the law adversely impacts on trade',[66] and (2) the GATT does not allow (at least under Art. III:4) that parties take into account NPR PPMs. Here, the US was under the obligation, in the view of the Panel, to treat imports equally, regardless of how they were produced or whether there are identical restrictions on domestic products. While one Panel believed that the extraterritorial reach of a measure excluded it from the purview of Art. XX altogether, the other said that the measures were of the sort that could fall under Art. XX but that they failed to do so in this case as they did not meet the specific requirements of the specific exceptions, largely on the basis of this extraterritorial reach.

As processing and production occur before export, the issue of territoriality is key to any inquiry as to the status of NPR PPMs under the GATT/WTO. As can be seen from these two reports from the last years of the GATT, this issue was not addressed consistently. Allowing for the fact that the GATT had no appellate review system and bearing in mind that these reports were not adopted, it should still be clear that the provision lacks any clear indication of territorial limitation in its application. It may be desirable for the Panel to have established this point on the basis of evolutionary interpretation—which could be indicated in a treaty by means of preambular purposes or in the DSU itself—but the text of the provision lacks formal realisability. It was not clear if there is a territorial limitation, and the jurisprudence (if not *acquis*) of the GATT did not make this any clearer. States were not in a position to be able to understand the breadth of their obligations, and thus it was not possible for them to legislate accordingly:

> The PPM debate reflects the WTO Members' unwillingness to deal with contentious issues within the negotiating process. The two *US – Tuna/Dolphin* disputes in the early 1990s clearly made the PPM question a central issue in the trade and environment discussions. However, Members did not address the issue during the Uruguay Round [. . .]. Instead, they left the PPM-related ambiguities for the WTO tribunals to resolve.[67]

How this issue has been dealt with under the WTO will be addressed below.

---

[66]*Carol J. Beyers*, The U.S./Mexico Tuna Embargo Dispute: a Case Study of the GATT and Environmental Progress, Maryland JIL 16 (2) (1992), 229, 246.

[67]*Nathalie Bernasconi-Osterwalder/Daniel Magraw/Maria Julia Olivia/Morcos Orellana/Elizabeth Tuerk*, Environment and Trade: A Guide to WTO Jurisprudence (London, 2006), 203.

6.4   United States – Standards for Reformulated and Conventional Gasoline

6.4.1   Facts and Arguments of the Parties

In 1993, the United States put into place regulations that were designed to further environmental policies in relation to emissions in certain areas of the country. These regulations, entitled 'Regulation on Fuels and Fuel Additives – Standards for Reformulated and Conventional Gasoline' (WT/DS4/1), were created by the US Environmental Protection Agency (EPA) under the auspices of the Clean Air Act 1963 (amended 1990) in order to 'improve air quality in the most polluted areas of the country by reducing vehicle emissions of toxic air pollutants and ozone-forming volatile organic compounds'.[68] In order to further this objective, in nine metropolitan areas of the United States where in the period 1987–1989 the worst summertime ozone pollution occurred, only 'reformulated gasoline'[69] could be sold to consumers.[70] In the rest of the United States, 'conventional gasoline' could still be sold.[71] Gasoline from 1990 was to be used as a baseline comparator in assessing reformulated and conventional gasoline.[72] Various methods were used to calculate separate baselines for domestic refiners, foreign refiners and importers, alongside a statutory baseline that was calculated by the EPA. The 75% rule dictated:

> An importer which is also a foreign refiner must determine its individual baseline using Methods 1, 2 and 3 if it imported at least 75 percent, by volume, of the gasoline produced at its foreign refinery in 1990 into the United States in 1990.[73]

Further:

> If actual 1990 data are not available, which is, as for domestic refiners, anticipated by EPA, importers and blenders are assigned to the statutory baseline.

---

[68]Panel Report, *United States – Standards for Reformulated and Conventional Gasoline*, para. 2.1.

[69]Following the Clean Air Act with regard to reformulated gasoline: 'The oxygen content must not be less than 2.0 percent by weight, the benzene content must not exceed 1.0 percent by volume and the gasoline must be free of heavy metals, including lead or manganese. The performance specifications of the CAA require a 15 percent reduction in the emissions of both volatile organic compounds ("VOCs") and toxic air pollutants ("toxics") and no increase in emissions of nitrogen oxides ("NOx"). These requirements are measured by comparing the performance of reformulated gasoline in baseline vehicles (representative model year 1990 vehicles) against the performance of "baseline gasoline" in such vehicles', *ibid.*, para. 2.3. 'Conventional gasoline' was also subject to 'anti-dumping rules' to prevent 'refiners, blenders or importers from dumping into conventional gasoline fuel components that are restricted in reformulated gasoline and that cause environmentally harmful emissions', *ibid.*, para. 2.4.

[70]*Ibid.*, para. 2.2.

[71]*Ibid.*

[72]*Ibid.*, para. 2.5.

[73]*Ibid.*, para. 2.7.

With regard to reformulated gasoline, 'the parameters sulphur, olefins and T-90 are measured against each US refiner's individual 1990 baseline and must be maintained at or below these 1990 levels',[74] whereas 'importers cannot use individual 1990 baseline for sulphur, olefins and T-90, but have to comply with levels specified in the statutory baseline for these parameters'.[75] With regard to 'conventional gasoline', domestic refiners were required 'to measure non-degradation requirements for conventional gasoline against their individual baselines while importers of foreign gasoline are assigned to the statutory baseline'.[76] Although there was a proposal to allow foreign refiners to set their own baselines (though with stricter requirements than domestic refiners), US Congress denied funding to such an amendment.[77]

In this case, brought by Venezuela and later joined by Brazil, it was argued that the US 'Gasoline Rule' was contrary to Arts. I and III of the GATT, not covered by the exceptions in Art. XX and contrary to Art. 2 of the TBT Agreement.[78] With regard to Art. I:1, Venezuela and Brazil argued that the 75% rule granted advantages to certain third countries and was thus a violation of the MFN rule[79] as only refineries in Canada were likely to be able to meet the criteria.[80] The US argued that the 75% rule did not grant an advantage and was available to all refineries, regardless of origin, if they met its two objective criteria.[81] With regard to the national treatment obligation, Venezuela and Brazil argued that the US Gasoline Rule was inconsistent with Art. III:4 GATT[82] as it accorded less favourable treatment to imported gasoline, both reformulated and conventional, than to gasoline from US refineries.[83] The US argued that there was no discrimination against foreign refineries as each 'importer had to satisfy on average the statutory baseline, which approximated average gasoline quality consumed in the US in 1990'.[84]

Importantly in the context of the potential extraterritorial effect of TREMs, the US argued that the Gasoline Rule did not affect foreign refineries, but rather just importers. The refineries were, in principle, 'not required to produce gasoline that met any baseline at all, but could produce gasoline which was cleaner or dirtier than the statutory baseline', and it was only the importers of gasoline that were engaged

---

[74]*Ibid.*, para. 2.9.

[75]*Ibid.*, para. 2.9.

[76]*Ibid.*, para. 2.11.

[77]*Ibid.*, para. 2.13.

[78]*Ibid.*, para. 3.1.

[79]*Ibid.*, para. 3.5.

[80]*Ibid.*, para. 3.6.

[81]*Ibid.*, para. 3.8.

[82]And later with also with regard to Art. III:1, see *ibid.*, paras. 3.34–3.36.

[83]*Ibid.*, para. 3.12.

[84]*Ibid.*, para. 3.17.

by the baseline rule.[85] Thus, the arguments of the complainants were misguided as the measures applied to imported products and not producers.[86]

If the US measures were deemed to be inconsistent with Art. I or III of the GATT, then the US argued that they would fall under the Art. XX general exceptions.[87] The US claimed that the measures aimed to

> protect public health and welfare by reducing emissions of toxic pollutants, VOCs and NOx for reformulated gasoline, and to avoid degradation of air quality for emissions of NOx and toxic air pollutants for conventional gasoline[88]

and thus fell under the Art. XX (b) exception. The crux of the matter was whether the measures were 'necessary'. While the US argued that industry-related practicalities and the level of protection desired demonstrated the necessity of their measures,[89] Venezuela attempted to make the case that the 'necessity' threshold was not met because the US had not demonstrated that there were no less trade-restrictive measures available to achieve the desired policy outcome.[90]

With regard to the Art. XX (d) exception, while the US argued that the 'baseline establishment system was necessary to enforce the non-degradation requirements aiming at preventing deterioration of air quality' and thus fell under the paragraph (d) exception,[91] the complainants argued, *inter alia*, that, similar to Art. XX (b), the necessity requirement was not fulfilled.[92]

With regard to the Art. XX (g) exception, the US argued that clean air was an exhaustible natural resource in the meaning of Art. XX (g) and that the measures in question therefore fell under this exception.[93] Venezuela argued, however, that this was not in line with the original purpose of Art. XX (g), and there was no textual basis for the inclusion of 'clean air' under the term 'exhaustible natural resources'.[94] With regard to the requirement that measures falling under the Art. XX (g) exception are also made effective in conjunction with restrictions on domestic consumption, Brazil argued that even if air could be considered an exhaustible natural resource, 'the Gasoline Rule did not restrict domestic production or consumption of clean air. At best, the Gasoline Rule sought to increase production if not consumption of clean air'[95] and thus failed to meet the requirements of Art. XX (g).

---

[85] *Ibid.*, para. 3.18.
[86] *Ibid.*
[87] *Ibid.*, para. 3.37.
[88] *Ibid.*, para. 3.39.
[89] *Ibid.*, para. 3.40–3.44.
[90] *Ibid.*, 3.45.
[91] *Ibid.*, para. 3.55.
[92] *Ibid.*, para. 3.56–3.57.
[93] *Ibid.*, para. 3.59.
[94] *Ibid.*, para. 3.60.
[95] *Ibid.*, para. 3.65.

The requirements of the chapeau were argued to be met by the US as they claimed that 'differences in treatment were neither arbitrarily nor unjustifiably discriminatory, but were based on valid, legitimate policy reasons'.[96] However, Venezuela argued that the US measures were clearly a 'disguised restriction on international trade',[97] while Brazil was of the view that

> the Gasoline Rule constituted a means of arbitrary or unjustifiable discrimination between countries where the same conditions prevailed. Since the discrimination of imported products was so blatant, Brazil considered that the restrictions on trade were not disguised.[98]

6.4.2 Panel Report

The Panel began its consideration of the case with Art. III:4. The Panel found that the Gasoline Rule was a 'law, regulation or requirement affecting the internal sale, offering for sale, purchase, transportation, distribution or use of an imported product'[99] and thus proceeded to assess its consistency with Art. III:4. The Panel established that under Art. III:4, the 'likeness' of the products was at issue and found that the 'chemically-identical imported and domestic gasoline are like products under Article III:4'.[100] The Panel further decided that as under the baseline establishment methods 'imported gasoline was effectively prevented from benefitting from as favourable sales conditions as were afforded domestic gasoline[...], imported gasoline was treated less favourably than domestic gasoline'.[101] Although the US put forward the argument that this was justified as 'imported gasoline is treated similarly to gasoline from *similarly situated* domestic parties', this was rejected by the Panel.[102] The Panel noted the US argument that imported gasoline was treated on the whole no less favourably than domestic gasoline but, following the reasoning of the Panel in *US – Section 337*, found that 'the "no less favourable" treatment requirement of Article III:4 has to be understood as applicable to each individual case of imported products'[103] and thus rejected the US argument and found a violation of Art. III:4.[104] As a violation was found under Art. III:4, the

---

[96]*Ibid.*, para. 3.67.

[97]*Ibid.*, para. 3.69

[98]*Ibid.*, para. 3.70.

[99]*Ibid.*, para. 6.5.

[100]*Ibid.*, para. 6.9.

[101]*Ibid.*, para. 6.10.

[102]*Ibid.*, paras. 6.11–6.13.

[103]GATT Panel Report *United States – Section 337 of the Tariff Act of 1930*, para. 5.14; Panel Report *United States – Standards for Reformulated and Conventional Gasoline*, para. 6.14.

[104]Panel Report *United States – Standards for Reformulated and Conventional Gasoline*, paras. 6.14–6.16.

Panel, following *US – Malt Beverages*, declined to assess Art. III:1.[105] With regard to Art. I:1, the Panel established that the rule was no longer in force and thus declined to address this issue.[106]

The Panel then went on to assess the Gasoline Rule under the general exceptions under Art. XX. Beginning with Art. XX (b), the Panel agreed that the policy aim of the measure meant that it fell within the remit of Art. XX (b).[107] With regard to the necessity requirement under Art. XX (b), the Panel stated that it was

> not the necessity of the policy goal that was to be examined, but whether or not it was necessary that imported gasoline be effectively prevented from benefitting from as favourable sales conditions as were afforded by an individual baseline tied to the producer of a product.[108]

Following the interpretation of necessary under Art. XX (d) in *US – Section 337*, and reaffirmed in *Thailand – Cigarettes*,[109] the Panel agreed that measures falling under Art. XX (b) could only be deemed to be 'necessary' where 'there were no alternative measures consistent with the General Agreement, or less inconsistent with it'.[110] After a review of the Gasoline Rule, the Panel agreed that there existed possible alternative measures that 'would entail a lesser degree of inconsistency'[111] and thus found that the US measure was inconsistent with Art. III:4 and could not fall under the Art. XX (b) exception as the 'necessity' element had not been fulfilled.[112] The measures were not deemed to be the type that fell under Art. XX (d) and were thus not assessed by the Panel under that exception.[113]

The Panel then went on to assess whether the measure in question fell under the Art. XX (g) exception invoked by the United States. The Panel agreed that clean air is a natural resource that can be depleted and thus 'that a policy to reduce the depletion of clean air was a policy to conserve a natural resource within the meaning of Article XX(g)'.[114] The next step for the Panel was then to assess whether the measure in question was 'related to' the policy goal. Following the GATT Panel in *Canada – Herring and Salmon*, the Panel agreed that the proper

---

[105]GATT Panel Report *United States — Measures Affecting Alcoholic and Malt Beverages*, para. 5.2; Panel Report *United States – Standards for Reformulated and Conventional Gasoline*, para. 6.17.

[106]Panel Report *United States – Standards for Reformulated and Conventional Gasoline*, paras. 6.18–6.19.

[107]*Ibid.*, para. 6.21.

[108]*Ibid.*, para. 6.22.

[109]GATT Panel Report *United States – Section 337 of the Tariff Act of 1930*, para. 5.26.

[110]GATT Panel Report Thailand – Restrictions on Importation and Internal Taxes on Cigarettes, para. 75; Panel Report *United States – Standards for Reformulated and Conventional Gasoline*, para. 6.24.

[111]Panel Report *United States – Standards for Reformulated and Conventional Gasoline*, para. 6.28.

[112]*Ibid.*, paras. 6.28–6.29.

[113]*Ibid.*, paras. 6.30–6.31.

[114]*Ibid.*, paras. 6.37.

interpretation of 'relating to' in Art. XX (g) was 'primarily aimed at'[115] but found that 'it could not be said that the baseline establishment methods that afforded less favourable treatment to imported gasoline were primarily aimed at the conservation of natural resources'.[116] The Panel thus found that this element had not been fulfilled and that the measures at hand did not fall under the Art. XX (g) exception.[117]

6.4.3   Appellate Body Report

The United States appealed certain conclusions on issues of law and legal inter-pretations in the Panel Report pursuant to Art. 16 DSU. In its Notice of Appeal, the US claimed that the Panel erred in law, 'firstly, in holding that the baseline esta-blishment rules of the Gasoline Rule are not justified under Article XX(g) of the General Agreement and, secondly, in its interpretation of Article XX as a whole'.[118]

The Appellate Body agreed with the Panel that the measure fell within the scope of Art. XX (g) as clean air was a resource that could be depleted.[119] The real problem with the Panel Report began, according to the Appellate Body, with the interpretation of 'necessity' and its application in this case.[120] While the Panel was of the view that the issue to be addressed was whether the "'less favourable treatment" of imported gasoline was "primarily aimed at" the conservation of natural resources',[121] the Appellate Body found that the appropriate question was rather whether the "'measure", i.e. the baseline establishment rules, were "primarily aimed at" conservation of clean air'.[122] The Body thus found that the Panel had erred in law 'in referring to its legal conclusion on Article III:4 instead of the measure in issue'.[123] The Body further concluded that the reasoning of the Panel in the application of the 'primarily aimed at' test appeared to confuse this test with the necessary test under Art. XX (b).[124] The Appellate Body took issue with the Panel's

---

[115]GATT Panel Report *Canada – Measures Affecting Exports of Unprocessed Herring and Salmon*, para. 4.6; Panel Report *United States – Standards for Reformulated and Conventional Gasoline*, para. 6.39–6.40.

[116]Panel Report *United States – Standards for Reformulated and Conventional Gasoline*, para. 6.40.

[117]*Ibid.*, para. 6.41.

[118]Appellate Body Report *United States – Standards for Reformulated and Conventional Gasoline*, pg. 9.

[119]*Ibid.*, pg. 14.

[120]*Ibid.*, pg. 16.

[121]*Ibid.*

[122]*Ibid.*

[123]*Ibid.*

[124]*Ibid.*

method of treaty interpretation and failure to properly apply Art. 31 VCLT ('A treaty shall be interpreted in good faith in accordance with the ordinary meaning to be given to the terms of the treaty in their context and in the light of its object and purpose'—considered to be part of customary law).[125] The Appellate Body then pointed to the differing language used in the Art. XX general exceptions[126] and stated that it 'did not seem reasonable' to conclude that the differing language was intended by WTO Members to be interpreted as requiring 'the same kind or degree of connection or relationship between the measure under appraisal and the state interest or policy sought to be promoted or realized'.[127] The Appellate Body viewed the baseline establishment rules as being 'primarily aimed at' the conservation of natural resources for the purposes of Art. XX (g).[128]

The Appellate Body then went on to analyse the rules further under Art. XX (g), next assessing whether the baseline establishment rules were 'made effective in conjunction with restrictions on domestic production or consumption'.[129] The Body sought to answer the question: do 'the measures concerned impose restrictions, not just in respect of imported gasoline but also with respect to domestic gasoline'?[130] The Body confirmed that there was no textual basis for identical treatment under Art. XX (g), nor was an 'effects test' called for under this article.[131] The Appellate Body was thus of the view that the baseline rules in place for domestic refineries demonstrated to the required extent 'restrictions on domestic production or consumption' and thus met the requirements of this part of the test under Art. XX (g).[132]

The Appellate Body then went on to assess the measures under the chapeau of Art. XX. The Body noted that the burden of demonstrating that the measure in question was in conformity with the requirements of the chapeau rested on the party invoking the exception and that this proved to be a heavier burden than demonstrating that the measure in question fell under Art. XX (a)–(j).[133] After conducting a thorough review of the measures, the Appellate Body found

> two omissions on the part of the United States: to explore adequately means, including in particular cooperation with the governments of Venezuela and Brazil, of mitigating the administrative problems relied on as justification by the United States for rejecting

---

[125]*Ibid.*, pg. 15.

[126]'"necessary" – in paragraphs (a), (b) and (d); "essential" – in paragraph (j); "relating to" – in paragraphs (c), (e) and (g); "for the protection of" – in paragraph (f); "in pursuance of" – in paragraph (h); and "involving" – in paragraph (i)', *ibid.*, pg. 17.

[127]*Ibid.*, pg. 18.

[128]*Ibid.*, pg. 19.

[129]*Ibid.*, pg. 19.

[130]*Ibid.*, pg. 20. A requirement that the Appellate Body refers to later as a requirement for '*even-handedness*', *ibid.*, pg. 21.

[131]*Ibid.*, pg. 21.

[132]*Ibid.*, pg. 22.

[133]*Ibid.*, pg. 22–23.

individual baselines for foreign refiners; and to count the costs for foreign refiners that
would result from the imposition of statutory baselines.[134]

These were omissions that in their view went 'well beyond what was necessary
for the Panel to determine that a violation of Article III:4 had occurred in the first
place' and thus constituted unjustifiable discrimination and a disguised restriction
on international trade.[135] The Appellate Body thus found that the US measures
failed to meet the requirements of the chapeau, and thus Art. XX, and were in violation of Art. III:4.

6.4.4 Analysis

Although this case did not directly involve NPR PPMs, and thus 'likeness', as the
environmental effects of gasoline imports occur in the importing country and not
the country where the gasoline is produced, it nonetheless proves helpful in this
study as the issue of extraterritoriality of environmental measures is raised.
Although this issue was not addressed directly by the DSS in this case, the
arguments put forward by the parties and the final resolution of the case provides
some illumination as to the changing attitude of the WTO to extraterritoriality and
Art. XX. Although the US argued that the measures in question affected importers
and not refineries per se, this is not convincing when taking into account US
petroleum consumption[136]—it is unreasonable to expect that refineries will not
change their policies in order to ensure market access to the world's biggest
petroleum-product-consuming nation. Although the measure in question may not
have been aimed at persuading Brazil to change its national regulation of pollutants
in petroleum (a case that would have been more suited to this study), it is nonetheless interesting to see that the extraterritorial application of the rules went largely
without comment.

Furthermore, though the products in question are 'like' and do not differ in their
NPR PPMs, this case is also interesting in that it directly addresses production
methods and industry standards. The rejection of the US appeal by the Appellate
Body based on the failure of the US to meet the requirements of the chapeau can be
seen as judicial overreach on the part of the DSS as they required an adequate
exploration of means 'in particular cooperation with the governments of Venezuela
and Brazil, of mitigating the administrative problems[...]'—while this requirement
to cooperate may be seen as a reasonable way in which the US could have met the
requirements of the chapeau, such specific pronouncements by the Appellate Body
on how to fulfil this obligation that have no textual basis are questionable. This

---

[134]*Ibid.*, pg. 28.

[135]*Ibid.*, pg. 29.

[136]See http://www.indexmundi.com/g/r.aspx?v=91 for recent consumption comparator; https://
www.cia.gov/library/publications/the-world-factbook/geos/us.html (last accessed on 05/03/2017).

preference for cooperation and multilateralism will be discussed further in relation
to the *US – Shrimp/Turtle* case, below.

6.5   United States – Import Prohibition of Certain Shrimp and Shrimp Products

6.5.1   Facts and Arguments of the Parties

In 1996, India, Malaysia, Pakistan and Thailand,[137] acting jointly, requested consultations with the US, pursuant to Art. 4 DSU and Art. XXII:1 GATT 1994 with
regard to a ban 'imposed upon importation of certain shrimp and shrimp products
from the respective countries by the United States'.[138] After the failure of the
consultations to bring about a satisfactory outcome, it was requested that a Panel
be established in order to examine

> the partial embargo on the importation of certain shrimp and shrimp products implemented
> through a series of actions, including enactment of Section 609, promulgation of regu
> lations and issuance of judicial decisions interpreting the law and regulations.[139]

This case concerned an import ban and partial embargo on shrimp caught by
shrimp trawlers without the use of turtle excluder devices (TEDs).[140] After instituting a ban on shrimping without TEDs domestically, in 1991 the US issued guidelines for assessing foreign regulations and comparing them with those in place in
the US. In order to be found comparable, such regulations had to include:

> *inter alia*, a commitment to require all shrimp trawl vessels to use TEDs at all times
> (or reduce tow times for vessels under 25 feet), or, alternatively, a commitment to engage in
> a statistically reliable and verifiable scientific programme to reduce the mortality of sea
> turtles associated with shrimp fishing.[141]

The guidelines allowed a 3-year 'phase-in period' and limited the ban to shrimp
products from certain countries.[142] In 1994, the guidelines were adjusted to remove
the second possibility for certification (the commitment to engage in a statistically

---

[137]While for the most part, the arguments of India, Pakistan and Thailand were given together, and
Malaysia separately, here the word 'complainants' without differentiation is generally preferred as
it is not operative who put forward the specific argument.

[138]Under: 'Section 609 of U.S. Public Law 101-1621 ("Section 609") and the "Revised Notice of
Guidelines for Determining Comparability of Foreign Programs for the Protection of Turtles in
Shrimp Trawl Fishing Operations"': Panel Report *United States – Import Prohibition of Certain Shrimp and Shrimp Products*, para. 1.

[139]*Ibid.*, paras. 1–2.

[140]*Ibid.*, para. 17.

[141]*Ibid.*, para. 18.

[142]Mexico, Belize, Guatemala, Honduras, Nicaragua, Costa Rica, Panama, Colombia, Venezuela,
Trinidad and Tobago, Guyana, Suriname, French Guyana, and Brazil, *ibid.*

reliable and verifiable scientific programme). The 1996 guidelines extended the ban to all foreign nations and provided the definition for shrimp or shrimp products harvested in conditions that do not affect sea turtles (i.e., those not subject to the ban if properly certified) as

> (a) Shrimp harvested in an aquaculture facility [...]; (b) Shrimp harvested by commercial shrimp trawl vessels using TEDs comparable in effectiveness to those required in the United States; (c) Shrimp harvested exclusively by means that do not involve the retrieval of fishing nets by mechanical devices or by vessels using gear that, in accordance with the US programme [...] would not require TEDs; (d) Species of shrimp, such as the pandalid species, harvested in areas in which sea turtles do not occur.[143]

'Other certifications' were also permitted under the 1996 guidelines and included

> a regulatory program governing the incidental taking of sea turtles in the course of commercial shrimp trawl harvesting that is comparable to that of the United States and if the average take rate of that incidental taking by vessels of the harvesting nation is comparable to the average take rate of incidental taking of sea turtles by United States vessels in the course of such harvesting.[144]

It is important to note that the certification programme under Section 609 only issued certificates in instances where the importing nation used TEDs in all of its shrimp trawlers and not only those whose produce was destined for the US.[145] It was thus argued by the complainants that the certification regime was an attempt to 'dictate the environmental policy that was to be followed by other Members with respect to all shrimp caught within their jurisdiction if they wished to export any shrimp to the United States'.[146]

In this case, India, Malaysia, Pakistan and Thailand complained that the US measures were contrary to Arts. XI:1 and XIII:1 of the GATT, were not justified under Art. XX (b) or (g) and nullified or impaired benefits within the meaning of Art. XXIII:1(a) of GATT 1994.[147] India, Pakistan and Thailand additionally requested the Panel to find that Section 609 was contrary to Art. I:1 of the GATT.[148] The US, on the other hand, requested that the Panel find its measures fell within the scope of the exceptions contained in Art. XX (b) and (g).[149]

India put forward a series of arguments describing the protection and conservation efforts being made in India for sea turtles and thoroughly rejected the US assumption that the only method for protecting sea turtles was the use of TEDs.[150] While India sympathised with the aim of the US measures, it was nevertheless of

---

[143]*Ibid.*, para. 22.

[144]*Ibid.*, para. 24.

[145]*Ibid.*, para. 140.

[146]*Ibid.*

[147]*Ibid.*, para. 27.

[148]*Ibid.*

[149]*Ibid.*, para. 29.

[150]*Ibid.*, paras. 31–32.

the view that such a goal could not justify such a 'taking [of] unilateral actions that infringed upon India's sovereign right to formulate its own environmental and conservation policies'.[151] Malaysia also pointed to its long history and comprehensive regulatory regime aimed at the protection and conservation of sea turtles.[152] It further argued that '[c]onservation efforts were better achieved through bilateral or multilateral agreements rather than resorting to trade sanctions under the WTO'.[153] Similarly, Pakistan viewed its own cultural relationship with turtles and its comprehensive legal regime in relation to them to prove that the US methods were not the only way in which sea turtle species could be protected.[154] On this basis, Pakistan argued that 'there was no need for the United States to impose its own agenda on third parties through the use of far-reaching, extraterritorial measures such as the one imposed by Section 609'.[155] Likewise, Thailand was also able to point to its own interaction with this issue at the national, regional and global levels, giving a comprehensive legal regime aimed at the protection of sea turtles.[156] Thailand argued that it had 'found that measures other than the use of TEDs could be made effective in preserving sea turtles in Thai waters'.[157]

The US, however, was of the view that 'the incidental mortality of sea turtles in shrimp trawl nets constituted the largest cause of human-induced sea turtle mortality'[158] and that '[a]ny effective programme to allow the recovery of these endangered species had to include the required use of TEDs by shrimp trawl vessels'.[159] Furthermore, the US argued that sea turtles are a 'shared global resource'[160] and that '[e]fforts by one nation to protect sea turtles would not succeed unless other nations in whose waters these species also occurred took comparable measures'.[161] The US put forward that the use of TEDs was a cheap and effective solution to the problems faced in sea turtle conservation.[162]

The complainants (India, Pakistan and Thailand) argued that the Section 609 programme violated Art. XI:1 of the GATT as it 'constituted a prohibition or restriction on the importation of shrimp and shrimp products from the complainants'.[163] The complainants made reference to the decisions of the Panels in *Tuna/Dolphin I and II*, describing the measures involved as 'virtually identical to the

---

[151]*Ibid.*, para. 32.
[152]*Ibid.*, paras. 33–34.
[153]*Ibid.*, para. 36.
[154]*Ibid.*, paras. 37–38.
[155]*Ibid.*, para. 38.
[156]*Ibid.*, paras. 38–42.
[157]*Ibid.*, para. 41.
[158]*Ibid.*, para. 45.
[159]*Ibid.*
[160]*Ibid.*, para. 62.
[161]*Ibid.*
[162]*Ibid.*, para. 105.
[163]*Ibid.*, para. 162.

restriction on shrimp imports at issue in this dispute'[164] and referring to the fact that the Panels had both found a violation of Art. XI:1.[165] The complainants further argued that Art. XIII was violated by the measure as it constituted a 'differential treatment of "like products" from certified and non-certified countries'.[166]

With regard to the alleged inconsistencies with Arts. I:1, XI:1 and XIII, the US pointed out that the complainants bore the burden of proving the violation[167] but did not dispute the Art. XI:1 violation (although it did with regard to Arts. I:1 and XIII:1).[168] The US was of the view that

> Since under Article XX nothing in the GATT 1994 was to be construed to prevent the adoption or enforcement of the measures at issue, there was little practical significance to attempts by the complainants to establish an inconsistency between these measures and other provisions of GATT.[169]

With regard to the Art. XX general exceptions, the complainants first noted that the US bore the burden of proving that the measures fell under one of the specific exceptions of Art. XX (a)–(j) and argued that with regard to Art. X (b) and (g), they had failed to do so.[170]

The US put forward the argument that 'This dispute dealt with issues that were central to how the rules of the multilateral trading system interacted with the ability of Members, both individually and collectively, to meet critical environmental objectives'.[171] The complainants, on the other hand, were of the view that it was not about conservation but rather 'it was about the imposition of unilateral trade measures designed to coerce other Members to adopt environmental policies that mirrored those in the United States'.[172]

The crux of the matter in this case was the jurisdictional application of Art. XX (b) and (g). The complainants put forward that Art. XX was expressly limited in its coverage to humans, animals or plants located within the jurisdiction of the member taking the measure, and Art. XX (b) did not 'expressly permit a Member to take measures concerning humans, animals or plants located within the jurisdiction of another Member'.[173] Citing Art. 31 (3)(c) of the VCLT, they argued that the

---

[164]*Ibid.*; see *supra*, 6.2 and 6.3.

[165]Panel Report *United States – Import Prohibition of Certain Shrimp and Shrimp Products*, para. 162.

[166]*Ibid.*, para. 163.

[167]Panel Report *United States – Import Prohibition of Certain Shrimp and Shrimp* Products, para. 169, quoting Appellate Body Report *United States – Measure Affecting Imports of Woven Wool Shirts and Blouses from India*, pg. 16.

[168]Panel Report *United States – Import Prohibition of Certain Shrimp and Shrimp Products*, para. 169.

[169]*Ibid.*

[170]*Ibid.*, para. 170.

[171]*Ibid.*, para. 171.

[172]*Ibid.*, para. 174.

[173]*Ibid.*, para. 183.

relevant rules of international law to be taken into account when interpreting Art. XX certainly included Arts. 1 (2), 2 (1) and 2 (7) of the Charter of the United Nations:

> which recognized the sovereign equality of states and the principle of non -interference in the internal affairs of another state. In light of these general rules of international law, it should be presumed that Article XX(b) did not extend to measures taken by one Member that affected the life or health of the people, animals and plants within the jurisdiction of another Member, absent specific treaty language to the contrary.[174]

For the same reason, the complainants believed that the lack of reference to where the 'exhaustible natural resources' were situated should not be interpreted so as to refer to resources located outside the territory of the party creating the measure.[175]

The US put forward that the argument that a jurisdictional limit should be imposed on Art. XX (b) and (g) was entirely without merit and should be rejected by the Panel, nor should a jurisdictional limit be read into Art. XX when it does not exist.[176] The US further rejected the sovereignty arguments as without merit in the case of conservation issues,[177] citing the general approach in international law as clearly not 'prohibiting countries from taking measures to conserve endangered species located in the jurisdiction of other countries'.[178] The US also pointed to previous case law that addressed similar jurisdictional nexuses but did not address the issue of whether 'the resource to be protected was outside the jurisdiction of the country taking the measure'.[179]

With regard to Art. XX (g), the complainants argued that interpreting 'exhaustible' in good faith in accordance with the ordinary meaning to be given to the terms of the treaty in their context and in the light of its object and purpose,[180] then it was clear that only 'finite natural resources' should be included and that sea turtles did not fall under this definition.[181] The US disagreed with this point and made extensive arguments[182] based on case law, international agreements[183] and the logic of the premise that sea turtles were similarly finite resources as 'Once a

---

[174]Panel Report *United States – Import Prohibition of Certain Shrimp and Shrimp Products*, para. 183.

[175]*Ibid.*

[176]*Ibid.*, para. 185–186.

[177]*Ibid.*, para. 187.

[178]*Ibid.*

[179]Panel Report *United States – Standards for Reformulated and Conventional Gasoline*; GATT Panel Report *Canada – Measures Affecting Exports of Unprocessed Herring and Salmon*; GATT Panel Report *United States – Prohibition of Imports of Tuna and Tuna Products from Canada*.

[180]Art. 31 (c) VCLT.

[181]Panel Report *United States – Import Prohibition of Certain Shrimp and Shrimp Products*, para. 263.

[182]*Ibid.*, paras. 268–270.

[183]E.g. Convention on International Trade in Endangered Species of Wild Fauna and Flora of 3 March 1973, UNTS 993, 14537.

species was extinct, it was gone forever, just as oil from a well or ore from a mine'.[184] The fulfilment of the 'with regard to' requirement of Art. XX (g) by the US was dismissed by the complainants, which stated: 'the United States could not credibly contend that the objective of the embargo was to protect the lives of sea turtles'.[185] Citing the reasoning of the *Tuna/Dolphin II* GATT Panel, the complainants argued that 'the shrimp embargo was not a measure "relating to" the conservation of sea turtles because it was effective only if it forced other nations to change their policies and practices'[186] and stuck firmly with the 'primarily aimed at' interpretation.[187] The US argued that it met the criteria for 'relating to' whether it was deemed to be 'primarily aimed at' or 'having a substantial relationship'.[188] With regard to the chapeau, the complainants were of the view that the US measure would fail to meet its requirements based on, *inter alia*, the fact that although all countries were currently treated equally, the newly affected nations had been given substantially less notice than other countries before being forced to comply with TED use.[189] In their view, this constituted arbitrary or unjustifiable discrimination, and thus Section 609 failed to meet the requirements of the chapeau.

6.5.2   Panel Report

The Panel began its assessment of the case by assessing the consistency of the US measure with Art. XI:1. All complainants had alleged a violation of this obligation, and the US 'basically admit[ted]' to a violation. The Panel considered that even if the admission was not a full admission to the violation of Art. XI:1, 'the evidence made available to the Panel is sufficient to determine that the United States prohibition of imports of shrimp from non-certified Members violates Article XI:1'.[190] Due to the found violation of Art. XI:1, the Panel chose not to examine the claims of the complainants under Arts. I:1 and XIII:1.[191]

The Panel then moved on to assess the US measure under Art. XX general exceptions, stating:

> The arguments of the parties raise the general question of whether Article XX(b) and (g) apply at all when a Member has taken a measure conditioning access to its market for a

---

[184]Panel Report *United States – Import Prohibition of Certain Shrimp and Shrimp Products*, para. 268.

[185]*Ibid.*, para. 276.

[186]*Ibid.*, para. 277.

[187]*Ibid.*, para. 278.

[188]*Ibid.*, para. 279.

[189]*Ibid.*, paras. 294–296.

[190]*Ibid.*, para. 7.16.

[191]*Ibid.*, paras. 7.18–7.23.

given product on the adoption of certain conservation policies by the exporting Member (s).[192]

The Panel thus began its assessment by first determining the scope of Art. XX before moving on to the specific requirements under Art. XX (b) and (g). The Panel, noting that previous Panels had assessed the chapeau after evaluating the measures at hand under the specific exceptions, decided in this case that it was 'equally appropriate' to first assess the chapeau and then the particular exceptions. The Panel found that although there was discrimination between countries where the same conditions prevail, it was not arbitrary.[193] The Panel then went on to assess whether such discrimination was nonetheless unjustifiable, noting that this word had never 'actually been subject to any precise interpretation'.[194] The Panel further noted that this word in its ordinary meaning could be interpreted both broadly and narrowly and thus sought to interpret it in its context and in light of the object and purpose of the agreement to which it belongs.[195]

Following Art. 31 (2) VCLT, the Panel was of the view that the context here clearly included the paragraphs of Art. XX.[196] After assessing some relevant case law on Art. XX, the Panel concluded that

> when invoking Article XX, a Member invokes the right to derogate to certain specific substantive provisions of GATT 1994 but that, in doing so, it must not frustrate or defeat the purposes and objects of the General Agreement and the WTO Agreement or its legal obligations under the substantive rules of GATT by abusing the exception contained in Article XX.[197]

The Panel further assessed the preamble in light of the object and purpose of the agreement and concluded that although environmental concerns are recognised in the preamble, the central focus 'remains the promotion of economic development through trade; and the provisions of GATT are essentially turned toward liberalization of access to markets on a nondiscriminatory basis'.[198]

The Panel thus concluded that Art. XX 'only allows Members to derogate from GATT provisions so long as, in doing so, they do not undermine the WTO multilateral trading system, thus also abusing the exceptions contained in Article XX,'[199] and that as allowing Members to adopt measures conditioning market access upon

---

[192]*Ibid.*, para. 7.26.

[193]*Ibid.* para. 7.28.

[194]*Ibid.*, para. 7.34.

[195]*Ibid.*

[196]*Ibid.*, para. 7.35.

[197]*Ibid.*, para. 7.40.

[198]*Ibid.*, para. 7.42. The first preambular paragraph states: 'in accordance with the objective of sustainable development, seeking both to protect and preserve the environment and to enhance the means of doing so in a manner consistent with [Members'] respective needs and concerns at different levels of economic development'.

[199]Panel Report *United States – Import Prohibition of Certain Shrimp and Shrimp Products*, para. 7.44.

the adoption of certain policies by the exporting Members would mean that the 'GATT 1994 and the WTO Agreement could no longer serve as a multilateral framework for trade among Members',[200] as the security and predictability of trade relations under those agreements would be threatened, then the US measure was 'unjustifiable' under Art. XX.[201]

With regard to the arguments put forward by the US in relation to jurisdiction, the Panel noted that 'environmental protection through international agreements – as opposed to unilateral measures – have for a long time been a recognized course of action for environmental protection'[202] but that 'this argument bears no direct relation to our finding, which rather addresses the inclusion of certain unilateral measures within the scope *ratione materiae* of Article XX'.[203] The Panel further made reference to Principle 2 of the Rio Declaration on Environment and Development, which states:

> States have, in accordance with the Charter of the United Nations and the principles of international law, the sovereign right to exploit their own resources pursuant to their *own* environmental and developmental policies, and the responsibility to ensure that activities within their jurisdiction or control do not cause damage to the environment of other States or of areas beyond the limits of national jurisdiction.[204]

The Panel highlighted that this 'recognises the right of States to design their own environmental policies on the basis of their particular environmental and developmental situations and responsibilities', which 'also stresses the need for international cooperation'.[205] The Panel made reference to the US argument that nothing in Art. XX requires WTO Members to seek negotiations 'instead of, or before adopting unilateral measures'[206] but further invoked the reasoning that

> the WTO multilateral trading system would be undermined if Members were allowed to adopt measures making access of other Members to their market conditional upon the adoption by the exporting Members of certain conservation policies because it would not be possible for Members to meet conflicting requirements of such a nature.[207]

On this basis, the Panel found that 'the US measure at issue is not within the scope of measures permitted under the chapeau of Article XX'.[208] Due to this

---

[200]*Ibid.*, para. 7.45.

[201]*Ibid.*, para. 7.49.

[202]*Ibid.*, para. 7.50.

[203]*Ibid.*

[204]UNCED, The Rio Declaration on the Environment and Development, UN Doc. A/CONF.151/5/REV.1 (1992), ILM 31, 874.

[205]Panel Report *United States – Import Prohibition of Certain Shrimp and Shrimp Products*, para. 7.52.

[206]*Ibid.*, para. 7.54.

[207]*Ibid.*, para. 7.55.

[208]*Ibid.*, para. 7.62.

conclusion, the measure was not assessed by the Panel under the individual requirements of Art. XX (b) or (g).[209]

6.5.3   Appellate Body Report

Following the circulation of the Panel Report, the United States notified the DSB of its decision to appeal certain issues of law in the Report and legal interpretations by the Panel and filed a Notice of Appeal with the Appellate Body.[210] The US appealed on the basis, *inter alia*, that the Panel erred in finding that the measure at issue was outside of the scope of Art. XX, that the measure constituted 'unjustified discrimination' and that the chapeau required the Panel to determine if the measure was a threat to the multilateral trading system.[211]

The Appellate Body thus addressed

> whether the Panel erred in finding that the measure at issue constitutes unjustifiable discrimination between countries where the same conditions prevail and thus is not within the scope of measures permitted under Article XX of the GATT 1994.[212]

With regard to the Panel's interpretation and application of Art. XX, the Appellate Body began by pointing out that the Panel did not follow the customary rules regarding treaty interpretation as 'it is in the words constituting that provision, read in their context, that the object and purpose of the states parties to the treaty must first be sought',[213] and rather than assess the application of the measure under the chapeau (as laid out by the Appellate Body in *US – Gasoline*), the Panel looked at the design of the measure.[214] The Appellate Body made clear that the design of the measure is to be considered when assessing whether the measure at hand falls within the scope of one of the Art. XX (a)–(j) exceptions and not with regard to the chapeau.[215] The Body also criticised the fact that the Panel assessed the object and purpose of the GATT 1994 and the WTO Agreement but failed to do so with regard to Art. XX itself.[216] In evaluating these errors in law, the Appellate Body found that they were to be expected as the Panel had 'disregarded the sequence of steps essential for carrying out such an analysis'.[217] The Appellate Body fully supported the foregoing sequence of interpretation regarding Art. XX and pointed out that it

---

[209] *Ibid.*, para. 7.63.

[210] Appellate Body Report *United States – Import Prohibition of Certain Shrimp and Shrimp Products*, para. 8.

[211] *Ibid.*, para. 10.

[212] *Ibid.*, para. 98.

[213] *Ibid.*, para. 114.

[214] *Ibid.*, paras. 115–116.

[215] *Ibid.*

[216] *Ibid.*

[217] *Ibid.*, para. 117.

would be difficult, if not impossible, to properly apply the chapeau of Art. XX
without having first assessed the measure at hand under the particular exceptions
under Art. XX.[218] On this basis, the Appellate Body considered that the Panel had
erred in law with regard to this issue and reversed its findings.[219]

Article 17 DSU states that '[a]n appeal shall be limited to issues of law covered
in the panel report and legal interpretations developed by the panel'. Nevertheless,
the Appellate Body, believing it was its duty and its responsibility,[220] went on to
complete the legal analysis where the Panel had failed to do so due to their error.
Citing previous cases in which the Body had executed such a function,[221] the Body
claimed that in doing so it was fulfilling the requirement of Art. 3.2 DSU 'to secure
a positive solution to a dispute'.

Beginning with Art. XX (g), the Appellate Body found that the exhaustible
natural resources are not limited to mineral or non-living natural resources[222] and,
pointing to the evolutionary nature of the generic term 'natural resources',[223] found
that the sea turtles involved here could be safely subsumed in this category.[224] At
this juncture, the Appellate Body also mentioned the jurisdictional nexus between
the US and the sea turtles specified in Section 609 and found that they 'are all
known to occur in waters over which the United States exercises jurisdiction'.[225]

The Body then moved on to an assessment of whether the measure at issue
'related to' the conservation of exhaustible natural resources. Citing *US – Gasoline*,
the Appellate Body sought to apply a test of substantial relationship between the
measure and the policy,[226] stating: 'we must examine the relationship between the
general structure and design of the measure here at stake, Section 609, and the
policy goal it purports to serve, that is, the conservation of sea turtles'.[227] Focusing
on the design of the measure, the Appellate Body found that the measure was 'not
disproportionately wide in its scope and reach in relation to the policy objective of
protection and conservation of sea turtle species'.[228] They were of the view that 'the
means [were], in principle, reasonably related to the ends'[229] and that thus the

---

[218]*Ibid.*, para. 120.

[219]*Ibid.*, para. 122.

[220]*Ibid.*, para. 123.

[221]E.g. Appellate Body Report *European Communities – Measures Affecting the Importation of Certain Poultry Products*.

[222]Appellate Body Report *United States – Import Prohibition of Certain Shrimp and Shrimp Products*, para. 128.

[223]*Ibid.*, para. 130. The Appellate Body also made reference to the definition of natural resources under UNCLOS and the CBD: *ibid.*

[224]Appellate Body Report *United States – Import Prohibition of Certain Shrimp and Shrimp Products*, para. 134.

[225]*Ibid.*, para. 133.

[226]*Ibid.*, paras. 136–168.

[227]*Ibid.*, para. 137.

[228]*Ibid.*, para. 141.

[229]*Ibid.*

measure was 'a measure "relating to" the conservation of an exhaustible natural resource within the meaning of Article XX(g) of the GATT 1994'.[230] As the requirements for Art. XX (g) had been met, the Appellate Body did not then go on to assess the measure under Art. XX (b).[231]

The provisional justification of the US measure under Art. XX (g) was then followed by an assessment of it with the requirements of the chapeau, with the Appellate Body confirming that this was the second tier of the two-tier test required under the Art. XX general exceptions.[232] Disregarding the US argument that the policy goal of the measure in question could be used for justification of a measure under the requirements of the chapeau,[233] the Appellate Body began its assessment by examining the ordinary meaning of the wording of the chapeau.[234] The Body then stated that there were three standards contained in the chapeau: (1) arbitrary discrimination between countries where the same conditions prevail, (2) unjustifiable discrimination between countries where the same conditions prevail and (3) a disguised restriction on international trade.[235] The Body stated that the purpose of the chapeau can be described thus:

> it embodies the recognition on the part of WTO Members of the need to maintain a balance of rights and obligations between the right of a Member to invoke one or another of the exceptions of Article XX, specified in paragraphs (a) to (j), on the one hand, and the substantive rights of the other Members under the GATT 1994, on the other hand.[236]

The Body further described the Art. XX exceptions as providing 'limited and conditional' exceptions to the substantive obligations contained in the GATT[237] and that the task of the DSS in interpreting and applying the chapeau is essentially a delicate one of 'locating and marking out a line of equilibrium between the right of a Member to invoke an exception under Article XX and the rights of the other Members under varying substantive provisions'.[238] Following such general considerations, the Appellate Body moved on to assess whether the application of the measure could be deemed to constitute arbitrary or unjustifiable discrimination between countries where the same conditions prevail or a disguised restriction on international trade.[239]

As the Appellate Body was persuaded that the application of the measure in question 'require[d] other WTO Members to adopt a regulatory program that is not

---

[230] *Ibid.*, para. 142.
[231] *Ibid.*, para. 146.
[232] *Ibid.*, para. 147.
[233] *Ibid.*, para. 148.
[234] *Ibid.*, para. 149.
[235] *Ibid.*
[236] *Ibid.*, para. 156.
[237] *Ibid.*, para. 157.
[238] *Ibid.*, para. 159.
[239] *Ibid.*, para. 160.

merely *comparable*, but rather *essentially the same*, as that applied to the United States shrimp trawl vessels'[240] and as such could constitute discrimination as

> We believe that discrimination results not only when countries in which the same conditions prevail are differently treated, but also when the application of the measure at issue does not allow for any inquiry into the appropriateness of the regulatory program for the conditions prevailing in those exporting countries.[241]

The Body then pointed to the conclusion of the Panel that there was no evidence that the US undertook serious negotiations on a (global) multilateral level to conclude an agreement on sea turtle conservation and cited, *inter alia*, Principle 12 of the Rio Declaration in support of the preference for multilateralism in environmental protection. Principle 12 states:

> Unilateral actions to deal with environmental challenges outside the jurisdiction of the importing country should be avoided. *Environmental measures addressing transboundary or global environmental problems should, as far as possible, be based on international consensus.*[242]

The Appellate Body then pointed to the Inter-American Convention for the protection of sea turtles and the US's failure to negotiate such a treaty with the parties to the case.[243]

Assessing the application of the measure against this background, and with particular reference to the differing treatment of different countries in the phase-in period, the Appellate Body thus decided that the measures constituted 'unjustifiable discrimination' within the meaning of the chapeau.[244] Furthermore, due to the fact that the rigidity of the certification system meant that only essentially identical regulatory systems would be certified without inquiring into the appropriateness of the system for the conditions prevailing in the exporting country, the Appellate Body also found the application of the measure to constitute 'arbitrary discrimination'.[245] As the measure was found to constitute both unjustifiable and arbitrary discrimination, it was not necessary for the Appellate Body to assess it under the third chapeau standard (disguised restriction on international trade).[246]

---

[240]*Ibid.*, para. 165.

[241]*Ibid.*

[242]*Ibid.*, para. 167–168. UNCED, The Rio Declaration on the Environment and Development, UN Doc. A/CONF.151/5/REV.1 (1992), ILM 31, 874; UNCED, Report of the United Nations Conference on the Environment and Development, UN Doc. A.CONF/151/26/REV.1 (Vol. I) (1992), 9 (Agenda 21), 2.22(i); Art. 5 CBD; Convention on the Conservation of Migratory Species of 23 June 1979, 1651 UNTS 333, Annex 1.

[243]Appellate Body Report *United States – Import Prohibition of Certain Shrimp and Shrimp Products*, para. 170–172.

[244]*Ibid.*, paras. 174–176.

[245]*Ibid.*, para. 177.

[246]*Ibid.*, para. 184.

6.5.4   Compliance Panel

In October 2000, Malaysia requested the formation of a Panel and asked the Panel to find

> that by not lifting the import prohibition and not taking the necessary measures to allow the importation of certain shrimp and shrimp products in an unrestrictive manner, the United States has failed to comply with the 6 November 1998 recommendations and rulings of the Dispute Settlement Body.[247]

The US had, since the Appellate Body Report was adopted, and pursuant to Art. 21.6 DSU, submitted regular status reports regarding the implementation of the recommendations of the DSB.[248] The reports set out that the US was taking steps to 'introduce greater flexibility in considering the comparability of foreign programs and the US programme' and 'elaborate a timetable and procedures for certification decisions' and that the US was engaged in efforts to 'negotiate an agreement on the conservation of sea turtles with the Governments of the Indian Ocean region, and that the United States had offered and was providing technical assistance on the design, construction, installation and operation of TEDs'.[249] Malaysia laid out its view of the mandate of the Panel as being 'to examine the consistency with Articles XI and XX of the GATT 1994 of measures taken by the United States to comply with the recommendations and rulings of the Dispute Settlement Body'.[250]

With regard to Art. XI:1, Malaysia argued that the continued enforcement of Section 609 had the effect of an import prohibition and seriously undermined the Malaysian shrimp export industry.[251] The US argued, on the other hand, that in the 13-month period agreed upon by the parties for implementation, it had modified the 'application of the measure in order to address the specific problems identified by the Appellate Body'.[252] The US did not, however, claim that the measure was not an import prohibition or that it was now compatible with Art. XI:1.[253]

With regard to Art. XX (g), the US identified these compliance steps:

(a) Revised Guidelines that provide more flexibility in decision-making;
(b) enhanced due process protections for exporting countries;
(c) efforts to negotiate a sea turtle conservation agreement in the Indian Ocean region; and
(d) enhanced offers of technical assistance[254]

---

[247]Panel Report *United States – Import Prohibition of Certain Shrimp and Shrimp Products* (Recourse to Article 21.5 by Malaysia), para. 1.4.

[248]*Ibid.*, para. 2.21.

[249]*Ibid.*

[250]*Ibid.*, para. 3.1.

[251]*Ibid.*, para. 3.28.

[252]*Ibid.*, para. 3.29.

[253]*Ibid.*, para. 3.30.

[254]*Ibid.*, para. 3.33.

The US also claimed that it had addressed the defects in the application of Section 609 in the interim period.[255] Malaysia, however, argued that 'since the imposition of the import prohibition is not justified under Article XX of the GATT 1994, it should be removed in order for the United States to bring the measure into conformity with its obligations under that Agreement'.[256]

With regard to the chapeau of Art. XX, Malaysia further argued that the US had mischaracterised the findings of the Appellate Body 'by erroneously stating that the Appellate Body's detailed findings under the Article XX chapeau are addressed not to the Section 609 statute itself, but to the United States' application of the measure'.[257] The US then explicitly recalled the Appellate Body's findings with regard to the failure to negotiate a multilateral agreement with all exporting nations. In this respect, the US pointed to its continued efforts in the interim period to launch such negotiations.[258] Countering this argument, Malaysia claimed that it would only be in line with the Appellate Body's recommendations if the US were to suspend its import prohibition while the negotiations were taking place[259] and that 'that no unilateral actions to deal with environmental measures may be imposed before any international consensus is reached'[260] as '[i]n the absence of any mutually agreed international standard to conserve and protect sea turtles, recognition of each country's sovereign right to manage and maintain its own conservation programme for sea turtles should be respected'.[261] The US countered this point by arguing that such a 'rule is flatly inconsistent with the Appellate Body Report and would effectively eviscerate the Article XX(g) exception'.[262]

The Compliance Panel followed the Appellate Body in finding the measure provisionally justified under Art. XX (g).[263] After a thorough examination of the Appellate Body Report and the comparison of the measure with the recommendation, the Compliance Panel also found that the measure is 'now applied in a manner that no longer constitutes a means of unjustifiable or arbitrary discrimination'[264] nor as a disguised restriction on international trade.[265]

---

[255]Ibid., para. 3.46.

[256]Ibid., para. 3.36.

[257]Ibid., para. 3.55.

[258]Ibid., paras. 3.67–3.75.

[259]Ibid., para. 3.99.

[260]Ibid., para. 3.104.

[261]Ibid.

[262]Ibid., para. 3.105.

[263]Ibid., paras. 5.39–5.42.

[264]Ibid., para. 5.137.

[265]Ibid., para. 5.144.

6.5.5   Compliance Appellate Body

Malaysia went on to appeal this decision before the Appellate Body on the basis that the Compliance Panel had erred in law in its examination of the new US measure as it compared it with the recommendations of the Appellate Body DSB Report[266] and not with the provisions of the GATT.[267] The Appellate Body, however, agreed with the Compliance Panel on the basis that the measure was essentially unchanged, and thus the DSB Report could be referred to when examining consistency with Art. XX (g).[268] The Appellate Body further found that the Panel ought to have in this case examined the application of the measure and that it did in fact do so and fully understood its mandate.[269]

With regard to the 'arbitrary or unjustified discrimination' criteria, the Appellate Body found that, contrary to the Malaysian argument that an international agreement must be concluded in order to meet the requirements of the chapeau, it was sufficient if comparable negotiations were offered (with no obligation of result).[270] Malaysia also argued that the inflexible 'unilateral nature' of the certification scheme meant that it could not meet the requirements of the chapeau as this constituted arbitrary discrimination, but, quoting itself, the Appellate Body recalled:

> conditioning access to a Member's domestic market on whether exporting Members comply with, or adopt, a policy or policies unilaterally prescribed by the importing Member may, to some degree, be a common aspect of measures falling within the scope of one or another of the exceptions (a) to (j) of Article XX.[271]

With regard to flexibility, the Appellate Body recalled that it was inappropriate to require 'essentially the same' regulatory programme as the US and reiterated that a scheme that was 'comparable in effectiveness' was flexible enough that it 'gives sufficient latitude to the exporting Member with respect to the programme it may adopt to achieve the level of effectiveness required'.[272] The Appellate Body found that, on this basis, the certification scheme allowed for sufficient flexibility and 'will enable the United States to consider the particular conditions prevailing in Malaysia if, and when, Malaysia applies for certification'.[273] The Compliance Panel Report

---

[266]Appellate Body Report *United States – Import Prohibition of Certain Shrimp and Shrimp Products* (Recourse to Article 21.5 by Malaysia).

[267]*Ibid.*, paras. 12–13.

[268]*Ibid.*, para. 96.

[269]*Ibid.*, paras. 99–106.

[270]*Ibid.*, paras. 122–123.

[271]*Ibid.*, para. 137. Appellate Body Report *United States – Import Prohibition of Certain Shrimp and Shrimp Products*, para. 121.

[272]Appellate Body Report *United States – Import Prohibition of Certain Shrimp and Shrimp Products* (Recourse to Article 21.5 by Malaysia), para. 144.

[273]*Ibid.*, para. 148 (emphasis added).

was thus upheld, and the US measures were now found to meet the requirements of the chapeau and thus fall under the Art. XX (g) general exception.

6.5.6   Analysis

This case, probably the most famous from the WTO, gained its reputation through its interaction with the environmental community—particularly the shift in approach by the Appellate Body, described as one that 'swept away almost all the pillars of the GATT anti-environmentalist edifice'.[274] The factual background of this case is clearly similar to *Tuna/Dolphin I and II* and demonstrates the shifting interpretation of the GATT Panels to the WTO DSS.

The issues that are central to this study are very clearly in evidence here: 'like products' and NPR PPMs based on TREMs under the WTO. What also becomes particularly apparent through this case is the relationship between these issues and the jurisdictional extent of the Art. XX exceptions and unilateralism vs. multilateralism under the WTO. Furthermore, while this study focuses on the impacts on sovereignty (in the political science sense) of the WTO in the realm of TREMs based on NPR PPMs on the importing State, this case brings very clearly to light that there are also significant concerns under the current system that allowing exceptions on the basis of NPR PPMs may interfere with the sovereignty of the exporting State.

The parties raised these issues in their argument before the Panel, with India pointing to its own efforts to protect sea turtles and claiming that the US's unilateralism infringed India's sovereignty, while Malaysia similarly highlighted its own regulatory program and expressed its preference for bilateral or multilateral negotiations to unilateral action. Pakistan also expressed its disapproval at such far-reaching unilateral measures. The invocation of the UN Charter (and the Rio Declaration) by the complainants and the argument that if Art. XX measures were to permissibly extend beyond national jurisdiction it would constitute an infringement of the internal affairs of another State certainly raises significant questions about the interpretation of Art. XX in such a manner. The issue of likeness was also addressed by the complainants, with India, Pakistan and Thailand stressing that the products were 'physically identical' to those caught without TEDs. These issues were largely ignored by the Panel, whose focus on an interpretation beginning with the chapeau of Art. XX centered on whether the measure invoking an Art. XX exception as a threat to the multilateral system was overturned by the Appellate Body.

---

[274]*Robert Howse*, The Appellate Body Rulings in the Shrimp/Turtle Case: A New Legal Baseline for the Trade and Environment Debate, Columbia Journal of Environmental Law 27 (2009), 489, 514.

Significantly, in terms of possible limitations of the influence of this case for environmental cases in the future, the Appellate Body found a jurisdictional nexus between the United States and the sea turtles at issue in this case. Had it not done so, the bar might have been set for the inclusion of NPR PPM extraterritorial environmental measures under Art. XX. As it stands, extraterritorial measures where there is some jurisdictional nexus can be included under Art. XX. How far 'jurisdictional nexus' could be extended when thinking of harm to the environment and especially global commons is not fixed and may further adapt with time.

The Appellate Body then overturned the Panel's interpretation of the chronology of the application of Art. XX. Despite the fact that it is more than questionable whether Art. 17 DSU properly allows for such 'completion of the legal analysis' (clearly constituting judicial overreach and bringing into question the Appellate Body's role in the standard of review), the Body did so and began with the sub-paragraphs. The decision of the Appellate Body differs vastly from that of the GATT Panels in *Tuna/Dolphin I and II*. In this case, the Body was persuaded that the means were reasonably related to the ends and that the US measures could be deemed related to the conservation of natural resources. Although this alternate interpretation by the DSS was largely lauded by the environmental community, such varying interpretations on very similar factual backgrounds demonstrate the imprecise nature and lack of formal realisability of the legal provisions. As demonstrated above, such a lack of formal realisability is more damaging to smaller economies as the relative cost of litigation may prevent them from enacting legislation that at differing times would be found either to meet or not to meet the exception under Art. XX (g). What *Tuna/Dolphin* and *Shrimp/Turtle* rather demonstrate is that strong economies, such as the United States, have less to lose relatively and therefore can legislate as they choose despite the lack of formal realisability.

The Appellate Body then moved on to try to find the equilibrium between the rights of the other Members under varying substantive provisions and the specific exceptions contained in Art. XX through the application of the chapeau. While it is understandable that the exceptions should be limited by 'arbitrary and unjustifiable discrimination' qualifiers, it is surely here that the balance should be struck— otherwise the exceptions are no exceptions at all. The Body found that there had been both arbitrary and unjustifiable discrimination, based partly on the finding that the chapeau should cover situations not only where the same conditions prevail but also where the measures in question fail to allow for differing conditions—despite no textual basis for such an assertion. The Body furthermore professed the WTO preference for multilateralism by highlighting the failure of the US to negotiate another international treaty that would have included the complainants. Indeed, the position of the Body has been summed up as 'no state may have recourse to the taking of unilateral measures before exhausting first means of international negotiation'.[275] While such a preference (or requirement) makes sense for a trade body,

---

[275]*Pierre-Marie Dupuy*, The Place and Role of Unilateralism in Contemporary International Law, EJIL 11 (2000), 19–29.

it is difficult to find any textual basis for such a conclusion and thus should be considered judicial overreach.

The findings of the DSB in the compliance part of the *Shrimp/Turtle* case serve to demonstrate that it is unlikely that this case was a 'one off' in the jurisprudence of the DSS. The firm adherence of the Appellate Body in both the appeal and compliance stages to the preference for multilateralism and clear approval of measures falling under Art. XX to be applied extraterritorially appears to support this. Furthermore, the pronouncement by the compliance Appellate Body that it may be inherent in the nature of the measures that come under Art. XX (b) and (g) that they apply extraterritorially also speaks to this. The fact that turtles are a common good and do not necessarily stay within the territory(ial sea) of any given party (and thus create jurisdictional nexus) may serve to differentiate this case from those involving NPR PPMs that cause pollution or harm to biodiversity (as they do not have such a jurisdictional nexus as migratory species), but the conclusion of the DSS with regard to this issue is clearly instructional as a basis for future cases based on TREMs.

6.6   EC – Asbestos

6.6.1   Facts and Arguments of the Parties

On 8 October 1998, Canada requested that the DSB form a Panel to assess certain measures taken by France for the prohibition of asbestos and products containing asbestos, alleging that the measure in question was in violation of Arts. 2 and 5 of the SPS Agreement, Art. 2 of the TBT Agreement, Arts. III and XI of the GATT 1994 and constituted a nullification or impairment under Art. XXIII:1(b) of the GATT 1994.[276] The measure in question was a French decree enacted in 1996[277] that banned 'the manufacture, processing, sale, import, placing on the domestic market and transfer under any title whatsoever of all varieties of asbestos fibres'[278] except 'on an exceptional and temporary basis' to products containing chrysotile fibre which 'poses a lesser occupational health risk than chrysotile fibre to workers handling those materials, products or devices'[279] and 'provides all technical guarantees of safety corresponding to the ultimate purpose of the use'.[280]

---

[276]Panel Report *EC – Measures Affecting Asbestos and Asbestos -Containing Products*, para. 1.2.

[277]Decree No. 96-1133 banning asbestos, issued pursuant to the Labour Code and the Consumer Code (décret no. 96-1133 relatif à l'interdiction de l'amiante, pris en application du code de travail et du code de la consommation).

[278]*Ibid.*, Art. 1.

[279]*Ibid.*, Art. 2.

[280]*Ibid*; Panel Report *EC – Measures Affecting Asbestos and Asbestos -Containing Products*, paras. 2.3–2.5.

In view of the facts and arguments put forward, Canada asked the Panel to find the French measure to be contrary to Arts. 2.2, 2.4, 2.8, 2.1 TBT Agreement (dealt with in the following chapter on the TBT Agreements) and Arts. XI:1 and III:4 GATT.[281] The European Communities, on the other hand, requested that the Panel find that the measure (1) should not be examined in relation to the scope of Art. XI of the GATT 1994; (2) did not establish less favourable treatment for similar imported products than for domestic products, within the meaning of Article III:4 of the GATT 1994; and (3) was necessary in any event, to protect human health, within the meaning of Article XX(b) of the GATT 1994.[282]

In seeking to establish the French measure as inconsistent with its obligations under the WTO, Canada argued that the 'ban on asbestos does nothing to correct the problems resulting from past asbestos use'[283] and thus failed to address the problem it sought to. Further, Canada criticised the French reliance on the Institut National de la Science et de la Recherche Médicale (INSERM) report recommendations[284] as they viewed the critique of this report by other experts (who stated that the report was 'not a credible basis for justifying a total ban on all varieties and all uses of asbestos for public health purposes'[285]) as being more valuable. Canada further argued that '[t]he undetectable risk from chrysotile is thus replaced by the unknown risk from substitutes. This results in inconsistencies in the regulation of potentially hazardous products in France',[286] and the ban was thus 'irrational and disproportionate'.[287] The EC argued, on the other hand, that 'confusion is systematic in the Canadian arguments' on the basis of their analysis of health risks,[288] coupled with an inaccurate depiction of asbestos use in France.[289] Rejecting the complainant's arguments about substitutes, the EC argued that 'the risks from chrysotile are not only detectable, but have been detected for a long time because they are so great if there is a high level of exposure; [and] the EC assert[ed] that this is still the case today, even with "modern" products'[290] and further that '[n]o substitute product for chrysotile in fibro-cement is recognized as carcinogenic at the international level'.[291]

The complainants argued that the French decree presented a two-pronged measure and thus violated both Arts. XI:1 and III:4 as on one hand 'it prohibits imports

---

[281]Panel Report *EC – Measures Affecting Asbestos and Asbestos -Containing Products*, para. 3.1.
[282]*Ibid.*, para. 3.4.
[283]*Ibid.*, para. 3.10.
[284]Institut National de la Science et de la Recherche Médicale. INSERM, Effects on Health of the Main Types of Exposure to Asbestos (1996).
[285]Panel Report *EC – Measures Affecting Asbestos and Asbestos-Containing Products*, para. 3.11.
[286]*Ibid.*
[287]*Ibid.*, para. 3.12.
[288]*Ibid.*, para. 3.13.
[289]*Ibid.* paras. 3.13–3.14.
[290]*Ibid.*, para. 3.17.
[291]*Ibid.*, para. 3.18.

and, on the other, it contains discriminatory internal regulations'.[292] The EC put forward that the measure was an internal regulation and thus fell under Art. III:4 but did not discriminate against foreign products and was thus not inconsistent with this obligation under the GATT.[293] Moreover, as the measure was an internal regulation in the meaning of Art. III:4, it did not fall under Art. XI:1, which is concerned with border and importation measures.[294] The EC firmly denied that the measure in question had two aspects and should be assessed under both Art. XI:1 and Art. III:4.[295]

With regard to Art. III:4, Canada argued that the measure in question constituted an internal measure and thus fell under Art. III:4. The measure violated Art. III:4 as (1) products 'like' Canadian chrysotile fibre and chrysotile cement exist, (2) these 'like products' are of French origin and (3) they benefit from treatment more favourable than that accorded to imported Canadian chrysotile fibre and chrysotile cement products.[296]

Basing its argument on previous case law and the fulfillment of the 'end-use of the product, consumers' tastes and habits, the physical properties, the nature and quality of the product, as well as tariff classification'[297] quantifiers of likeness, Canada argued that 'the substitute fibres are like chrysotile fibre and fibro-cement products are like chrysotile cement products'.[298]

The EC, on the other hand, argued that 'like products' had to be determined on the basis of (1) their properties, nature and quality; (2) their tariff classification; (3) their end use; and (4) consumers' tastes and habits.[299] The EC put forward that Canada was mistaken in its interpretation of 'like products' under Art. III:4 and the similar but not identical 'directly competitive or substitutable products' under Art. III:2.[300] With regard to the consumers' taste and habit qualifier, the EC was of the view that

> As far as the tastes and habits of consumers are concerned, the EC consider that, while this criterion may be relevant in certain cases (everyday consumer goods), it is not relevant in the case of asbestos and asbestos-containing products.[301]

---

[292]*Ibid.*, para. 3.394.

[293]*Ibid.*, para. 3.395.

[294]*Ibid.*

[295]For the competing arguments, see *ibid.*, paras. 3.394–3.406.

[296]*Ibid.*, para. 3.410.

[297]*Ibid.*, para. 3.411. See further *ibid.*, paras 4.12–4.25.

[298]*Ibid.*, para. 3.411.

[299]*Ibid.*, para. 3.426.

[300]*Ibid.*, para. 3.427.

[301]*Ibid.*, para. 3.429.

The EC furthermore pointed to the 'characteristics of asbestos fibres' that make them 'particularly dangerous to health as they increase the risk of cancer'[302] as being definitive in the examination of 'like products'.

As Canada viewed the products in question as 'like', it found the differential treatment for the asbestos substitutes to violate the national treatment obligation of Art. III:4.[303] With regard to the substitute products, the EC pointed to France's negative trade balance in these products as demonstrating that the measure in question did not discriminate against them. The EC was firmly of the view that there was a complete absence of *de jure* and *de facto* discrimination in the application of the measure.[304]

Concerning Art. XI:1, Canada put forward the argument that as one aspect of the measure in question addressed the importation of asbestos or asbestos-containing products, it was incompatible with the prohibition on quantitative restrictions contained in Art. XI:1.[305] The EC reiterated the view that as Art. III:4 applied in this case, Art. XI:1 was excluded.[306] The complainant then went on to point out that even if the French decree was considered an internal measure, this did not necessarily rule out the application of Art. XI:1 in this case as 'Article XI:1 can apply to an internal regulation that has the effect of restricting or prohibiting imports'.[307]

The EC then contended that if the decree was found to be in contravention of its obligations under Art. III:4, then it would be nonetheless permissible as it fell within the Art. XX (b) exception.[308] Canada pointed to the 'limited and exceptional' nature of the exceptions and argued that the EC failed to discharge the burden of proof in demonstrating that the measure qualified as an exception under Art. XX (b).[309] The EC argued:

> The measure taken is the only possible one that enables the spread of the risks due to asbestos exposure to be halted effectively. It therefore falls under the heading of measures for the purposes described in Article XX(b).[310]

Concerning the 'necessity' requirement of Art. XX (b), the EC argued:

> (i) the ban is justified by the existence of risks to the health of the population; and (ii) the ban is the only measure that enables the objective set by the French authorities (halting the spread of the risk) to be attained.[311]

---

[302]*Ibid.*, para. 3.431.

[303]*Ibid.*, paras. 3.454 *et seq.*

[304]*Ibid.*, paras. 3.460–3.466.

[305]*Ibid.*, para. 3.467.

[306]*Ibid.*, para. 3.469.

[307]*Ibid.*, para. 3.472.

[308]*Ibid.*, para. 3.474.

[309]*Ibid.*, paras. 3.475–3.476; see also Appellate Body Report *United States – Import Prohibition of Certain Shrimp and Shrimp Products*, para. 157.

[310]Panel Report *EC – Measures Affecting Asbestos and Asbestos-Containing Products*, para. 3.477.

[311]*Ibid.*, para. 3.479; ibid., 3.479–3.491.

Canada, on the other hand, reiterated its view that 'chrysotile in high-density non-friable products do not constitute a detectable risk to human health'[312] while also highlighting that whatever is the French level of protection chosen, the *Thailand – Cigarettes* interpretation that '[a] measure will be deemed necessary "[...] only if there were no alternative measure consistent with the General Agreement, or less inconsistent with it, which [the party] could reasonably be expected to employ to achieve its health policy objectives"'[313] was clearly not fulfilled in this case.

With regard to the chapeau, the EC argued 'that the Decree is not applied as a means of imposing arbitrary or unjustifiable discrimination between countries where the same conditions prevail'[314] as it did not involve any discrimination between countries where the same conditions prevail.[315]

In this case, the Panel sought the opinion of scientific experts to assist in its judgment.[316] Four *amicus curiae* briefs were received, and the Panel, following the Appellate Body in *US – Shrimp/Turtle*, forwarded them to the parties and then took two of them into consideration.[317]

6.6.2   Panel Report

With regard to the claims made by Canada and the EC over the applicability of Arts. III and XI, the Panel found that Art. III was *prima facie* applicable and thus began its analysis under the GATT with Art. III.[318]

The 'likeness' of the products in question was identified by the Panel as the first point to be addressed,[319] followed by 'the identification of the products which have to be compared pursuant to Article III:4'.[320] The Panel chose to first assess whether 'PVA, cellulose and glass fibres, taken separately (i.e. not incorporated in a product), are products like to chrysotile fibre'.[321] Next, the Panel sought to assess

---

[312]*Ibid.*, para. 3.493.

[313]*Ibid.*, para. 3.492; GATT Panel Report *Thailand – Restrictions on Importation and Internal Taxes on Cigarettes*, para. 75.

[314]Panel Report *European Communities – Measures Affecting Asbestos and Asbestos-Containing Products*, para. 3.501.

[315]*Ibid.*, para. 3.503.

[316]*Ibid.*, para. 8.10.

[317]*Ibid.*, paras. 8.12–8.13.

[318]Panel Report *European Communities – Measures Affecting Asbestos and Asbestos-Containing Products*, para. 8.100.

[319]*Ibid.*, para. 8.103 (a).

[320]*Ibid.*, para. 8.103 (b).

[321]*Ibid.*, para. 8.111 (a).

the likeness of 'products containing asbestos or substitute fibres'.[322] Relying on the Appellate Body Reports in *Japan – Alcohol, US – Gasoline* and the Working Party in *Border Tax Adjustments*, the Panel sought to make its assessment of 'likeness' on a case-by-case basis,[323] taking into account the product's end uses in a given market, consumers' tastes and habits -which change from country to country- and the product's properties, nature and quality[324] and tariff classification[325]—while noting that 'panels must use their best judgement when determining whether, products are in fact like products, and this would always inevitably involve a degree of discretionary judgement'.[326]

In the assessment of product characteristics, the Panel found that '[t]heir properties are then equivalent, if not identical' and thus judged them to be like.[327] The Panel then recalled the US argument that the risk of a product to human health should be the basis for distinguishing products. The Panel stated, however, that 'the risk of a product for human or animal health has never been used as a factor of comparison by Panels entrusted with applying the concept of "likeness" within the meaning of Article III'[328] and that introducing such a criterion would largely invalidate Art. XX (b).[329] As such, it was not to be included in any assessment of likeness. With regard to end uses, the products in question 'allowed certain identical or at least similar end uses' and were thus also considered to be like under this criterion.[330] As consumers' tastes and habits were deemed by the Panel to be too varied in this case, this criterion was not taken into account.[331] Although the EC did provide different tariff classifications for these products, the Panel did not judge it to be decisive in this case[332] and thus decided that the products in this case (when taken separately) were 'like'.[333] In assessing likeness between 'products containing asbestos and certain other products', the Panel was of the view that the main argument put forward by the EC was based on 'risk' being a factor to be taken

---

[322]*Ibid.*, para. 8.111 (b).

[323]*Ibid.*, para. 8.112; Appellate Body Report *Japan –Taxes on Alcoholic Beverages*, pg. 18.

[324]Panel Report *European Communities – Measures Affecting Asbestos and Asbestos-Containing Products*, para. 8.112.

[325]*Ibid.*, para. 8.113; Appellate Body Report *United States – Standards for Reformulated and Conventional Gasoline*, paras. 6.8–6.9.

[326]Panel Report *European Communities – Measures Affecting Asbestos and Asbestos-Containing Products*, para. 8.114.

[327]*Ibid.*, para. 8.125–8.126.

[328]*Ibid.*, para. 8.129.

[329]*Ibid.*, para. 8.130.

[330]*Ibid.*, para. 8.136.

[331]*Ibid.*, para. 8.140.

[332]*Ibid.*, para. 8.143.

[333]*Ibid.*, para. 8.144.

into consideration,[334] and as this criterion had already been ruled out, they were also persuaded that these products were also 'like'.[335]

In assessing whether there was less favourable treatment of the Canadian products, the Panel found that the decree did 'not place an identical ban on PVA, cellulose or glass fibre and fibro-cement products containing PVA, cellulose or glass fibres' and thus constituted *de jure* discrimination.[336] The Panel therefore felt that the requirements had been satisfied to find a violation of Art. III:4.[337]

Having found a violation of Art. III:4, the Panel concluded that it was not necessary to assess the measure under Art. XI:1[338] and thus moved on to an assessment of the measure under Art. XX (b). The Panel began by assessing whether the 'policy in respect of the measures for which Article XX is invoked falls within the range of policies designed to protect human life or health'.[339] The Panel viewed this part of Art. XX (b) as entrusting them to decide whether a health risk was posed by the products in question, stating: '[w]e must therefore determine, on the basis of the relevant rules of evidence, whether chrysotile-asbestos, in the various forms we have considered so far, poses a risk to human life or health'.[340] The Panel reiterated the point made in *US – Gasoline* that it was not its job to decide whether the measure was necessary but stated rather that it 'must simply determine if the French policy of prohibiting the use of chrysotile-asbestos falls within the range of policies designed to protect human life or health'.[341] Considering the evidence put before it by both parties, the Panel was of the view that it 'tended to show' health risks from asbestos and asbestos-containing products.[342] Thus, it found the measure fitted *prima facie* under Art. XX (b).[343]

In its assessment of the 'necessity' of the measure in protecting human, animal or plant life or health, the Panel, following the Panel in *Thailand – Cigarettes*,[344] sought 'a measure that would be consistent, or less inconsistent, with the GATT 1994 and would allow the objective pursued by France to be achieved'.[345] The Panel also cited *US – Section 337* and laid out that such an alternate measure should

---

[334]*Ibid.*, para. 8.149.

[335]*Ibid.*, para. 8.150.

[336]*Ibid.*, para. 8.155.

[337]*Ibid.*, para. 8.158.

[338]*Ibid.*, para. 8.159.

[339]*Ibid.*, para. 8.169.

[340]*Ibid.*, para. 8.170.

[341]*Ibid.*, para. 8.171.

[342]*Ibid.*, para. 8.193.

[343]*Ibid.*, para. 8.194.

[344]GATT Panel Report *Thailand – Restrictions on Importation and Internal Taxes on Cigarettes*, para. 75.

[345]Panel Report *European Communities – Measures Affecting Asbestos and Asbestos-Containing Products*, para. 8.204.

be 'reasonably available',[346] as well as sufficiently effective.[347] Canada's suggestion of an alternate measure involving the controlled use of asbestos and asbestos-containing products was deemed by the Panel, however, to be neither sufficiently effective nor reasonably available in this case.[348] The measure was thus deemed to meet the requirements of Art. XX (b); the Panel then moved on to assess it under the chapeau of Art. XX.

In the application of the measure, the Panel did not find any discrimination and thus did not go on to assess the 'arbitrary or unjustifiable' qualifiers.[349] With regard to the requirement of the chapeau that the measure not constitute a 'disguised restriction on international trade', the Panel noted that this phrase had never been clearly defined.[350] Following the Appellate Body in *Japan – Alcohol*, the Panel assessed the 'design, architecture and revealing structure of the Decree' and found 'nothing that might lead us to conclude that the Decree has protectionist objectives'.[351] The Panel found that although there was a possibility that the measure might end up favouring domestic manufacturers of substitute products, this 'is a natural consequence of prohibiting a given product and in itself cannot justify the conclusion that the measure has a protectionist aim, as long as it remains within certain limits'.[352] The Panel thus found that the French decree met the requirements of the chapeau and was justified as an exception under Art. XX (b).[353]

6.6.3   Appellate Body Report

Both Canada and the EC appealed the Report of the Panel on various grounds. The issues addressed by the Appellate Body in its Report, *inter alia*, included whether the Panel erred in its interpretation and application of the term 'like products' in Art. III:4 of the GATT 1994 and whether the Panel erred in finding that the measure at issue is 'necessary to protect human [. . .] life or health' under Art. XX (b) of the GATT 1994.[354]

---

[346]GATT Panel Report *United States – Section 337 of the Tariff Act of* 1930, para. 5.26; Panel Report *European Communities – Measures Affecting Asbestos and Asbestos-Containing Products*, para. 8.206.

[347]Panel Report *European Communities – Measures Affecting Asbestos and Asbestos-Containing Products*, para. 8.208.

[348]*Ibid.*, para. 8.217.

[349]*Ibid.*, para. 8.230.

[350]*Ibid.*, para. 8.233.

[351]*Ibid.*, para. 8.236–8.238; Appellate Body Report *Japan – Taxes on Alcoholic Beverages*, pg. 31.

[352]*Ibid.*, para. 8.239.

[353]*Ibid.*, paras. 8.240–8.241. The Panel also found no nullification or impairment under Art. XXIII:1(b) GATT; *ibid.*, para. 8.304.

[354]Appellate Body Report *European Communities – Measures Affecting Asbestos and Asbestos-Containing Products*, para. 58.

With regard to the Panel's interpretation of 'likeness', the Appellate Body similarly invoked the four criteria that should be taken into account when assessing likeness under Art. III:4[355] while bearing in mind that they are neither treaty mandated nor 'a closed list of criteria that will determine the legal characterization of products'.[356] The Body emphasised that Panels must 'examine fully the physical properties of products'[357] and noted that while the Panel recognised certain physical characteristics (carcinogenicity, or toxicity), it did not share the view that they should not be included in a comparison of likeness.[358] In fact, the Body stated:

> We do not see how this highly significant physical difference cannot be a consideration in examining the physical properties of a product as part of a determination of 'likeness' under Article III:4 of the GATT 1994.[359]

The Body further did not agree that including health risks in the evaluation of likeness under Art. III:4 nullified Art. XX (b).[360] The Appellate Body then went on to find that the Panel had erred in its interpretation of likeness under Art. III:4 on the basis that

> the Panel disregarded the quite different 'properties, nature and quality' of chrysotile asbestos and PCG fibres, as well as the different tariff classification of these fibres; it considered no evidence on consumers' tastes and habits; and it found that, for a 'small number' of the many applications of these fibres, they are substitutable, but it did not consider the many other end-uses for the fibres that are different. Thus, the only evidence supporting the Panel's finding of 'likeness' is the 'small number' of shared end-uses of the fibres.[361]

The Body thus reversed the Panel's finding that the products were 'like' under Art. III:4[362] and, completing the legal analysis under Art. III:4, found that the 'evidence rather tends to suggest that these products are not "like products" for the purposes of Article III:4 of the GATT 1994'.[363]

The Appellate Body then went on to address Canada's appeal claim regarding the Panel's interpretation of Art. XX (b).[364] In this instance, the Body found that the

---

[355]'(i) the physical properties of the products; (ii) the extent to which the products are capable of serving the same or similar end-uses; (iii) the extent to which consumers perceive and treat the products as alternative means of performing particular functions in order to satisfy a particular want or demand; and (iv) the international classification of the products for tariff purposes', *ibid.*, para. 101.

[356]*Ibid.*, para. 101.

[357]*Ibid.*, para. 114.

[358]*Ibid.*

[359]*Ibid.*

[360]*Ibid.*, para. 115.

[361]*Ibid.*, para. 125.

[362]*Ibid.*, paras. 126, 131.

[363]*Ibid.*, paras. 141, 148.

[364]It should be noted that Canada also claimed that the Panel breached Art. 11 DSU in failing to make an objective assessment under Art. XX (b). Although this was an important point in the proceedings, for the sake of space it will not be addressed here. See *ibid.*, para. 155, 176–181.

Panel remained within the bounds of its discretion with regard to its assessment of whether the measure fell under Art. XX (b)[365] and agreed that the EC had demonstrated that there was no reasonably available alternative, thus meeting the necessity requirement[366] and upholding the Panel's decision. Overall, the Body found that Canada had not succeeded in 'establishing that the measure at issue is inconsistent with the obligations of the European Communities under the covered agreements and, accordingly, [did not] make any recommendations to the DSB under Art. 19.1 of the DSU'.[367]

6.6.4   Analysis

Although this case is not strictly environmental, and as with *US – Reformulated Gasoline* the 'harm' relating to asbestos and asbestos-containing products would occur in the importing country and not the country of origin, some of the issues raised here are still of relevance in this study. The differing interpretations of the 'likeness' of the products clearly demonstrate impreciseness of the obligations under the GATT, and while the result may have granted more regulatory space to France, it is not clear that the guidance given by the Appellate Body in this case will ensure any consistency or predictability of 'likeness' in the future. Moreover, this case demonstrates that such imprecise wording in the substantive provisions of the GATT and a 'case-by-case' approach to likeness can produce unpredictable and damaging results.

Despite the fact that the Appellate Body rectified the Panel's blunder, the fact that it was possible for the Panel to make such an interpretation at first instance demonstrates the deficiencies of the imprecise treaty texts. The 'accordion of likeness' may be squeezed differently at different times in order to avoid arbitrary rulings but certainly should not be done to implement them. The strength of a case by-case approach is the flexibility to avoid arbitrary or unjust outcomes—if outcomes such as the Panel Report in this case are produced, then the basis text must be made more precise or explicit, or the implementing body must have better guidelines as to the interpretation and application of the law. *EC – Asbestos* may have little to do with NPR PPMs, but the insights gained from assessing the interpretation of 'likeness' in this case are helpful and relevant to this study.

---

[365]*Ibid.*, para. 162–163.
[366]*Ibid.*, para. 175.
[367]*Ibid.*, para. 193.

6.7 Summary

The preceding summary of the GATT case law to date with primary focus on cases relevant to NPR PPMs based on TREMs demonstrates the complexity of the topic itself and the jurisprudence of the DSS on this matter. The issue is not clearly covered (or clearly not covered) by the GATT but has been taken into account in varying ways under the treaty since environmental issues first began to be raised before the GATT DSS.

Through this brief overview of relevant case law, it is clear that many of the criticisms drawn out from the analysis of the provisions the previous chapter are born out in the cases that have thus far come before the DSS. Imprecise formulations and a lack of formal realisability lead to a lack of legal certainty. A lack of legal certainty is disproportionately burdensome to developing countries. A jurisdictional limitation of Art. XX would appear to rule out the use of TREMs based on NPR PPMs being lawful under the GATT, but allowing for an extraterritorial application of such measures under Art. XX could potentially interfere with the internal affairs or sovereignty of exporting States. Further to this, such interference would disproportionately affect net exporting States and weaker economies that would be coerced into changing their policies so as not to lose out on market access. The preference for multilateralism can also be seen to be more beneficial to stronger economies as they have the wealth and influence to begin negotiations and bring about their desired results, whereas developing countries lack both the expertise and substantial financial backing necessary for such ventures. In other words, developed countries can afford to use the Art. XX exceptions, but developing countries probably cannot.

A tentative suggestion at this point is that the progression towards not recognising products with differing (and on one side environmentally damaging) NPR PPMs as being 'like' may eliminate some of the problems raised in this chapter. It may disproportionately affect developing States in some ways,[368] but as has been demonstrated in this chapter, the status quo is also detrimental to them and does not provide legal certainty for any WTO Members. While institutional reform and reform to the treaties would be more desirable than an interpretative change of stance from the DSS, this is highly unlikely for manifold reasons. It may be that, rather than the Art. XX (a) moral exception or further use of Art. XX (b) and (g), this change in the interpretation of 'likeness' would be a positive influence on the system and improve legal certainty and predictability—although, as 'like products' would still be assessed on a case-by-case basis, this is perhaps overly ambitious.

The following chapters will go on to assess NPR PPMs under the TBT and SPS Agreements in the field of environmental protection, and related case law.

---

[368]*Abhinay Kapoor*, Product and Process Methods (PPMs): 'a Losing Battle for Developing Countries', International Trade Law and Regulation 17 (2011), 131 *et seq.*

Chapter 7
Trade-Related Environmental Measures and the TBT

7.1 Overview

Following on from analysis under the GATT, it is necessary in turn to look at how different types of TREMs are regulated by the TBT Agreement. As the name would suggest, the Agreement on Technical Barriers to Trade establishes a regulatory regime to ensure that technical regulations about products, i.e. voluntary standards, mandatory requirements and conformity assessment procedures, 'are not prepared, adopted or applied with the view or effect of creating unnecessary obstacles to international trade'.[1] As highlighted previously, following Interpretative Note to Annex 1A of the WTO Agreement, in the event of a conflict between the GATT and a provision of one of the other agreements listed in Annex 1A to the WTO Agreement, 'the provision of the other agreement shall prevail to the extent of the conflict'.[2] In cases where there is no conflict, measures falling within the scope of one of the covered agreements will also be assessed under the GATT, so that, for example, a measure deemed TBT compliant would still be assessed under the provisions of the GATT. If a violation of the TBT is found, however, the DSS would exercise judicial economy and not carry out an assessment under the GATT.[3]

The TBT Agreement applies to a 'limited class of measures'[4] and maintains the conventional GATT disciplines of MFN and national treatment in relation to technical regulations, while 'drawing a distinction between a standard and a

---

[1]*Gary P. Sampson*, Trade, Environment and the WTO: The Post-Seattle Agenda (2000), 71–72.

[2]See *supra*, Chap. 3.

[3]Unlike under the SPS Agreement, there is no presumption of GATT consistency if a measure is found consistent with the TBT, *Peter Van den Bossche/Werner Zdouc*, The Law and Policy of the World Trade Organization (Cambridge, 3rd ed. 2013), 862.

[4]Appellate Body Report *European Communities – Measures Affecting Asbestos and Asbestos-Containing Products*, para. 80.

© Springer International Publishing AG 2017
A.R. Maggio, *Environmental Policy, Non-Product Related Process and Production Methods and the Law of the World Trade Organization*, European Yearbook of International Economic Law 1, DOI 10.1007/978-3-319-61155-6_7

technical regulation on the basis of compliance and enforcement'.[5] While mandatory technical regulations and conformity assessment procedures are governed by the main text of the TBT, voluntary standards are covered by an annex (Code of Good Practice for the Preparation, Adoption and Application of Standards). The TBT Agreement mainly addresses central governmental bodies but also covers local government and non-governmental bodies.[6] With regard to local government and non-governmental bodies, the TBT places an obligation on members to take such reasonable measures as are available to them to ensure compliance with the TBT by such entities and to refrain from measures that might encourage actions inconsistent with the TBT by these entities.[7]

Whether the TBT covers NPR PPMs at all has long been a point of contention for WTO members and has been discussed often in the Committee on Trade and Environment and the TBT Committee. Even with regard to voluntary labelling schemes, it was contested whether labels that did not refer to product characteristics but only production methods would be covered by this agreement at all.[8] The developments in the interpretation of the application of the TBT Agreement will be laid out below both in reference to interpretation of the provisions of the agreement in this chapter and with reference to case law in the following chapter. This chapter will address the MFN and national treatment obligations contained in the TBT, followed by the obligation in the agreement not to create unnecessary obstacles to international trade and the obligation to base measures under the TBT on international standards.[9]

The TBT Agreement came into effect on 1 January 1995 and has, by comparison, far less practice under the DSS than the GATT.[10] Although often invoked by parties seeking the formation of a Panel, it is cited less often in the Panel phase, perhaps for the very reason that there is little practice and thus less certainty in possible/probable interpretative choices by the DSS. Therefore, this chapter, although addressing different and equally important issues to this work, will necessarily be more brief than the previous concerning the GATT.

---

[5]*Sampson* (note 1), 72.

[6]*Van den Bossche/Zdouc* (note 3), 860.

[7]*Ibid.*; Arts. 3, 7, 8 and Annex 3.B TBT Agreement.

[8]*Sampson* (note 1), 75–76.

[9]Based on the breakdown of the agreement in *Van den Bossche/Zdouc* (note 3), 863–883.

[10]Although the Tokyo Round TBT Agreement was its precursor, this did not provide any jurisprudence.

7.2   Article 2.1 TBT: MFN and National Treatment

7.2.1   Content of the Norm

Although similar obligations are contained in the GATT and the TBT Agreement, the form and structure are decidedly different. Article 2.1 TBT states:

> Members shall ensure that in respect of technical regulations, products imported from the territory of any Member shall be accorded treatment no less favourable than that accorded to like products of national origin and to like products originating in any other country.

Article 2.1 thus lays out two three-tier tests:

MFN test
- the measure at issue must be a technical regulation;
- the products at issue must be like;
- the treatment accorded to imported products from any member must be less favourable than that accorded to like products originating in any other country.

National treatment test
- the measure at issue must be a technical regulation;
- the products at issue must be like;
- the treatment accorded to imported products must be less favourable than that accorded to like domestic products.[11]

Although this only applies to technical regulations, pursuant to Annex 3.D and Art. 5.1.1 TBT, the MFN and national treatment obligations also apply to 'standards' and 'conformity assessment procedures'.[12]

With regard to interpretation of the terms 'technical regulation', 'standards' and 'conformity assessment procedures', definitions are given in Annexes 1.1, 1.2 and 1.3 of the TBT thus:

- **Technical regulation**: 'Document which lays down product characteristics or their related processes and production methods, including the applicable administrative provisions, with which compliance is mandatory. *It may also include or deal exclusively with terminology, symbols, packaging, marking or labelling requirements as they apply to a product, process or production method.*[13]
- **Standard**: 'Document approved by a recognized body, that provides, for common and repeated use, rules, guidelines or characteristics for products or related processes and production methods, with which compliance is not mandatory. *It may also include or deal exclusively with terminology, symbols, packaging,*

---

[11] See also Appellate Body Report *United States – Measures Affecting the Production and Sale of Clove Cigarettes*, para. 87.

[12] See further *Van den Bossche/Zdouc* (note 3), 864.

[13] Annex 1.1 TBT (emphasis added).

marking or labelling requirements as they apply to a product, process or production method.[14]

- **Conformity assessment procedure**: 'any procedure used, directly or indirectly, to determine the relevant requirements in technical regulations or standards are fulfilled.[15]

The major difference between technical regulations and standards is that compliance with regulations is mandatory, whereas standards are voluntary. Conformity assessment procedures refer to monitoring and inspection procedures and are thus not of relevance to this work. It should be noted that both the 'technical regulation' and 'standard' definitions make reference to a 'document', broadly defined, which in *US – Tuna II (Mexico)* was elaborated on by the Appellate Body, which stated that 'the use of the term "document" could therefore cover a broad range of instruments or apply to a variety of measures'.[16]

In the definitions given above, the highlighted sections are central to this study. The applicability of Art. 2.1 TBT to TREMs based on NPR PPMs hinges upon the interpretation of these sections. Due to the inclusion of the word 'related' when referencing PPMs, the sections highlighted in bold could be read to indicate that technical regulations and standards based on NPR PPMs do not fall within the scope of the TBT.[17] If so, the GATT rules as laid out in the previous chapter would apply instead. However, with regard to the sections relating to labelling, highlighted in italics, the word 'related' is not included and thus could be interpreted to include NPR PPMs in relation to 'terminology, symbols, packaging, marking or labelling requirements'.

Due to the fact that the coverage of the TBT was so controversial among members, the WTO Secretariat put together a document for the Committee of Trade and Environment and the Committee on Technical Barriers to Trade entitled 'Negotiating History of the Coverage of the Agreement on Technical Barriers to Trade with Regard to Labelling Requirements, Voluntary Standards, and Processes and Production Methods Unrelated to Product Characteristics'.[18] This paper lays out that the negotiating history of the TBT suggests 'that many participants were of the view that standards based *inter alia* on PPMs unrelated to a product's characteristics should not be considered eligible for being treated as being in conformity with the TBT Agreement'[19] and reports that although it was suggested (unopposed) that the language contained in the definitions in Annex 1 should be changed to make

[14]Annex 1.2 TBT (emphasis added).

[15]Annex 1.3 TBT.

[16]Appellate Body Report *United States – Measures Concerning the Importation, Marketing and Sale of Tuna and Tuna Products*, para. 185; *Van den Bossche/Zdouc* (note 3), 853.

[17]*Van den Bossche/Zdouc* (note 3), 854.

[18]WTO, Negotiating History of the Coverage of the Agreement on Technical Barriers to Trade with regard to Labelling Requirements, Voluntary Standards, and Processes and Production Methods Unrelated to Product Characteristics, Doc. WT/CTE/W/10 (29 August 1995).

[19]*Ibid.*, pg. 2 (lit. (c)).

it unambiguously clear that NPR PPMs were not included, it was not possible to find the relevant consensus required to make the change.[20] In this paper, the Secretariat laid out that '[d]eveloping countries pointed out that labelling requirements were more onerous to their products than to others and thus represented a disproportionate burden to their trade'.[21]

At the Tokyo Round (producing the Tokyo Round Agreement on Technical Barriers to Trade, the precursor to the TBT under the WTO), the applicability of the agreement to PPMs was discussed at length, and the discussions 'showed a divergence of views'.[22] PPMs were not covered except in Art. 14.25, which only applied 'if there was a deliberate attempt to escape or circumvent obligations under the Agreement by drafting requirements in terms of PPMs rather than product characteristics'.[23]

Article 14.25 of the Tokyo TBT read:

> The dispute settlement procedures set out above can be invoked in cases where a Party considers that obligations under this Agreement are being circumvented by the drafting of requirements in terms of processes and production methods rather than in terms of characteristics of products.

It was suggested that if the agreement were to apply to PPMs, the definitions contained in it would have to be altered, but this did not take place.[24] The issue was repeatedly raised in the Tokyo TBT Committee, but no consensus could be reached about the applicability of the Tokyo TBT to PPMs.[25]

At the Uruguay Round, the US put forward a proposal to explicitly include PPMs in the agreement and argued:

> Lack of full coverage of PPMs seriously weakened the effectiveness of the Agreement by excluding a growing body of regulations from its disciplines. The intention was not to discourage the use of PPMs but rather to eliminate potential trade barriers to both industrial and agricultural trade posed by PPM-based requirements. Full extension of the provisions of the Agreement to PPM-based requirements would strengthen the Agreement and make it more effective in reducing arbitrary or unnecessary technical barriers to trade.[26]

Support was expressed for the US position and the idea of preventing PPM-based measures from creating unnecessary obstacles to trade, although there were also some concerns.[27] It was noted that if PPMs were to be included under the TBT, then Art. 14.25 would become redundant. There were significant discussion and a number of proposals as to how best to explicitly include PPMs under the

---

[20]*Ibid.*

[21]*Ibid.*, pg. 4 (para. 9).

[22]*Ibid.*, pg. 36 (para. 112).

[23]*Ibid.*, pg. 37 (para. 114).

[24]*Ibid.*

[25]*Ibid.*, paras. 111–118.

[26]*Ibid.*, pg. 39 (para. 121).

[27]*Ibid.*, para. 122.

TBT,[28] both in the main text and in the Annexes. By 1990, the majority of main text references were dropped but retained in the Annexes.[29]

At that stage, the draft Annex 2.1 read:

> Document which lays down characteristics for products, processes and production methods including the applicable administrative provisions, with which compliance is mandatory. It may also include or deal exclusively with terminology, symbols, packaging, marking or labelling requirements as they apply to a product, process or production method.[30]

At the final stage of the negotiations, Mexico introduced a proposal that sought to clarify the scope of application of the agreement by inserting 'related' before the first reference to PPMs in order to make it clear 'that the intent was to exclude PPMs unrelated to the characteristics of a product from the coverage of the Agreement'.[31] This was then adopted into the draft Annex for standards, as well as technical regulations.[32] From the negotiating history, it thus appears clear that there was no intention for NPR PPMs to be included in the expanded inclusion of the treaty's application to PPMs.

With regard to labelling, the Tokyo TBT made reference to technical specifications that 'may include or deal exclusively with terminology, symbols, testing and test methods, packaging, marking or labelling requirements as they apply to a product',[33] without reference to PPMs. There was no recorded discussion of the coverage of labelling under the TBT at the Uruguay Round.[34] It is thus not clear from the negotiations what the intentions of the parties were with regard to the wording 'labelling requirements as they apply to a product, process or production method', though the tendency would appear to be that that was not envisaged. However, the argument that the difference in wording regarding the inclusion of 'related' (on the basis of the Mexican Proposal) with regard to technical regulations and standards but not their labelling counterparts could be reinforced by questioning why it was felt necessary to include such a distinction with regard to the first part of the Annex definitions but not regarding labelling.

This point was hotly contested in literature and in the TBT Committee after the birth of the WTO. However, *US – Tuna II (Mexico)*,[35] decided by the Appellate Body in 2012, involved labelling requirements based on NPR PPMs, and the respondent did not put forward the argument that the measures at issue did not fall within the scope of the TBT.[36] It may, however, be notable that the US was a

---

[28]See *ibid.*, paras. 122–137.

[29]*Ibid.*, para. 140.

[30]*Ibid.*, pg. 49.

[31]*Ibid.*, para. 146.

[32]*Ibid.*, pg. 50.

[33]*Ibid.*, pg. 5.

[34]*Ibid.*, para. 16.

[35]Appellate Body Report *United States – Measures Concerning the Importation, Marketing and Sale of Tuna and Tuna Products (US – Tuna II (Mexico))*.

[36]*Van den Bossche/Zdouc* (note 3), 855.

firm defender of the inclusion of PPMs into the coverage of the TBT Agreement, and they may therefore also have more lenient views relating to labelling and NPR PPMs than other WTO members. This case is discussed in further detail in Part II of this chapter.

Returning to Art. 2.1, following the Appellate Body in *EC – Asbestos*, technical regulations must be mandatory,[37] lay down 'product characteristics' that include 'any objectively definable "features", "qualities", "attributes", or other "distinguishing mark" of a product',[38] as well as intrinsic and extrinsic features.[39] Furthermore, the product must be identifiable.[40]

The voluntary versus mandatory distinction used for distinguishing standards and technical regulations was at issue in *US – Tuna II (Mexico)*, where the Appellate Body laid out that such a distinction could only be made on a case-by-case basis by examining the measure at hand but may involve considering

- whether the measure consists of a law or a regulation enacted by a WTO member;
- whether it prescribes or prohibits particular conduct;
- whether it sets out specific requirements that constitute the sole means of addressing a particular matter;
- the nature of the matter addressed by the measure.[41]

After assessing the first element of the test of consistency under Art. 2.1 (technical regulation/standard/conformity assessment procedure), the DSS must go on to assess the 'likeness' of the products involved in the dispute. Only if the products in question are considered 'like' can the measure in question be said to fall under Art. 2.1. The MFN and national treatment obligations are thus only applicable to 'like products'.

The 'likeness' of the products concerned was particularly at issue in *US – Clove Cigarettes*, a case brought following the US ban on flavoured cigarettes.[42] While the Panel in this case took a 'purpose based' approach[43] on the basis that 'the measure at issue was a technical regulation having the immediate purpose of

---

[37]Appellate Body Report *European Communities – Measures Affecting Asbestos and Asbestos-Containing Products*, para. 68.

[38]*Ibid.*, para. 67.

[39]*Ibid.*

[40]*Ibid.*, para. 70.

[41]*Van den Bossche/Zdouc* (note 3), 859; Appellate Body Report *United States – Measures Concerning the Importation, Marketing and Sale of Tuna and Tuna Products (US – Tuna II (Mexico))*, para. 188.

[42]Panel Report *United States – Measures Affecting the Production and Sale of Clove Cigarettes*; Appellate Body Report *United States – Measures Affecting the Production and Sale of Clove Cigarettes*.

[43]Panel Report *United States – Measures Affecting the Production and Sale of Clove Cigarettes*, para. 7.119; *Van den Bossche/Zdouc* (note 3), 866.

regulating flavoured cigarettes for public health reasons',[44] the Appellate Body rejected this approach in favour of a competition-based approach. The Body stated that a determination of likeness under Art. 2.1 is 'a determination about the nature and extent of a competitive relationship between and among the products at issue'.[45]

The final element of the test for Art. 2.1 is the 'treatment no less favourable' requirement. This applies as both an MFN and national treatment obligation. With regard to the national treatment obligation contained in Art. 2.1, in *US – Clove Cigarettes* the Appellate Body laid out that the case law and interpretation of the term 'treatment no less favourable' under Art. III:4 GATT should be considered 'instructive'[46] and should include both *de facto* and *de jure* discrimination.[47] With regard to legitimate regulatory distinctions versus discrimination under Art. 2.1, the Appellate Body stated that Panels must assess such matters on a case-by-case basis, looking particularly at the 'design, architecture, revealing structure, operation and application' of the measure at issue.[48]

7.2.2 Analysis

Article 2.1 TBT contains simplified versions of the MFN and national treatment obligations contained in the GATT. The MFN rule contained in Art. 2.1 TBT constitutes a Hohfeldian duty as it contains an absence of permission to discriminate between trading partners and thus a right for exporting WTO members. Although there is no case law exploring the subject, this duty is limited in a similar way to that of Art. I:1 GATT in relation to the privilege of States to create preferential trade agreements and regional trade areas. As highlighted above, this privilege has a disproportionate negative effect on developing countries, as developed countries have the resources and bargaining power to enter more of these arrangements and on better terms, meaning they can choose who they discriminate against. The national treatment rule contained in Art. 2.1 TBT also constitutes a Hohfeldian duty, and the analysis of Arts. III:2 and III:4 GATT is referenced here in that connection. Both duties contained in Art. 2.1 TBT require the presence of 'like products', highlighting that if the products in question were not deemed to be like (perhaps by a progressive interpretation of the term by the DSS), then the provisions

---

[44]*Van den Bossche/Zdouc* (note 3), 866.

[45]Appellate Body Report *United States – Measures Affecting the Production and Sale of Clove Cigarettes*, para. 120.

[46]*Van den Bossche/Zdouc* (note 3), 868; Appellate Body Report *United States – Measures Affecting the Production and Sale of Clove Cigarettes*, para. 180.

[47]Appellate Body Report *United States – Measures Affecting the Production and Sale of Clove Cigarettes*, paras. 179–182.

[48]*Ibid.*, para. 2.15.

would not apply. As this is not currently the interpretative position of the DSS (or members), products subject to differing technical regulations based on NPR PPMs should be considered 'like'.

However, it appears clear from both the genesis and the wording of Art. 2.1 TBT that it was not intended to cover NPR PPMs in technical regulations that lay down product characteristics or standards that create rules, guidelines or characteristics for products. Thus, in general, technical barriers to trade in the shape of technical regulations or standards that are based on NPR PPMs appear to be outside of the scope of the TBT, except in the case of those that 'include or deal exclusively with terminology, symbols, packaging, marking or labelling requirements as they apply to a product, process or production method'.

Such labelling requirements (whether phrased as technical regulations or standards) may be the only NPR-PPM-based measures that presently engage the TBT Agreement and are subject to its rigours. However, that is not to underplay their significance. Despite the fact that a true environmental agenda may be better served through border measures such as import bans, the political reality of the situation is that it may be preferable for many governments to allow consumer choice to regulate this issue. In doing so, however, they must ensure that both mandatory and voluntary labelling schemes under central governmental authority respect the rules contained in the TBT. Furthermore, under Art. 3, TBT members must 'take reasonable measures' with respect to their local government and *non-governmental bodies* within their territories to ensure their compliance with Art. 2 TBT. Although the obligation to 'take reasonable measures' does not set a particularly high bar, the fact that WTO members are obligated to ensure that non-governmental entities obey the rules laid down in Art. 2 TBT, even with regard to *voluntary* standards, demonstrates that this is indeed a far-reaching obligation. Thus, for example, if an environmental NGO set up a voluntary labelling standard to encourage the purchase of sustainably fished tuna and it was found that this only applied to tuna products caught using methods used by only a handful of trading partners, or only by the member itself, then this issue could be raised before the DSS.

While it may seem reasonable that government agencies should be obligated not to discriminate in the creation of labelling requirements for imported products sold in their territories, it is more tenuous to extend this application to NGOs—which themselves have no 'protectionist' motives. NGO-led labelling schemes that are on their face origin neutral but may *de facto* cause consumer prejudice between or against products from trading partners can equally be seen as a way to inform the consumer about issues that may be of relevance to them. This is particularly the case as consumers' tastes and habits are taken into account in the assessment of 'like products' but cannot be said to be fairly assessed if consumers are not well informed about their choices. The rigours of the TBT on this point could be argued to limit consumer choice, and there is no underlying argument of eliminating protectionism, which is the case for labelling schemes put in place by governments themselves.

7.3   Article 2.2 TBT

7.3.1   Content of the Norm

Article 2.2 of the TBT reads:

> Members shall ensure that technical regulations are not prepared, adopted or applied with a view to or with the effect of creating unnecessary obstacles to international trade. For this purpose, technical regulations shall not be more trade restrictive than necessary to fulfil a legitimate objective, taking into account the risks non-fulfilment would create. Such legitimate objectives are, *inter alia*: [...]; protection of human health or safety, animal or plant life or health, or the environment. In assessing such risks, relevant elements are, *inter alia*: available scientific and technical information, related processing technology or intended end-uses of products.

By virtue of Art. 5.1.2 and Annex 3.E TBT, the same obligations apply to standards and conformity assessment procedures. To date, the DSS has not found any party to have acted inconsistently with Art. 2.2 TBT.

Although there is no equivalent to the Art. XX GATT general exceptions contained in the TBT Agreement, there are some echoes of its rules in Art. 2.2. The invocation of legitimate objectives (along with the non-exhaustive list that includes human, animal and plant life or health and the environment) and the particular language that seeks for the measure in question to be not more trade restrictive than necessary all have strong similarities with the wording, interpretation and jurisprudence related to Art. XX. However, Art. 2.2 TBT does not function as an exception clause, and thus, although conformity with the provision is required, it cannot be invoked as an exception in the case where another provision of the TBT has been violated by a WTO member. It should be noted that, despite the fact that the TBT has no exception clause, the content of Art. XX is largely reproduced in Preamble 6, which reads:

> *Recognizing* that no country should be prevented from taking measures necessary [...] for the protection of human, animal or plant life or health, of the environment [...] at the levels it considers appropriate, subject to the requirement that they are not applied in a manner which would constitute a means of arbitrary or unjustifiable discrimination between countries where the same conditions prevail or a disguised restriction on international trade, and are otherwise in accordance with the provisions of this Agreement.

The Preamble cannot create any legal obligations on either the WTO members or the DSS, but its interpretative function is well established.[49] Thus, the combination of the inclusion of Preamble 6 and Art. 2.2 may, while not going as far as providing a clear exception clause, be argued to provide a presumption that such measures (i.e., those necessary for the protection of human, animal or plant life or health or the environment) are permissible under the TBT if they meet the requirements of Art. 2.2. Clearly, however, there is a lack of legal certainty here, and despite some

---

[49]*M Makane Moïse Mbengue*, Preamble, in: Rüdiger Wolfrum (ed.) The Max Planck Encyclopaedia of Public International Law, vol. VIII (Oxford, 2012), 397 (paras. 3 *et seq.*).

misgivings it may in fact be preferable for States using TREMs based on NPR PPMs to have them assessed under the GATT. With regard to the labelling requirements that would fall under the TBT, if they do not fall foul of Art. 2.1 (for which Art. 2.2 does not constitute an exception), then they must also meet the specific requirements of Art. 2.2.

The specific requirement under Art. 2.2 that the measure be no 'more trade restrictive than necessary' shows that trade-restrictive measures fall under Art. 2.2 but that some trade-restrictive measures are permitted if they are not more restrictive than necessary to carry out a legitimate objective. Regarding the legitimate objective, Panels are not bound by the characterisation of the measure given by the member.[50] The list given in Art. 2.2 is non-exhaustive, but for the purposes of this study the inclusion of human, animal or plant life or health and the environment is sufficient for TREMs (particularly with regard to environmental labelling). A member should be free to choose the 'level it considers appropriate' for the legitimate objective,[51] while Panels 'must seek to ascertain to what degree, or if at all, the challenged technical regulation, as written and applied, actually contributes to the legitimate objective pursued by the Member'.[52] The 'no more trade restrictive than necessary' test here appears to echo the interpretation given to the 'necessity' requirement in Art. XX (b)[53]: the 'least-trade-restrictive' approach. This approach, it has been noted, was 'failing to give adequate consideration to societal values other than trade'.[54] With regard to Art. 2.2, the Appellate Body laid out that an assessment of measures conforming with the 'not more trade restrictive than necessary' element should

> begin by considering factors that include: (i) the degree of contribution made by the measure to the legitimate objective at issue; (ii) the trade-restrictiveness of the measure; and (iii) the nature of the risks at issue and the gravity of consequences that would arise from non-fulfilment of the objective(s) pursued by the Member through the measure. In most cases, a comparison of the challenged measure and possible alternative measures should be undertaken.[55]

As noted above, no measure has as yet been found to violate Art. 2.2, and thus there is no further elaboration from the DSS to enlighten one to their approach in this context.

---

[50]*Van den Bossche/Zdouc* (note 3), 874; Appellate Body Report *United States – Measures Concerning the Importation, Marketing and Sale of Tuna and Tuna Products (US – Tuna II (Mexico))*, para. 314.

[51]Appellate Body Report *United States – Measures Concerning the Importation, Marketing and Sale of Tuna and Tuna Products (US – Tuna II (Mexico))*, para. 316.

[52]*Ibid.*, para. 3.17.

[53]See Sect. 5.5.2.

[54]*Nathalie Bernasconi-Osterwalder/Daniel Magraw/Maria Julia Olivia/Morcos Orellana/Elizabeth Tuerk*, Environment and Trade: A Guide to WTO Jurisprudence (London, 2006), 149.

[55]Appellate Body Report *United States – Measures Concerning the Importation, Marketing and Sale of Tuna and Tuna Products (US – Tuna II (Mexico))*, para. 322.

7.3.2 Analysis

Article 2.2 clearly creates a Hohfeldian duty, along with several privileges that restrict the scope of that duty. The duty that technical regulations shall not be more trade restrictive than necessary to fulfil a legitimate objective is limited itself as the obligation not to create trade-restrictive technical regulations is limited by the exclusion of those that are necessary to fulfil a legitimate objective (and even further by the reference to the risks of non-fulfilment). Further application of the provision is required before more in-depth analysis can be carried out, particularly in reference to labelling requirements based on NPR PPMs.

7.4 International Standards

7.4.1 Content of the Norm

Article 2.4 TBT creates an obligation on WTO members to base technical regulations on international standards, when they are available. Art. 2.4 states:

> Where technical regulations are required and relevant international standards exist or their completion is imminent, Members shall use them, or the relevant parts of them, as a basis for their technical regulations except when such international standards or relevant parts would be an ineffective or inappropriate means for the fulfilment of the legitimate objectives pursued, for instance because of fundamental climatic or geographical factors or fundamental technological problems.

By virtue of Art. 5.4 Annex 3.F TBT, a similar obligation applies with respect to standards and conformity assessment procedures.

Article 2.4 lays out a three-part test:

- Is there a relevant international standard?
- Is this standard used as a basis for the measure in question?
- Is the standard an effective and appropriate means for the fulfilment of the legitimate objective pursued?[56]

Following the Appellate Body in *US – Tuna II (Mexico)*, such standards originate in international bodies but need not be from international organisations.[57] Such a body must be 'a body that has recognized activities in standardization and whose membership is open to the relevant bodies of at least all Members'.[58] Following the

---

[56]*Van den Bossche/Zdouc* (note 3), 879.

[57]Appellate Body Report *United States – Measures Concerning the Importation, Marketing and Sale of Tuna and Tuna Products (US – Tuna II (Mexico))*, paras. 353–359.

[58]*Ibid.*, para. 359. For example the World Wide Web Consortium or the Universal Postal Union, who develop international standards and are open for membership but are not 'international organizations' in the traditional sense.

Panel in *EC – Sardines (2002)*, the relevance of such standards will be based on the products at issue and any product requirements such as labelling, presentation and packaging.[59]

When assessing whether the relevant international standard had been used as a basis for the measure in question, the Panel in *EC – Sardines* relied on the interpretation of the Appellate Body in the *EC – Hormones* case in relation to the wording 'based on' in Art. 3.2 SPS.[60] On this basis, the international standard has to be employed or applied as 'the principal constituent or fundamental purpose of enacting the technical regulation'.[61] In this case, the Appellate Body believed that it came down to 'whether there was a contradiction' between the measure in question and the relevant international standard,[62] an apparently looser standard than that given by the Panel.

To determine whether the relevant international standard is an effective and appropriate means for the fulfilment of the legitimate objective pursued requires first that the objective pursued by the technical regulation is legitimate. While the effectiveness of the measure bears upon the results given by the means employed, the appropriateness relates to the nature of the means employed.[63] Thus, a measure would be considered 'effective if it had the capacity to accomplish [. . .] the[. . .] objectives, and it would be appropriate if it were suitable for the fulfilment of [. . .] the[. . .] objectives'.[64] The complainant has the burden of proof in establishing that the relevant international standard is both an effective and appropriate means to fulfil the legitimate objective at hand.[65]

7.4.2 Analysis

The inclusion of a requirement to base any technical regulations or standards on international standards aims at harmonisation of standards used within the WTO but also provides for situations where the international standard in question would be an ineffective or inappropriate means of fulfilling the legitimate objective at hand. While this appears to allow for higher protection standards to be chosen by members than those achieved by international standards, the examples given in the

---

[59]Panel Report *European Communities – Trade Description of Sardines*, paras. 7.69–7.70; *Van den Bossche/Zdouc* (note 3), 880–881.

[60]Panel Report *European Communities – Trade Description of Sardines*, para. 7.110; Appellate Body Report *EC – Measures Concerning Meat and Meat Products (Hormones)*, para. 171; see further *Van den Bossche/Zdouc* (note 3), 881, 910–913.

[61]Panel Report *European Communities – Trade Description of Sardines*, para. 7.110.

[62]Appellate Body Report *European Communities – Trade Description of Sardines*, para. 249.

[63]Panel Report *European Communities – Trade Description of Sardines*, para. 7.116.

[64]Appellate Body Report *European Communities – Trade Description of Sardines*, para. 288.

[65]*Ibid.*, paras. 274–275.

provision ('fundamental climatic or geographical factors or fundamental techno-
logical problems') demonstrate a more extreme interpretation of 'ineffective or
inappropriate' than the mere desire for a higher level of protection. However, in *US
– Tuna II (Mexico)*, this issue was addressed by the Panel and found to be
unproblematic—this case is addressed in detail in the following chapter.

WTO members are also obligated under Art. 2.4 in conjunction with Art. 3.1
TBT to ensure that NGOs within their territory that set up voluntary standards base
those standards on international standards. The scope of this obligation is as yet
unclear as it would also depend on the interpretation of 'ineffective or inappropriate', as above. If this were deemed to also include the desire for higher environmental protection standards, then the extension of this provision appears relatively
unproblematic. However, if such measures were not deemed to fall under this
definition, then such restrictions on the freedom of non-governmental bodies
creating voluntary standards is questionable.

7.5 Summary

This short overview of the most relevant provisions of the TBT Agreement should
demonstrate that there is still considerable uncertainty regarding the scope and
application of this agreement. While it is often put forward in the application phase,
it appears less often in the submissions before Panels for this very reason. Its
application to NPR PPMs is currently limited to labelling schemes due to a
complete lack of consensus from WTO members. It is worth noting once more
the comments of the United States during negotiations in this context, which stated
in regard to PPMs generally in the Tokyo Round Agreement on Technical Barriers
to Trade:

> Lack of full coverage of PPMs seriously weakened the effectiveness of the Agreement by
> excluding a growing body of regulations from its disciplines. The intention was not to
> discourage the use of PPMs but rather to eliminate potential trade barriers to both industrial
> and agricultural trade posed by PPM-based requirements. Full extension of the provisions
> of the Agreement to PPM-based requirements would strengthen the Agreement and make it
> more effective in reducing arbitrary or unnecessary technical barriers to trade.[66]

Although the TBT Agreement now covers PPMs, this criticism could be levelled
mutatis mutandis at its non-coverage of NPR PPMs. Furthermore, although it is
clear that developing countries fear excessive technical regulations based on NPR
PPMs being used as a form of protectionism, and failing to take into account their
special and different positions in terms of development needs, refusing to have

---

[66]WTO, Negotiating History of the Coverage of the Agreement on Technical Barriers to Trade
with regard to Labelling Requirements, Voluntary Standards, and Processes and Production
Methods Unrelated to Product Characteristics, Doc. WT/CTE/W/10 (29 August 1995),
pg. 39 (para. 121).

these issues addressed under the TBT Agreement is not necessarily the most beneficial way forward for them, as the preceding chapter addressing the GATT has demonstrated.

Article 11 TBT provides for technical assistance for developing countries in their preparation of technical regulations, providing for preparations, advice and conformity assessment. Furthermore, Art. 12 TBT provides for special and differential treatment for developing country members under the TBT Agreement. According to this article, members are obliged, *inter alia*, to provide 'differential and more favourable treatment' and to take their 'special development, financial and trade needs' into account. Although it is questionable whether developed countries have 'lived up to their commitments'[67] under such provisions under the WTO, their inclusion demonstrates that there is a way in which the potential rigours of the application of these provisions could be somewhat blunted for developing and least-developed countries, while at the same time their application to NPR PPMs could create further legal certainty and a strengthening of the Agreement to make it more effective in reducing arbitrary or unnecessary technical barriers to trade.

The problems with the TBT Agreement highlighted above include a lack of legal certainty, an unclear scope of application and a lack of consistent jurisprudence. These factors clearly interfere with 'the ability of public authorities to regulate the flow of information, ideas, goods, people, pollutants, or capital across borders', one of *Krasner's* pillars of sovereignty. It is clear from the foregoing that the TBT Agreement requires additional interpretation or more clarity in the scope of its provisions from members. The case law in the following chapter should serve to illustrate these points further.

---

[67] *Constantine Michalopoulos*, The Role of Special and Differential Treatment for Developing Counties in the GATT and the World Trade Organisation, Policy Work Research Papers (1999), 18.

Chapter 8
Environmental Cases Under the TBT

8.1 Overview

This chapter will now go on to provide a summary of the relevant case law of the WTO DSS under the TBT Agreement along with analysis. The cases that will be assessed are the following:

- *European Communities – Measures Affecting Asbestos and Asbestos-Containing Products,*[1]
- *United States – Measures Concerning the Importation, Marketing and Sale of Tuna and Tuna Products (US – Tuna II (Mexico)).*[2]

8.2 EC – Asbestos

8.2.1 Facts and Arguments of the Parties

The facts of this case are laid out in Chap. 6.[3] In this case, Canada asked the Panel to find the French measure to be contrary to, *inter alia*, Arts 2.1. 2.2 and 2.4 TBT Agreement. Canada characterised the French decree as discriminatory and an

---

[1]Panel Report *European Communities – Measures Affecting Asbestos and Asbestos-Containing Products*; Appellate Body Report *European Communities – Measures Affecting Asbestos and Asbestos-Containing Products*.

[2]Panel Report *United States – Measures Concerning the Importation, Marketing and Sale of Tuna and Tuna Products (US – Tuna II (Mexico))*; Appellate Body Report *United States – Measures Concerning the Importation, Marketing and Sale of Tuna and Tuna Products (US – Tuna II (Mexico))*.

[3]See Sect. 6.7.1.

© Springer International Publishing AG 2017
A.R. Maggio, *Environmental Policy, Non-Product Related Process and Production Methods and the Law of the World Trade Organization*, European Yearbook of International Economic Law 1, DOI 10.1007/978-3-319-61155-6_8

unnecessary barrier to trade that was not based on international standards 'nor on the performance of asbestos fibres and products containing such fibres'.[4] Canada argued that the decree was a 'technical regulation' in the meaning of Annex 1 TBT on the basis that it prohibits chrysotile products where there is a substitute that presents a 'lesser occupational health risk', which gives a 'technical guarantee of safety'.[5] Furthermore, Canada was of the view that the French decree was a technical regulation as

> It is a document that sets forth a characteristic of a product, a process and a production method for a product, and administrative provisions applicable to a product. The document also deals with labelling requirements. Moreover, compliance with the contents of the document is mandatory.[6]

The existence of the exceptions was cited as evidence that the decree was a technical regulation.[7]

On the other hand, the EC argued that the TBT was not applicable in this case as it 'does not cover general prohibitions on the use of a product for reasons to do with the protection of human health'.[8] Referring to the VCLT, the preamble to the TBT and the history of the agreement, the EC argued that the TBT Agreement does not cover general prohibitions.[9] In contrast, the EC argued that the measure ought not to fall under the definition of 'technical regulation' as the 'definition of technical regulation should not [...] apply to prohibition measures that cover all products in general'.[10] Furthermore, the EC argued that the measure 'specifies neither the characteristics nor the production processes and methods for asbestos fibres, asbestos-containing products nor the products exempted from the prohibition measure'.[11]

With regard to Art. 2.1 TBT, Canada argued that the French measure was incompatible with it on the basis that it subjected 'chrysotile fibre and chrysotile-cement products imported from Canada and from any other country to less favourable treatment than like PVA, cellulose and glass fibres, and like fibro-cement products, of French or foreign origin'.[12] As this was the first examination of Art 2.1 by a Panel, Canada recalled the MFN and national treatment non-discrimination obligations incorporated into Art. 2.1 and argued that the Panel should take into account the 'precedents' from Arts. I:1 and III:4 of the

---

[4]Panel Report *European Communities – Measures Affecting Asbestos and Asbestos-Containing Products*, para. 3.245.

[5]*Ibid.*, para. 3.246.

[6]*Ibid.*

[7]Ibid.

[8]*Ibid.*, para. 3.250.

[9]*Ibid.*, paras. 3.251–3.252.

[10]*Ibid.*, para. 3.253.

[11]*Ibid.*, para. 3.254.

[12]*Ibid.*, para. 3.266.

GATT.[13] Canada, similarly characterising the products in question as 'like',[14] argued that 'chrysotile fibres and the products containing them are subject to less favourable treatment than substitute products of French or foreign origin'[15] and on the basis of Art. 2.1's similarity in language with Arts. I:1 and III:4 GATT that the same obligations apply.[16] Canada thus concluded that that the French measure banning asbestos was 'incompatible with the provisions of Article 2.1 [...] because it discriminates against chrysotile fibre and chrysotile products, as opposed to PVA, cellulose and glass fibre and fibro-cement products'.[17]

Moving on to Art. 2.2 TBT, Canada put forward that, for a technical regulation to be in conformity with the obligation laid out in Art. 2.2, the Panel must first 'determine if the objective that the regulation is supposed to fulfil is part of the range of legitimate objectives listed in Article 2.2'. If it is not on the list, it is incompatible with Art. 2.2.[18] The EC, on the other hand, outlined that a proper interpretation of Art. 2.2 implies a two-part test: (1) there must first be a legitimate objective, such as the protection of human health, and (2) then the Member's technical regulation must not be more trade restrictive than is necessary to fulfil this legitimate objective, taking account of the risks that non-fulfilment would create.[19] Canada viewed the obligation in Art. 2.2 differently (a rational link between the objective and the measure and if the trade effects of the measure are necessary)[20] and was of the view that there was no rational link and, further, that due to the alternate regulatory system of 'controlled use', neither of the criteria for Art. 2.2 was met.[21] The EC found Canada's interpretation of Art. 2.2 artificial and at variance with the wording of the provision.[22] The EC was particularly critical of the Canadian 'controlled use' alternative, finding it both insufficient and ineffective.[23]

Canada, on the other hand, provided stark criticism for the EC's invocation of the preamble, stating:

> the preamble to the TBT Agreement cannot be invoked to justify noncompliance of a technical regulation with Article 2.2. The preamble to the TBT Agreement cannot be used to justify the Decree. The preamble outlines the goals and rationale of a treaty. It does not confer any rights and does not impose any obligations.[24]

---

[13]*Ibid.*

[14]*Ibid.*, para. 3.267; See Sect. 6.7.1.

[15]Panel Report *European Communities – Measures Affecting Asbestos and Asbestos-Containing Products*, para. 3.268.

[16]*Ibid.*, para. 3.269.

[17]*Ibid.*

[18]*Ibid.*, para. 3.273.

[19]*Ibid.*, para. 3.274.

[20]*Ibid.*, para. 3.279.

[21]*Ibid.*

[22]*Ibid.*, para. 3.290.

[23]*Ibid.*, para 3.291.

[24]*Ibid.*, para. 3.310.

Furthermore, the Canadian position rejected any possible invocation of the precautionary principle in connection with the TBT Agreement on the basis of the Appellate Body's decision in *Japan – Agricultural Products*.[25] In response, the EC stated that it was 'important to be aware that a Member of the WTO can establish the level of health protection it deems appropriate in its territory' and that the preamble of the TBT stated this clearly.[26]

Moreover, the EC argued that the 'necessity' test involved in Art. 2.2 TBT was a formalisation of previous practice related to Art. XX (b) GATT,[27] although noted that the burden of proof falling on the party invoking Art. 2.2 distinguished it from Art. XX (b), as with Art. XX (b) this would exclusively be the defendant but under Art. 2.2 almost exclusively the complainant.[28] The EC argued that there was a similarity in the necessity in Art. XX (b) GATT and Art. 2.2 TBT, and the second sentence of Art. 2.2 ought to be interpreted as to mean that 'a restrictive measure is "necessary" only if there are risks associated with the non-adoption of the measure in question'.[29] Canada, on the other hand, contended that the ban was not necessary as there was a less trade-restrictive measure available[30] and that the 'ban is the most extreme and restrictive trade measure available',[31] which in this case was not based on a credible risk assessment.[32]

Moving on to Art. 2.4 TBT, Canada asserted in this case that the French decree was not in line with the obligation contained in Art. 2.4 as there existed relevant international standards[33] that were 'effective and appropriate for fulfilling the

---

[25] Appellate Body Report *Japan – Measures Affecting Agricultural Products*, para. 81. Here the Appellate Body reaffirmed that although elements of the precautionary principle were included in the SPS Agreement (Arts. 3.3 and 5.7), there was no basis for the conclusion that the precautionary principle could be invoked as justification for a measure that was otherwise SPS inconsistent. Canada argued in *EC – Asbestos* that if it was not the case for the SPS then it certainly would not be for the TBT: Panel Report *European Communities – Measures Affecting Asbestos and Asbestos-Containing Products*, para. 3.311.

[26] Panel Report *European Communities – Measures Affecting Asbestos and Asbestos-Containing Products*, para. 3.313.

[27] See Sect. 5.5.2.

[28] Panel Report *European Communities –Measures Affecting Asbestos and Asbestos-Containing Products*, para. 3.316.

[29] *Ibid.*, para. 3.319.

[30] *Ibid.*, para. 3.328.

[31] *Ibid.*, para. 3.330.

[32] *Ibid.*, para. 3.331. Canada argued further on this point that if a risk assessment had been carried out, then France would have led the French authorities to conclude that these products are not dangerous to workers, *ibid.*, para. 3.337.

[33] *Ibid.*, para. 3.359. Convention Concerning Safety in the Use of Asbestos of 24 June 1986 – (International Labour Organisation Convention 162); ILO, Recommendation Concerning Safety in the Use of Asbestos, ILO Rec. 172 (1986); ILO; Safety in the Use of Asbestos: Code of Practice (1984).

objectives of promoting public health'[34] while providing for safe and controlled use of asbestos.[35] Canada further asserted that the ban was not in compliance with international standards.[36] The EC, on the other hand, asserted that the standards provided by Canada did not meet the definition of 'standards' in Annex 1 TBT and that '[i]n any event, the EC consider that the French authorities used the texts referred to by Canada in its submission "as a basis" for their Decree, within the meaning of Article 2.4 of the TBT Agreement'.[37] Further, the EC argued that

> the level of protection deemed appropriate by the Member could be a factor in making international standards ineffective or inappropriate. Within the context of the TBT Agreement, a Member is free to choose the level of protection it deems appropriate. An international standard is only effective or appropriate if it enables the Member to achieve the legitimate objective it has set itself.[38]

8.2.2   Panel Report

The Panel's evaluation of the TBT Agreement began with an assessment of the applicability of the TBT to the French decree.[39] The Panel noted the complainant's claim that the exceptions to the ban on asbestos contained in the decree confirmed that it was technical regulation, while the defendant claimed that neither the ban nor the exceptions were within the scope of the TBT Agreement.[40] The Panel evaluated the decree to contain a general prohibition (Arts. 1 and 5) and exceptions (Arts. 2–4) and felt that thus the next appropriate action would be to determine if the prohibition and exceptions should be considered as one single measure or different measures which may come under different agreements.[41]

The Panel defined a technical regulation as 'a regulation which sets out the specific characteristics of one or more identifiable products in comparison with general characteristics that may be shared by several unspecified products'.[42] The Panel then noted that the decree in question did not set out specific characteristics of one or more identifiable products but rather 'was generally applicable both to asbestos and products containing it, in other words, a very large number of products

---

[34]Panel Report *European Communities – Measures Affecting Asbestos and Asbestos-Containing Products*, para. 3.360.

[35]*Ibid.*

[36]*Ibid.*, para. 3.361.

[37]*Ibid.*, para. 3.362.

[38]*Ibid.*, para. 3.374.

[39]*Ibid.*, para. 8.18 *et seq.*

[40]*Ibid.*, para. 8.30.

[41]*Ibid.*, para. 8.31.

[42]*Ibid.*, para. 8.39.

which the Decree does not identify by name nor even by function or category'.[43] Pointing to the history of the TBT Agreement, the Panel concluded that it was not intended to cover import bans, which are covered by Art. XI:1 GATT, but rather had the object and purpose 'to prevent much more complex situations than a straightforward unconditional ban on a product'.[44] The major difference in this case between the ban with exceptions and a technical regulation was found by the Panel to be that 'none of the products covered by the Decree can be imported, with the exception of those given a temporary exemption', whereas 'a technical regulation [...] defines the characteristics of one or more given products'.[45]

The Panel thus concluded that the decree was not a 'technical regulation' within the meaning of Annex 1 TBT and that it thus did not fall within the scope of the agreement.[46]

Additionally, with regard to Art. 2.2, the Panel noted:

> the criteria on the preparation, adoption or application of technical regulations in Article 2.2 of the TBT Agreement are very similar to those in Article XX of the GATT 1994. The preamble to the TBT Agreement in fact repeats some of the wording of Article XX of the GATT.[47]

The exceptions contained in the French decree were deemed by the Panel to be technical regulations, despite their temporary, transitional nature,[48] and thus fell within the scope of the TBT Agreement.[49] Having already rejected the Canadian claims that the exceptions characterised the entire decree as a technical regulation, the Panel noted that Canada made no specific claims on the basis of the exceptions in the terms of reference, and it thus did 'not have to reach any findings concerning the exceptions'.[50]

8.2.3   Appellate Body Report

As noted in Chap. 6, both parties to this dispute appealed against the recommendations contained in the Panel Report. With regard to the TBT, the particular issue raised on appeal was

> whether the Panel erred in its interpretation of the term 'technical regulation' in Annex 1.1 of the TBT Agreement in finding, in paragraph 8.72(a) of the Panel Report, that 'the part of

---

[43]*Ibid.*, para. 8.40.

[44]*Ibid.*, para. 8.49.

[45]*Ibid.*, para. 8.51.

[46]*Ibid.*, para. 8.58.

[47]*Ibid.*, para. 8.55.

[48]*Ibid.*, para. 8.66.

[49]*Ibid.*, para. 8.70.

[50]*Ibid.*, para. 8.72.

the Decree relating to the ban on imports of asbestos and asbestos-containing products' does not constitute a 'technical regulation'.[51]

Canada appealed the Panel's decision to treat the decree not as one single unified measure but as separate components of the prohibition and exceptions.[52] Canada also claimed that the Panel had erred in law as general prohibitions should also be considered 'technical regulations'.[53]

The Appellate Body began its analysis by stating that 'the proper legal character of the measure at issue cannot be determined unless the measure is examined as a whole'.[54] In examining the measure, the Body noted that it was not a general prohibition as it included provisions that permitted some imports of asbestos-containing products (albeit for a limited time) and that characterising it as a general prohibition overlooked the complexities of the measure.[55] The Appellate Body thus reversed the Panel's two-step approach to the assessment of the decree.[56]

The Body then went on to assess the applicability of the TBT to the measure. In doing so, it first focused on the definition of 'product characteristics' as laid out in Annex 1.1 TBT. It clarified that these characteristics can be either positively or negatively defined in the document in question as the legal result is the same.[57] The Body then went on to emphasise that a technical regulation must be applicable to an *identifiable* product, but, 'in contrast to what the Panel suggested, this does not mean that a "technical regulation" must apply to "given" products which are actually named, identified or specified in the regulation'.[58] In this instance, the Appellate Body found that the products at issue were identifiable—those that contained asbestos.[59] With regard to the exceptions in the French decree, the Appellate Body found that they 'apply to a narrowly defined group of products with particular "characteristics"'.[60] The combination of these with the mandatory character of the decree led the Appellate Body to thus reverse the findings of the Panel that the measure in question was not a 'technical regulation' under the TBT Agreement.[61]

The Appellate Body was not able to make any further pronouncements on the decree under the TBT Agreement as the issues were not explored in any depth by

---

[51] Appellate Body Report *European Communities – Measures Affecting Asbestos and Asbestos-Containing Products*, para. 58 (a).
[52] *Ibid.*, para. 62.
[53] *Ibid.*
[54] *Ibid.*, para. 64.
[55] *Ibid.*
[56] *Ibid.*, para. 65.
[57] *Ibid.*, para. 69.
[58] *Ibid.*, para. 70.
[59] *Ibid.*, para. 72.
[60] *Ibid.*, para 74,
[61] *Ibid.*, paras. 75–76.

the Panel, and thus there were no 'issues of law' or 'legal interpretations' for the
Appellate Body to review.[62]

8.2.4 Analysis

As highlighted in the previous chapter, this case did not concern NPR PPMs and
thus has limited relevance in this study. However, it has been included for various
reasons. In relation to the TBT Agreement, its inclusion demonstrates the lack of
clarity in the scope of application of the agreement and the definition of 'technical
regulation'. The issues raised in this case are also indicative of the lack of clarity in
the provisions, particularly demonstrated through the arguments of the parties.
Although labelling is only briefly mentioned, this overview of the interpretation
of the provisions by the parties provides an illustrative overview of litigation under
the provision and enlightens as to the possibility of future 'relevant' cases being
brought to the DSS under the TBT Agreement. Moreover, the facts and arguments
of the parties are further enlightening and enable one to build a bigger picture of the
interpretative problems of the DSS under the TBT Agreement and the WTO and
covered agreements as a whole.

8.3   US – Tuna II (Mexico)

8.3.1   Facts and Arguments of the Parties

Following the failure of consultations to resolve the dispute, Mexico requested the
formation of a Panel on 9 March 2009 pursuant to Arts. 4 and 6 DSU, Art. XXIII
GATT 1994 and Art. 14 TBT Agreement. As with the previous GATT *Tuna/
Dolphin* cases,[63] this case concerned measures adopted by the US concerning the
importation, marketing and sale of tuna and tuna products.[64]

The Dolphin Protection Consumer Information Act (DPCIA) barred the use of
any 'dolphin-safe' label or 'any other term or symbol that falsely claims or suggests
that the tuna contained in the product were harvested using a method of fishing that

---

[62]*Ibid.*, para. 82.

[63]See Sects. 6.2–6.3.

[64]Specifically at issue were: the United States Code, Title 16, Section 1385 ('Dolphin Protection
Consumer Information Act'); Code of Federal Regulations, Title 50, Section 216.91 ('Dolphin-
safe labelling standards') and Section 216.92 ('Dolphin-safe requirements for tuna harvested in the
ETP [Eastern Tropical Pacific Ocean] by large purse seine vessels'); and the ruling in *Earth Island
Institute v. Hogarth*, 494 F.3d 757 (9th Cir. 2007): Panel Report *United States – Measures
Concerning the Importation, Marketing and Sale of Tuna and Tuna Products (US – Tuna II
(Mexico)*, para. 2.1.

is not harmful to dolphins' in the US if the product contains tuna harvested (1) on the high seas by a vessel engaged in driftnet fishing, (2) outside the ETP by a vessel using purse-seine nets, (3) in the ETP by a vessel using purse-seine nets (with some exceptions).[65] The rules provided in the Act prohibited the sale of tuna with a dolphin-safe label, '*unless* certain conditions established by the DPCIA provisions themselves are met'.[66] For tuna caught outside the ETP using purse-seine nets, differentiations were made in the DPCIA for fisheries that had comparable 'regular and significant tuna-dolphin association' and those without—although it was noted by the US that no such similar association existed.[67]

Under the Act, it was only permissible to apply a 'dolphin safe' label to tuna products if (1) no dolphins are killed or seriously injured in the sets or other gear deployments in which the tunas were caught, (2) the label is supported by a tracking and verification program that is comparable in effectiveness to that under the DPCIA, (3) the label complies with all applicable labelling, marketing and advertising laws and regulations of the Federal Trade Commission, including any guidelines for environmental labelling.[68]

Mexico requested the Panel to find the US measures inconsistent with Arts. I:1 and III:4 of the GATT and Arts. 2.1, 2.2 and 2.4 TBT.[69]

Mexico began by making reference to the history of market access problems encountered regarding yellowfin tuna from the ETP: the embargo that was at issue in *Tuna/Dolphin I* and the more recent non-tariff barriers to trade, described as the US having 'found a new way to prevent Mexican tuna from competing in the US market'.[70] It laid out the essence of the dispute as being 'the prohibition of the use of a US dolphin-safe label on imports of tuna products from Mexico, while such a label is permitted to be used on tuna products from other countries, including the United States'.[71] Mexico claimed that although it had maintained a 'sound and environmentally sustainable method for fishing for tuna' and 'participated in all multilateral initiatives to protect dolphins while fishing for tuna', its tuna products were nevertheless 'prohibited by the US measures from using a dolphin-safe label, while tuna caught in other fisheries that have not adopted comparable measures to protect dolphins are able to benefit from a dolphin-safe label'.[72]

Mexico began by characterising 'the statutory and regulatory provisions that make up the labelling provisions' as a document[73] while claiming that it also met

---

[65]*Ibid.*, para. 2.3.

[66]*Ibid.*, para. 2.6.

[67]*Ibid.*, paras. 2.21–2.23.

[68]*Ibid.*, para. 2.27.

[69]*Ibid.*, para. 3.1. Claims relating to Art. 2.4 TBT are of limited relevance to this work and will not be addressed here.

[70]*Ibid.*, para. 4.1.

[71]*Ibid.*, para. 4.2.

[72]*Ibid.*, para. 4.3.

[73]*Ibid.*, para. 4.54.

the other requirements for a technical regulation.[74] With regard to Art. 2.2 TBT, Mexico alleged violation as the 'technical regulation' in question did not fulfil a legitimate objective or, in the alternative, was more trade restrictive than necessary to fulfil a legitimate objective.[75]

Mexico argued that the more limited objective of protecting dolphins in the ETP was not fulfilling the legitimate objective of protection of animal life or health or the environment as it was too narrow. In Mexico's view:

> measures that trade off the life or health of different animal species and which undermine broader environmental objectives that are enshrined in a successful multilateral environmental agreement cannot be found to 'fulfil a legitimate objective' within the meaning of Article 2.2 of the TBT Agreement.[76]

With regard to Art. 2.2, Mexico further argued that the 1998 Agreement on the International Dolphin Conservation Program (AIDCP) created a system that would fulfil the objectives sought by the US and that the negative trade effects of the US measures where thus more trade restrictive than necessary as the objective would be fulfilled without them and no such restrictions on trade would be incurred.[77]

With regard to Art. 2.1, Mexico put forward that, on the basis of the arguments made with regard to violations of Arts. I:1 and III:4 GATT, the technical regulation in question was similarly in violation of the MFN and national treatment obligations contained in Art. 2.1 TBT.[78]

The US began its counterclaim by aggressively denying that the main thrust of Mexico's argument—that the US measures prohibited use of the dolphin-safe label on Mexican tuna—was in any way correct.[79] The US put forward that its certification scheme was a voluntary labelling scheme and it did not deny market access to Mexico, despite Mexico's claims.[80] The US argued that Mexico had *prima facie* failed to establish violation of Arts. I:1 and III:4 GATT as the labelling scheme was voluntary and did not discriminate based on origin, and accordingly it was not possible for Mexico to establish that Arts. 2.1, 2.2 and 2.4 TBT even applied to US measures.[81]

---

[74]*Ibid.*

[75]*Ibid.*, para. 4.55.

[76]*Ibid.*

[77]*Ibid.*, para. 4.59.

[78]Under the GATT, Mexico alleged *inter alia* that the measures were contrary to the MFN clause because they grant an advantage, favour or privilege 'to tuna products and tuna originating in certain WTO Members that has not been accorded immediately and unconditionally to the like products originating in Mexico' (*ibid.*, para. 4.45). Furthermore, with regard to the Art. III:4 national treatment clause, Mexico argued 'accord less favourable treatment to Mexican tuna products and tuna than that accorded to the like products of US origin' (*ibid.*, para. 4.36).

[79]*Ibid.*, para. 4.73.

[80]*Ibid.*, para. 4.74.

[81]*Ibid.*, para. 4.76.

Specifically regarding the definition of the US measures as a 'technical regulation' within the meaning of Annex 1 TBT, the US put forward that the Mexican
claim was incorrect on the basis that the US measures did not lay out product
characteristics (or PPMs) but rather 'specif[ied] the conditions under which tuna
products may be labelled dolphin-safe.' Further, these measures were not mandatory but rather 'constitute[d] a voluntary labelling measure and such voluntary
labelling measures are not covered by the definition of a technical regulation'.[82]

With regard to Art. 2.2 TBT, the US laid out its legitimate objectives as

(1) ensuring that consumers are not misled or deceived about whether tuna prod-
    ucts contain tuna that was caught in a manner that adversely affects dolphins;
    and
(2) to the extent that consumers choose not to purchase tuna without the dolphin-
    safe label, the US provisions ensure that the US market is not used to encourage
    fishing fleets to catch tuna in a manner that adversely affects dolphins.[83]

Criticising the Mexican argument that the US measures were too narrow in their
approach to marine conservation in the ETP, as they only addressed dolphins and
not 'preserving other marine species and the environment of the ETP as a whole',
the US argued that it was not for Mexico to decide what its legitimate objectives
were to be.[84]

With regard to the AIDCP system and the 'more trade restrictive than necessary'
criterion, the US put forward that its labelling scheme was supplemental and
extended protection of dolphins in the ETP beyond what was achievable under
this system. Furthermore, it argued that 'eliminating the US dolphin-safe labelling
provisions in lieu of the AIDCP would not fulfil the objective of ensuring that
consumers are not misled or deceived about whether or not tuna products contain
tuna that was caught in a manner that adversely affects dolphins'.[85] The US also
emphatically stated that such voluntary labelling schemes have a minimal effect on
trade as they do not require tuna imported into the US to carry a dolphin-safe label
or to be dolphin safe: any effects on trade are due to the fact that 'consumers have a
preference for tuna products that contain tuna that is not caught by setting on
dolphins'.[86]

---

[82]*Ibid.*, para. 4.84.
[83]*Ibid.*, para. 4.88.
[84]*Ibid.*, para. 4.90.
[85]*Ibid.*, para. 4.99.
[86]*Ibid.*, para. 4.100.

8.3.2 Panel Report

The Panel began by highlighting that Mexico made claims under Arts. 2.1, 2.2 and
2.4 TBT, all of which address 'technical regulations', and then went on to address
whether the measures at hand constituted a 'technical regulation' within the meaning of Annex 1 of the TBT Agreement. Thus, beginning with the definition of
'technical regulation' as laid out in Annex 1.1 TBT, the Panel identified the three-
tier test required:

(a) the measure applies to an identifiable product or group of products;
(b) it lays down one or more characteristics of the product; and
(c) compliance with the product characteristics is mandatory.[87]

   With regard to the first tier, the Panel concluded that both sides appeared to agree
(and were correct in agreeing) that the measures in question applied to an identifiable group of products (tuna products).[88] The second tier of the test (product
characteristics) was assessed by the Panel to also involve labelling requirements
and thus was fulfilled.[89] The final tier, the mandatory requirement, was the point
contested by the parties to the dispute. The Panel noted that the Appellate Body had
previously laid out that such mandatory requirements could be laid out positively or
negatively[90] and laid emphasis on the differentiation between voluntary and mandatory given in the Explanatory Note to Annex 1.2 TBT.[91] In this context, the Panel
noted that it was

> mindful of the fact that the term 'mandatory' expresses the single characteristic that defines
> the key conceptual distinction between two of the three types of measures covered under
> the TBT Agreement (technical regulations and standards) and therefore plays a central role
> in preserving the balance between the different sub-regimes coexisting within that
> Agreement.[92]

   While recognising that Mexico did not allege a *de jure* obligation for products to
carry a dolphin-safe label, the Panel decided the measures in question legally and
bindingly prescribed 'the manner in which a dolphin-safe label can be obtained in
the United States, and disallow any other use of a dolphin-safe designation, the US
tuna labelling measures "regulate" dolphin-safe labelling requirements "in a binding or compulsory fashion".'[93] The Panel viewed the US measures as creating a
negative requirement that no tuna be labelled dolphin friendly if it did not meet the

---

[87]*Ibid.*, para. 7.53.

[88]*Ibid.*, paras. 7.56–7.62.

[89]*Ibid.*, para. 7.79.

[90]Appellate Body Report *European Communities – Measures Affecting Asbestos and Asbestos-
Containing Products*, para. 69.

[91]Panel Report *United States – Measures Concerning the Importation, Marketing and Sale of Tuna
and Tuna Products (US – Tuna II (Mexico)*, paras. 7.107–7.108.

[92]*Ibid.*, para. 7.109.

[93]*Ibid.*, para. 7.131.

requirements set out in the measure and thus imposed 'a prohibition on the offering for sale in the United States of tuna products bearing a label referring to dolphins and not meeting the requirements that they set out'.[94] The Panel furthermore pointed out that there was no discretion to resort to other means to inform consumers about the dolphin safety of tuna products. The Panel thus found that the measures were *de jure* mandatory.[95]

However, one of the Panellists was unable to agree with the majority and issued a separate opinion.[96] In the separate opinion, it was laid out that an agreement was not reached on whether the measures at issue required mandatory compliance with the prescribed product characteristics or process and production methods. The major difference between mandatory and voluntary labelling schemes was identified as being '[i]n a voluntary labelling scheme, labelling requirements are thus not mandatory for marketing products'.[97] As the measures in question did not impose a general requirement for tuna products to bear a dolphin-safe label, and tuna without such a label could still enter and be sold on the US market, the Panellist was of the view that the labelling requirements remained voluntary and were not mandatory within the meaning of Annex 1.1 TBT,[98] and the fact that the labelling requirements were legally enforceable was not enough to change this.[99]

The Panellist further found that the measures in question were neither *de jure* or *de facto* mandatory and therefore failed to meet all the requirements to be considered a 'technical regulation', meaning that Art. 2 TBT was not applicable in this case.[100] It was then clarified that this pronouncement would not affect the possible applicability, in the view of the Panellist, of other provisions of the TBT, but 'since Mexico did not submit any claims based on other provisions of the TBT Agreement, no determinations in this regard can be made'.[101]

Returning to the recommendations of the Panel where the requirements for 'technical regulation' under Annex 1.1 TBT had been found, the Panel then went on to assess the conformity of the measure under Art. 2.1 TBT. Although the 'likeness' of the products was not disputed by the parties to the case, the Panel assessed whether the products could be considered 'like' under Art. 2.1.[102] In doing so, the Panel made reference to customary rules of interpretation and previous decisions of the DSS-particularly the 'accordion of likeness' described by the

---

[94]*Ibid.*

[95]*Ibid.*, paras. 7.144–7.145.

[96]*Ibid.*, paras. 7.146 *et seq.*

[97]*Ibid.*, para. 7.149.

[98]*Ibid.*, para. 7.153.

[99]*Ibid.*, para. 7.158.

[100]*Ibid.*, para. 7.186.

[101]*Ibid* , para. 7.187.

[102]*Ibid.*, paras. 7.215 *et seq.*

Appellate Body in *Japan – Alcohol*.[103] How the accordion should be squeezed in this case was described by the Panel thus: 'it must be informed by the fact that our examination takes place under Article 2.1 of the TBT Agreement, as well as by the context and circumstances that prevail in this case'.[104] However, the Panel did rely on the reasoning of the Appellate Body in *EC – Asbestos* in coming to the conclusion that the products in question must be in a 'competitive relationship' to be considered 'like'.[105] The Panel also deemed that the interpretation of the term should be informed by the fact that the TBT Agreement only applies to a limited set of measures and that it aimed to preserve the competitive opportunities.[106] The Panel relied on Mexico's criteria for the determination of like products under Art. 2.1 TBT and concluded that the tuna products were like.[107] In this context, the Panel noted that 'A comparison on the basis of dolphin-safe status would imply that Mexican tuna products are assumed not to be dolphin-safe while US tuna products and tuna products originating in any other country would be assumed to be dolphin-safe'[108]—an assumption which the Panel felt was unfounded at that stage.

In assessing whether the products in question received 'less favourable treatment', the Panel laid out that the essence of the measures covered by Art. 2.1 would necessitate distinctions (as they set out product characteristics or related PPMs), but such distinctions 'must not be designed or applied to the detriment of imports or imports of certain origins'.[109] The Panel sought to assess (1) whether the US measures granted an advantage on the US market for dolphin-friendly tuna and (2) whether Mexico was denied access to this advantage—resulting in disadvantageous and discriminatory treatment.[110] Although the Panel agreed that it was not the measures themselves but rather consumer preferences that granted the advantage for dolphin-friendly tuna products, they were nonetheless of the view that an advantage was afforded to products that were eligible for the label, and it was the measures that controlled access to the label.[111] After first concluding that the measures did not in themselves create a disadvantage for Mexican tuna vis-à-vis domestic tuna and tuna imported from third countries, the Panel went on to assess

---

[103]See Appellate Body Report *Japan – Taxes on Alcoholic Beverages*, pg. 21; Panel Report *United States – Measures Concerning the Importation, Marketing and Sale of Tuna and Tuna Products (US – Tuna II (Mexico)*, para. 7.221.

[104]Panel Report *United States – Measures Concerning the Importation, Marketing and Sale of Tuna and Tuna Products (US – Tuna II (Mexico)*, para. 7.222.

[105]Appellate Body Report, EC – Asbestos, para. 99; Panel Report *United States – Measures Concerning the Importation, Marketing and Sale of Tuna and Tuna Products (US – Tuna II (Mexico)*, para. 7.224.

[106]Panel Report *United States – Measures Concerning the Importation, Marketing and Sale of Tuna and Tuna Products (US – Tuna II (Mexico)*, para. 7.225.

[107]*Ibid.*, para. 7.250.

[108]*Ibid.*

[109]*Ibid.*, para. 7.276.

[110]*Ibid.*, para. 7.284.

[111]*Ibid.*, para. 7.287.

the application of the measure and 'whether less favourable treatment nonetheless arises from the application of the measures, by reason of the practices of the fleets'.[112] In this regard, the Panel was also not persuaded that the Mexican tuna products were disadvantaged and moved on to an assessment of Mexican tuna products on the US market.[113] In this respect, the Panel sought to assess 'whether the measures have modified the relative position on the market of US and Mexican tuna products, to the detriment of Mexican tuna products'.[114] However, it was not persuaded that this was evidenced in this case and thus found no violation of Art. 2.1 TBT.[115]

Moving on to Art. 2.2 TBT, the Panel agreed with the US analysis that the two requirements of Art. 2.2 are that (1) technical regulations pursue a legitimate objective, and (2) they must not be more trade restrictive than necessary to fulfil that legitimate objective, taking into account the risks that non-fulfilment would create.[116] The Panel established that the burden of proof lay on the complaining party to establish violation and that 'this necessarily involves a determination of what such objective is and its legitimacy within the meaning of Article 2.2'.[117] As the legitimate objective pursued was a contentious point between the parties, the Panel found it necessary to clarify what it was.[118] Relying on the Appellate Body's analysis in regard to Art. XIV GATS, the Panel stated that 'a panel's analysis is not bound by a Member's characterization of the objectives of its own measures'.[119] The Panel agreed that the measures aimed, *inter alia*, to ensure that consumers were not misled or deceived about whether tuna products contain tuna that was caught in a manner that adversely affected dolphins.[120]

With regard to the Mexican contention that the US objective was narrower than the protection of animal life or health or the environment, meaning that it was not a legitimate objective under Art. 2.2, the Panel described it thus: 'the ulterior objective is contributing to the protection of dolphins, whereas the means chosen to achieve this objective is to ensure that the US market is not used to encourage certain fishing techniques'.[121] The Panel rejected the Mexican assertion that this ulterior motive was limited geographically to the ETP and noted that it rather seemed 'directed to discouraging, more generally, the use of fishing techniques

---

[112]*Ibid.*, para. 7.311.
[113]*Ibid.*, paras. 7.350 *et seq.*
[114]*Ibid.*, para. 7.359.
[115]*Ibid.*, para. 7.374.
[116]*Ibid.*, para. 7.387.
[117]*Ibid.*, para. 7.392.
[118]*Ibid.*, para. 7.405.
[119]*Ibid.*; Appellate Body Report *United States — Measures Affecting the Cross-Border Supply of Gambling and Betting Services*, para. 304.
[120]Panel Report *United States – Measures Concerning the Importation, Marketing and Sale of Tuna and Tuna Products (US – Tuna II (Mexico)*, para. 7.413.
[121]*Ibid.*, para. 7.416.

that have harmful effects on dolphins'.[122] The Panel also identified the US objective of ensuring that consumers are not 'misled or deceived' about whether products contain tuna that was caught in a manner that adversely affected dolphins.[123]

Having established what the objectives behind the US measures were, the Panel moved on to assess whether they were 'legitimate' within the context of Art. 2.2. The Panel found that the US objectives related to 'genuine concerns in relation to the protection of the life or health of dolphins and deception of consumers', which could both be seen to be legitimate objectives under Art. 2.2.[124] Thus, the Panel found that the measures met the requirements of the first part of the test contained in Art. 2.2.[125]

The Panel then moved on to the second part of the test: whether the US dolphin-safe provisions are more trade restrictive than necessary to fulfil their objectives, taking into account the risks that non-fulfilment would create. With the regard to this requirement, the Panel espoused the interpretation that 'while a degree of "trade-restrictiveness" may be justified, where it is "necessary to fulfil a legitimate objective", a measure could not be justified under Article 2.2 if it is more trade restrictive than is necessary to achieve the objective at issue',[126] meaning that 'trade-restrictiveness is only permissible to the extent that it is necessary to the achievement of the objective'.[127] In assessing this requirement, while being informed by the interpretation of 'necessity' under Art. XX GATT by the DSS, the Panel recognised that the difference in wording of the provisions may have an effect, particularly as Art. 2.2 TBT is formulated as a positive obligation and not an exception.[128] Furthermore, the Panel identified that, under Art. 2.2, the 'necessity' in question was the 'necessity of the trade restrictiveness' and not the 'necessity of the measure'.[129] However, the Panel also recognised that, under the TBT Agreement, it is also for WTO members to set their own levels of protection as 'the preamble of the TBT Agreement makes clear that a Member is entitled to take measures "at the level it considers appropriate"', meaning that the enquiry to be made by the Panel was to determine 'whether such trade-restrictiveness is required to fulfil the legitimate objectives pursued by the Member *at its chosen level of protection*'.[130] Thus, taking into account the level of protection chosen by the US, the Panel sought to analyse to what extent the measure is capable of contributing to the objective, stating that 'it would be more trade-restrictive than necessary if an

---

[122]*Ibid.*, paras. 7.419 and 7.424.

[123]*Ibid.*, para. 7.435.

[124]*Ibid.*, para. 7.438.

[125]*Ibid.*, para. 7.444.

[126]*Ibid.*, para. 7.454.

[127]*Ibid.*, para. 7.456.

[128]*Ibid.*, para. 7.458.

[129]*Ibid.*, para. 7.460.

[130]*Ibid.*

alternative measure that is less trade-restrictive is reasonably available, that would achieve the challenged measure's objective at the same level'.[131]

As the burden of proof lay on Mexico under this article, the Panel then went on to assess whether Mexico had established that the US dolphin-safe provisions were more trade restrictive than necessary, taking account of the risks that non-fulfilment would create. The Panel first assessed the manner and the extent to which the US measures contributed to their objective, then went on to assess whether 'this objective could be similarly fulfilled by allowing the AIDCP standard to be applied in addition to the existing US standard'.[132]

In carrying out this assessment, the Panel pointed to the opinion poll submitted by Mexico, which demonstrated that US consumers largely failed to understand the current dolphin-safe certification to mean the same as what the US dolphin-safe provisions define it to mean.[133] The Panel further highlighted the Mexican argument regarding the disparity in certification requirements for tuna caught within and outwith the ETP. After lengthy analysis, the Panel first concluded that

> certain tuna fishing methods other than setting on dolphins have the potential of adversely affecting dolphins, and that the use of these other techniques outside the ETP may produce and has produced significant levels of dolphin bycatch, during the period over which the US dolphin-safe provisions have been in force[134]

despite the fact that such tuna products may be eligible for a dolphin-safe label. Thus, tuna caught in the ETP would have fulfilled the objective sought by the US, as consumers could be 'completely assured that no dolphin was adversely affected during the catching of that tuna in the ETP'.[135] However, this was not the case for tuna caught outside the ETP, which could not offer such certainty, meaning that 'the US measures [could] only *partially* ensure that consumers [were] informed about whether tuna was caught by using a method that adversely affects dolphins'.[136]

With regard to whether the alternative measure proposed by Mexico provided 'a reasonably available less trade restrictive means of achieving the same level of protection', the Panel was of the view that (similar to the application of the US measure alone) the combination of AIDCP and current US measures would also lead to consumers bearing a certain level of uncertainty as to whether dolphins were adversely affected when buying tuna products but that the extent to which consumers were likely to be misled was not greater than under the US measures alone.[137] Thus, the Panel concluded that Mexico had put forward a less trade-

---

[131]*Ibid.*, para. 7.465.
[132]*Ibid.*, para. 7.475.
[133]*Ibid.*, para. 7.482.
[134]*Ibid.*, para. 7.531.
[135]*Ibid.*, para. 7.545.
[136]*Ibid.*, para. 7.563.
[137]*Ibid.*, para. 7.573.

restrictive measure that fulfilled their objective relating to the misleading of consumers, and the US had not successfully rebutted this claim.[138]

With regard to the objective of the US measure to ensure that the US market is not used to encourage fishing fleets to catch tuna in a manner that adversely affects dolphins, the Panel concluded again that the US measure was only partially able to fulfil this objective.[139] As to whether the Mexican suggestion provided a reasonably available less trade-restrictive means of achieving the same level of protection, the Panel also decided that it would provide the same level of protection as the current US measure.[140] In light of these considerations, the Panel found the US measure to be inconsistent with Art. 2.2 TBT on the basis that it was more trade restrictive than necessary to fulfil their legitimate objectives.

8.3.3   Appellate Body Report

Beginning with the US appeal claim relating to the definition of 'technical regulation' and the characterisation of the US measure as such, the Appellate Body highlighted the meaning of 'requirement'[141] and that this did 'not imply therefore that the measure is for that reason alone a "technical regulation" within the meaning of Annex 1.1'.[142] The Appellate Body was thus of the view that in order to determine whether a particular measure constitutes a 'technical regulation' in the meaning of Annex 1.1, a Panel must assess the 'characteristics of the measure at issue and the circumstances of the case',[143] i.e. on a case-by-case basis.

In carrying out its assessment, the Appellate Body recalled the US argument that the enforceability of the measure should not affect its characterisation as a 'technical regulation' or 'standard' as both can be enforceable. While the Body agreed with this point, it pointed to the fact that in this case it was not only enforceable but also enforceable to the exclusion of other standards as it 'enforce[d] a prohibition against the use of any other label'.[144] Indeed, to the Appellate Body, 'the mere fact that there is no requirement to use a particular label in order to place a product for sale on the market does not preclude a finding that a measure constitutes a "technical regulation" within the meaning of Annex 1.1'. Indeed, the Body stated:

---

[138]*Ibid.*, para. 7.578.

[139]*Ibid.*, paras. 7.599–7.600.

[140]*Ibid.*, para. 7.618.

[141]'provisions that set out criteria or conditions to be fulfilled in order to use a particular label', *ibid.*, para. 186.

[142]*Ibid.*, para. 187.

[143]*Ibid.*, para. 188.

[144]*Ibid.*, para. 195.

while it is possible to sell tuna products without a 'dolphin-safe' label in the United States, any 'producer, importer, exporter, distributor or seller' of tuna products must comply with the measure at issue in order to make any 'dolphin-safe' claim[145]

and therefore agreed with the Panel that the measure in question could be deemed 'mandatory' and thus fit under the Annex 1.1 definition of 'technical regulation'.[146]

Moving on Mexico's appeal of the Panel's findings regarding Art. 2.1 TBT, the Appellate Body began by noting that the US did not appeal the Panel's findings that the products in question were 'like products' under Art. 2.1.[147] Regarding Mexico's point of contention over the 'treatment no less favourable', the Appellate Body highlighted that by their very nature, technical regulations (covered by Art. 2.1) 'establish distinctions' between products based on product characteristics or their related process and production methods and that this meant that the interpretation of Art. 2.1 TBT should not 'mean that any distinctions, in particular ones that are based exclusively on particular product characteristics or on particular processes and production methods, would *per se* constitute "less favourable treatment"'.[148]

The Appellate Body was of the view that the previous findings of the DSS were instructive in assessing the meaning of 'treatment no less favourable'. It thus adopted the approach of 'examining whether a measure modifies the *conditions of competition* in the relevant market to the detriment of imported products' from the *Korea – Beef* Appellate Body Report[149] while also taking into account the statement of the Body in *US – Clove Cigarettes* that it is necessary to 'further analyze whether the detrimental impact on imports stems exclusively from a legitimate regulatory distinction rather than reflecting discrimination against the group of imported products'.[150] The Body also recognised the importance of how the preamble to the TBT Agreement informs the interpretation of Art. 2.1 but rejected the Mexican approach that all the elements contained in the sixth recital must be met by the US measure in order not to fall foul of its obligation under Art. 2.1.[151] The Appellate Body found on, *inter alia*, these bases that the approach of the Panel had not been correct regarding Art 2.1 and thus went on to assess themselves whether the US measure was consistent with Art. 2.1.[152]

---

[145]*Ibid.*, para. 196.

[146]*Ibid.*, para. 199.

[147]*Ibid.*, para. 202.

[148]*Ibid.*, para. 210.

[149]*Ibid.*, para. 214. Appellate Body Report *Korea – Measures Affecting Imports of Fresh, Chilled and Frozen Beef*, para. 137.

[150]Appellate Body Report *United States – Measures Concerning the Importation, Marketing and Sale of Tuna and Tuna Products (US – Tuna II (Mexico)*, para. 215; Appellate Body Report *United States – Measures Affecting the Production and Sale of Clove Cigarettes*, para. 182.

[151]Appellate Body Report *United States – Measures Concerning the Importation, Marketing and Sale of Tuna and Tuna Products (US – Tuna II (Mexico)*, para. 219.

[152]*Ibid.*, paras. 227 *et seq.*

The Appellate Body concluded that the measure created a clear detrimental modification in the conditions of competition while also siding with Mexico in its determination that it was 'the measure at issue, rather than private actors, that denie [d] most Mexican tuna products access to a "dolphin-safe" label in the US market'.[153]

In the assessment of whether this detrimental modification also amounted to discrimination, the Appellate Body also addressed the US's claims in relation to the Panel's conduct and Art. 11 DSU. The Appellate Body clarified that in order for a claim under Art. 11 to succeed, it was necessary for the Body to be satisfied that 'the Panel has exceeded its authority as the initial trier of facts'.[154] If the Panel is fulfilling its obligations under Art. 11, then it must 'provide "reasoned and adequate explanations and coherent reasoning"'.[155] On this point, the Appellate Body was not convinced that the contradictions and failures alleged by the US were in existence.[156] The Body found that the Panel had acted consistently with its obligations under Art. 11 DSU 'in its analysis of the arguments and evidence before it',[157] and its analysis could therefore be used in the Body's determination as to whether discrimination had occurred under Art. 2.1 TBT.[158]

The Appellate Body found that Mexico had established *prima facie* that the measures modified the conditions of competition to the detriment of Mexican tuna products as they were not 'even-handed in the way in which they address the risks to dolphins arising from different fishing techniques in different areas of the ocean'.[159] On the basis that the Appellate Body was not convinced by the US arguments that the Panel had acted contrary to Art. 11 DSU, it could not conclude that the US had rebutted the *prima facie* case established by Mexico.[160] Thus, the Body reversed the decision of the Panel and found that the US measure provided less favourable treatment to Mexican tuna products and was thus in contravention of their obligation under Art. 2.1.

Moving on to the US appeal under Art. 2.2, the Appellate Body began with the 'legitimate objective' criterion. The Body confirmed that '[a] panel is not bound by a Member's characterization of the objectives it pursues through the measure, but must independently and objectively assess them' on the basis of the objectives listed in Art. 2.2, those in the sixth and seventh recitals of the preamble and

[153]*Ibid.*, paras. 235 and 239.

[154]*Ibid.*, para. 254.

[155]*Ibid.*, quoting Appellate Body Report *United States – Subsidies on Upland Cotton (Article 21.5 – Brazil)*, para 293 (footnote 618).

[156]Appellate Body Report *United States – Measures Concerning the Importation, Marketing and Sale of Tuna and Tuna Products (US – Tuna II (Mexico)*, paras. 258 *et seq.*

[157]*Ibid.*, para. 281.

[158]*Ibid.*

[159]*Ibid.*, para. 298.

[160]*Ibid.*

objectives recognised in other WTO agreements.[161] The Appellate Body also highlighted that any assessment by a Panel of whether a measure 'fulfils' a legitimate objective should also be 'concerned with the degree of contribution that the technical regulation makes toward the achievement of the legitimate objective'[162] and noted that '[t]he degree of achievement of a particular objective may be discerned from the design, structure, and operation of the technical regulation, as well as from evidence relating to the application of the measure'.[163] With regard to the 'necessity' criterion, the Appellate Body recalled its previous interpretation in *Korea – Beef* that 'the word "necessary" refers to a range of degrees of necessity, depending on the connection in which it is used'[164] and concluded that in this case 'necessity' involves a 'relational analysis of the trade-restrictiveness of the technical regulation, the degree of contribution that it makes to the achievement of a legitimate objective, and the risks non-fulfilment would create'.[165]

The Appellate Body here first noted that the Panel had found that the US measure only partially fulfilled their two stated objectives while agreeing that Mexico's proposed alternative would do so to the same extent.[166] The Appellate Body, however, found that this conclusion of the Panel was based on an improper comparison of the AIDCP measures applied alone rather than in coexistence with the US measure. Further, the application of the AIDCP would not result in any difference in standard outside the ETP (as it is limited to the ETP), but within the ETP the two standards would not provide the same coverage as under the US measure no tuna caught using methods where dolphins were set upon would be permitted to bear the label, but under Mexico's proposed AIDCP, this would not be the case.[167] The Body thus disagreed 'that the proposed alternative measure would achieve the United States' objectives "to the same extent" as the existing US "dolphin-safe" labelling provisions', reversed the finding of the Panel that the measure at issue was more trade restrictive than necessary to fulfil the US' legitimate objectives[168] and therefore held that the US measure was inconsistent with Art. 2.2 TBT.

With regard to Mexico's conditional appeal regarding the 'objective of contributing to the protection of dolphins by ensuring that the US market is not used to encourage fishing fleets to catch tuna in a manner that adversely affects

[161]*Ibid.*, paras. 313–314.

[162]*Ibid.*, para. 315.

[163]*Ibid.*, para. 317.

[164]*Ibid.*, para. 318; Appellate Body Report *Korea – Measures Affecting Imports of Fresh, Chilled and Frozen Beef*, para. 161, '[a]t one end of this continuum lies "necessary" understood as "indispensable"; at the other end, is "necessary" taken to mean as "making a contribution to"'.

[165]Appellate Body Report *United States – Measures Concerning the Importation, Marketing and Sale of Tuna and Tuna Products (US – Tuna II (Mexico)*, para. 318.

[166]*Ibid.*, paras. 327–328.

[167]*Ibid.*, para. 329.

[168]*Ibid.*, para. 331.

dolphins',[169] the Appellate Body felt that Mexico's invocation of the sixth recital of the preamble was misguided as its prohibition referred to the measure and not to the objective.[170] The Body thus rejected the Mexican appeals under Art. 2.2.[171]

8.3.4 Analysis

As is apparent from the extensive coverage above, this case is of central importance to an understanding of NPR PPMs and the TBT Agreement. Not only that, but it is also instructional in terms of policy choices for States. As is clear from the previous chapters, WTO membership severely constrains the regulatory freedom of States. Although wealthy diverse economies can effectively buy themselves out of their WTO obligations, this can only be done as the 'Bad Man': by weighing up which of the options is least detrimental or by paying a 'tax' for choosing to regulate as they wish and not how their obligations dictate they should. For weaker economies, such 'taxes' are less feasible, and thus the WTO rules become *de facto* more binding upon them. This case serves to demonstrate the consequences of policy choices and whether the 'lighter option' of labelling rather than other trade-restrictive measures (particularly import bans) is a feasible option for States seeking to prevent the consumption of products with environmentally damaging PPMs within their polities. Leaving aside the fact that an import ban would in most cases be legislated by a democratically elected government and would thus already in some ways demonstrate the 'will of the people', the idea that labelling and consumer choice is preferable to unilateral trade restrictions is one that is floated often in literature on trade and the environment. Looking more closely at this case should show that this is not necessarily the case, at least from an environmental policy perspective (although perhaps from a trade policy one).

This case in some ways has its genesis in *Tuna/Dolphin I and II*, discussed above. Rather than instituting an import ban, however, as had been done previously in relation to tuna products caught using purse-seine nets, in this instance the US chose to create a labelling scheme in order to inform consumers. As highlighted above, there is to date little jurisprudence of the DSS on the TBT Agreement (certainly in comparison to the GATT), and lessons from the review of GATT jurisprudence certainly show that one interpretation by the DSS does not necessarily become the prevailing interpretation over time. Nevertheless, this case represents the foundations of the future evolution of the interpretation of the TBT Agreement, and the criticisms levelled in this chapter seek to address budding problems.

---

[169]*Ibid.*, para. 95.

[170]*Ibid.*, para. 339.

[171]*Ibid.*, para. 342.

Beginning with the definition of 'technical regulation' and the arguments of the parties, perhaps the most controversial element of this case is the debated nature as to whether a scheme with which participation was voluntary but the requirements to participate were mandatory was 'mandatory' within the meaning of Annex 1 TBT. It should be remembered that the wording of Annex 1.1 defines 'technical regulation' as

> Document which lays down product characteristics or their related processes and production methods, including the applicable administrative provisions, with which compliance is mandatory. It may also include or deal exclusively with terminology, symbols, packaging, marking or labelling requirements as they apply to a product, process or production method.

Whereas, Annex 1.2 defines 'standard' as

> Document approved by a recognized body, that provides, for common and repeated use, rules, guidelines or characteristics for products or related processes and production methods, with which compliance is not mandatory. It may also include or deal exclusively with terminology, symbols, packaging, marking or labelling requirements as they apply to a product, process or production method.

While the Annex 3 Code of Good Practice for the Preparation, Adoption and Application of Standards reduces the importance of the differentiation significantly, as it replicates many of the substantive obligations contained in the main text of the TBT for standards, it is still problematic that the DSS has chosen such an interpretative direction—as it goes clearly against the idea of legal certainty. If 'with which compliance is mandatory' does not in fact mean a technical regulation with which compliance is mandatory but rather a regulation that has mandatory elements in order to utilise a label, then including labelling in 'standards' appears redundant. If compliance with the requirements for a standard is not mandatory in order to use a standard, then the labelling scheme is meaningless and cannot be used for environmental protection standards. The problems with the Panel's interpretation of 'technical regulation' were indeed brought up by one of the Panellists, who (in quite the coup within the WTO DSS, where separate opinions are far from standard procedure) expressly disagreed with the Panel's interpretation.

This issue was barely addressed by the Appellate Body, which sidestepped the issue and failed to engage in any comparative analysis of 'technical regulation' and 'standard'—weakly claiming that the issue is best assessed on a case-by-case basis (i.e., unpredictably and with no legal certainty) and pointing to the fact that if an exporting State wished to make use of the term 'dolphin safe', then it must comply with the measure in question, and thus compliance is mandatory. Whether the outcome of the case would have been different if assessed under 'standard' is less clear, but the massive oversight in the appropriate characterisation of measures under the TBT cannot inspire confidence for States seeking regulatory options to pursue environmental objectives to create labelling schemes.

With regard to the Art. 2.1 obligation, the interpretations of the Panel and the Appellate Body both recognised that by their nature 'technical regulations' would create distinctions between products and rightly focused on whether their application created discrimination in the MFN or national treatment sense. Whether such products should be treated as 'like' is of course a matter of opinion, and changing attitudes may lead in the future to changing the interpretation of 'likeness'. However, for the moment, it is clear that NPR PPMs are not determinative for the 'likeness' of products, even under the TBT Agreement.

With regard to Art. 2.2, the legitimacy of the Panel's examination of the 'legitimate objective', confirmed by the Appellate Body, raises some questions. While in cases where a measure clearly does not fulfil a legitimate objective it must be necessary for the Panel to assess this, and likewise in borderline cases, it is important for the efficacy of the multilateral trading system that it can do so; nevertheless, questions are raised about the standard of review and who is best placed to decide what a legitimate objective is (particularly in the field of environmental protection), which in turn raises questions about the legitimacy of such imprecise obligations having influence on the policy space left for governmental decision-making.

Chapter 9
NPR PPMs and the SPS

9.1 Overview

The SPS Agreement addresses sanitary and phytosanitary measures instituted by WTO members. While previous chapters have focused on TREMs or labelling and NPR PPMs under the WTO, this chapter will take a slightly different focus in order that this study can encapsulate both the environmental and health concerns relating to the most controversial of NPR PPMs: GMOs. GMOs may also be covered by labelling under the TBT agreement, but it is under the SPS that they are predominantly addressed. The approach of this chapter and the next is necessarily different to that taken in the preceding four chapters due to the nature of SPS measures, which are typically based on the effects (or potential effects) of products within the territory of the importing State.

The reason that such issues concern both NPR PPMs and SPS measures is that with regard to GMOs (particularly, although other SPS measures are also relevant, as will be seen later in relation to the *EC – Hormones* case), the potential risk of these products in the territory of the importing State is based on the NPR PPM of the product—i.e., its genetic modification. Clearly, if the risk materialises into actual harm, genetic modification is no longer an NPR PPM but a PPM. Further, as the SPS Agreement does not concern itself with 'like products', the scope of the debate around this issue is evidently of a different nature. The issue of GMOs and the SPS Agreement has already been litigated before a WTO Panel, but the results of the case are far from enlightening, as will be demonstrated in the next chapter. This chapter will first address the relevant provisions of the SPS Agreement.

The Agreement on the Application of Sanitary and Phytosanitary Measures addresses the question:

> How do you ensure that your country's consumers are being supplied with food that is safe to eat – 'safe' by the standards you consider appropriate? And at the same time, how can

© Springer International Publishing AG 2017

A.R. Maggio, *Environmental Policy, Non-Product Related Process and Production Methods and the Law of the World Trade Organization*, European Yearbook of International Economic Law 1, DOI 10.1007/978-3-319-61155-6_9

you ensure that strict health and safety regulations are not being used as an excuse for protecting domestic producers?[1]

SPS measures often take the form of technical barriers to trade but are to be addressed under the rules of the SPS Agreement[2] on the basis that 'the preservation of domestic regulatory autonomy was, and still is, considered of particular importance where health risks are at issue'.[3] The charge has been levelled that developed countries increasingly use SPS measures as a form of protectionism, something that could be very detrimental to developing countries without diversified economies that rely on the export of food products. On the other hand, the import and consumption of GM foodstuff is seen by some, particularly in Europe, to be inherently unsafe and thus deserving of the strictest regulation.

Under the SPS Agreement, members have a right to take SPS measures, so long as they are not inconsistent with the Agreement (Art. 2.1 SPS). The basic rights and obligations are contained in Art. 2 SPS and are followed by, *inter alia*, obligations relating to harmonisation (Art. 3 SPS), equivalence (Art. 4 SPS) and risk assessment and management (Art. 5 SPS). These rules will be discussed below.

9.2 SPS Measures

SPS measures are defined in Annex A (1) SPS as follows:

Any measure applied:

(a) to protect animal or plant life or health within the territory of the Member from risks arising from the entry, establishment or spread of pests, diseases, disease-carrying organisms or disease-causing organisms;

(b) to protect human or animal life or health within the territory of the Member from risks arising from additives, contaminants, toxins or disease-causing organisms in foods, beverages or feedstuffs;

(c) to protect human life or health within the territory of the Member from risks arising from diseases carried by animals, plants or products thereof, or from the entry, establishment or spread of pests; or

(d) to prevent or limit other damage within the territory of the Member from the entry, establishment or spread of pests.

Sanitary or phytosanitary measures include all relevant laws, decrees, regulations, requirements and procedures including, inter alia, end product criteria; processes and production

---

[1]https://www.wto.org/english/tratop_e/sps_e/spsund_e.htm (last accessed on 05/03/2017).

[2]*Peter Van den Bossche/Werner Zdouc*, The Law and Policy of the World Trade Organization (Cambridge, 3rd ed. 2013), 894.

[3]*Ibid.*, 895.

methods; testing, inspection, certification and approval procedures; quarantine treatments including relevant requirements associated with the transport of animals or plants, or with the materials necessary for their survival during transport; provisions on relevant statistical methods, sampling procedures and methods of risk assessment; and packaging and labelling requirements directly related to food safety.

What is immediately noteworthy, particularly in the context of the foregoing discussion about the jurisdictional reach of permissible TREMs under the Art. XX GATT general exception, is the repeated reference to 'within the territory of the Member' in the Annex A (1) definition, a point that removes any possibility of extraterritorial SPS measures that fall under the SPS Agreement. Indeed, such measures are by their very nature territorial. As highlighted above, this also affects the NPR PPM description as it is hotly debated whether genetic modification affects the products as such. If it does, they are no longer NPR PPMs—but this issue is not yet resolved and centres around *potential* risk.

The definition demonstrates that SPS measures are to be determined on the basis of their objective or purpose, a point that was confirmed by the Appellate Body in *Australia – Apples*, which stated:

the relationship of the measure and one of the objectives listed in Annex A (1) must be manifest in the measure itself or otherwise evident from the circumstances related to the application of the measure. This suggests that the purpose of a measure is to be ascertained on the basis of objective considerations.[4]

While it is clear from the wording of lits (a)–(d) of Annex A (1) that health is directly addressed as an objective for SPS measures, the Panel in *EC – Biotech* included environmental damage in its interpretation of lit (d) as 'encompassing adverse effects on biodiversity, population dynamics of species or biogeochemical cycles'.[5] Following the Appellate Body in *US – Poultry (China)*, only an objective determination that the measure in question aims at one of the Annex A (1) purposes is required for the measure to be considered an SPS measure.[6] '[I]t is not necessary to demonstrate that an SPS measure actually has an effect on trade'[7]—it is sufficient that the measure in question may affect international trade.[8]

---

[4]Appellate Body Report *Australia – Measures Affecting the Importation of Apples from New Zealand*, para. 172.

[5]*Van den Bossche/Zdouc* (note 2), 898.

[6]*Ibid.*, 899; Panel Report *United States – Certain Measures Affecting Imports of Poultry from China*, paras. 7.119–7.120.

[7]Panel Report *European Communities – Approval and Marketing of Biotech Products*, para. 7.435.

[8]*Van den Bossche/Zdouc* (note 2), 901.

9.3   Article 2 SPS

9.3.1   Content of the Norm

Article 2 SPS contains the basic rights and obligations of WTO members under the SPS Agreement. Paragraph 1 contains the general pronouncement, referred to above, that WTO members have the right to take SPS measures provided that they are not inconsistent with the SPS Agreement. The second paragraph contains an obligation that SPS measures are only applied 'to the extent necessary' and that they are based on scientific evidence and not maintained without sufficient scientific evidence. Paragraph 3 aims to ensure that SPS measures do not discriminate between WTO members in an arbitrary or unjustifiable manner and to ensure that the application of SPS measures does not constitute a disguised restriction on international trade. Paragraph 4 contains the proviso that if measures are found to conform with the provisions of the SPS Agreement, then they shall be presumed to also be in accordance with the GATT, particularly Art. XX (b).

9.3.2   Analysis

The Hohfeldian breakdown of Art. 2 demonstrates that importing States have the privilege to institute SPS measures, and that other States are exposed to the limit of this privilege, but that this privilege is limited by the many duties contained in the SPS Agreement, and particularly in Art. 2, in how this privilege is exercised (as duties and privileges are mutually limiting principles). Thus, exporting States have the right that when an importing State exercises its privilege, it does so in a certain way. The extent of the privilege is thus determined by the number and severity of its limitations—i.e., the duties contained in the SPS Agreement. This is of importance to this study as it is clear in the case of SPS measures that both the domestic and interdependence elements of *Krasner's* sovereignty paradigm are engaged. More so than when thinking about environmental protection standards with regard to extraterritorial effects, SPS measures are designed to protect territory under the sovereign jurisdiction of a State. If their 'right' (a Hohfeldian privilege) to prevent potentially harmful substances or products coming onto their territory is severely limited by the duties contained in this Agreement, then significant questions are raised about the appropriateness of such an agreement and the legitimacy of a trade body making decisions related to it.

9.4   Article 2.2 SPS

9.4.1   Content of the Norm

Article 2.2 SPS states:

> Members shall ensure that any sanitary or phytosanitary measure is applied only to the extent necessary to protect human, animal or plant life or health, is based on scientific principles and is not maintained without sufficient scientific evidence, except as provided for in paragraph 7 of Article 5.

This paragraph contains a general necessity requirement but has not, as of yet, been subject to interpretation by the WTO DSS.[9]

The second element of Art. 2.2 is the requirement for a scientific basis for SPS measures, a requirement that 'introduce[s] science as a touchstone against which SPS measures will be judged'.[10] Although this is also covered in more detail in Art. 5 SPS, it has been subject to interpretation by the DSS. In *Japan – Apples*, the Panel considered that Art. 2.2 formed part of the context for the interpretation of evidence when creating SPS measures, stating that in the context of Art. 2.2 'the evidence to be considered should be evidence gathered through scientific methods'.[11] Following the Appellate Body in *Japan – Agricultural Products II*, the sufficiency of the scientific evidence will be assessed on the basis of a 'rational relationship' test,[12] while '[w]hether there is a rational relationship between an SPS measure and the scientific evidence is to be determined on a case-by-case basis [. . .], including the characteristics of the measure at issue and the quality and quantity of the scientific evidence'.[13] It appears that the DSS will carry out this assessment on the basis that 'the more serious the risks to life or health, the less demanding the requirement of "sufficient scientific evidence"'.[14]

Article 2.2 contains an exception to this general rule, in that if an SPS measure meets the requirements of Art. 5.7, it does not have to be based on sufficient scientific evidence. This 'qualified exception'[15] will be discussed further below, but it should be noted that it is not an exception in the sense that it provides a defence to violation of Art 2.2 but operates as an 'autonomous right of the importing member'.[16]

---

[9]*Ibid.*, 905.

[10]*Van den Bossche/Zdouc* (note 2), 905.

[11]Panel Report *Japan – Measures Affecting the Importation of Apples*, para. 8.92.

[12]Appellate Body Report *Japan – Measures Affecting Agricultural Products*, para. 84.

[13]*Ibid.*

[14]*Van den Bossche/Zdouc* (note 2), 906.

[15]Appellate Body Report *Japan – Measures Affecting Agricultural Products*, para. 80.

[16]Panel Report *European Communities – Approval and Marketing of Biotech Products*, para. 7.2962, though not a Hohfeldian 'right'.

9.4.2 Analysis

The introduction of 'scientific principles' and 'sufficient scientific justification' into the SPS Agreement through Art. 2.2 raises questions about the standard of review, explored in more detail in relation to risk below. It is more than questionable if a trade body is better placed to review the sufficiency of scientific evidence than a specialised governmental body that likely drafted the legislation/SPS measure in question. The fact that such sufficiency will be assessed on 'rational relationship' criteria may sound reasonable, but this phrase has no textual basis, and the inclusion of mention of a case-by-case basis is also problematic. While a case-by-case approach can provide necessary flexibility in the application of legal obligations, it is problematic in instances where the obligations themselves are vague and imprecise as there can be no predictability, formal realisability or legal certainty. When thinking about pollutants, pests and other potentially harmful substances or products crossing borders, it must be a priority for a system to provide predictability and stability and allow States to protect human, animal and plant life and health, as well as the environment in general, within their borders in the best and easiest way.

9.5 Article 2.3 SPS

9.5.1 Content of the Norm

Article 2.3 SPS states:

> Members shall ensure that their sanitary and phytosanitary measures do not arbitrarily or unjustifiably discriminate between Members where identical or similar conditions prevail, including between their own territory and that of other Members. Sanitary and phytosanitary measures shall not be applied in a manner which would constitute a disguised restriction on international trade.

This article, similar to Art. 2.1 TBT, includes loose MFN and national treatment obligations that are central to the GATT within the SPS regime, and its wording 'replicates part of the chapeau of Article XX'.[17] Unlike in the obligations contained in the GATT and TBT Agreements, however, the wording of Art. 2.3 SPS does not centre around 'like products' (or 'directly competitive or substitutable products') and 'may also include discrimination between *different* products'.[18] This difference reflects the nature of the SPS Agreement and 'recognises that it is the similarity of the risks, rather than the similarity of the products, that matters'.[19] This implies of

---

[17]*Van den Bossche/Zdouc* (note 2), 908.

[18]Panel Report *Australia – Measures Affecting Importation of Salmon (Recourse to Article 21.5 by Canada)*, para. 7.112 (emphasis in original).

[19]*Van den Bossche/Zdouc* (note 2), 909.

course that the obligation on Members is to apply their SPS measures to all products that incur the same risks—a task that becomes more difficult if attempting to include potential risks.

9.5.2   Analysis

Article 2.3 includes a series of obligations that limit the privilege of WTO members to institute SPS measures. The constellation of obligations is familiar and similar to that under the GATT and TBT Agreements. The fact that arbitrary or unjustifiable discrimination must not occur under Art. 2.3 between different products demonstrates this obligation to be of a slightly different nature and potentially much broader. While further litigation is required before the true scope of Art. 2.3 can be determined, it is instructive that it is the 'similarity of the risks' that is important. This could lead to problems in comparable assessment of risk, with possible unjustifiable discrimination being found as a member did not create an SPS measure for a product deemed to be at a similar risk level by another State, but not itself. The inherent subjectivity of risk from a cultural and societal perspective (explored in more detail below) means that it is a difficult bedfellow for non-discrimination provisions as where risk is assessed and measured differently, some may see blatant and unjustifiable discrimination, while others only see policies enacted to address risk. Such indeterminacy clearly does not provide for legal certainty (or for States to understand the breadth of their obligations under the SPS Agreement) and constitutes a potentially very significant limitation on the privilege of members to institute SPS measures.

9.6   Article 3 SPS

9.6.1   Content of the Norm

As mentioned above, Art. 3 SPS contains obligations for WTO members introducing SPS measures with regard to harmonisation. The goal of harmonisation, mentioned in the preamble to the SPS Agreement,[20] is contained as a firm obligation in Art. 3.1 ('Members shall base their sanitary and phytosanitary measures on

---

[20]Stating: '*Desiring* to further the use of harmonized sanitary and phytosanitary measures between Members, on the basis of international standards, guidelines and recommendations developed by the relevant international organizations, including the Codex Alimentarius Commission, the International Office of Epizootics, and the relevant international and regional organizations operating within the framework of the International Plant Protection Convention, without requiring Members to change their appropriate level of protection of human, animal or plant life or health.'

international standards, guidelines or recommendations'), except where provided for elsewhere in the Agreement. The main alternative to this general obligation arises under Art. 3.3 (specifically mentioned in Art. 3.1), which gives Members the right (a Hohfeldian privilege) to introduce or maintain SPS measures aiming at higher levels of protection than those based on the relevant international standards, guidelines or recommendations 'if there is scientific justification' and they are not inconsistent with other provisions of the SPS Agreement. Article 3.2 further provides that where measures *do* conform to international standards, guidelines or recommendations, then they shall be presumed to be consistent with the relevant provisions of the SPS.

With regard to Art. 3.1 and the general obligation to base SPS measures on international standards, the Appellate Body confirmed in *EC – Hormones* that this did not create a situation where these voluntary international standards were 'transformed' into binding norms.[21] Rather, measures that are 'based on' international standards, following Art. 3.1, do not have to conform to the standard in question 'since not all of the elements of the standard need to be incorporated into the measure'.[22] However, in this case, the presumption of consistency with the SPS Agreement contained in Art. 3.2 would not apply.

In *EC – Hormones*, the Appellate Body specifically declared with regard to Art 3.3 that

> this right of a Member to establish its own level of sanitary protection under Article 3.3 of the *SPS Agreement* is an autonomous legal right and *not* an 'exception' from a 'general obligation' under Article 3.1.[23]

While SPS measures that conform to international standards under Art. 3.2 are excused from this, those that are based on or are more stringent than international standards under Arts. 3.1 and 3.3 must meet the requirements relating to risk assessment contained in Art. 5 SPS.

9.6.2   Analysis

Article 3 SPS demonstrates once again the WTO preference for multilateralism over unilateral action. While the structure of the provision appears to provide for circumstances in which SPS measures can be introduced that aim at a higher level of protection than the relevant international standard, the extra hurdles for members may mean that particularly developing countries will be encouraged to use the

---

[21] Appellate Body Report *European Communities – Measures Concerning Meat and Meat Products (Hormones)*, para. 165.

[22] *Van den Bossche/Zdouc* (note 2), 911; Appellate Body Report *European Communities – Measures Concerning Meat and Meat Products (Hormones)*, para. 163.

[23] Appellate Body Report *European Communities – Measures Concerning Meat and Meat Products (Hormones)*, para. 172.

international standard, even where they believe a higher standard may be more appropriate. A presumption of consistency is a meaningful promise that speaks to governments of a reduced likelihood of litigation before the DSS (a very costly process). Moreover, countries with less material and intellectual resources may find the requirement of additional scientific justification much more burdensome than developed countries with an abundance of these resources. Thus, the 'Bad Man' developing country, looking only at the consequences, will be more likely to choose to base their regulations on international standards than the 'Bad Man' developed country on the basis of what they can afford. This means that developing countries may be coerced into choosing a level of protection that may be less than their desired level due to the potential consequences—once again demonstrating how WTO norms do not create just burdens for members across the scope of development.

9.7   Article 5 SPS

9.7.1   Content of the Norm

Article 5 SPS is a long provision detailing the risk assessment obligations relevant for WTO members seeking to implement SPS measures. Risk assessment is defined in Annex A (4) SPS as

> The evaluation of the likelihood of entry, establishment or spread of a pest or disease within the territory of an importing Member according to the sanitary or phytosanitary measures which might be applied, and of the associated potential biological and economic consequences; or the evaluation of the potential for adverse effects on human or animal health arising from the presence of additives, contaminants, toxins or disease-causing organisms in food, beverages or feedstuffs.

The risk assessment obligation is made up of two parts: risk analysis and risk management.[24] The risk analysis obligations are set out in Arts. 5.1–5.3. Article 5.1 contains the general obligation ('Members shall ensure') that SPS measures are based on an assessment of risks to 'human animal or plant life or health' while also

---

[24]*Van den Bossche/Zdouc* (note 2), 914. As noted by Van den Bossche and Zdouc, the firm distinction between these two elements has been rejected by the Appellate Body. However, this appears to be largely on the basis that the use of this distinction by the Panels in both cases (*EC – Hormones* and *US/Canada – Continued Suspension*) resulted in the same '"restrictive notion of risk assessment"', which the Appellate Body felt had no textual basis. On the other hand, following Van den Bossche and Zdouc, it appears that there is a clear distinction in the nature of the obligations contained in the various provisions of Art. 5 SPS. While making such a distinction is helpful for understanding the nature of the obligations contained in the SPS, it is not materially affected by the fact that the DSS will label all of these obligations together 'risk assessment'. See: *ibid.*, 914 (footnote 85); Appellate Body Report *Canada – Continued Suspension of Obligations in the EC – Hormones Dispute*, para. 542.

'taking into account risk assessment techniques developed by relevant international organizations'. Article 5.2 requires members to take, *inter alia*, 'available scientific evidence; relevant process and production methods; relevant inspection, sampling and testing methods [. . .]; relevant ecological and environmental conditions' into account when carrying out risk assessment under Art. 5.1. Article 5.3 obliges members to take into account 'relevant economic factors' when assessing risk.

The main risk management provisions are Arts. 5.4 and 5.5: Art. 5.4 obliges members to take into account the objective of minimising trade effects when determining the appropriate level of protection, while Art. 5.5 obliges members to avoid 'arbitrary or unjustifiable distinctions in the levels it considers appropriate in different situations'. Annex A (5) defines the appropriate level of sanitary or phytosanitary protection as 'The level of protection deemed appropriate by the Member establishing a sanitary or phytosanitary measure to protect human, animal or plant life or health within its territory'.

9.7.2   Analysis

Article 5 contains a conglomeration of duties that limit the privilege of WTO members to institute SPS measures. The breadth and complexity of these duties, alongside any inherent uncertainty or impreciseness, together serve to incrementally limit the privilege, or freedom of action, that WTO members have to attempt to protect human, animal and plant life and health within their borders. As will be seen in the following, the duties contained in Art. 5 are complex and taken together represent a serious and significant limitation on this privilege.

9.8   Risk Analysis

9.8.1   Article 5.1 SPS

Article 5.1 states:

> Members shall ensure that their sanitary or phytosanitary measures are based on an assessment, as appropriate to the circumstances, of the risks to human, animal or plant life or health, taking into account risk assessment techniques developed by the relevant international organizations.

As can be seen from the above definition of risk assessment, given in Annex A (4) SPS, there are two different types of risk assessment that can be carried out in order to fulfil the obligation contained in Art. 5.1 SPS. Following the Appellate Body in *Australia – Salmon*, the first test involves the following:

(1) identifying pests or diseases;
(2) evaluating the likelihood of their entry, establishment or spread and the asso-
    ciated biological and economic consequences;
(3) evaluating this likelihood again but in light of the SPS measure to be applied.[25]

According to *Van den Bossche/Zdouc*, the second test can be deduced from the
EC – Hormones Panel Reports and involves the following:

(1) identifying the adverse effects on human or animal health from food-borne
    risks[26];
(2) evaluating the potential for such adverse effects.[27]

In order to fulfil the obligation under Art. 5.1 SPS, WTO members do not have to
carry out a risk assessment themselves but may rather rely on those carried out by
other members or international organisations.[28]

9.8.2   Articles 5.2 and 5.3 SPS

Although there is no express methodology required for the risk assessment to be
carried out by members implementing SPS measures, Arts. 5.2 and 5.3 do lay out
some requirements that must be taken into account when carrying out a risk assessment under Art. 5.1.[29]

Article 5.2 requires members to take into account, *inter alia*, 'available scientific
evidence; relevant process and production methods; relevant inspection, sampling
and testing methods, prevalence of specific diseases or pests; existence of pest- or
disease-free areas; relevant ecological and environmental conditions'. The main
factor to be taken into account is scientific evidence,[30] but the other factors
demonstrate that the assessment is based not only on laboratory science but also
on 'real-world factors that affect risk'.[31] While Art. 5.2 does not provide a 'closed
list', no definitive list has been articulated by the DSS (and this is likely not
possible).

The Appellate Body stated in *Canada – Continued Suspension*:

---

[25] Appellate Body Report *Australia – Measures Affecting Importation of Salmon*, para. 121; see
further *Van den Bossche/Zdouc* (note 2), 915.

[26] Additives, contaminants, toxins or disease carrying organisms in foodstuffs or beverages.

[27] *Van den Bossche/Zdouc* (note 2), 915–916.

[28] *Ibid.*, 917; Appellate Body Report *European Communities – Measures Concerning Meat and
Meat Products (Hormones)*, para. 190.

[29] *Van den Bossche/Zdouc* (note 2), 917.

[30] Appellate Body Report *Australia – Measures Affecting the Importation of Apples from
New Zealand*, para. 208.

[31] *Van den Bossche/Zdouc* (note 2), 918.

The risk assessment cannot be entirely isolated from the appropriate level of protection. There may be circumstances in which the appropriate level of protection chosen by a Member affects the scope or method of the risk assessment. [...] However, the chosen level of protection must not affect the rigour or objective nature of the risk assessment, which must remain, in its essence, a process in which possible adverse effects are evaluated using scientific methods. Likewise, whatever the level of protection a Member chooses does not pre-determine the results of the risk assessment. Otherwise, the purpose of performing the risk assessment would be defeated.[32]

Article 5.3 SPS requires that members take into account economic factors when carrying out risk assessments to create SPS measures designed concerning animal or plant life or health—though not for those concerning human life or health.[33]

9.8.3   Analysis

The Art. 5.1 obligation to base SPS measures on a risk assessment constitutes a significant (if logically justifiable) restriction on the privilege of States to implement SPS measures. Article 5.2 SPS places a firm obligation on members to base their risk assessments on scientific evidence. While this also seems reasonable, it is called into question when thinking about the realm of scientific uncertainty. This issue is dealt with in connection with Art. 5.7, below. A further problematic point in relation to Arts. 5.1 and 5.2 is raised when thinking about the potential standard of review employed by the DSS to the scientific evidence relied upon—particularly its 'relevance'. As there is no textual basis for standard of review under the SPS Agreement, and, as demonstrated in Chap. 4, the standard of review employed by the DSS is characterised by inherent indeterminacy, it is not clear how much deference will be shown to members' decision-making in regard to risk assessment.[34] Indeed, as the Appellate Body's review of the Panel's standard of review appears to only apply where there exists an "egregious error that calls into question the good faith" of the Panel',[35] this raises huge problems of legitimacy in relation to SPS measures, where arguably the greatest amount of deference should be shown. Although this is hypothesised to be the case, it is again argued here that a firm

---

[32]Appellate Body Report *Canada – Continued Suspension of the Obligations in the EC – Hormones Dispute*, para. 534.

[33]Art. 5.3 states: In assessing the risk to animal or plant life or health and determining the measure to be applied for achieving the appropriate level of sanitary or phytosanitary protection from such risk, Members shall take into account as relevant economic factors: the potential damage in terms of loss of production or sales in the event of the entry, establishment or spread of a pest or disease; the costs of control or eradication in the territory of the importing Member; and the relative cost-effectiveness of alternative approaches to limiting risks.

[34]Ch. 4.3.

[35]Appellate Body Report *Australia – Measures Affecting Importation of Salmon*, pg. 78 (para. 266).

textual basis is required in order to prevent the possibility of Panels replacing governmental decisions with their own regarding SPS measures.

With regard to Art. 5.3, the examples of relevant economic factors given are the potential damage in terms of loss of production or sales in the event of the entry, establishment or spread of a pest or disease; the costs of control or eradication in the territory of the importing Member; and the relative cost-effectiveness of alternative approaches to limiting risks. It is worrying from an environmental perspective that such economic factors need to be taken into account. For example, one of the perceived threats from GMO crops (and thus the import of GMO seeds, etc.) is the harm to biodiversity. Such harm may have little to absolutely no economic impact or one that is unforeseeable in the short term but may have long-term effects. The inclusion of these factors demonstrates the potential dangers of a trade body issuing binding reports on topics that involve priorities that are outwith their sphere of competence. The fact that the terms of the treaty itself encourage the DSS to think about economic incentives is an issue that should be addressed by members in any future negotiations.

The quotation from the Appellate Body in *Canada – Continued Suspension* demonstrates the difficulty in separating the risk analysis from risk management in terms of chronology and policy choices. It can only be seen as positive that the DSS recognises that due to the nature of politics, sometimes the level of protection may be a foregone conclusion, before the risk analysis part of the process has properly taken place.

9.9 Risk Management

9.9.1 Articles 5.4 and 5.5 SPS

The second part of the risk assessment obligation[36] under Art. 5 SPS is made up of risk management. It cannot be entirely extracted from risk analysis, but the focus of certain articles is certainly more on management. Risk management does not concern the level of risk entailed by a certain product but rather the amount of risk tolerated in a society on a policy level. This requires decisions about both how much risk can be tolerated and what kind of measures to put in place to ensure that this risk ceiling is not breached. Articles 5.4 and 5.5 SPS deal with the appropriate level of protection chosen by members, defined in Annex A (5) as 'The level of protection deemed appropriate by the Member establishing a sanitary or phytosanitary measure to protect human, animal or plant life or health within its territory'.

---

[36]For a treatment of the 'false distinction' between risk analysis and risk management, see *supra*, note 1189.

Article 5.4 SPS contains a general obligation to take into account 'the objective of minimizing negative trade effects' when determining the appropriate level of protection, while Art. 5.5 obliges members to avoid 'arbitrary or unjustifiable distinctions in the levels it considers appropriate in different situations, if such distinctions result in discrimination or a disguised restriction on international trade'. It can be seen from the language of the two provisions that Art. 5.4 is more hortatory in nature[37] ('should [. . .] take into account'), while Art. 5.5 provides a firm obligation ('shall avoid'). However, it should be noted that Art 5.4 has been regarded by the DSS as an element that must be respected in carrying out the risk assessment obligation under Art. 5.[38] Further, the firm obligation in Art. 5.5 has been tempered in its interpretation by the DSS as it 'recognised that countries establish their levels of protection *ad hoc* as risks arise. Absolute consistency in levels of protection is neither realistic nor required by Article 5.5 SPS'.[39]

9.9.2 Analysis

As highlighted above in relation to risk analysis, the appropriateness of being obligated to take trade concerns (or 'minimizing trade effects') into consideration when carrying out a risk assessment is questionable in the context of the protection of human, animal and plant life and health and the environment generally. The fact that absolute consistency is no longer required under Art. 5.5 shows that the DSS is at least partially aware of the myriad of restrictions that limit the privilege of members to implement SPS measures. It should be highlighted that this privilege is not granted to States by being parties to the WTO, but rather it is a part of their inherent sovereignty that has been preserved while becoming parties to the WTO. The restrictions on this privilege should thus rightly be seen as restrictions on a fundamental part of statehood and not simply limitations on a freedom granted under the treaty.

---

[37]*Van den Bossche/Zdouc* (note 2), 921.

[38]See *ibid.*, citing Appellate Body Report *Canada – Continued Suspension of the Obligations in the EC – Hormones Dispute*, para. 523 (footnote 1088), which lists Art. 5.4 as one of the elements contained in the SPS Agreement provides 'that a Member must respect'.

[39]*Van den Bossche/Zdouc* (note 2), 922, citing: Appellate Body Report *European Communities – Measures Concerning Meat and Meat Products (Hormones)*, para. 213, which further states that Art. 5.5 'does not establish a *legal obligation* of consistency of appropriate levels or protection'. Emphasis in original.

9.10 Article 5.6 SPS

Article 5.6 provides that members must 'ensure that such measures are not more trade-restrictive than required to achieve their appropriate level of sanitary or phytosanitary protection, taking into account technical and economic feasibility' when establishing or maintaining SPS measures. A footnote to Art. 5.6 clarifies:

> For the purposes of paragraph 6 or Article 5, a measure is not more trade-restrictive than required unless there is another measure, reasonably available taking into account technical and economic feasibility, that achieves the appropriate level of sanitary or phytosanitary protection and is significantly less restrictive to trade.

This footnote creates a three-tier test, laid out by the Panel in *Australia – Salmon* as being the following:

(1) 'reasonably available taking into account technical and economic feasibility';
(2) 'achieves [Australia's] appropriate level of sanitary ... protection'; and
(3) 'significantly less restrictive to trade' than the sanitary measure contested.[40]

9.11 Provisional Measures: Art. 5.7 SPS

9.11.1 Content of the Norm

As laid out above, in cases where there is insufficient scientific evidence for an SPS measure to be implemented under Arts. 5.1 and 5.2, Art. 5.7 SPS provides that

> a Member may provisionally adopt sanitary or phytosanitary measures on the basis of available pertinent information, including that from the relevant international organizations as well as from sanitary or phytosanitary measures applied by other Members In such circumstances, Members shall seek to obtain the additional information necessary for a more objective assessment of risk and review the sanitary or phytosanitary measure accordingly within a reasonable period of time.

This gives members the right (Hohfeldian privilege) to adopt provisional measures in instances where scientific evidence is insufficient, if such measures are based on available pertinent information. It provides a secondary duty to seek additional information, while provisional measures are in place in order to carry out a more objective risk assessment, as well as the secondary duty to review the provisional SPS measure 'within a reasonable period of time'. The provisional measures implemented under Art. 5.7 cannot be maintained if the member does not seek this additional information or carry out this review.[41]

Although the precautionary principle is not directly referenced in Art. 5.7, the Appellate Body in *EC – Hormones*, while deeming it imprudent to make any ruling

---

[40]Panel Report *Australia – Measures Affecting Importation of Salmon*, para. 8.167.
[41]*Van den Bossche/Zdouc* (note 2), 927.

in relation to the status of the precautionary principle in international law (and thus its status within the WTO),[42] found that the precautionary principle 'indeed finds reflection in Article 5.7 of the SPS Agreement'[43] and, although this may not be the full extent of the relevance of the principle under the SPS,[44] that 'the principle has not been written into the SPS Agreement as a ground for justifying SPS measures that are otherwise inconsistent with the obligations of Members set out in particular provisions of that Agreement'[45]

Article 5.7 'cannot be used to justify measures that are adopted in disregard of reliable scientific evidence'[46] as, following the Panel and Appellate Body in *Japan – Apples*, Art. 5.7 is 'triggered not by the existence of scientific uncertainty, but rather the insufficiency of scientific evidence'.[47] This means that where there is scientific uncertainty, then the rigours of Arts. 5.1–5.6 must be followed. This clearly demonstrates that while the precautionary principle may be deemed by the DSS to be 'reflected' in Art. 5.7, it is certainly not encapsulated by it. This approach was confirmed by the Panel in *EC – Biotech*, which further highlighted that the 'provisional adoption of an SPS measure is not a condition for the applicability of Article 5.7. Rather, the provisional adoption of an SPS measure is permitted by the first sentence of Article 5.7'.[48]

9.11.2 Analysis

Article 5.7 is perhaps the most controversial provision in the SPS, and certainly from the European perspective. It covers situations slightly different to those discussed above, in that it seeks to address areas where scientific evidence is insufficient to complete a risk assessment under Arts. 5.1–5.6. What is crucial here from the perspective of environmental sovereignty is that the interpretation of this provision by the DSS excludes areas of scientific uncertainty from the possibility of provisional measures. When thinking about GMOs, many of the perceived risks are hypothetical, and the desire to exclude such products from markets comes from the perspective of fear that such products or crops could have dramatic, damaging and as of yet unforeseeable consequences. Whatever the merits of such arguments are, it is clear that the court of public opinion in many (predominantly European) States is against the import and cultivation of GMOs. Furthermore, it is predominantly

---

[42]Appellate Body Report *European Communities – Measures Concerning Meat and Meat Products (Hormones)*, para. 123.

[43]*Ibid.*, para. 124.

[44]*Ibid.*

[45]*Ibid.*

[46]*Van den Bossche/Zdouc* (note 2), 928.

[47]Panel Report *Japan – Measures Affecting the Importation of Apples*, para. 184.

[48]Panel Report *European Communities – Approval and Marketing of Biotech Products*, para. 7.2939.

within Europe and the EU that the precautionary principle has found a firm legal grounding.[49] This raises the issue in relation to Art. 5.7 as to whether such an interpretation can be deemed consequent from the wording of the provision. If it cannot, then serious issues of legitimacy and interference with sovereignty become apparent.

Recalling that the provision states '[i]n cases where scientific evidence is insufficient', the question becomes whether that phrase adequately covers or on the other hand clearly excludes situations in which there may be sufficient evidence to carry out a risk assessment in the view of some States but not others. If one State implements a provisional SPS measure on the basis that it finds the wider uncertainty of such new technologies to be too big a risk within its territory, can this situation also be covered by the phrase 'where scientific evidence is insufficient'? There have been many studies that come out in favour of GMOs, and experience from outside Europe over the last several decades demonstrates that the fears within Europe are perhaps exaggerated. However, if governments seek to reflect the will of their people and legislate in order to show utmost precaution, this is democracy in action. When thinking about whether Art. 5.7 encapsulates such instances, it becomes clear that unless it specifically excludes them, such interpretations as have come from the DSS to date are problematic in terms of legitimacy. If such cases are excluded from Art. 5.7, then they will inevitably fail to meet the requirements of Arts. 5.1–5.6, as such far-reaching uncertainty does not necessarily have scientific backing, whereas the competing risk assessment would provide evidence of a lack of or low risk.

While it is difficult to provide impartial analysis of which is the better position, it is clear from the foregoing that the wording of the provision is not firm enough to come down squarely on either side of the debate. The current interpretation by the DSS serves to bring the legitimacy of the DSS itself into question in its capacity to make such decisions, which involve health and environmental concerns, science, scientific uncertainty, policy, politics and democratic will. If the DSS were to find that such measures were permissible, this may partially undermine 'the right of market access' of other WTO members in some instances, but its overall implications would be less damaging to the system.

The issue of developing countries and the production of GMO crops is also raised here as it is often claimed that the use of SPS measures to exclude such products from domestic markets in Europe is a form of disguised protectionism. While it may be very damaging to the economies of developing countries to 'lose' the right of market access in respect of such crops, it must be highlighted that, particularly with respect to GMOs, public opinion appears to be the prime motivator rather than protectionism. In order to combat such concerns, any further treaty could include strong mechanisms to investigate protective purposes, without preventing States legislating on the basis of the precautionary principle.

Article 5.7 SPS creates a privilege for importing States that in instances of insufficient scientific evidence, they may implement provisional SPS measures.

---

[49] See, e.g., Art. 191 Treaty on the Functioning of the European Union.

This privilege is limited by the additional duty to seek more information for a more objective assessment of the risk. The scope of the privilege is currently limited by the interpretation of the DSS as to what constitutes 'insufficiency'. This raises the further issue of discretion to governmental decision-making. Although the Panel must offer a legal interpretation of the meaning of this phrase, it is also clear that when such polarised interpretations are held by different sides, the broader interpretation may be more appropriate, particularly in view of the lack of precision in the provision.

9.12   Summary

This overview of the SPS Agreement seeks to highlight some of the structural and interpretative problems with this covered agreement. While its relevance to NPR PPMs is different in nature to the GATT and TBT Agreements, how it interacts with such issues helps us gain a better understanding of this issue in the wider context of the WTO. The specific issues raised in the foregoing should serve to further illustrate that WTO membership comes at significant costs to States, even while the global trade system provides them with many benefits. Lack of legal certainty, the requirement to include trade concerns when legislating environmental and health issues, problematic interpretation and legitimacy problems all serve to raise concerns over how much sovereignty (in the political science sense) was ceded under the SPS Agreement.

More jurisprudence is required before this question can be definitely answered, but it is clear from the foregoing that the answer is likely to be this: more than States envisaged when they became parties to the WTO. The cases explored in the next chapter should serve to flesh out these preliminary conclusions and better explain the functional application of this agreement.

Chapter 10
Overview Relevant Case Law Under the SPS Agreement

10.1 Overview

This chapter will now go on to summarise some of the relevant case law under the SPS Agreement. For reasons of space and more limited relevance, it is not possible to summarise these cases to the same extent as in previous chapters. However, the facts will be summarised, as will the most important conclusions of the DSS.

The cases that will be assessed in this part are as follows:

- *European Communities – Measures Concerning Meat and Meat Products (Hormones)*,[1]
- *European Communities – Approval and Marketing of Biotech Products.*

---

[1]Panel Report *European Communities – Measures Concerning Meat and Meat Products (Hormones) (Canada)*; Panel Report *European Communities – Measures Concerning Meat and Meat Products (Hormones) (US)*; Award of the Arbitrator, *EC – Hormones (Article 21.3(c))*; Appellate Body Report *EC – Measures Concerning Meat and Meat Products (Hormones)* Appellate Body Report *Canada – Continued Suspension of Obligations in the EC- Hormones Dispute*; Appellate Body Report *United States – Continued Suspension of Obligations in the EC- Hormones Dispute.*

© Springer International Publishing AG 2017
A.R. Maggio, *Environmental Policy, Non-Product Related Process and Production Methods and the Law of the World Trade Organization*, European Yearbook of International Economic Law 1, DOI 10.1007/978-3-319-61155-6_10

10.2   EC – Hormones

10.2.1   Facts and Arguments of the Parties

On 25 April 1996, the United States[2] requested the establishment of a Panel on the basis that EC measures adversely affected imports of meat and meat products and appeared to be inconsistent with the obligations of the European Communities under the GATT, TBT and SPS Agreements, as well as under the Agreement on Agriculture. With regard to the SPS Agreement, the US alleged violation of Arts. 2, 3 and 5 SPS[3] on the basis of Council Directive 81/602/EEC, Council Directive 88/146/EEC and Council Directive 88/299/EEC.[4]

Specifically:

> Directive 81/602/EEC prohibits the administering to farm animals of substances having a *thyrostatic action* or substances having an *oestrogenic, androgenic or gestagenic* action; the placing on the market or slaughtering of farm animals to which these substances have been administered; the placing on the market of meat from such animals; the processing of meat from such animals and the placing on the market of meat products prepared from or with such meat.[5]

This Directive included two exceptions,[6] which were largely removed by Directive 88/146/EEC.[7] Article 7 of the Directive provides for derogations for trade in 'those animals and meat from those animals treated for therapeutic or zootechnical purposes, including imports from third countries'.[8] The specifics of these derogations are laid out in Directive 88/299/EEC and would also be applied to imports from third countries.[9]

---

[2]A parallel Panel was requested by Canada with respect to the same measures. Although were separate, they related to the same EC measures, were dealt with by the same Panel members and were assisted by the same scientific experts. For reasons of space, only the US case will be dealt with in this work.

[3]Panel Report *European Communities – Measures Concerning Meat and Meat Products (Hormones) (Canada)*; Panel Report *European Communities – Measures Concerning Meat and Meat Products (Hormones) (US)*, para. 1.4.

[4]*Ibid.*, para. 2.1

[5]*Ibid.*, para. 2.2.

[6]One where oestrogenic, androgenic or gestagenic substances were used for 'therapeutic or zootechnical purposes and administered by a veterinarian or under a veterinarian's responsibility', and another 'for oestradiol-17, progesterone, testosterone, trenbolone acetate (or TBA) and zeranol – when they were used for growth promotion purposes and their use was governed according to the individual regulatory schemes maintained by EC member States', *ibid.*

[7]The Directive extended 'the prohibition imposed by Directive 81/602/EEC to the administration to farm animals of trenbolone acetate and zeranol for any purpose, and oestradiol-17, testosterone and progesterone for fattening purposes' while maintaining the exception for zootechnical and therapeutic purposes, *ibid.*, para. 2.3.

[8]*Ibid.*

[9]*Ibid.*, para. 2.4.

At issue in this case was the following:

In the United States, the three natural hormones may be used for medical treatment (therapeutic). Oestradiol-17 is also permitted for zootechnical purposes. In the United States the six hormones are also approved for growth promotion purposes. Three of the hormones used for growth promotion purposes, trenbolone, zeranol, and MGA, have no zootechnical or therapeutic uses. For growth promotion purposes, five of these hormones (except MGA) are formulated as pellets (with approved and fixed amounts of compound) designed to be implanted in the ear of the animal. The ear is discarded at slaughter. MGA is administered as a feed additive.[10]

Standards for five of the substances (two synthetic and three natural hormones) at issue had been developed and adopted by the Codex Alimentarius Commission.[11]

On the basis of hormone scandals in France in the 1970s (concerning the illegal use of dethylstilboestrol, commonly known as DES, in the production of veal) and Italy (where adolescents had been reported to be suffering from hormonal irregularities, and veal had come under suspicion as a possible cause), concerns about hormones in meat became a big issue for European consumers.[12] After boycotts, the EC Council of (Agriculture) Ministers 'adopted a declaration in favour of a ban on the use of oestrogen',[13] which was followed by measures by the EC Commission and the EC Council of Ministers, which eventually led to the directives at issue.[14]

Attempts were made by the US to bring this case before a GATT Panel on the basis of the Tokyo Round Agreement on Technical Barriers to Trade, but they were ultimately unsuccessful as the EC claimed that they were based on PPMs and thus were only not permitted under the Tokyo Round TBT if used to 'circumvent the Agreement'.[15] The US introduced retaliatory measures against EC imports, which were maintained until the EC requested a Panel regarding this element of the dispute.[16] The case was then brought by the US before a WTO Panel.

The US claimed that

the EC ban on the importation and sale of animals, and meat derived from animals, that had been administered any of the six hormones at issue for growth promotion purposes (oestradiol-17, progesterone, testosterone, trenbolone, zeranol and melengestrol acetate (MGA)) was inconsistent with the SPS Agreement and the GATT.[17]

Particularly with regard to the SPS Agreement, the US claimed that the measures in question were sanitary measures and:

directly and indirectly affected international trade; were not based on an assessment of risk and were consequently inconsistent with Article 5.1 of the Agreement; were maintained

---

[10]*Ibid.*, para. 2.10.

[11]*Ibid.*, paras. 2.20–2.23.

[12]*Ibid.*, para. 2.26.

[13]*Ibid.*

[14]For a full account of the European measures and legislation, see *ibid.*, paras. 2.26–2.33.

[15]*Ibid.*, para. 2.34.

[16]*Ibid.*, para. 2.35.

[17]*Ibid.*, para. 3.1.

without sufficient scientific evidence in contravention of Article 2.2; were not justified as a 'provisional' measure under Article 5.7; breached Articles 2.2 and 5.6 in that they were not based on scientific principles; were not applied only to the extent necessary to protect human life or health and were more trade-restrictive than required to achieve the appropriate level of sanitary protection; arbitrarily or unjustifiably discriminated between Members where identical or similar conditions prevailed, in contravention of Article 2.3; constituted a disguised restriction on international trade, in breach of Article 2.3; contravened Article 3.1 because they were not based on the relevant international standards, guidelines or recommendations and that this departure from international standards was not justified by Article 3.3; and were based on arbitrary or unjustifiable distinctions in the levels of protection in different situations, resulting in discrimination or a disguised restriction on international trade in contravention of Article 5.[18]

Thus, the US variously alleged the violation of Arts. 2.1, 2.2, 2.3, 3.1, 3.3, 5.1 and 5.6, while refuting that the measure fell under the Art 5.7 provisional measures.

The EC submitted that the assessment of the measures under the SPS should only take place if the Panel first established a violation of the GATT and its defences were thus based, in the first instance, on the GATT.[19] Further, with regard to the SPS Agreement, the EC put forward that its measures did not violate any obligations under the agreement as its measures satisfied the conditions imposed by it,[20] particularly, as '[t]he measures were based on scientific principles as required by Article 2.2 of the SPS Agreement, and a risk assessment had been performed which established the scientific basis for regulatory action'.[21] The EC argued that their chosen level of protection was higher than that contained in the Codex standards, that the US specifically attacked the EC's chosen level of protection and not its measures and further that 'WTO dispute settlement panels were not competent to judge its level of sanitary protection nor the scientific evidence upon which it was based, but only whether its measures were in conformity with the provisions of the SPS Agreement'.[22] The EC also argued that its measures were based on the precautionary principle, that the US had failed to discharge its burden of proving that the measures were more trade restrictive than necessary and that the measures themselves were applied in a non-discriminatory manner.[23]

10.2.2   Panel Report

Before making its findings, and in consultation with the parties to the dispute, the Panel put together a series of questions and addressed them, along with the written

---

[18]*Ibid.*, para. 3.2.

[19]*Ibid.*, para. 3.4.

[20]*Ibid.*, para. 3.6.

[21]*Ibid.*

[22]*Ibid.*

[23]*Ibid.*

submissions of the parties, to six experts, as well as to the Codex Commission Secretariat.[24] The responses of the experts are included in the Panel Report.[25] The Panel expressly pointed out: 'we made clear to the experts advising the Panel that we were not seeking a consensus position among the experts but wanted to hear all views'.[26]

In the dispute, both parties and the Panel agreed that the measures in question were 'sanitary measures in the sense of Paragraph 1(b) of Annex A of the SPS Agreement'.[27] The Panel began by rejecting the argument of the EC that the applicability of the SPS depended on the prior violation of a provision of the GATT.[28] The Panel also pointed out the structural difference between the GATT and the SPS: whereas the GATT provides substantive obligations and exceptions for certain measures under Art. XX, the SPS provides a series of 'specific obligations to be met in order for a Member to enact or maintain specific types of measures'.[29]

Beginning with Art. 3 SPS, the Panel first identified the relevant Codex Alimentarius standards that applied to five of the six hormones at issue.[30] The Panel noted the EC's protest that these standards applied to maximum residue levels rather than the use of hormone growth promoters and that the standards were adopted by a very slim margin in what was ordinarily a consensus-based adoption system within the Codex Alimentarius.[31] The Panel then rejected the need to consider by what margin any relevant standard was adopted on the basis that it is only necessary for the Panel to establish whether they exist at all and then if the SPS measure at issue is based on them, under Art. 3.1.[32] The Panel further rejected the distinction made between the purposes standards and the SPS measure, finding that they were relevant international standards in the meaning of Art. 3.1.[33] The Panel then compared the levels of sanitary protection afforded by the Codex standards and the EC measures and found that as they afforded differing levels of protection, the EC measures were not 'based on' the relevant international standards within the meaning of Art. 3.1.[34] On the basis of the text of Art. 3.3, the Panel concluded that it was necessary to first determine the consistency of the SPS measure in question with, *inter alia*, Art. 5 SPS before making any pronouncement on the consistency of the measure with Art. 3.3.[35]

---

[24] *Ibid.*, para. 3.8.

[25] *Ibid.*, paras. 6.11 *et seq.*

[26] *Ibid.*, para. 8.9.

[27] *Ibid.*, paras. 8.21–8.22.

[28] *Ibid.*, para. 8.36.

[29] *Ibid.*, para. 8.39.

[30] *Ibid.*, paras. 8.58 *et seq.*

[31] *Ibid.*, paras. 8.66–8.67.

[32] *Ibid.*, para. 8.69.

[33] *Ibid.*, para 8.70,

[34] *Ibid.*, paras. 8.75–8.77.

[35] *Ibid.*, para. 8.89.

Moving on then to its assessment of the measure under the Art. 5 risk assessment obligation, the Panel began with a clear differentiation between the risk assessment obligations, which the Panel clarified as 'a scientific examination of data and factual studies; it is not a policy exercise involving social value judgments made by political bodies',[36] and risk management requirements, in which the member seeking to impose an SPS agreement must decide 'the extent to which it can accept the potential adverse effects related to a specific substance which have been identified in the risk assessment';[37] 'the risk management phase involves *non-scientific* considerations, such as social value judgments'.[38] The Panel made a special express note that Art. 5.3 SPS does not have any application in this case as it refers to 'animal and plant life and health', and the case at hand was centred on human health.[39]

The Panel found that the EC had met its burden under Art. 5 of demonstrating that it had carried out a risk assessment[40] and then went on to consider whether the SPS measure at hand was 'based on' said risk assessment,[41] a consideration with both procedural and substantive aspects.[42] The procedural aspect of the obligation was deemed by the Panel to include the submission of evidence that the party imposing the SPS measure had taken the risk assessment into account in order to demonstrate that it was based on this risk assessment.[43] This obligation was deemed by the Panel not to have been discharged by the EC in this case, who the Panel found thus to be in contravention of its obligations under Art. 5.1.[44]

Moving on to the substantive obligation, after assessing some of the specific and general evidence put forward as the EC's 'risk assessment', the Panel disagreed that the SPS measure was based on this evidence as

> none of the scientific evidence referred to by the European Communities which specifically addresses the safety of some or all of the hormones in dispute when used for growth promotion, indicates that an identifiable risk arises for human health from such use of these hormones if good practice is followed.[45]

The Panel went on to conclude that the EC had

> not demonstrated that the scientific evidence it referred to, which generally addresses the safety of some or all of the hormones in dispute, would indicate that an identifiable risk arises for human health from the use of these hormones for growth promotion purposes if good practice is followed.[46]

---

[36]*Ibid.*, para. 8.94.

[37]*Ibid.*, para. 8.95.

[38]*Ibid.*, para. 8.97.

[39]*Ibid.*, para. 8.106.

[40]*Ibid.*, para. 8.111.

[41]*Ibid.*, paras. 8.112 *et seq.*

[42]*Ibid.*, para. 8.112.

[43]*Ibid.*, para. 8.113.

[44]*Ibid.*, paras. 8.114–8.116.

[45]*Ibid.*, para. 8.124.

[46]*Ibid.*, para. 8.134.

The Panel then went on to assess whether the scientific conclusion that underpinned the SPS measure in question was reflected in the evidence put forward by the EC. This 'scientific conclusion' was determined by the Panel as being 'the use of the hormones in dispute for growth promotion purposes, even in accordance with good practice, poses an identifiable risk to human health'.[47] The Panel concluded that this 'scientific conclusion' '[did] not conform to any of the scientific conclusions reached in the evidence referred to by the European Communities'.[48] Other categories of risk put forward by the EC were also deemed by the Panel not to be supported by scientific evidence or an appropriate risk assessment.[49] The invocation of the precautionary principle by the EC was similarly rejected by the Panel on the basis that it could not override the explicit wording of Arts. 5.1 and 5.2 SPS or the findings of the Panel in relation to this issue.[50]

Moving on to the risk management obligations, the Panel noted: 'we consider that if there is no scientific evidence of an identifiable risk, there is no basis on which to adopt a measure to achieve a level of sanitary protection under the SPS Agreement' (except as provided in Article 5.7).[51] As the Panel had already established that the EC had not 'provided evidence of an identifiable risk related to the presence of five of the six hormones at issue', it concluded that 'it is not possible for the European Communities to ban the use of these hormones as growth promoters in accordance with good practice'.[52]

The Panel also found the EC to be in breach of, *inter alia*, Arts. 5.5 and 5.7 SPS.[53]

10.2.3   *Appellate Body Report*

Both the EC and the US appealed points of law in the Panel Report. The Report of the parallel Panel dealing with the dispute between Canada and the EC was also appealed by both parties to the dispute. The appeals were dealt with by the Appellate Body in one report. For reasons of space, only the points raised in the EC/US dispute will be dealt with in detail.

The EC appealed with regard to the allocation of the burden of proof by the Panel in regard to Arts. 3.3 and 5.1 SPS, as well as the general allocation by the Panel under the SPS to the member imposing the measure.[54] The EC further

---

[47]*Ibid.*, para. 8.136.

[48]*Ibid.*, para. 8.137.

[49]*Ibid.*, paras. 8.139–8.156.

[50]*Ibid.*, paras. 8.157–8.158.

[51]*Ibid.*, para. 8.161.

[52]*Ibid.*, para. 8.162.

[53]*Ibid.*, para. 8.245.

[54]Appellate Body Report *European Communities – Measures Concerning Meat and Meat Products (Hormones)*, paras. 9–11.

appealed with regard to the standard of review imposed by the Panel, claiming that 'the Panel erred in law by not according deference to the [. . .] EC measures' and that 'WTO panels should adopt a deferential "reasonableness" standard when reviewing a Member's decision to adopt a particular science policy or a Member's determination that a particular inference from the available data is scientifically plausible'.[55]

The EC further disagreed with the Panel's interpretation of the precautionary principle, which it claimed was part of customary international law or at least a general principle of law and should thus have been taken into account by the Panel not only in the risk management but also in the risk assessment stage.[56] The EC also alleged that the Panel did not comply with its obligations under Art. 11 DSU as it did not carry out an objective assessment of the facts.[57] These claims were summarily refuted by Canada and the United States.[58] The United States then went on to appeal the Panel Report on the basis that the Panel ought to have also found the EC measures to be inconsistent with Arts. 2.2 and 5.6 SPS.[59]

The Appellate Body began by agreeing with the EC in their criticism of the allocation of an evidentiary burden of proof on the member imposing the measure, finding no basis for this in the SPS Agreement.[60] With regard to the standard of review employed by the Panel, the Appellate Body reasoned that it 'must reflect the balance established in that Agreement between the jurisdictional competences conceded by the Members to the WTO and the jurisdictional competences retained by the Members for themselves'.[61] The Body then pointed to the 'objective assessment of the facts' test laid out in Art. 11 DSU and highlighted that a deferential standard of review would make it impossible for a Panel to fulfil its obligations under this provision.[62] The Appellate Body did not go on to examine if the 'objective assessment of the facts' required under Art. 11 DSU had been fulfilled and was satisfied that the EC claims relating to deference (and the standard contained in the Anti-Dumping Agreement) were not relevant claims of appeal.[63]

The Appellate Body also upheld the findings of the Panel with regard to the precautionary principle, finding that while it may have crystallised in the field of international environmental law, its status as customary international law or a general principle of law generally was less certain.[64] The relationship between

---

[55] *Ibid.*, paras. 13–14.

[56] *Ibid.*, para. 16.

[57] *Ibid.*, paras. 17–18.

[58] *Ibid.*, paras. 40–71.

[59] *Ibid.*, paras. 72–76.

[60] *Ibid.*, para. 102.

[61] *Ibid.*, para. 115.

[62] *Ibid.*, para. 117.

[63] *Ibid.*, para. 119.

[64] *Ibid.*, para. 123, stating further: 'We consider, however, that it is unnecessary, and probably imprudent for the Appellate Body in this appeal to take a position on this important, but abstract, question.'

the SPS Agreement and the precautionary principle was confirmed by the Body being focused in its reflection in Art. 5.7, with any broader sphere of application that did not follow the text of the agreement being outwith the remit of the DSS, stating that 'the precautionary principle does not, by itself, and without a clear textual directive to that effect, relieve a panel from the duty of applying the normal (i.e. customary international law) principles of treaty interpretation in reading the provisions of the SPS Agreement'.[65]

Regarding the Panel's alleged failure to fulfil its obligation under Art. 11 DSU on the basis that 'the Panel disregarded or distorted or misrepresented the evidence submitted by the European Communities and even the opinions expressed by the Panel's own expert advisors',[66] the Appellate Body began by recognising the importance of this claim as the failure by a Panel to do so as 'den[ying] the party submitting the evidence fundamental fairness, or what in many jurisdictions is known as due process of law or natural justice'.[67] However, after finding that the Panel 'failed to make reference' to an evaluation and a statement by two experts, the Appellate Body then stated that 'it is generally within the discretion of the Panel to decide which evidence it chooses to utilize in making findings',[68] a statement that is at least partially hard to reconcile with its previous statements. With regard to certain points, the Appellate Body did agree that the Panel had at times erred in law by not taking certain evidence into account,[69] but although 'the Panel did not in fact represent the opinions of its experts accurately', 'this mistake [did] not amount to [an] egregious disregarding or distorting of evidence'.[70]

Moving on to assess the EC claim regarding the interpretation of Art. 3 SPS, the Appellate Body rejected the Panel's interpretation that led to an assimilation of the term 'based on' to 'conform to'.[71] The Body also rejected the Panel's characterisation of the ability of members to choose their own level of sanitary protection under Art. 3.3 as an 'exception' to the general rule, describing it rather as an autonomous right,[72] though not an absolute or unqualified one.[73] However, the Body agreed with the Panel's interpretation that Art. 3.3 requires that the member imposing an SPS measure also fulfil the risk assessment obligation under Art. 5.1 and thus upheld the Panel's findings.[74]

With regard to the 'risk assessment' and 'risk management' distinction elaborated by the Panel, the Appellate Body noted that there was no textual basis for

---

[65] *Ibid.*, para. 124.

[66] *Ibid.*, para. 133.

[67] *Ibid.*

[68] *Ibid.*, para. 133.

[69] *Ibid.*, para. 143.

[70] *Ibid.*, para. 144.

[71] *Ibid.*, paras. 163–166.

[72] *Ibid.*, para. 172.

[73] *Ibid.*, para. 173.

[74] *Ibid.*, para. 177.

this.[75] While not agreeing with several further interpretative points by the Panel regarding Art. 5.1,[76] the Body nonetheless agreed that for an SPS measure to be based on risk assessment, it must have a rational relationship with it.[77] The Body recognised that the risk assessment in question need not just follow the 'main-stream' view within the scientific community but could also set out divergent views.[78] With regard to the EC measures, the Appellate Body did not find the necessary rational relationship,[79] and while recognising that there was a divergent opinion, the Body nevertheless deemed this 'not reasonably sufficient to overturn the contrary conclusions reached in the scientific studies referred to by the [EC]'.[80] Other studies relied on by the EC were found by the Panel to be too general, and this was supported by the Body.[81] On the basis of, *inter alia*, these points, the Body found that the EC had not carried out a risk assessment within the meaning of Arts. 5.1 and 5.2 SPS[82] and was thus also in contravention with the obligation contained in Art. 3.3 SPS.[83]

10.2.4   Resolution of the Dispute

As mentioned in the foregoing, the EC measures were kept in place despite the recommendations of the DSS in 1998. The United States therefore suspended concessions under Art. 22 DSU. The dispute continued until

> On 25 September 2009, the European Communities and the United States notified the DSB of a Memorandum of Understanding regarding the importation of beef from animals not treated with certain growth-promoting hormones and increased duties applied by the United States to certain products of the European Communities, agreed by the United States and the European Communities on 13 May 2009, in relation to this dispute. On 14 April 2014, the European Union and the United States notified the DSB of a revised Memorandum of Understanding dated 21 October 2013.[84]

---

[75]*Ibid.*, para. 180.

[76]*Ibid.*, paras. 181–192.

[77]*Ibid.*, para. 193.

[78]*Ibid.*, para. 194.

[79]*Ibid.*, para. 197.

[80]*Ibid.*, para. 198.

[81]*Ibid.*, paras. 199–200.

[82]*Ibid.*, para. 208.

[83]*Ibid.*, para. 209.

[84]See https://www.wto.org/english/tratop_e/dispu_e/cases_e/ds26_e.htm (last accessed on 05/03/2017).

10.2.5   Analysis

As can be seen from this short summary of the *EC – Hormones* case, the issues raised in the previous chapter are not merely academic. The practical implementation of the SPS Agreement has led to the issues of policy decision-making and deference to such decision-making being decided upon by a trade tribunal. The interpretation of scientific evidence and the weight that the precautionary principle is given in creating SPS measures was removed from the decision-making State and replaced by the judgment of the DSS.

What is particularly worrying in this case is the long period of non-fulfilment by the EC following the recommendations of the Panel and Appellate Body. From an environmentalist perspective, this can be seen positively as the EC fully utilising the 'Bad Man' position and paying the tax in order to exercise the precautionary principle in defiance of the DSS. Indeed, the fact that the EC/EU has the economic strength and relative bargaining power means that it can choose to exercise precaution even when it is not permissible under the SPS (positive for GMO campaigners). However, from the perspective of developing and least-developed countries, this is particularly problematic. On the one hand, if a developing country wanted to implement SPS measures on the basis of precaution in a similar way to the EC, it would not have the possibility to withstand the suspension of concessions as this would be too damaging to its economy. On the other hand, the possibility of a developing country litigating against a developed country in such a case would also be prejudicial due to the costs involved and particularly the fact that even if the recommendations of the DSS were issued in their favour they would have little to no chance of having their opponent remove the SPS-inconsistent measures and no hope of coercing them to do so with the suspension of concessions. Moreover, developing countries implementing 'retaliatory' suspension of concessions may further damage their own economies and would likely be dissuaded from doing so—meaning that the 'Bad Man' developed country would not even have to properly take this factor into account.

Looking more specifically at the case at hand, it is clear that the obligations of the Panels in assessing, interpreting and giving weight to evidence presented to them are not specific enough. Furthermore, the Appellate Body, in reviewing the actions of the Panel, found multiple instances in which the Panel did not fulfil its obligations and yet was largely unwilling to see that this amounted to something prejudicial to the EC. This raises again the issue of deference and standard of review, particularly as even where the Appellate Body finds problems with the Panel Report, it still fails to recognise that where a Panel purports to replace the interpretation and weight given to evidence by a member, each instance of an error in law should be taken seriously as a potential egregious disregarding or distorting of evidence. The competence to review such decisions is questionable in the context of such large policy questions, and the fact that the Panel did 'not in fact represent the opinions of its experts accurately' brings it further into question.

This criticism can also be echoed in relation to the Appellate Body's 'rational relationship' test and treatment of the divergent opinion in this case. While the Body superficially recognised that SPS measures could be based on the divergent view put forward in a risk assessment, when assessing this case it found that this had in fact occurred but that it was 'not reasonably sufficient to overturn the contrary conclusions'. This again appears to undermine the statement put forward first that it was indeed possible to base measures on the divergent opinion and represents another instance where deference would arguably have been the more appropriate response.

Such problems as are highlighted in this case clearly tear at the legitimacy of the regime in the context of SPS measures. Although this case does not deal with potential environmental but rather deals with potential public health risks, it is nonetheless instructive as to the position of the WTO DSS and the inherent problems of the text of the SPS Agreement.

10.3   EC – Biotech

10.3.1   Facts and Arguments of the Parties

The final case to be discussed is the *EC – Biotech* Panel Report.[85] This Panel Report reaches more than 1200 pages and for reasons of space cannot be analysed in such detail as the previous cases covered in this work. Some of the most salient points of contention that are relevant to the theme of this work will be addressed, but it should be noted that this is necessarily not an in-depth summary or analysis of this dispute.

In this case, in May 2003, the United States requested consultations with the EC concerning certain measures taken by the EC (and its member States) affecting imports of agricultural and food imports from the United States. The United States asserted that the moratorium applied by the EC in 1998 (and maintained) on the approval of biotech (also called GM) products restricted imports of agricultural and food products from the United States. Further, the United States asserted that a number of EC member States maintained national marketing and import bans on biotech products even though those products had already been approved by the EC for import and marketing in the EC.[86] The US alleged breach, *inter alia*, of Arts. 2, 5, 7 and 8 and Annexes B and C of the SPS Agreement. Australia, Argentina, Brazil, Canada, Chile, Colombia, India, Mexico, New Zealand and Peru joined the consultations.[87] In March 2004, a Panel was composed upon the request of the United States, Canada and Argentina.

---

[85]Panel Report *European Communities – Approval and Marketing of Biotech Products.*

[86]See https://www.wto.org/english/tratop_e/dispu_e/cases_e/ds291_e.htm (last accessed on 05/03/2017).

[87]*Ibid.*

The issues raised in this dispute concerned two distinct matters: (1) the operation and application of the EC regime for approval of biotech products and (2) certain measures adopted and maintained by EC member States prohibiting or restricting the marketing of biotech products.[88] 'Biotech products' are defined in the Panel Report as 'plant cultivars that have been developed through recombinant deoxyribonucleic acid ("recombinant DNA") technology'.[89] The EC regime (based on EC Directive 2001/18, EC Directive 90/220 and EC Regulation 258/97) involved a 'case-by case evaluation of the potential risks biotech products might pose to human health and the environment. On the basis of that evaluation, the marketing of a particular biotech product [was] either approved or not.'[90] However, EC Regulation 258/97 'under certain conditions permit[ted] EC member States to adopt "safeguard" measures in respect of biotech products that [had] obtained approval for EC-wide marketing'.[91]

However, the complainants argued that the current application of these measures by the EC amounted to a *de facto* moratorium on the approval of biotech products,[92] including 'the suspension by the European Communities of approval of biotech products and on the other, the failure by the European Communities to consider for approval applications for the biotech products'.[93] While up to October 1998 the approval procedures were in use and 10 biotech products were approved,[94] after this the EC suspended its approval procedures and 'failed to allow any new biotech product to move to final approval'.[95] This *de facto* moratorium, alleged the US, was not adopted in a transparent fashion or published but nevertheless was 'widely-recognized, including by leading EC officials'.[96] It was not the approval system itself that was contested by the complainants in this case but rather the failure of the EC to apply it without delay.[97]

The second part of the dispute concerned not EC measures but those from EC member States, six of whom, according to the United States:

> adopted marketing or import bans on biotech products that previously have been approved by the European Communities. These product-specific bans, like the moratorium, are not based on science and are thus inconsistent with the European Communities' obligations under the WTO Agreement.[98]

---

[88]Panel Report *European Communities – Approval and Marketing of Biotech Products*, para. 2.1.
[89]*Ibid.*, para. 2.2.
[90]*Ibid.*, para. 2.4.
[91]*Ibid.*, para. 2.5, 'More particularly, individual EC member States may provisionally restrict or prohibit the use and/or sale of an approved biotech product in their own territory if these member States have detailed grounds for considering, based on new or additional information or scientific knowledge, that the particular product poses a risk to human health or the environment.'
[92]*Ibid.*, para. 4.10.
[93]*Ibid.*
[94]*Ibid.*, para. 4.130.
[95]*Ibid.*, para. 4.131.
[96]*Ibid.*, para. 4.132.
[97]*Ibid.*, para. 4.133.
[98]*Ibid.*, para. 4.134.

The EC pointed out that the factual background of this case was more complex than the submissions of the complainants (characterised as seeking 'to evade or ignore the whole sociopolitical, legal, factual and scientific complexity of the case'[99]), which the EC accused, while also denying the existence of a *de jure* or *de facto* moratorium,[100] of 'avoid[ing] to discuss the specific steps taken in the authorization procedures for GMOs in connection with each individual product, and they instead blur the picture referring to the existence of a "moratorium"'.[101] The EC further stated:

> Finally, the complaining parties try to artificially compress this complex dispute into the SPS framework, ignoring the fact that the aims of the European Communities' policies on GMOs go beyond the protection against the specific risks covered by the *SPS Agreement*.[102]

10.3.2 Panel Report

In providing its conclusions, the Panel first began by pointing out what it did not decide on in this dispute. To the disappointment of environmentalists and those seeking definitive answers in the case of GMOs, the Panel did not decide on, *inter alia,* 'whether biotech products in general are safe or not' and[103] 'whether the biotech products at issue in this dispute are "like" their conventional counterparts'[104] and did not evaluate the 'conclusions of the relevant EC scientific committees regarding the safety evaluation of specific biotech products'.[105]

Rather, regarding the complaints of the US, the Panel concluded that there had indeed been a *de facto* moratorium in the EC approval process,[106] which was inconsistent with 'Annex C(1)(a), first clause, of the SPS Agreement and, consequently, with its obligations under Article 8 of the SPS Agreement',[107] though not with any of the other provisions of the SPS raised by the complainants.[108] The Panel further found a breach of Annex C (1)(a) and Art. 8 SPS with regard to 24 product-specific measures[109] and further that all 9 EC member State safeguard measures were not based on risk assessments and were thus inconsistent with Art. 5.1 SPS.[110]

---

[99] *Ibid.*, para. 4.332.
[100] *Ibid.*, para. 4.334.
[101] *Ibid.*, para. 4.332.
[102] *Ibid.*
[103] *Ibid.*, para. 8.3.
[104] *Ibid.*
[105] *Ibid.*
[106] *Ibid.*, para. 8.13 (a).
[107] *Ibid.*, para. 8.14 (a).
[108] *Ibid.*, para. 8.14 (b)-(g).
[109] *Ibid.*, para. 8.18 (a).
[110] *Ibid.*, paras. 8.21–8.31.

The safeguard measures were found not to fall under Art. 5.7 SPS as the Panel deemed that there was sufficient evidence to carry out a risk assessment based on the fact that risk assessments had been carried out by the EC in relation to the products concerned.

The conclusions of the Panel regarding the complaints of Canada and Argentina follow the same reasoning.[111]

This case was not appealed by any of the parties.

10.3.3 Analysis

As will be clear from this short summary, this case did not address the most fundamental issue in relation to NPR PPMs and GMOs—are they 'like' non-GMO products? Part of the reason for this was that the case concerned the SPS Agreement, where like products are not relevant. Litigation on GMOs may eventually come before the DSS on the basis of infringements of the GATT or the TBT, but due to the nature of the measures involved any restrictions on them will likely be encompassed by the SPS Agreement at first instance.

With regard to the 25 product-specific measures, the Panel found a breach of Annex C (1)(a) SPS and Art. 8—both of which provide for procedural requirements in relation to 'Control, Inspection and Approval Procedures'.[112] This was also closely related to the moratorium and does not provide any further insight into the substantive provisions of the SPS. Although the risk assessment procedures are also procedural, their prescribed content relates directly to the problem at hand, and thus they can be distinguished from these provisions.

The fact that the 'insufficiency' of scientific evidence element of Art. 5.7 was viewed by the Panel as not being met (due to the fact that there had been other risk assessments carried out), it failed to properly engage with the idea of 'insufficiency' and the policy decisions surrounding such a characterisation.

The found inconsistency of the nine safeguard measures with, *inter alia*, Art. 5.1 relates to the problem at hand— but, as the measures at hand were found not to be based on a risk assessment on the ground that they invoked an insufficiency of scientific evidence despite the existence of other risk assessments with regard to the same products, this point was also not dealt with by the Panel in a way that is

---

[111] *Ibid.*, paras. 8.32–8.63.

[112] Art. 8 SPS states: Members shall observe the provisions of Annex C in the operation of control, inspection and approval procedures, including national systems for approving the use of additives or for establishing tolerances for contaminants in foods, beverages or feedstuffs, and otherwise ensure that their procedures are not inconsistent with the provisions of this Agreement. Annex C (1) (a) states: 1. Members shall ensure, with respect to any procedure to check and ensure the fulfilment of sanitary or phytosanitary measures, that: (a) such procedures are undertaken and completed without undue delay and in no less favourable manner for imported products than for like domestic products.

enlightening about their approach to GMOs or other NPR PPMs under the SPS Agreement.

In fact, despite being long awaited, this case tells us surprisingly little about the position of the DSS on the SPS that we did not already know from *EC – Hormones*. The main crux of the case was essentially a moot point as the *de facto* moratorium had already been lifted before the Panel Report was issued, and this is reflected in the judgment. The findings that the member State safeguard measures were all found to be inconsistent with the SPS on the ground that they were not based on risk assessments show only a continuation of the interpretative canon that began in *EC – Hormones*, and raise similar issues of legitimacy.

While this case has, particularly in comparison to the others cited in this work, little extra to add to the general regime critique of the WTO, it is important in the context of the SPS Agreement and to a lesser extent in relation to the issues raised in the rest of this book.

Chapter 11
Conclusion

This work has uncovered and evaluated the true position of members under the WTO through the particular lens of NPR PPMs and the environment. The use of Hohfeldian legal analysis, coupled with influences from *Holmes* and *Hale*, and through the prism of *Krasner's* sovereignty, has proven its worth in untangling the complexity of the legal relationships and highlighting some of the institutional problems facing the WTO in its 20th year. By breaking down the complex web of WTO obligations in relation to NPR PPMs into their constituent parts and using them to describe the legal relationships that they create, as well as looking at the obligations through the lens of consequence and on the basis of coercion, this work has produced greater clarity in the assessment of WTO membership.

This assessment began by tracing the history of the organisation and its progressive judicialisation. Although this process began under the GATT, it was cemented by the birth of the WTO and, with it, the DSU and its DSS. Many of the concerns raised in this work are only of particular relevance due to the hyper-judicialised nature of this trade body. While the ambiguity that characterised the GATT years was 'important as a way of ensuring sufficient flexibility in the law to permit it to express whatever informal community consensus existed at any particular point in time',[1] the compulsory, binding dispute settlement procedures of the WTO—an international organisation with almost universal membership—show a rigid judicial organisation and mean that the WTO DSS is the most powerful international tribunal that exists to date.

The short overview of the institutional make-up of the WTO and some of the more influential rules laid out the main points to be borne in mind when assessing the DSS in its first two decades of existence. Central to that is the reverse consensus rule in the DSU, which ensures that decisions that may be *de jure* capable of being

---

[1]*Andrew Lang*, World Trade After Neoliberalism: Re-imagining the Global Economic Order (Oxford, 2011), 204.

© Springer International Publishing AG 2017
A.R. Maggio, *Environmental Policy, Non-Product Related Process and Production Methods and the Law of the World Trade Organization*, European Yearbook of International Economic Law 1, DOI 10.1007/978-3-319-61155-6_11

reversed by the DSB are adopted *de facto* automatically. Furthermore, the factor that members have no other choice of forum in instances where trade concerns arise means that, even where other fora may be better placed to rule on issues such as environment and health, this not permissible under the WTO system. Finally, the fact that it is essentially possible for members to buy their way out of their obligations by awarding compensation or allowing for the suspension of concessions against them means that the entire system is weighted in favour of developed countries with strong diverse economies and against developing countries.

While the consent argument can always be put forward to any of the charges laid out in this work, it is important to note that due to the almost universal membership of the WTO and the fact that it could be economically incredibly damaging for States to leave the WTO, this argument lacks some of the force that it would have in other areas of international law. Thus, while legal sovereignty has been limited in an agreed, consent-based way, other factors that make up sovereignty in the broader sense have been impinged upon in often unforeseeable and largely undesirable ways. This work, therefore, rather assessed the impact of the WTO on sovereignty in the political science sense of the term. In doing so, *Krasner's* four conceptions of sovereignty were repeatedly brought up in order to demonstrate when and how this 'sovereignty' had been ceded—with the results showing that it has been ceded often and generally to the DSS itself.

Following the institutional critique of the WTO DSS came a more in-depth assessment of the judicial function of the WTO. This chapter highlighted some of the shortcomings of the DSS in its role as the settler of disputes under the WTO and covered agreements. With regard to treaty interpretation, the particular problems of overreach of competence and judicial lawmaking were addressed. The problem of the standard of review under the GATT, TBT and SPS Agreements was explored, and the lack of consensus, even from academics, about the standard of review that has been applied and should be applied helped to demonstrate the underlying problems of competence and legitimacy in this area. Likewise, the particular problem of the interpretation of 'like products' was summarised and evaluated with a view to providing some analytical backdrop for the coming chapters. Importantly, it was noted that 'the broader the concept [of like products], the broader the jurisdiction of international trade law becomes (narrowing the scope of national regulatory autonomy)'[2] and deduced that just how broad the concept is uncertain and largely in the hands of the DSS on a case-by-case basis, meaning the DSS itself largely decides upon the limitations on its own power. This chapter also highlighted the potential of Art. XI:2 of the WTO Agreement in possibly remedying some of the many difficulties inherent in the WTO system, without having to conclude a new negotiation round while also providing for greater legitimacy in the current operation of the organisation.

---

[2]*Won-Mog Choi*, Like Products in International Trade Law: Towards a Consistent GATT/WTO Jurisprudence (Oxford, 2003), ix.

After this scene setting, the methodological analysis of the three most relevant covered agreements and their related case law was carried out. Beginning in Chaps. 5 and 6 with the GATT, which forms the analytical backbone of this work, and moving on in Chaps. 7–10 to the TBT and SPS Agreements, this analysis looked more closely at the role of NPR PPMs under the WTO.

While Chaps. 5, 7 and 9 addressed the provisions of the treaties in detail and provided Hohfeldian analysis in order to uncover the true position of WTO members from the tangle of their obligations, Chaps. 6, 8 and 10 were designed not only to assess the problems in practice but also to give the reader a better understanding of WTO members' own engagement with these issues. This aim was pursued by providing not only the facts of the cases and the judgments of the DSS but also the most salient arguments of the parties that had some relevance to the issues raised elsewhere in this volume.

The examination of the GATT in Chap. 5 determined that in the area of NPR PPMs based on TREMs under the GATT, WTO members are faced with judicial lawmaking, overreach, a lack of formal realisability and thus a large amount of uncertainty. Power distributive analysis showed that the combination of Arts. I, III and XI with Art. XX places yet more power in the hands of the DSS. The examination also went on to show that national regulatory space in the area of environmental regulation is clearly and significantly encroached upon, at least in the application of TREMs, under the WTO. Despite the growing recognition of consumers' tastes and habits in any assessment of 'likeness', the chapter also definitively demonstrated that products that differ only on their NPR PPMs will still be treated as 'like' under the GATT. The possibility of their inclusion under the Art. XX general exceptions, and particularly the environmental exceptions, was explored and the various problems with each exception and the chapeau outlined. It was also tentatively suggested that some future environmental TREMs based on NPR PPMs may potentially, depending on the facts of the case, be best subsumed under the Art. XX (a) moral exception—although it is not likely that many societies could make such claims in reference to most NPR PPMs (although some European States in reference to GMOs, for example, may have a chance). It was further noted that while stricter interpretation of the substantive obligations (i.e., less case by case) would provide for legal certainty, this is not the case under the general exceptions, which serve the purpose of preserving some regulatory freedom for States to implement policy choices and thus should be applied with greater flexibility to the differing factual situations that arise.

Chapter 6 closely assessed the relevant case law under the GATT and demonstrated the practical application of the provisions evaluated in the abstract in the previous chapter. This chapter also served to demonstrate the evolution of the treatment of NPR PPMs from the GATT to the WTO and to the present day. Changing values, interpretation cannons and definitions transport this issue under Art. XX from being treated very restrictively in the *Tuna/Dolphin I and II* cases to being permissible in *US Shrimp/Turtle Compliance*. The issue of extraterritorial application of national measures as a problem was not immediately apparent when assessing the text of Art. XX but was demonstrated to be crucial in the proper application of this provision by the DSS. The legitimacy of the manifestation of the preference for multilateralism in *US – Shrimp/Turtle* raises questions of judicial lawmaking and legitimacy, and the relevance of the judgment in cases where there is no conceivable jurisdictional nexus is not certain, both demonstrating further issues that ought to be addressed by WTO members. PPM-based measures were excluded from the rigours of the WTO regime, but '[r]ecently [. . .] it has become clear that PPM-based measures affecting trade are not prohibited by WTO rules per se'.[3] This may be a preferable outcome when assessing TREMs based on NPR PPMs, but from the position of States it also shows how much power has been ceded to the DSS, which can now change the coverage of the agreement without impunity. Furthermore, regarding TREMs based on NRP PPMs, the sovereignty of the exporting State may also be impinged upon by measures falling under the exceptions, posing further problems for the legitimacy of such measures.

The examination of the TBT Agreement, on the other hand, revealed its current restricted applicability in the case of NPR PPMs. Only with regard to labelling requirements can it be definitively said to be truly relevant, though its scope is still characterised by uncertainty. Moreover, the main advocates for its non-applicability to NPR PPMs are developing countries, and this examination also demonstrated that it may not be more beneficial for them to have the decision rendered under the GATT. The problems with the TBT Agreement highlighted in this work include an unclear scope of application, an absence of consistent juris- prudence and, thus, a lack of legal certainty. These factors clearly interfere with 'the ability of public authorities to regulate the flow of information, ideas, goods, people, pollutants, or capital across borders', one of *Krasner's* pillars of sover- eignty. It is clear that the TBT Agreement requires additional interpretation or more clarity in the scope of its provisions from members.

The exploration of the case law relating to the TBT Agreement expanded on these points, with *EC – Asbestos* evidencing interpretative problems and *US – Tuna II (Mexico)* exposing the dangers incumbent on members that choose the trade- friendly option of labelling rather than instituting a ban or other TREM. The *US – Tuna II (Mexico)* case furthermore had its genesis in the GATT *Tuna/Dolphin* cases and thus demonstrated the full circle of this regulatory issue from a GATT Panel applying the GATT to the WTO DSS applying the TBT.

The treatment of the SPS Agreement in Chap. 9 acknowledged that its coverage is inherently different from that of the GATT or TBT as NPR PPMs with effects outside the jurisdiction of the importing State are not relevant; rather, the issue at hand becomes the potential risk of particular groups of products based on NPR PPMs. This chapter, however, exposed far more serious problems for members. This is the case as the consequences of an envisaged measure being found not in conformity with the GATT or TBT could lead to products being offered on the market that were previously banned or had a different labelling scheme (potentially

---

[3]*Nathalie Bernasconi-Osterwalder/Daniel Magraw/Maria Julia Olivia/Morcos Orellana/Eliza- beth Tuerk*, Environment and Trade: A Guide to WTO Jurisprudence (London, 2006), 203.

with more products being allowed to use a label), whereas the risk of pests, pollutants or other harm to the human, animal and plant life or health of the importing member is the consequence of an SPS measure being found inconsistent. This is clearly a much bigger potential assault on 'sovereignty' than under the GATT or TBT Agreement. The standard of review that would hope to protect members under the SPS from having their decisions replaced by the DSS has no textual basis and has been demonstrated not to offer the deference that some members desire.

Although the case law relating to the SPS Agreement did not prove to be particularly instructive, the fact that the ban in the *EC – Hormones* case continued for over a decade after the Appellate Body gave its report further demonstrates the structural benefits of such a system of dispute resolution for strong diverse economies and thus also the disadvantages for developing and least-developed countries.

Overall, this work has not only addressed the legal position of NPR PPMs under the three agreements in question but shown the structural deficiencies of the agreements and the WTO DSS through the prism of NPR PPMs. The problems raised in this volume were largely unforeseen by States in the negotiations at the Uruguay Round, nor were the consequences of the radical judicialisation necessarily clear. It is the combination of provisions that lack clarity and the new position of the DSS as the most powerful (trade) tribunal on the international plane that makes the issues raised here so important. Automatic, binding, compulsory dispute settlement coupled with imprecise obligations, judicial lawmaking and overreach should be a concern to all States. Furthermore, as has been demonstrated in this work, these issues all cut to the heart of the legitimacy of the WTO DSS in its current emanation. With the failed Doha Round looming over any discussion of reform at the WTO, the suggestion that the GATT and the TBT and SPS Agreements, as well as the DSU, should be reformed may seem little more than a pipe dream. Nevertheless, such pipe dreams can still be instructive for States when assessing what they hope to achieve at any future round.

Finally, it should be once more noted that

> The PPM debate reflects the WTO Members' unwillingness to deal with contentious issues within the negotiating process. The two *US – Tuna/Dolphin* disputes in the early 1990s clearly made the PPM question a central issue in the trade and environment discussions. However, Members did not address the issue during the Uruguay Round [...]. Instead, they left the PPM-related ambiguities for the WTO tribunals to resolve.[4]

This study has shown that this has not been conducted in a coherent manner and much uncertainty still remains. Perhaps now is the time for States to revisit the issue, rather than allowing the WTO DSS to impinge further upon their sovereignty by deciding the breadth of their obligations.

---

[4] *Ibid.*, 203.

Bibliography

Books and Journal Articles

Georges Abi-Saab, The Appellate Body and Treaty Interpretation, in: Malgosia Fitzmaurice/ Olufemi Elias/Panos Merkouris (eds.), Treaty Interpretation and the Vienna Convention on the Law of Treaties: 30 Years On (Leiden, 2010), 97–110

Alberto Alemanno, Public Perception of Food Safety Risks Under WTO Law: A Normative Perspective, in: Geert Van Calster/Denise Prevost (eds.), Research Handbook on Environment, Health and the WTO (Cheltenham, 2013)

Jose E. Alvarez, Multilateralism and Its Discontents, EJIL 11 (2000), 393–411

Antony Anghie, Imperialism, Sovereignty and the Making of International Law (Cambridge, 2004)

Arthur E. Appleton, Shrimp/Turtle: Untangling the Nets, JIEL 2 (1999), 477–496

Christopher Arup, The New World Trade Organisation Agreements: Globalising Law Through Services and Intellectual Property; (Cambridge, 2000)

Jeffrey Atik, On the Efficiency on Health Measures and the 'Appropraite Level of Protection', Geert Van Calster/Denise Prevost (eds.), Research Handbook on Environment, Health and the WTO (Cheltenham, 2013), 116–138

R. Rajesh Babu, Interpretation of the WTO Agreements, Democratic Legitimacy and Developing Nations, Indian Journal of International Law 50 (2010), 45–90

James Bacchus, WTO Appellate Body Roundtable, ASIL Proceedings (2005), 175–187

Robert Baldwin, Nontariff Distortions of International Trade (Washington DC, 1970)

John J. Barcello III, Product Standards to Protect the Local Environment - The GATT and the Uruguay Round Sanitary and Phytosanitary Agreement, Cornell International Law Journal 27 (1994), 755–776

Ross Becroft, The Standard of Review in WTO Dispute Settlement: Critique and Development (Cheltenham, 2012)

Ross Becroft, The Standard of Review Strikes Back: The US-Korea DRAMS Appeal, JIEL 9 (2006), 207–217

Wolfgang Benedek, General Agreement on Tariffs and Trade (1947 and 1994), in: Rüdiger Wolfrum (ed.) The Max Planck Encyclopaedia of Public International Law, vol. IV (Oxford, 2012), 312–323

Nathalie Bernasconi-Osterwalder/Daniel Magraw/Maria Julia Olivia/Morcos Orellana/Elizabeth Tuerk, Environment and Trade: A Guide to WTO Jurisprudence (London, 2006)

© Springer International Publishing AG 2017

A.R. Maggio, *Environmental Policy, Non-Product Related Process and Production Methods and the Law of the World Trade Organization*, European Yearbook of International Economic Law 1, DOI 10.1007/978-3-319-61155-6

Steven Bernstein/Erin Hannah, Non-State Global Standard Setting and the WTO: Legitimacy and the Need for Regulatory Space, JIEL 11 (2008), 575–608

Carol J. Beyers, The U.S./Mexico Tuna Embargo Dispute: a Case Study of the GATT and Environmental Progress, Maryland JIL 16 (2) (1992), 229–253

Jagdish Bhagwati/Robert E. Hudec (eds.), Fair Trade and Harmonization: Prerequisites for Free Trade?, vol. II Legal Analysis (London, 1997)

Jagdish Bhagwati/T. N. Srinivasan, Trade and the Environment: Does Environmental Diversity Detract from the Case for Free Trade,? Columbia University Academic Commons (1995), available at: http://hdl.handle.net/10022/AC:P:15611 (last accessed on 05/03/2017)

Niels M. Blokker, International Organizations or Institutions, Implied Powers, in: Rüdiger Wolfrum (ed.) The Max Planck Encyclopaedia of Public International Law, vol. VI (Oxford, 2012), 18–26

Armin von Bogdandy/Ingo Venzke, Beyond Dispute: International Judicial Institutions as Lawmakers, in: Armin Von Bogdandy/Ingo Venzke (eds.), International Judicial Lawmaking (Heidelberg, 2012)

Laurence Boisson de Chazournes, Unilateralism and Environmental Protection: Issues of Perception and Reality of Issues, EJIL 11 (2000), 315–383

Brandon L. Bowen, The World Trade Organisation and its Interpretation of Article XX Exceptions to the General Agreement on Tariffs and Trade, in Light of Recent Developments, GA, J Int'L & Comp. L. 29 (2000), 181–202

Matthew Bramley/Marc Huot/Simon Dyer/Matt Horne, Responsible Action? An Assessment of Alberta's Greenhouse Gas Policies (Pembina Institute, 2011)

Tomer Broude, Principles of Normative Integration and the Allocation of International Authority: The WTO, The Vienna Convention on the Law of Treaties, and the Rio Declaration, Loyola International Law Review 6 (2008), 173–207

Tomer Broude, The Rule(s) of Trade and the Rhetos of Devlopment: Reflections on the Functional and Aspirational Legitimacy of the WTO, Columbia Journal of Transnational Law 45 (2006–2007), 221–261

Ian Brownlie, Principles of Public International Law (Oxford, 7th ed. 2008)

Marc J. Busch/Krzysztof J. Pelc, The Politics of Judicial Economy at the World Trade Organization, International Organization 64 (2010), 257–279

Marlo Pfister Cadeddu, Turtles in the Soup? An Analysis of the GATT Challenge to the United States Endangered Species Act Secion 609 Shrimp Harvesting Nation Certification Program for the Conservation of Sea Turtles, Geo. Int'l Envtl. L. Rev 11. (1998–1999), 179–207

Barry E. Carter, Economic Coercion, in: Rüdiger Wolfrum (ed.) The Max Planck Encyclopaedia of Public International Law, vol. III (Oxford, 2012), 291–294

Deborah Z. Cass, The Constitutionalization of the World Trade Organisation: Legitimacy, Democracy and Community in the International Trading System (Oxford, 2005)

Ha-Joon Chang, Kicking Away the Ladder: Development Strategy in Historical Perspective (London, 2002)

Seung Wha Chang, GATTing a Green Trade Barrier: Ecolabelling and the WTO Agreement on Technical Barriers to Trade, Journal of World Trade 31 (1997), 137–159

Steve Charnovitz, A New WTO Paradigm for Trade and the Environment, SYBIL 11 (2007), 15–40

Steve Charnovitz, GATT and the Environment: Examining the Issues, International Environmental Affairs 4 (1992), 203–233

Steve Charnovitz, The WTO's Environmental Progress, JIEL 10 (2007), 685–706

Simon Chesterman, The Rule of Law, in: Rüdiger Wolfrum (ed.) The Max Planck Encyclopaedia of Public International Law, vol. VIII (Oxford, 2012), 1014–1022

Ilona Cheyne, Law and Ethics in the Trade and Environment Debate: Tuna, Dolphins and Turtles, JEL 12 (2000), 293–316

Ilona Cheyne, Proportionality, Proximity and Environmental Labelling in WTO Law, JIEL 12 (2009), 927–952

Won-Mog Choi, Like Products in International Trade Law: Towards a Consistent GATT/WTO Jurisprudence (Oxford, 2003)

William R. Cline, Evaluating the Uruguay Round, The World Economy 18 (1995), 1–23

Juscelino F. Colares, A Theory of WTO Adjudication: From Empirical Analysis to Biased Rule Development, Vanderbilt Journal of Transnational Law 42 (2009), 383–439

John R. Commons, The Legal Foundations of Capitalism (Madison, 1923)

Christine R. Conrad, Processes and Production Methods (PPMs) in WTO Law: Interfacing Trade and Social Goals (Cambridge, 2011)

Olivier Corten, Article 52 Convention of 1969, in: Olivier Corten/Pierre Klein (eds.), The Vienna Conventions on the Law of Treaties: A Commentary, vol. II (Oxford, 2011), 1201–1220

C. Coughlin/G. E. Wood, An Introduction to Non-Tariff Barriers to Trade, 71 Federal Reserve Bank of St Louis (1989), 31

James R. Crawford, State Responsibility, in: Rüdiger Wolfrum (ed.) The Max Planck Encyclopaedia of Public International Law, vol. IX (Oxford, 2012), 517–533

Steven P. Croley/John H. Jackson, WTO Dispute Proceudres, Standard of Review and Deference to National Governments, AJIL 90 (1996), 193–213

William J. Davey, Has the WTO Dispute Settlement System Exceeded its Authority?: A Consideration of Deference Shown By the System to Member Government Decisions and its Use of Issue-Avoidance Techniques, JIEL (2001), 79–110

William J. Davey, Non-discrimination in the World Trade Organization (The Hague, 2012)

Claudia Dorninger, Der Stellenwert der Umwelt im Recht der WTO (Saarbrücken, 2008)

Pierre-Marie Dupuy, The Place and Role of Unilateralism in Contemporary International Law, EJIL 11 (2000), 19–29

Oliver Dörr, Article 31, in: Oliver Dörr/Kirsten Schmalenbach (eds.), The Vienna Convention on the Law of Treaties: A Commentary (Heidelberg, 2012), 521–570

Claus-Dieter Ehlermann/Lothar Ehring, The Authoritative Interpretation Under Article IX:2 of the Agreement Establishing the World Trade Organization: Current Law, Practice and Possible Improvements, JIEL 8(2005), 803–824

Marsha A. Echols, Equivalence of Risk Regulation under the World Trade Organisation's SPS Agreement, in: Geert Van Calster/Denise Prevost (eds.), Research Handbook on Environment, Health and the WTO (Cheltenham, 2013), 79–115

Daniel C. Etsy, Good Governance at the World Trade Organization: Building a Foundation of Administrative Law, JIEL 10 (2007), 509–527

John Errrico, The WTO in the EU: Unwinding the Knot, Cornell International Law Journal 44 (2011), 179–208

Alexander M. Feldman, Evolving Treaty Obligations: A Proposal for Analyzing subsequent Practice Derived from WTO Dispute Settlement, NYU Journal of International Law and Politics 41 (2008–2009), 655–706

Malgosia Fitzmaurice, Third Parties and the Law of Treaties, MPUNYBL 6 (2002), 37–138

Malgosia Fitzmaurice/Panos Merkouris, Canons of Treaty Interpretation, in Malgosia Fitzmaurice/Olufemi Elian/Panos Merkouris (eds.), Treaty Interpretation and the Vienna Convention on the Law of Treaties: 30 Years On (Leiden, 2010), 153–237

Luca Fiorito, John R. Commons, Wesley N. Hohfeld, and the Origins of Transactional Economics (2008), available at: http://repec.deps.unisi.it/quaderni/536.pdf (last accessed on 05/03/2017)

Barbara Fliess/Frederic Gonzales/Jeonghoi Kim/Raymnd Schonfeld, The Use of International Standards in Technical Regulation, OECD Trade Policy Papers 102 (2010)

Caroline E. Foster, Science and the Precautionary Principle in International Courts and Tribunals (Cambridge, 2011)

Kevin P. Gallagher (ed.), Handbook on Trade and the Environment (Cheltenham, 2008)

Nita Ghei, Evaluating the WTO's Two Step Test for Environmental Measures Under Article XX, Colorado Journal of International Environmental. Law & Policy 18 (2007), 117–150

Stephen Gill, Globalisation, Market Civilisation and Disciplinary Neoliberalism, Journal of International Studies 24 (1995), 399–423

Andrew Green/Michael Trebilcock, Enforcing WTO Obligations: What Can We Learn From Export Subsidies, JIEL 10 (2007), 653–683

Andrew Green/Tracey Epps, The WTO, Science and the Environment: Moving Towards Consistency, JIEL 10 (2007), 285–316

Leena Grover, A Call to Arms: Fundamental Dilemmas Confronting the Interpretation of Crimes in the Rome Statute of the International Criminal Court, EJIL 21(3) (2010), 543–583

Lukasz Gruszczyski, Regulating Health and Environmental Risks under WTO Law: A Critical Analysis of the SPS Agreement (Oxford, 2010)

Andrew T. Guzman, Food Fears: Health and Safety at the WTO, Virginia Journal of International Law 45 (2004–2005), 1–39

Robert Lee Hale, Force and the State: A Comparison of 'Political' and 'Economic' Compulsion, Columbia Law Review 35 (1935), 149–201

Robert Lee Hale, Coercion and Distribution in a Supposedly Non-Coercive State, Political Science Quarterly 38 (1924), 470–494

Caroline Henckels, GMOs in the WTO: A Critique of the Panel's Legal Reasoning in EC - Biotech, Melbourne Journal of International Law 7 (2006), 278–305

Wesley Newcomb Hohfeld, Fundamental Legal Conceptions as Applied in Judicial Reasoning and Other Legal Essays (London, 1923)

Oliver Wendell Holmes, The Path of Law, 10 Harvard Law Review (1897)

Robert Howse, The Appellate Body Rulings in the Shrimp/Turtle Case: A New Legal Baseline for the Trade and Environment Debate, Columbia Journal of Environmental Law 27 (2009), 489–519

Robert Howse/Joanna Langille, Permitting Pluralism: The Seals Products Dispute and Why the WTO Should Accept Trade Restrictions Justified by Noninstrumental Moral Values, YJIL 37 (2011), 367–432

Robert Howse/Donald Regan, The Product/Process Distinction – An Illusory Basis for Disciplining 'Unilateralism' in Trade Policy, EJIL 11 (2000), 249–289

Rob Howse/Elizabeth Tuerk, The WTO Impact on Internal Regulations: A Case Study of the Canada-EC Asbestos Dispute, in: Grianne De Burca/Joanne Scott (eds.), The EU and the WTO: Legal and Constitutional Issues (Oxford, 2006), 283–329

Robert E. Hudec, 'Like Product': The Differences in Meaning in GATT Articles I and III, in: Thomas Cottier/Petros Mavroidis (eds.), Regulatory Barriers and the Principle of Non-Discrimination in World Trade Law (Ann Arbor, 2000), 101–123

Robert E. Hudec, Enforcing International Trade Law: The Evolution of the Modern GATT Legal System (London, 1993)

Robert E. Hudec, The GATT Legal System and World Trade Diplomacy (London, 2nd edn. 1990)

Robert E. Hudec, Developing Countries in the GATT Legal System (Cambridge, 1987)

Douglas A. Irwin/Joseph Weiler, Measures Affecting the Cross-Border Supply of Gambling and Betting Servces (DS 285), World Trade Review 7 (2008), 71–113

John H. Jackson, International law Status of WTO Dispute Settlement Reports: Obligation to Comply or Option to "Buy Out"?, AJIL 98 (2004), 109–125

John H. Jackson, The Evolution of the World Trading System: The Legal and Institutional Context, in: Daniel Bethlehem/Isabelle Van Damme/Donald McRae/Rodney Neufeld (eds.), The Oxford Handbook of International Trade Law (Oxford, 2009), 30–54

John H. Jackson, Sovereignty, The WTO and Changing Fundamentals of International Law (Cambridge, 2006), 169

John H. Jackson, WTO and the New Sovereignty, ASIL Proceedings 88 (1994)

Michael Jeffery, Environmental Imperatives in a Globalised World: The Ecological Impact of Liberalising Trade, Macquarie Law Journal 7 (2007), 25–51

Miles Kahler, International Institutions and the Political Economy of Integration (Washington DC, 1995)

Abhinay Kapoor, Product and Process Methods (PPMs): "a Losing Battle for Developing Countries", International Trade Law and Regulation 17 (2011), 131–134

Kenneth Keith, Governance, Sovereignty and Globalisation, Victoria University of Wellington Law Review 28 (1998), 477–492

Trish Kelly, The Impact of the WTO: The Environment, Health and Sovereignty (Cheltenham, 2007)

Benedict Kingsbury, Sovereignty and Inequality, EJIL 9 (1998), 599–625

Albert Kocourek, Various Definitions of Jural Relation, Columbia Law Review 20 (1920), 394–412

John H. Knox, The Judicial Resolution of Conflicts Between Trade and the Environment, Harvard Environmental Law Review 28 (2004), 1–78

Stephen Krasner, Sovereignty: Organized Hypocrisy (Princeton, 1999)

Kati Kulovesi, The WTO Dispute Settlement System: Challenges of the Environment, Legitimacy and Fragmentation (Croydon, 2011)

Pascal Lamy, The Place and Role of the WTO in the International Legal Order: Address before the European Society of International Law (May 2006), available at: http://www.wto.org/english/news_e/sppl_e/sppl26_e.htm (last accessed on 05/03/2017)

Andrew Lang, World Trade After Neoliberalism: Re-imagining the Global Economic Order (Oxford, 2011)

Lekha Laxman/Abdul Haseeb Ansari, GMOs, Safety Concerns and International Trade: Developing Countries Perspective, Journal of International Trade Law and Policy 10 (2011), 281–307

Michael Lennard, Navigating by the Stars: Interpreting the WTO Agreements, JIEL (2002), 17–89

George Lestas, Strasbourg's Interpretive Ethic: Lessons for the International Lawyer, EJIL 21 (2010), 509–541

Peter Lichtenbaum, Dispute Settlement and Institutional Issues, JIEL 3 (2000), 173–176

Oliver Long, Law and its Limitations in the GATT Multilateral Trading System (Heidelberg, 1985)

Andreas F. Lowenfeld, International Economic Law (Oxford, 2002)

Makane Moïse Mbengue, Preamble, in: Rüdiger Wolfrum (ed.) The Max Planck Encyclopaedia of Public International Law, vol. VIII (Oxford, 2012), 397–400

Arnold D. McNair, The Law of Treaties (Oxford, 1961)

Patrick F. J. Macrory/Arthur E. Appleton/Michael G. Plummer (eds.), The World Trade Organization: Legal, Economic and Political Analysis, vol. I (USA, 2005)

Patrick F. J. Macrory/Arthur E. Appleton/Michael G. Plummer (eds.), The World Trade Organization: Legal, Economic and Political Analysis, vol. II (USA, 2005)

Panos Merkouris, Interpretation is an Art, is a Science, is an Art, in Malgosia Fitzmaurice/Olufemi Elian/Panos Merkouris (eds.), Treaty Interpretation and the Vienna Convention on the Law of Treaties: 30 Years On (Leiden, 2010), 1–16

Constantine Michalopoulos, The Role of Special and Differential Treatment for Developing Counties in the GATT and the World Trade Organisation, Policy Work Research Papers (1999)

Mike Moore (ed.), Doha and Beyond: The Future of the Multilateral Trading System (Cambridge, 2004)

Eric Neumayer, Greening Trade and Investment: Environmental Protection without Protectionism (London, 2001)

John S. Odell (ed.), Negotiating Trade: Developing Countries in the WTO and NAFTA (Cambridge, 2006)

Matthias Oesch, Standards of Review in WTO Dispute Resolution (Oxford, 2003)

Matthias Oesch, Standards of Review in WTO Dispute Resolution, JIEL 6 (2003), 635–659

Atsuko Okubo, Environmental Labelling Programs and the GATT/WTO Regime, Geo. Int'l Envtl. L. Rev. 11 (1998–1999), 599–646

Lassa Oppenheim, International Law: A Treatise, vol. I (London, 3rd edn. 1920–1921)

David Palmeter/Petros C. Mavroidis, Dispute Settlement in the World Trade Organization: Practice and Procedure (Cambridge, 2nd edn. 2004)

Joost Pauwelyn/Manfred Elsig, The Politics of Treaty Interpretation: Variations and Explanations across International Tribunals, in: Jeffrey L. Dunoff/Mark A. Pollack (eds.), Interdisciplinary Perspectives on International Law and International Relations (Cambridge, 2012), 445–474

Jacqueline Peel, A GMO by Any Other Name... Might be an SPS Risk!: Implications of
    Expanding the Scope of WTO Sanitary and Phytosanitary Measures Agreement, EJIL
    17 (2007), 1009–1031

Jacqueline Peel, Scope of Application of the TBT Agreement: A Post-*Biotech* Anaylsis, in: Geert
    Van Calster/Denise Prevost (eds.), Research Handbook on Environment, Health and the WTO
    (Cheltenham, 2013), 332–362

Jacqueline Peel/Rebecca Nelson/Lee Godden, GMO Trade Wars: The Submissions in the EC -
    GMO Dispute in the WTO, Melbourne Journal of International Law 6 (2005), 141–166

Oren Perez, Ecological Sensitivity and Global Legal Pluralism: Rethinking the Trade and Envi-
    ronmental Conflict (Oxford, 2004)

Ernst-Urlich Petersmann, International and European Trade and Environmental Law after the
    Uruguay Round (London, 1995)

Ernst-Ulrich Petersmann, International Trade Law and the GATT/WTO Dispute Settlement
    System 1948–1996: An Introduction, in: Ernst-Ulrich Petersmann (ed.), Studies in Transna-
    tional Economic Law: International Trade Law and the GATT/WTO Dispute Settlement
    System (Neuwied, 1997), 1–123

John Ragosta/Navin Joneja/Mikhail Zeldovich, WTO Dispute Settlement: The System is Flawed
    and Must Be Fixed, The International Lawyer 37 (2003), 697–752

Albrecht Randelzhofer/Oliver Dörr, Article 2(4), in Bruno Simma/Daniel-Erasmus Khan/Georg
    Nolte/Andreas Paulus (eds.) The Charter of the United Nations: A Commentary, vol. I (Oxford,
    3rd edn. 2012), 200–234

P. K. Rao, The World Trade Organization and the Environment (Basingstoke, 2000)

Cesare P. R. Romano (ed.), The Sword and the Scales: The United States and International Courts
    and Tribunals (Cambridge, 2008)

Gary P. Sampson, Trade, Environment and the WTO: The Post-Seattle Agenda (2000)

Gary Sampson/John Whalley (eds.), The WTO, Trade and the Environment (Cheltenham, 2005

Gregory Shaffer, Risk, Science and the Law in the WTO, ASIL Proceedings 104 (2010), 19–23

Joseph William Singer, Legal Realism Now, California Law Review 76 (1988), 465–544

Joseph William Singer, The Legal Rights Debate in Analytical Jurisprudence from Bentham to
    Hohfeld, Wisconsin Law Review (1982), 975–1059

Krzysztof Skubiszewski, Implied Powers of International Organizations, in: Yoram Dinstein (ed),
    International Law at a Time of Perplexity: Essays in Honour of Shabtai Rosenne (Leiden,
    1989) 855–68

Christian Tams, Unity and Diversity in the Law of State Responsibility, in: Andreas Zimmerman/
    Rainer Hofmann (eds.) Unity and Diversity in International Law (Berlin, 2006), 435–458

Jörg Philipp Terhechte, Non-Tariff Barriers to Trade, in: Rüdiger Wolfrum (ed.) The Max Planck
    Encyclopaedia of Public International Law, vol. VII (Oxford, 2012), 750–759

Anke Thiedemann, WTO und Umwelt: Die Auslegung des Art. XX GATT in der Praxis der GATT/
    WTO-Streitbeilegungsorgane (Hamburg, 2005)

Michael J. Trebilcock/Robert Howse, The Regulation of International Trade (London, 3rd edn.
    1995)

Tullio Treves, Customary International Law, in: Rüdiger Wolfrum (ed.) The Max Planck Ency-
    clopaedia of Public International Law, vol. II (Oxford, 2012), 937–957

Kenichiro Urakami, Unsolved Problems and Implications for the Chapeau of GATT Article XX
    After the Reformulated Gasoline Case, in: Edith Brown Weiss/John H. Jackson/Nathalie
    Bernasconi-Osterwalder (eds.), Reconciling Trade and Environment (2nd edn. 2008), 171–188

Isabelle Van Damme, Treaty Interpretation by the WTO Appellate Body (Oxford, 2009)

Peter Van den Bossche, The Law and Policy of the World Trade Organization (Cambridge, 2nd
    edn. 2008)

Peter Van den Bossche/Werner Zdouc, The Law and Policy of the World Trade Organization
    (Cambridge, 3rd ed. 2013)

Scott Vaughan, Trade and Environment, Some North-South Considerations, Cornell international
    Law Journal 27 (1994), 591–606

Ingo Venzke, Making General Exceptions: The Spell of Precedents in Developing Article XX
GATT into Standards for Domestic Regulatory Policy, in Armin Von Bogdandy/Ingo Venzke
(eds.), International Judicial Lawmaking (Heidelberg, 2012), 179–249

Tania Voon, Sizing Up the WTO: Trade-Environment Conflicts and the Kyoto Protocol, Journal of
Transnational Law and Policy 10 (2000), 71–79

Erich Vranes, Trade and the Environment: Fundamental Issues in International Law, WTO Law
and Legal Theory (Oxford, 2009)

James K. R. Watson, The WTO and the Environment: Development of Competence Beyond Trade
(Oxford, 2013)

Joseph H. H. Weiler, The Interpretation of Treaties- A Re-examination: Preface, EJIL 21 (2010),
507

Edith Brown Weiss/John H. Jackson/Nathalie Bernasconi-Osterwalder (eds.), Reconciling Trade
and Environment (2nd edn. 2008),

Johnathan B. Wiener, Whose Precaution After All? A Comment on the Comparison and Evolution
of Risk Regulatory Systems, Duke Journal of Comparative and International Law 13 (2003),
207–262

WTO Secretariat (eds.), Trade, Development and the Environment (London, 2000)

ZhongXiang Zhang, Trade in Environmental Goods, with Focus on Climate Friendly Goods and
Technologies, East West Center Working Papers120 (2011), 1–24

Stefan Zleptnig, Non-economic Objectives in WTO Law (Leiden, 2010)

Laylah Zuek, The European Communities Biotech Dispute: How the WTO Fails to Consider
Cultural Factors in the Genetically Modified Food Debate, Texas International Law Journal
42 (2006–2007), 345–368

Documents and Reports

Center for International Environmental Law, EC-Biotech: Overview and Analysis of the Panel's
Interim Report (2006)

Decision on Notification Procedures for Quantitative Restrictions from the Council for Trade in
Goods G/L/59 of 10 January 1996

EU, Summaries of EU Legislation: Glossary, available at http://europa.eu/legislation_summaries/
glossary/community_acquis_en.htm

GA, Economic Measures as a Means of Political and Economic Coercion against Developing
Countries; Note by the Secretary General, UN Doc. A/48/535 (1993)

ILC, Report of the Study Group of the International Law Commission - Fragmentation in
International Law: Difficulties Arising from the Diversification and Expansion of International
Law, UN Doc. A/CN.4/L.702 (2006)

ILC, Responsibility of States for Internationally Wrongful Acts, GA Res. 56/83 of 12 December
2001, Annex

ILO, Recommendation Concerning Safety in the Use of Asbestos, ILO Rec. 172 (1986)

ILO, Safety in the Use of Asbestos: Code of Practice (1984)

INSERM, Effects on Health of the Main Types of Exposure to Asbestos (1996)

ODI, The GATT Uruguay Round, Overseas Development Institute Briefing Paper (1987)

UN ECOSOC, Draft Report of the Technical Subcommittee of Committee II, UN Doc. E/PC/T/C.
II/54 (1946)

UNCED, Report of the United Nations Conference on the Environment and Development, UN
Doc. A.CONF/151/26/REV.1 (Vol. I) (1992), 9 (Agenda 21)

UNCED, The Rio Declaration on the Environment and Development, UN Doc. A/CONF.151/5/
REV.1 (1992), ILM 31, 874

WTO, Negotiating History of the Coverage of the Agreement on Technical Barriers to Trade with regard to Labelling Requirements, Voluntary Standards, and Processes and Production Methods Unrelated to Product Characteristics, Doc. WT/CTE/W/10 (1995)

WTO, The Future of the WTO: Addressing Institutional Challenges in the New Millennium (2004), (2004 Sutherland Report by *Peter Sutherland/Jagdish Bhagwati/Kwesi Botchwey/ Niall FitzGerald/Koichi Hamada/John J. Jackson/Celso Lafer/Thierry de Montbrial*)

WTO, Understanding the WTO (5th edn. 2011)

WTO, World Trade Report 2012: Trade and Public Policies: A Closer Look at Non-tariff Measures in the 21st Century (2012)

WTO, Negotiating History of the Coverage of the Agreement on Technical Barriers to Trade with regard to Labelling Requirements, Voluntary Standards, and Processes and Production Methods Unrelated to Product Characteristics, Doc. WT/CTE/W/10 (29 August 1995)